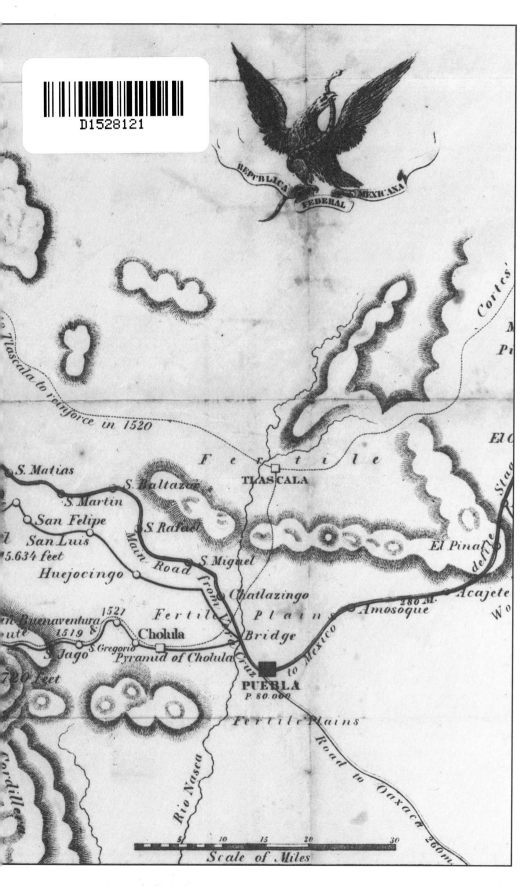

REPUBLICA FEDERAL MEXICANA

Cortes'

M
Pu

El C

Tlascala to reinforce in 1520

Fertile

El Pina

de

S. Matias

S. Baltazar

TLASCALA

S. Martin

S. Rafael

San Felipe

San Luis

5.634 feet

S. Miguel

El Pinal

Huejocingo

Main Road

from Vera

Chatlazingo

Fertile Plains

Amosoque

Acajete

280 M.

Buenaventura

1521

Cholula

Bridge

1519 &

S. Jago

S. Gregorio

Pyramid of Cholula

to Mexico

720 feet

PUEBLA
P. 80.000

Fertile Plains

Cordille

Rio Nasca

Road to Oaxaca 260m.

5   10   15   20   30

Scale of Miles

VOLUNTEERS

VOLUNTEERS

The Mexican War Journals
of Private Richard Coulter
and Sergeant Thomas Barclay,
Company E, Second Pennsylvania Infantry

EDITED BY
Allan Peskin

THE KENT STATE UNIVERSITY PRESS
Kent, Ohio, and London, England

© 1991 by The Kent State University Press, Kent, Ohio 44242
All rights reserved
Library of Congress Catalog Card Number 90-47704
ISBN 0-87338-432-6
Manufactured in the United States of America

Library of Congress Cataloging-in-Publication Data

Coulter, Richard, 1827?–1908.
    Volunteers : the Mexican War journals of Private Richard Coulter
and Sergeant Thomas Barclay, Company E, Second Pennsylvania Infantry
/ edited by Allan Peskin.
        p.   cm.
    Includes bibliographical references and index.
    ISBN 0-87338-432-6 (cloth : alk.) ∞
    1. United States—History—War with Mexico, 1845–1848—Personal
narratives.   2. Coulter, Richard, 1827?–1908—Diaries.   3. Barclay, Thomas,
1824?–1881—Diaries.   4. United States. Army. Pennsylvania Infantry, 2nd—Biography.
5. Pennsylvania—History—War with Mexico, 1845–1848—Personal narratives.
6. Soldiers—Pennsylvania—Diaries.   I. Barclay, Thomas, 1824?–1881.
II. Peskin, Allan.   III. Title.
E411.C77   1991
973.6′28—dc20   90-47704
[B]

British Library Cataloging-in-Publication data are available.

. . . history has for more than two thousand years preserved the memory of the ten thousand Greeks who effected their retreat from Persia without fighting a single battle; let our people not altogether forget the ten thousand American soldiers who landed at Vera Cruz, the victorious and triumphant march to the capital of Mexico, and which never retreated an inch.

John Jacob Oswandel
First Pennsylvania Infantry

This one is for Larry and Jim.

Contents

Acknowledgments

In the course of gathering material for a biography of Winfield Scott, I stumbled across the Mexican War journals of Richard Coulter and Thomas Barclay at the William L. Clements Library of the University of Michigan. After a cursory inspection, I routinely had them photocopied, hoping that they might contain some colorful nuggets useful for background material on Scott's Mexican War campaign. It was only somewhat later, after a careful reading, that it occurred to me that these diaries were of interest in their own right and that they ought to be shared with a wider public.

While engaged in this project I received assistance and encouragement from many quarters. Long-standing custom as well as common courtesy require that these debts be gratefully acknowledged. First, my thanks must go to Cleveland State University, which generously provided funds for travel and photocopying expenses. The Clements Library gave me permission to publish the diaries. Other libraries gave expert assistance, especially the Westmoreland County Historical Society, which supplied the photo of the young Coulter, and the Western Reserve Historical Society, which supplied the map of Mexico reproduced in the endpapers. Thanks must also be extended to the Beinecke Library at Yale University, the Western Pennsylvania Historical Society at Pittsburgh, and the military history staff at the National Archives in Washington, D.C. The battle maps are reprinted with permission of Macmillan Publishing Company, from *The Mexican War, 1846–1848* by K. Jack Bauer. Copyright © 1974 by K. Jack Bauer.

Finally, my thanks go to Barbara, simply for being there.

Allan Peskin

Introduction

Here is a pair of diaries from an episode many Americans would rather forget. From a twentieth-century standpoint, the Mexican War bears some of the hallmarks of an act of naked aggression against a weaker neighbor. This, after all, was the war that provoked James Russell Lowell to write his sardonic *Biglow Papers* and Henry David Thoreau to formulate his principles of *Civil Disobedience*. Even some of the participants in the war, from the young captain, Ulysses S. Grant, to his commanding general, Winfield Scott, held grave reservations about the justice of the cause for which they fought.

Most of their countrymen, including these two diarists, had no such misgivings. To them, the war with Mexico was both necessary and just, precipitated by a long series of provocations by Mexico. The friction point was Texas. This remote Mexican province lay in the path of the irresistible American westward tide, but Mexico, distracted by constant revolutions, could not defend it. Nor would she give it up, even after Texas had made good its independence in 1836. When the United States formally annexed Texas in 1845, Mexicans regarded this as an act of aggression and threatened war.

The newly elected American president, James Knox Polk, was not averse to war, particularly if it would further his dream of acquiring California and the desert Southwest, but he was not prepared to wage it. The United States had not fought a major war in over thirty years. It had low taxes, no national bank to mobilize credit, few battle-tested generals (unlike Mexico, whose civil wars had been a military training ground), and, the most serious deficiency of all, virtually no standing army.

In 1845 the United States Army numbered only 8,509 officers and men,[1] and even these meager ranks were perpetually thinned by endemic desertion ranging from 5 to 20 percent annually. When losses from disability, discharge, and death were taken into account, over a third of the army had to be replaced annually merely to maintain its authorized level.[2] In a

1. Russell F. Weigley, *History of the United States Army* (New York: Macmillan, 1967), 566–67.
2. Leonard D. White, *The Jacksonians: A Study in Administrative History, 1829–1861* (New York: Free Press, 1965), 202–3.

1

nation without much of a military tradition, where civilian opportunities for able-bodied men were ample, it was hard to find sufficient native-born recruits to fill the ranks. By the 1840s immigrants accounted for more than half of the "American" army, which was contemptuously described as consisting "either of the scum of the population of the older States, or the worthless German, English, or Irish emigrants."[3]

In emergencies, such as the crisis with Mexico, this sort of army was clearly inadequate. Thus the government turned to volunteers to augment the regulars. It was for this purpose that the militia system had been devised originally and, even though that system had demonstrated serious deficiencies during the War of 1812, state militias were still flourishing by the 1840s, despite their shortcomings in training and discipline. In some eastern states they had acquired a social éclat that the despised regulars sorely lacked. Small-town America provided few enough opportunities for distinction, comradeship, and masculine exertion. The militia companies offered all three. With their uniforms, titles, and parades they were especially attractive to budding politicians seeking some form of local renown.

The Westmoreland Guards of Greensburg, in western Pennsylvania, were a prime example of the caliber of men drawn to the army through the militia companies. Of its ninety-four members, sixteen were lawyers or law students, and there was a sprinkling of teachers, printers, and clerks. "They were the best educated young men in the county," declared an early chronicler, who added approvingly that they "in nearly every case came from what might be called our best families." Thomas Barclay himself proudly declared that his Mexican War comrades constituted "the *elite* of the county."[4]

No one exemplified the elite nature of the Westmoreland Guards better than these two diarists. Both Richard Coulter and Thomas Barclay were well born, well educated, and well connected. The first Westmoreland Coulter was a Pennsylvania boundary commissioner who helped lay out the county line, liked what he saw, and settled in Greensburg in 1792 as a well-to-do merchant. One of his sons, Richard (after whom his nephew, the diarist, was named), followed the law and became "in all probability the most eloquent member of the Westmoreland County bar in the nineteenth century."[5] Rising from mayor (or its equivalent) of Greensburg

3. Cited in Francis Paul Prucha, "The United States Army as Viewed by British Travelers, 1825–1860," *Military Affairs* 17 (Fall 1953): 115.

4. John Newton Boucher, *History of Westmoreland County, Pennsylvania*, 3 vols. (New York: Lewis, 1906), 1:271; Cited in George Dallas Albert, *History of the County of Westmoreland, Pennsylvania* (Philadelphia, 1882), 385.

5. John N. Boucher, *Old and New Westmoreland*, 4 vols. (New York: American Historical Society, 1918), 2:41.

through the Pennsylvania House of Representatives to four terms in the United States Congress (as a Democrat), he crowned his public career as justice of the state supreme court from 1846 until his death in 1852.

His brother Eli, the diarist's father, stayed at home, operating one of the area's first steam-powered mills. He became the brother-in-law of Major John B. Alexander, one of the county's most notable and eccentric public figures. An officer in the War of 1812, later a congressman, he was very rich and very boorish. One of his two sisters married Joseph Kuhns, himself a congressman (and father of Henry B. Kuhns, later a sergeant in the Westmoreland Guards). The other, Rebecca, married Eli Coulter. Coulter died in 1830, leaving his three-year-old son, Richard, fatherless. When the boy grew up, he followed his namesake uncle's profession, graduating from Washington and Jefferson College in 1845 and being admitted to the Westmoreland County bar the following year, when he was barely nineteen.

Thomas Barclay's early life was remarkably similar to that of Richard Coulter's. He too had a wealthy relative to whom he could turn when his father died after being thrown from a horse in 1841. His mother was a member of the prominent Johnston clan of eight brothers and two sisters who dwelt at Kingston House, an impressive stone mansion near Greensburg presided over by his grandfather, Alexander Johnston, a pioneer iron magnate. It was to Kingston House that the widowed Isabella Barclay brought her children. Thomas, the eldest son, lived with his uncles as if they were his brothers. The oldest, William F. Johnston, was usually off in Harrisburg, officiating over the state senate, a position next in line to the governor. In 1848, when Governor Francis R. Shunk was forced to resign due to ill health, William Johnston succeeded to the governor's office. The youngest uncle, Richard, was Thomas Barclay's age, and a close intimacy developed between them.

Like Richard Coulter, Barclay studied law and was admitted to the Westmoreland bar in 1844, at age eighteen. Later that year he was appointed district attorney. Both Coulter and Barclay were members of a Westmoreland militia company. To these young attorneys the outbreak of the Mexican War must have seemed like a reprieve from the adult burdens they had prematurely shouldered. Both eagerly volunteered: Barclay as a sergeant; Coulter as a private. John W. Johnston, one of Barclay's uncles, was captain and company commander; Richard Johnston, describing himself simply as a "laborer," joined the ranks briefly as a private. When a new regular regiment, the 11th Infantry, was organized, a place was found for him as a second lieutenant. A third uncle, James, enlisted as an assistant quartermaster.

Although their backgrounds were similar, Coulter and Barclay had distinctly different personalities. Quiet and introspective, Thomas Barclay was later described as "a man of deep thought, few words and little display or public demonstration."[6] His men toasted him, half-respectfully, half-mockingly as "The moral Philosopher of the Westmoreland Guards,"[7] but their preferred nickname would be "Daddy," for the fussy, paternalistic care he lavished on the company.

Richard Coulter, on the other hand, was active and outgoing. Barclay described him enviously as "a big broad shouldered fellow, and as hearty as a bear." Others, who warmed to his "particularly genial and unselfish disposition," discerned that "under a somewhat bluff exterior he possessed a heart as tender and sympathetic as a woman's."[8]

As early as June of 1845, a call was issued for citizens of Westmoreland County to assemble at the courthouse for the purpose of forming a military company in anticipation of imminent war with Mexico.[9] For almost a year thereafter the two North American republics shadowboxed along the Rio Grande, and it was not until the spring of 1846, following Zachary Taylor's battles at Palo Alto and Resaca de la Palma in northern Mexico, that a state of war between Mexico and the United States was officially declared.

By June of 1846, a company of would-be volunteers, taking the name Westmoreland Guards, was organized, but the government was not yet ready for their services.[10] President Polk, cautious and parsimonious, hoped to bring Mexico to terms on the cheap by occupying her remote northern provinces. The deluded president even allowed Mexican strong man Antonio López de Santa Anna, then in exile, to pass through the American blockade into Vera Cruz in the fond hope that once back in power the presumably grateful general would agree to peace terms. Consequently, the Westmoreland Guards were compelled to languish at home, even though an impatient local poet urged:

> Guards arouse! your country calls,
> Speed ye on to western lands,
> On! where tyranny enthrals;
> Where the trembling despot stands.[11]

By November, the inconclusive nature of the war in northern Mexico had convinced even the president that bolder measures were required "to conquer a peace" (as he described America's war aims). He approved a

6. Ibid., 49.

7. *Pennsylvania Argus* (Greensburg), 21 July 1848

8. Thomas Barclay to [?], 23 October 1847, in *Pennsylvania Argus*, 31 December 1847; Boucher, *Old and New Westmoreland*, 2:41; Albert H. Bell, *Memoirs of the Bench and Bar of Westmoreland County, Pennsylvania* (Batavia, N.Y.: n.p., 1925), 91.

9. *Pennsylvania Argus*, 13 January 1845.

10. Ibid., 19 June 1846.

11. Ibid., 26 June 1846.

Richard Coulter, 1827–1908. Courtesy of the Westmoreland County Historical Society.

plan that had long been urged by commanding general Winfield Scott: to land an army at Vera Cruz and retrace Cortes's route to Mexico City, striking at the enemy's heart rather than at his extremities. This expedition would require an additional infusion of soldiers, so a call went out authorizing the states to enlist more volunteer regiments.

Pennsylvania was allowed one regiment of ten companies, and the "stout hearted and patriotic young men" of Westmoreland, who had been waiting since summer for this opportunity, offered their services. Due to what was described vaguely as "some informality in the 'tender'," their services were not accepted, and the regiment was filled by ten other companies.[12] Seven or eight Westmorelanders were so disappointed at this apparently lost opportunity that they resigned from the Guards and enlisted in those companies that had been selected. They need not have been so rash; within a short time, Pennsylvania was allowed another regiment, and this time the Westmoreland Guards complied with all the necessary formalities and were enrolled as a company in the new regiment, formally designated as the 2d Pennsylvania Infantry.

"The young men of our town are nearly all gone to the war," lamented the local newspaper, which grimly (and correctly) predicted: "There are but few of our families who will not look over the reports . . . for the names of sons, brothers or other relatives or friends who have gallantly fought, or gallantly fallen in battle."[13]

All such forebodings were put aside as Greensburg prepared to give its young warriors a memorable send-off. The volunteers were all treated to a round of Christmas dinners at local homes, and "neatly bound" Bibles were presented to each departing soldier, along with appropriately pious admonitions. Wagons and coaches were placed at their disposal to transport them in style to Pittsburgh, where a final, and perhaps more practical, gift was bestowed—an unsheathed sword.[14]

A year and a half later, their mission accomplished, the Westmoreland Guards returned to Pennsylvania to an even more enthusiastic reception. "Addresses were made, dinners given, toasts drank, ballrooms festooned, fiddlers pensioned, and the fair were ready, everywhere ready, to honor the returning brave." Cannon boomed, bands played, the streets were laden with garlands, and innumerable toasts were given and consumed by the returning conquerors.[15]

Not all who had left returned. Of the ninety-four who had departed at Christmastime, only forty-four were mustered out with the company at war's end. Some of the others had been sent home earlier, in broken health, but many had been left behind in Mexican graves. Slightly over half of the company either died or had been discharged, usually because of illness. Volunteers in general had a significantly higher casualty rate than regular soldiers during the Mexican War, but the rate for the Westmoreland Guards was almost twice as high as that of the volunteers (though approximately the same as the overall rate for the 2d Pennsylvania Infantry). Not one member of Company E died in battle (Richard Johnston had

12. Ibid., 25, 18 December 1846.
13. Ibid., 1 January 1847.
14. Boucher, *History of Westmoreland County*, 1:272; *Pennsylvania Argus*, 8 January 1847.
15. Albert, *History of Westmoreland*, 386; Boucher, *History of Westmoreland County*, 1:278; *Pennsylvania Argus*, 21 July 1848.

already transferred to the 11th Infantry Regiment when he was killed at Molino del Rey, and Daniel Kuhns was felled by a sniper after Mexico City had surrendered). Instead they succumbed to measles, fever, and dysentery—not exactly the fate they had anticipated when they enlisted.

Of the four young men who had left Kingston House for Mexico, only Thomas Barclay returned unscathed. He apparently had had his fill of military life, for when the Civil War broke out Barclay would remain at home, tending to his business and his family. Both prospered. Abandoning the law in 1854, he opened a bank, becoming, in the judgment of an awed local chronicler, "the greatest financier Westmoreland County ever produced."[16] That same year he took to wife Rebecca Kuhns, sister of his old comrade-in-arms, Henry B. Kuhns. As she was a cousin of Richard Coulter, the two diary-keeping Mexican War messmates were finally linked in some sort of family connection. That connection was further strengthened when one of Barclay's ten children, John, married Coulter's daughter Rebecca. In 1881, his wanderlust apparently satisfied by his Mexican adventures, Thomas Barclay died, in the same house in which he had been born fifty-seven years earlier.

For Richard Coulter, however, the Mexican War was merely the prelude to future conflicts. Remaining active in local militia affairs, he rushed to the colors immediately after Fort Sumter, becoming captain and then lieutenant colonel of the 11th Pennsylvania Volunteer Infantry. When that three-month regiment was reorganized for a three-year term, Coulter became its colonel, winning the nickname "Fighting Dick," suffering three severe wounds at Fredericksburg, Gettysburg, and Spotsylvania and rising to brigadier general and finally brevet major general of volunteers. Returning home after Appomattox, he turned his energy to developing coal mines and founded the First National Bank, Barclay's chief competitor. In old age he grew a striking white beard, cultivated a gruff, no-nonsense manner, and became, surprisingly, a pillar of the local Presbyterian church. He died in 1908.

Coulter married late in life, at age forty-two, but managed to father six children. One of his sons, Richard, followed his father's footsteps, not only into banking but also into military service, first as a lieutenant in the Spanish-American War and then as a brigadier general, commanding a division in France during the First World War: two generations; four wars. He lived until 1955, dying just before his eighty-fifth birthday.

In his later years, this Richard Coulter became interested in preserving the memory of his father's exploits. He had someone type a transcript of the senior Coulter's Mexican War diary and, while he was at it, did the same for Thomas Barclay's journal. In the early 1940s, he prepared a brief article

16. Albert, *History of Westmoreland*, 524.

Thomas Barclay (1827–1908) became a successful banker after the Mexican War. Courtesy of the Westmoreland County Historical Society.

for a local historical journal, with tantalizing excerpts from both diaries and, for good measure, some choice entries from the already-published journal of George W. Hartman,[17] which he unaccountably attributed to Israel Uncapher. A copy of the Coulter-Barclay typescript was deposited

17. Richard Coulter, "The Westmoreland Guards in the War with Mexico, 1846–1848," *Western Pennsylvania Historical Magazine* 24 (1941): 101–26; George W. Hartman, *A Private's Own Journal* (Greencastle, Pa., 1849).

with the Westmoreland County Historical Society in Greensburg. Another copy, presumably identical, found its way to the Clements Library in Ann Arbor, Michigan, and was the basis for the text that follows.

The original manuscript diaries seem to have been irretrievably lost. Their absence raises unavoidable questions about the veracity of these documents. There is no way to be absolutely sure that these diaries have not been tampered with, but their remarkably candid descriptions of drunkenness, cowardice, and petty thievery seem to be presumptive evidence that the original text has not been bowdlerized. When someone tries to sanitize a document, generally he does not stop with halfway measures. It is, however, clear from internal evidence that the journals were polished somewhat by their authors in the interest of style and continuity. These entries are not artless observations jotted down on the spur of the moment, but (as is the case with most diaries) they were written in leisure from rough notes taken earlier.

A more serious cause for concern is the carelessness with which the typescripts were transcribed. Whoever prepared the typed copy had very little knowledge of the Mexican War and no patience with the intricacies of nineteenth-century handwriting. Mexican place names, as might be expected, are particularly treacherous, as Tacubaya, for example, becomes Lambaya in the transcription. Even relatively simple proper names become distorted. Thus General Worth is transformed into North, Quitman into Laitman, and Harney appears in a half-dozen different incarnations. These lapses have been corrected in the text without editorial comment. There seemed no compelling scholarly reason to perpetuate the errors of an anonymous typist or even to enshrine them within a footnote. Similarly, obvious errors in Spanish phrases, English spelling, and common sense (such as "log" for "fog") have been unobtrusively corrected, although characteristic misspellings such as "waggon" have been retained.

Mexican War diaries are not uncommon. The American soldier, especially the volunteer, was remarkably literate, and it is not surprising that he would want to record what was likely to be the most memorable experience of his life. A comprehensive Mexican War bibliography lists literally hundreds of diaries, memoirs, and journals to be found in books, articles, and manuscript collections.[18] Yet even within this substantial literature, the Coulter-Barclay diaries stand out for both their scope and their quality.

There are very few diaries written from the point of view of an enlisted man who served in the entire campaign from Vera Cruz to Mexico City, and of those none can match these diaries for either felicity of style or clarity of perception. Some are semiliterate, such as that of William McWilliams

18. Norman E. Tutorow, *The Mexican-American War: An Annotated Bibliography* (Westport, Conn.: Greenwood Press, 1981).

(also a Westmoreland Guard): "Brigade Drill to day at 3 oclock   By Col. Wyncoop   a mail cem in to day   I received one letter from my cuzin marry morrow   By it there was a grate many fur the company."[19] Others are embarrassingly high-flown and self-consciously "literary," such as this musing by Colonel John W. Geary: "At night nought was visible to the eye save the light house at the bar. 'It seemed like a star in lifes tremulous ocean.' So sweetly described, in the song I have rapturously listened to—so sweetly sung from the mellifluous lips of my beloved wife."[20]

Occasionally Barclay succumbed to this poetic urge, but Coulter could generally be counted on to bring things back to earth. Usually their concerns are of a more mundane nature—staying dry and finding something to eat. They may grumble about officers, Mexicans, Catholicism, and soldiers from all states other than Pennsylvania, but as a rule they accept their hardships with surprisingly good grace.

In so doing, they refuted the scornful slur of a regular officer that volunteers were "useless, useless, useless—expensive, wasteful—good for nothing." A contemporary British officer echoed that contempt. "The American," he said, "can never be made a soldier. His constitution will not bear the restraint of discipline, neither will his very mistaken notions about liberty allow him to subject himself to its necessary control."[21] These Westmoreland Guards, fresh from their law offices, demonstrated that Americans could combine liberty with discipline and become soldiers while remaining free men.

When the men of Company E returned to Greensburg, a subscription was undertaken to raise a monument in their honor. Partly because of ambivalence over the morality of the cause for which they had fought and partly because the Mexican War was soon overshadowed by an even greater conflict, that project was abandoned. These diaries are the true monument to those Pennsylvania volunteers who helped conquer a peace in Mexico.

19. John W. Larner, Jr., "A Westmoreland Guard in Mexico, 1847–1848: The Journal of William Joseph McWilliams," *Western Pennsylvania Historical Magazine* 52, no. 4 (October 1969): 405.

20. Harry Marlin Tinkcom, *John White Geary, Soldier-Statesman, 1819–1873* (Philadelphia: University of Pennsylvania Press, 1940), 9.

21. Robert W. Johannsen, *To the Halls of the Montezumas: The Mexican War in the American Imagination* (New York: Oxford University Press, 1985), 41.

1

Now to Foreign Land We Hie
Greensburg, Pennsylvania, to Vera Cruz, Mexico

1846

December 30

THOMAS BARCLAY. All the necessary preparations having been made the last few days, the Westmoreland Guards at an early hour this morning departed for Pittsburgh. The most comfortable arrangements had been made to carry the members of the Company to Pittsburgh. Crowds of citizens from the Borough and neighborhood had assembled to bid us good bye. There were many sad faces, many affectionate partings. Old friends in silence gave the farewell grasp and the father, brother and son dropt a tear in leaving the family circle. The bustle and confusion for a time drove away in a measure the melancholy impressions from our minds and those we left behind may be the sadder party. So farewell old Greensburgh— many happy days have we spent in thee. Liberally dost thou send forth thy young men to do battle for this Country. We love thee old town—thy old men and maidens. Happy and prosperous may you be in our absence. The kindness of the citizens has touched our hearts. And the ladies, God bless them! we always must remember and like true knights must maintain their beauty and goodness against all the knights in Christendom.

> "Tho now to foreign land we hie
> Pursuing fortunes slippery ———
> With a melting heart and brimful eye
> We'll mind you still where far ———."[1]

John Eicher[2] took Andy Huston, C. Sargent and myself in a carriage. Considering that we were leaving perhaps forever everything that was

1. Diligent search for the origins of this quatrain having proven unavailing, the possibility cannot be dismissed that it represents an attempt at versification by Barclay himself. If so, that would account for the missing words in lines two and four, which readers are invited to fill in for themselves.

2. John S. Eicher of Greensburg, born 1823, described by a Westmoreland chronicler as "one of the best auctioneers of the county and a leading democrat" (John W. Gresham, *Biographical and Historical Cyclopedia of Westmoreland County, Pennsylvania* [Philadelphia, 1890], 86).

dear to us in the world, our ride was pleasant. My companions were merry and jovial. The day cool and bracing. In every town on the road crowds were assembled to say good bye and God speed you. About 1 P.M. arrived at Chappan's and joined with a part of our company who had preceded us. Remained some time in East Liberty waiting for Captain Johnston. A short time before dark the train of carriages entered Pittsburgh. A majority of the Company met up at Bell's. Naylor's Company were there before us. This night was a *leetle* stormy.

December 31

BARCLAY. Paid a visit to the Barracks, a large three story warehouse on the Monongahela. Our Room the third story. An election was held today for 1st and 2nd Lieut. It resulted in the election of Sergt. James Armstrong as 1st Lt. and James Coulter as 2nd Lt. Jr. Lieut. Armstrong was unanimously elected. Campbell and McDermott were candidates for the 2nd Lieutenancy. Coulter's majority was 30 odd over Campbell. McDermott received but 6 votes. At the first organization of the Westmoreland Guards, J. W. Johnston[3] was chosen Captain, John C. Gilchrist[4] 1st Lieut. and Wash. Murry 2nd Lieut. The company were not fortunate enough to get into the 1st Pa. Regt. Lieut. Gilchrist volunteered as a private in the Duquesne Greys and it was necessary to fill the vacancy. Jas. Keenan, R. C. Drum,[5] W. Burns and Jos. Spencer and Henry Bates, all of Westmoreland County were also members of the Duquesne Greys. The Company generally are well pleased with the officers. H. C. Marchand is appointed 1st and myself 2nd Sergeant.

3. An uncle of Thomas Barclay's, John W. Johnston was colonel of the 14th Pennsylvania Volunteer Infantry during the Civil War.

4. Fearing that only one regiment would be allowed from Pennsylvania, Gilchrist, a Greensburg lawyer, resigned his commission in the Westmoreland Guards to join the 1st Pennsylvania Volunteers as a private. He was killed on 12 October 1847 at the siege of Puebla, "fighting like a tiger," only hours before that siege was lifted. (*Pennsylvania Argus*, 10 December 1847.)

5. After enlisting as a private in the 1st Pennsylvania Volunteers, Richard Coulter Drum won a commission in the regular army as second lieutenant of the 11th Infantry. Making the army his career, he rose steadily through the ranks, culminating in 1880 with his appointment as brigadier general and adjutant general, the chief administrative officer of the army. He held this position throughout the decade until his retirement. Not a fighting soldier, he spent the Civil War years on the Pacific coast and in 1878 commanded the troops in Chicago that intimidated the striking railroad workers.

He was the brother of Simon Drum, the artillery officer whom the Westmoreland Guards later encountered so dramatically outside the gates of Mexico City. Another brother, Augustus Drum, was a Democrat who represented Greensburg in the state senate. In 1852 he was elected to the United States Congress, partly due to a catchy campaign song in which the refrain of each verse said of his opponent: "He'll be left at home, because he can't beat a Drum."

1847

January 1

BARCLAY. This day we were mustered into the service of the United States to serve during the war with Mexico unless sooner discharged. The company passed before Lt. H. B. Field,[6] U.S.A., and Dr. King,[7] U.S.A., the mustering officers. The Doctor examined the outward appearance and asked each man questions as to his soundness, etc. (In examining regular recruits the regulations require a much greater strictness.) Our men all passed muster except David Serena who besides being advanced in life had not the free use of the fingers of one of his hands. The "Bounty" money was paid, each one receiving $21 in lieu of six months clothing. So we have today ceased to be "free and independent" citizens and are become the property of Uncle Sam, who has the sole and exclusive right to our labor, lives and all our energies.

RICHARD COULTER. Westmoreland Guards were mustered into the service of the United States at Pittsburg, Pa., by 1st Lt. H. B. Field, of the U.S.A. to serve during the Mexican War unless sooner discharged.

January 2, 3, 4, 5

BARCLAY. During these days our military duties have been rather agreeable. Plenty of good eating and drinking. "Col. Scott" drills us daily. He is a most amusing character. One of those whisky drinking military men, perfectly conversant with military matters, whose rank is doubtful. His perfect knowledge of his business at times induces us to believe his stories. He will accompany us to Mexico. An agreement has been entered into with Digby who furnishes our Company with uniforms—jacket and pants for $7. On the 3rd (Sunday) a part of the Company attended Dr. Riddle's Church.[8] Mr. Morrison Underwood accompanied us. That gentleman on every occasion showed the greatest kindness to his old Greensburgh friends. A great many citizens from Westmd are in the City. Their principal business is to see us off. Companies from different parts of the States are daily arriving and considerable intriguing is going on for Field Officers. Tonight I was Sergt. of the Guard at the Barracks, the first guard from the Company A Reg. was Corporal.

6. Horace B. Field (West Point, 1840) was brevetted as captain of the 3d Artillery for his part in the battle of Huamantla, Mexico, 9 October 1847. He was lost in a storm at sea in 1853.

7. Probably William Shakespeare King of Pennsylvania who had been an assistant surgeon in the army since 1837. His service in the Civil War earned him a brevet colonelcy. He died 18 May 1898. A member of the 1st Pennsylvania Volunteers, Jacob Oswandel, described him as "a jolly old fellow, who made some mirthful and joking remarks to nearly every one he mustered" (J. Jacob Oswandel, *Notes of the Mexican War* [Philadelphia, 1885], 17).

8. David D. Riddle, D.D., was pastor of the Third (Presbyterian) Church of Pittsburgh.

January 6

BARCLAY. The election for field officers takes place today. From our Company Montgomery wishes to run for Colonel, Murry for Lt. Colonel and Carpenter for Major. As it is not likely that all can be elected, they have agreed to submit to the Company which shall withdraw. The Company by a large majority decided that Murry and Carpenter shall withdraw. The prominent candidates for Colonel are Hambright,[9] Roberts[10] and [Charles] Naylor. Finding that Montgomery has no possible chance and believing that Hambright is much the most competent man our company determines to support Hambright. Great exertions are made by wire workers to induce us to vote for Roberts. With the exception of some 7 or 8 our Company all voted for Hambright. Roberts has 6 of a majority over Hambright. Geary[11] is elected by a large majority over Lt. Murry. [William] Brindle, Lt. in Co. C is chosen Major. Klotz[12] his opponent would have received the votes of our Company had he not shown himself. His appearance however was much against him. We voted for Brindle, tho we never had seen him. Dan'l Byerly, 4th Corporal, is very sick with the rheumatism. So low that he cannot accompany us. Thomas Simms is substituted in his place.

COULTER. The second Regiment of Pennsylvania Volunteers was organized composed of the following companies:
Company A.   Reading Artillery, Capt. Thos. S. Loeser.
Company B.   American Highlanders, Capt. Jno. W. Geary.
Company C.   Columbia Guards, Capt. Jno. S. Wilson.[13]
Company D.   Cambria Guards, Capt. James Murray.

9. Entering the Mexican War as a sergeant, Henry Augustus Hambright emerged with a lieutenant's commission. Enlisting in the Civil War as a captain, he became colonel of the 79th Pennsylvania Volunteer Infantry and a brigade commander in the Army of the Cumberland with the brevet rank of brigadier general of volunteers. Continuing in the postwar regular army as a major, he retired in 1879 and died in 1893.

10. William Barton Roberts, a businessman born in Uniontown, Pennsylvania, 2 January 1809, died 3 October 1847 in Mexico City of typhus.

11. John White Geary (1819–1873), the *bête noire* of the Westmoreland Guards, was himself born in Westmoreland County and had been a railroad construction engineer and active in state militia affairs before the Mexican War. The unremitting hostility he roused in some of the troops under his command hurt his subsequent career not in the slightest. After his Mexican service he was appointed postmaster of San Francisco and was soon elected the first American mayor of that boom town. In 1856 President Franklin Pierce, a fellow Democrat, named him governor of the Kansas Territory, then at the peak of the violence between free-soil and proslavery factions. He emerged from the Civil War a major general with a distinguished record for bravery and competence. Turning Republican, he was elected governor of Pennsylvania in 1866, acquired a reform reputation despite rumors of corruption, and was even considered presidential timber by the tiny Labor Reform party in 1872. Six feet five and one-half inches tall, he had a quick temper that often exploded into violence.

12. During the Civil War Robert Klotz was the colonel of the 19th Pennsylvania Militia.

13. Captain Wilson died at sea, 12 April 1847.

Company E.   Westmoreland Guards, Capt. Jno. W. Johnston.
Company F.   Philadelphia Rangers, Capt. Charles Naylor.
Company G.   Cameron Guards, Capt. Ed. C. Williams.[14]
Company H.   Fayette Volunteers, Capt. Wm. B. Roberts.
Company I.   Irish Greens, Capt. Robert Porter.
Company K.[15] Stockton Artillery, Capt. James Miller.[16]
Today we elected the following field officers: Colonel Wm. B. Roberts, captain Company "H"; Lieutenant Colonel John W. Geary, captain Company "B"; Major Wm. Brindle, lieutenant Company "C"; Lieutenant Benj. F. Dutton of Company "F," was appointed adjutant.

January 7

BARCLAY. Lt. Dutton of Co. F. is appointed Adjutant, McMichael[17] of Co. A. Sergeant Major and Jas. Johnston of our Company Qr Master Sergeant. The Westmoreland Guards are known as Co. E, the companies being alphabetically arranged according to the dates of each Captains Commission. The oldest commission being first on the alphabet taking the first letter. Orders to embark tomorrow evening on board the North Carolina Steamboat.

January 8

BARCLAY. S. H. Montgomery has received from the President the appointment of Assistant Quarter Master, an important and lucrative office.[18] Day extremely cold. Towards evening after a sorrowful farewell to the friends who had accompanied us to Pittsburgh, we went aboard. Our men were all sober and marched to the boat in the most orderly and decent manner, in this respect contrasting with Company H, many of whose members were drunk and it was necessary to carry some of them on board. General Bowman[19] visited us and made a very appropriate address. He then cordially shook hands with Company E, without noticing Company H.

14. Edward Charles Williams survived the severe wounds he received during the storming of Chapultepec to become colonel of the 9th Pennsylvania Cavalry during the Civil War and lived until 1900.

15. There was no Company J in American regimental organization since that letter could be too easily confused with I.

16. Severely wounded at Chapultepec, James Miller survived the Mexican War to become colonel of the 81st and 105th Pennsylvania Volunteers, only to fall at the Battle of Fair Oaks, Virginia, 31 May 1862.

17. During the Civil War, Richard McMichael was a lieutenant colonel in the 14th, 53rd, and 194th Pennsylvania Volunteer Infantry regiments.

18. An assistant quartermaster was paid over fifty dollars a month. Private soldiers made only seven dollars a month, plus a clothing allowance of three dollars.

19. Francis L. Bowman was adjutant general of the state of Pennsylvania. During the Mexican War, he served as major in the 1st Pennsylvania Infantry. He returned to the army in 1855 as captain of the 9th Infantry and died on 15 June 1856.

About an hour before dark the boat moved off and darkness soon shut out the shores of old Pennsylvania from our view. The boat was considerably crowded, two full companies being on board. The officers occupied the ladies cabin. The men slept in the cabins and on the tables and floor. Tonight we supped on government crackers and some tea (as strong as lye). The supper gave us an idea of a soldier's fare.

COULTER. Embarked on board the Steamboat "North Carolina," together with Company "H." Left the wharf same evening. Supped this evening on government rations, our first taste of a soldier's fare. Sea biscuits are perfect jaw breakers, especially after the soft raised bread of a Pittsburg Hotel.

January 9

BARCLAY. Day cold—uncomfortable away from the stove. Drill by Col. Scott. An arrangement made with the cook of the boat to cook for our company. Our bill of fare is hard crackers, pork and beans, with coffee twice a day. To an interested spectator the scene at eating hours would be very amusing. Notice being given, the companies take their seats at the table, each man armed with a knife, fork, spoon, tin plate and tin. It is the object of every one to make as much noise as possible, beating the tables, rolling tin and plate, etc. Sergeant Marchand who imagines his responsibility is immense is always busy. He enters with a kettle of coffee, the coffee steaming and the Sergeant sweating profusely. The other Sergeants are usually the attendants and severally enter duly loaded. Each man wants to be helped first and the majority insist that their neighbors have a larger share than themselves. The noise is terrible and there is any quantity of swearing. Bye and bye all are served and stuffed.

January 10

BARCLAY. Arrived at Cincinnatti. Lay there a short time. The "Anthony Wayne" which left Pittsburgh on the 7th lay here. By Col. Roberts orders no private is permitted to leave the Boat. Cincinnatti looks gloomy, the day is cold and the ground slightly covered with snow. Same Day—passed North Bend the residence of Gen'l Harrison.[20] Shortly after dark Boat passed Louisville, which was beautifully lit up. As the Boat flew rapidly by the sheets running at right angles with the River presented a splendid sight. The River is so high that the falls offer no impediment to navigation. The weather is still cold and unpleasant on deck.

20. William Henry Harrison, ninth president of the United States, died on 4 April 1841, only one month after his presidential inauguration.

January 11

BARCLAY. Passed many beautiful plantations. It is now winter and everything looks dull. In the summer season the banks of the Ohio must present most beautiful scenery. Besides police only regular details are made for guard duty, which is strictly performed. The amusements are dancing, card playing and some little whisky drinking which is slipped against orders from the Bar. At 12 o'clock at night entered the Mississippi. The mouth of the Ohio for a considerable distance was gorged with ice. The boat labored much in getting through. The wheel was broke. To those unaccustomed to river life things looked squally. During all the noise and confusion I slept soundly.

COULTER. Today I was detailed for guard and with another sentinel was posted in the stern of the boat—don't know what for—had no orders except to prevent soldiers from jumping overboard, as though any sane man would prefer a cold river in mid-winter with a very slim chance of ever getting ashore.

January 12

BARCLAY. Ran for some time among the fog and ice. Passed New Madrid. Weather becoming warmer. At 11 P.M. arrived at Memphis. Remained half an hour. Several letters written by our boys were here mailed. I mailed one to W[illiam] F. J[ohnston].

COULTER. Last night, while on post, entered the Mississippi about midnight. By the way, I think it was a very foolish piece of business to stick a fellow on the stern of a boat on a cold river in winter where every blast came whiff in one's face and for no other purpose than to keep *Volunteers* from deserting. The Mississippi is a large and magnificent river. It is very high now and running full of drift ice which is caused by a freshet in the upper waters.

January 13

BARCLAY. Day very pleasant. Drilled on deck and remained on deck the greater part of the day. The Mississippi was booming full, overflowing much of the surrounding country. As we were born rapidly along and contemplated the immense mass of moving water we could appreciate the propriety of the name given by the Indians to this glorious river. The color of the water is a dark yellow. After standing in a vessel for some time a sediment settles in the bottom and the water is pleasant to drink. Men who follow the river consider it the finest drinking water in the world. Where the Mississippi passes through the States of Indiana, Illinois and Arkansas, the shores present continued wilderness occasionally broken by an unhealthy looking settlement. Settlers shun the river shore on account of the prevalence of fever.

January 14

BARCLAY. So warm that jackets were thrown off. Usual police drilling, etc.

January 15

BARCLAY. Lovely day. Our trip had been rapid and we were approaching New Orleans. All were on the lookout. The country on both sides of the river for many miles above New Orleans is in a most excellent state of cultivation. Running back from the river for miles it is a perfect level. A great part of the land is recovered from the river which for over 50 miles is saved from the overflowing of the stream by artificial embankments. The planters here live like lords. The steeple of the St. Charles Hotel is visible long before we enter the City. Soon the number of passing boats and smaller craft inform us that we are approaching the great emporium of the West. Houses thicken. Business increases. The boat like a race horse nearing the stand flies like lightning and stops at a landing where there are hundreds of ships, sloops, boats and craft of every description from every quarter of the world. Here we are then in the City of Cotton, Sugar and niggers. Not *quite* in it, for guards are stationed and orders issued that no man shall leave the boat. The officers landed and reported themselves and are ordered to move down to Camp Jackson, 6 miles below the city. When we landed the 1st Pa. Regt. were about embarking. Gilchrist, Drum, Keenan, the Greensburgh boys obtain permission to be on shore. They look well. E. Young[21] also assists us in passing the evening. Towards night we pitch our tents.

COULTER. During the last two days the weather has greatly moderated and today we were welcomed with an exceeding warm sun. About noon came to New Orleans and lay about an hour at the wharf, but were not allowed to go ashore. Were ordered to the rendezvous, Camp Jackson, eight miles below the city, the old battle ground of Orleans, where we arrived about three o'clock P.M. Here landed, pitched tents and today we begin camp life.

January 16

BARCLAY. Rain and cold. Between Camp and the City are many wood-yards where a great number of negroes are employed. A certain quantity of work is allotted to each slave a day. It requires steady working during daylight. If they perform their allotted work, the slaves have Sunday to themselves. They are a most degraded set of beings and their appearance and submissive behavior (differing in this respect much from their brethren in

21. Probably a misprint for Montgomery P. Young, first lieutenant in the 1st Pennsylvania Infantry, who died 5 October 1847 at Puebla, Mexico.

the north) would excite the sympathy of any human being except a slave holder. The Company is divided into four messes, a Sergeant and Corporal at the head of each mess. The government rations of a good quality are regularly issued. Water and wood is daily furnished by a contractor.

COULTER. We had rather a cold time of it last night. No straw was provided us. Managed to get a few boards to lay in our tents, but had only one blanket apiece which is rather small allowance for a party just turned out of warm beds. Today we got some hay which will make it more comfortable. The company has been divided into four messes with a Sergeant and Corporal to each. We have about six men to a tent. My tent companions are McGinley, Campbell, Sargent, Brady and Uncapher. Our three adjoining tents form a mess with Sergeant McLaughlin and Corporal Bigelow. The Mississippi Volunteers, lately called out, are the only troops here now except ours and the First Pennsylvania Regiments.

January 17
BARCLAY. Many of the Company went to the City. I was Sergeant of the Camp Guard. Today I wrote to Grandfather. Ch. Painter from Westd. visited us. The Regt. from Mississippi is encamped between us and the River. They have been very unfortunate. By some bad arrangement they were compelled to encamp near Vicksburg without tents and exposed to the snow and rain. Diseases were contracted and they are dying off daily.[22] Their clothing is bad.

January 18
BARCLAY. Warm and pleasant. Travelled over the Battle ground where Andrew Jackson checked the progress of the British arms, saved the City of New Orleans from the British army and immortalised his own name. The plain on which the Battle took place is large, running about a mile from the river to the morass where Gen. Coffee was posted. The British troops landed on the right bank and gradually made their approaches. The American defences were mere field works, the ground offering no natural advantages. At this distance of time, in looking at the field I cannot see why the British army did not land on the left bank and leave the Americans in possession of their entrenchments. The spot is pointed out where Gen. Packenham fell while gallantly leading on his column. The ditches are now nearly filled up. While walking about I picked up an old musket ball probably one of those which flew fast and furious on the memorable 8th of January.[23]

22. Within six months of its formation, the ranks of the 2d Regiment of Mississippi Rifles, originally 850 men, had been reduced by 167 deaths and 134 discharges for disease.
23. On 8 January 1815, an American army under General Andrew Jackson repulsed a substantially larger British force commanded by Sir Edward Pakenham. The overwhelming

January 19

BARCLAY. Again cold and rainy. Considerable complaints among the men that while there is abundance of room both in the City and at Fort Jackson men should be obliged to lay out in the cold rain and mud.[24] Last night an Irish Green[25] was assasinated in his tent. Suspicion rests on another member of the Company who is under arrest. Col. Scott put Company E through the light infantry drill. As the ground was wet and muddy, it was very amusing, particularly to the Col. Very heavy rain at night—water running into the tents.

January 20

BARCLAY. Cold and wet. Several Mississipians dead. 3 buried. This continued cold and wet weather very disagreeable. It would have been intolerable had we not derived some consolation from divers French Taverns along the banks of the River, where besides eatables a very good article of Brandy could be had, which being mixed with honey was a most excellent preventive to colds, agues and rheumatism, etc.

January 21

BARCLAY. Cold and clear. Mississipians dying as usual. Ross, Taylor and Pease sick. The former has been sent to the City, the two latter to the hospital, A. Huston as their attendant.

January 22

BARCLAY. Cold and windy. An oyster boat sunk opposite camp.

January 23

BARCLAY. Commenced raining at 12 M. At 3 P.M. Company E went on board the J. N. Cooper Ship. It required some skill for us lubbers, armed and "knapsacked" to mount the ladder. The rain was pouring in torrents and as we descended into the hold of the vessel, dark and crowded, I experienced the first *"blueish"* sensation I felt since leaving home. Between 3 and 400 men were to be crowded into the hold of a vessel, which by the

---

victory, the last engagement of the War of 1812, not only saved New Orleans but also secured Jackson's reputation. John Coffee, mentioned by Barclay, had once been Jackson's partner in a Nashville business venture and was, in 1815, his comrade-in-arms. Barclay's criticism of British strategy is well taken.

24. Only for enlisted men. The officers, complained another member of the Guards, spent their time, not in the mud, but "in the _____ houses in New Orleans" ("A Westmoreland Guard in Mexico, 1847–1848: The Journal of William Joseph McWilliams," ed. John William Larner, Jr. *The Western Pennsylvania Historical Magazine* 52, no. 3 [July 1969], 217n.).

25. His name was Montgomery and he was from Lycoming County.

laws of some of the States and by every principle of right and justice should not have carried more than one half of the number.[26]

COULTER. The last seven days have been unusually dull. Has rained the greater part of the time and has been extremely cold for this climate and particularly cold to us being so suddenly and unusually exposed. Being but young cooks our fare has been poorly prepared, confined to crackers, fried bacon and the hardest kind of coffee. Nevertheless we can always do full justice to our rations. Hunger is a sure preventative against weak stomachs. However, our mess had a couple of chartered feasts at one time. One of the fellows stole a couple of fine large turkeys which were soon made way with and not many objections to the manner of obtaining them. At another time some of us managed to plunder a fish waggon which were dispatched as the former with as little regard to the moral tendency. Today the company embarked on board the transport ship "J. N. Cooper." I was detailed as one of the guard under Corporal Carpenter, to remain in camp tonight.

January 24
BARCLAY. It was fortunate we went aboard yesterday. The Camp this morning is entirely covered with water, it having rained all last night. As there is no provision on board, we have no breakfast. Companies A (Capt. Loeser), H ([William] Quail) and I (Porter) are our fellow passengers. The hold is much crowded.

COULTER. The last was a loud night. The entire company, except the guard, were embarked and building a large fire we had the camp to ourselves. One of the party left, but shortly returned with a fine large goose (of course we did not inquire how or where it was gotten, we only wanted two hours use of it) which was soon plucked, gutted, spitted and nicely roasting before the fire. Once prepared together with a quantity of potatoes (borrowed on the same terms as the goose) it served materially to lessen the weariness and, with some whisky, the stillness of a night guard. The latter article rather disturbed the gravity of our Corporal and one of the guard known as "Bould Archy Dougherty." During the night it rained extremely heavy. It hapened to be raining while "Archy" was on post, but he, considering a tent more comfortable, quietly betook himself to his bed, leaving the musket to do duty. Shortly afterward the Corporal, himself also pretty well fuddled, missed "Archy" off his post and went to his tent to hunt him, where he found his sentinel quietly enjoying a soldier's bed with his blanket wrapped around him. A few kicks quickly brought "Archy" to his feet with a loud "who's there." After considerable parleying (always the case among drunken men) and threatening to shoot him

26. The *James N. Cooper* was only 143-feet long and 30-feet broad in the beam.

in the morning, the Corporal ordered him to his post. It having rained very heavily in the meantime, the water was now running swiftly and with considerable noise through the ditches around the tents and "Archy," whose brain was still bewildered by the whisky, and who was not perfectly awake, did not understand where he was, refused to go out, but standing in the tent door swore right stoutly "By Jasus Christ, I ain't a goin' to stip over the side of the stameboat for any mon," and rolling himself up on his blanket was soon again fast asleep. "Archy" was afterwards again wakened and ordered to his post on penalty of being court martialed and shot in the morning, but fearlessly bared his breast and said "Shote me now, shote me now; I'm God damned if I care how soon." Neither threats nor entreaty could pursuade "Archy" and he was soon once more in the happy state. This morning, meeting "Archy" I asked him how he had rested. "Och" said he, "It is well that I happened to lay my head on a knapsack last night, for I was so God damned drunk that I would have drowned sure before waking, damn my soul, if the water didn't get up to my gills as it was." In fact "Archy" was pretty near correct. When I waked up myself I found that I was lying in water with blanket and clothes completely soaked. The camp ground presents a pretty spectacle. In many places men are wading through three feet of water and baggage is being taken away in canoes. We have fared better than the others, our camp being on an elevated spot apart from the rest. We who had remained in camp last night went on board today, where we found four companies (A.E.H.I.) stowed on the lower decks. It is rather crowded, but will not be so bad for the men as a wet camp.

January 25
    BARCLAY. Continues cold and wet. The men are in bad humour.

January 26
    BARCLAY. Still raining. Some of the Company go to the City against orders.

January 27
    BARCLAY. Day pleasant.

January 28
    BARCLAY. A guard sent after McDermott, who there is strong reason for believing has deserted. He was extremely noisy and patriotic at first and was a candidate for Lieutenant. Guard returned without finding him.

January 29
    BARCLAY. A great many complaints have been made for the last few days in the City papers in regard to outrages committed by volunteers in

and about the City.[27] I cannot judge of the truth of the complaints myself as I have only been in the City once and then but a short time in daylight (my business being to purchase coffee for the Company, the ration of coffee being exhausted). As there are only the two Regiments here, the blame must attach to either the Mississippians or Pennsylvanians. The Mississippian officers have assured the Editors that it is not their men who are guilty. The officers of our Regiment are silent and the Pennsylvania Regiment lies (in my opinion unjustly) under the imputation of being guilty of outrages upon the lives and property of their fellow citizens. Heard today that the City Council had passed an Ordinance to prevent all volunteers from entering the City. The papers are very abusive calling upon the citizens to arm, etc.

A high wind has been blowing for some days from the Gulf, the waves in the river roll and endanger the rafts which are drawn up to the shore. Col. Roberts is on board and everything is ready for our departure.

January 30

BARCLAY. Early in the morning the Sheriff came to arrest the murderer of a man killed in Orleans. He promised to publish a card exculpating the 2nd Penna. Regt. A slave holder came on board the Gen. Veazie and demanded from the Captain his boy. The Captain denied having any knowledge of him. The master said he could prove he was on board. As he was about taking his leave, he remarked to the Captain that he supposed he was aware of the Laws of Louisiana on the subject. This threat had the desired effect. The negro was produced and the little fellow, half frightened to death, followed his master. (I have been told that by the Laws of Louisiana a ship is liable to confiscation which carries off a slave.[)][28] At 10 A.M. the tow boat, having in tow the J. N. Cooper and another vessel, moved off. The country we passed was generally marshy. At times prairie land was visible. There were but few houses visible. At 10 o'clock at night arrived in the Gulf.

COULTER. Have spent the last five days on board the ship, daily expecting to leave, but as often disappointed. Had no sport of any account, except with "Archy" who had several scraps keeping the "Domned Irish Greens," as he calls them, out of our quarters. He also had some trouble

27. For example, the New Orleans *Bee* of 26 January 1847 reported the cold-blooded murder of a coffee-house proprietor by a Mississippi or Pennsylvania volunteer who shot the old man to death without any apparent provocation and then made good his escape. (*Pennsylvania Argus*, 19 February 1847.)

28. Under a Louisiana law passed 25 March 1840, a ship's captain was responsible for any runaway slave found on his vessel, whether there with his knowledge or not. That responsibility was limited to a fine and expenses (plus the value of the slave, if lost) and did not include the automatic confiscation of his ship.

smuggling his whisky aboard. This morning, to our great delight, weighed anchor and were towed down the river in company with the ship "Mayflower" carrying part of the Mississippi Regiment.

January 31
BARCLAY. Towed into the Gulf by two tow boats, there was considerable difficulty in crossing the Bar. The day is warm—no wind. We lay becalmed during the whole day, at evening the shore still visible.

COULTER. Last night about 12 o'clock anchored at the mouth of the Mississippi. This morning weighed anchor and were towed across the bar where we must now depend upon canvass and fair wind. When completely clear of land, Colonel Roberts, who is aboard our ship, opened his orders and found our destination to be the Island of Lobos, situate about sixty miles south of Tampico, after having reported himself at Tampico. The day has been very warm with little or no breeze so that at dark we were still within sight of land.

February 1
BARCLAY. Day warm. Made but little headway.

COULTER. About noon there sprang up a pleasant breeze and for the remainder of the day made considerable headway, though not perhaps the most favorable to our course. Some of the men are getting seasick.

February 2
BARCLAY. The wind springing up increased to a furious gale. The sea is rough and nearly all are sea sick. Cooking is out of the question. Consequently there is no eating save hard crackers. The safest position is on the broad of your back in the bunk. For landsmen it is somewhat dangerous to venture to walk even below. Dick Johnston manages to cook a kettle of rice for the Company. But few venture on deck. The sight amply repays the labour. The ocean in a storm once witnessed can never be forgotten. It certainly is the most magnificent sight in creation. All that has been written in poetry or prose falls far short of giving a full idea of a storm at sea. The traveller overwhelmed with terror and admiration at the grandeur of the works of nature, while he bows to the omnipotence of Deity, feels a conscious pride in the hardihood and skill of his fellow beings, who, casting their little bark to the wind and waters, fearlessly venture upon the great deep. The sublime above deck is in strange contrast with the ludicrous below. The oaths, laughter and songs of the hearty are mingled with the groans of the sick. (By all laws ancient and modern a sea sick subject may be made sport of.) From many of the bunks the boys are "calfring." The boxes and barrels loosed from their fastenings are merrily dancing and at every lurch, pitch and roll the length of the vessel. Provisions are

scattered in the most beautiful confusion over the floor. In the bow there is a large box or magazine filled with our munitions. A guard is here stationed to prevent anyone from approaching with lights. About 10 o'clock at night Tommy McGee, an Irishman in Co. I, is on guard. The box becomes loose by the rolling of the ship. Tommy throws down his gun and takes to his heels roaring at the top of his voice "Jasus the magazine, the magazine is afther me." However, everything must have an end. So had the night of the 2nd of February, a night which long wil be remembered by the soldiers on board the good ship J. N. Cooper.

COULTER. The breeze continued till about three o'clock this afternoon when it increased into a heavy gale and at dark we were riding under bare poles and tossing pretty heavy which has sickened many of the men.

February 3
BARCLAY. The wind is abating, though the sea is still rough. After noon becomes somewhat calmer.

COULTER. Last night was rather a mixture of odd scenes. The excessive tossing of the vessel affected most of the men with seasickness and it was one continual sound of pukeing, spitting, groaning and laughing mixed with the tumult of the gale. In one place would be a chap laughing at his neighbor's misery telling him to say "New York and go it," when suddenly he would feel an uneasiness himself at the stomach which a few more lurches would ripen and with a couple of preliminary "Oh God's" and a few groans, he would "York" it up himself; out it would come in spite of him, and with it a burst of laughter in the surrounding berths from those, who having previously laid out their rations on the deck, were now enjoying a short respite. So it went, each laughing at his fellows loss and in suspense lest he would be the subject of the next outbreak. Some of the companies had not secured their provisions with lashings to the vessel and during the night it caused quite an uproar of barrels sliding and dashing across the deck and Uncle Sam's provisions were scattered in glorious confusion. The boys in the lower berths were in some jeopardy from the loose barrels. A box some ten feet square lashed in the bows on the same deck with us constituted our powder magazine. This was torn from its fastenings by a heavy sea which struck the old ship broadside and laid her on her beam ends. At the same time the anchor chain was dashed through the fore hatch. For a short time, until the ship righted, the noise of box, chain, barrels and all things movable on the ship was terrible and every man was hanging on to his berth to prevent having his brains dashed out. At the same time High Corpulent Tommy McGee, (a celebrated character of Company I) who was the sentry over the magazine, frightened at seeing the box move off with him jumped off, dropped his musket and rushing down the gangway, yelled "Sergeant of the Guard, Boss Captain, Hold

Jasus, the magazine's loose and chasin' me through the hould," at the same time positively asserting that we had struck a chain bar, as he saw one coming through the bows. The magazine was secured and the chain taken up again, but Tommy lost his musket, which was destroyed in the melee. Uncomfortable as our situation was, this odd scene excited a universal shout of laughter. Our deck presented a pretty appearance this morning, covered with one promiscuous mess of coffee, sugar, flour and crackers mixed in a sea of slime and chewed rations. The gale blew all day and at night was still high. The pukeing continued with as little abatement. For my part I have not yet been sick and can therefore appreciate this scene.

February 4

BARCLAY. Calm. The sick boys are generally recovered. A good breeze springs up which bears us gaily on our course.

COULTER. Last night was passed in about the same manner as the previous, saving the "corpular's" performance. The gale which lasted since Tuesday abated today. Sailed the remainder of the day under a stiff breeze, although not very favorable to our course.

February 5

BARCLAY. Warm and pleasant. Good wind. The crew of our ship is composed of Dutch, French, Spanish, Swedish and English sailors. They are generally cross, gruff fellows, in a bad humour all the time. The soldiers are somewhat dirty in their habits, which makes the sailors still more ill humored than they naturally would be. The Englishman, who is one of the finest looking men I ever saw, differs from the rest. He is very kind and agreeable. He is a particular friend of mine, probably because we have had several talks about "Merrie old England," which like a true Englishman, he contends is by far the greatest country in the world. The mates of the ship are very impudent fellows who manage to be half drunk and in a bad humor all the time. The Capt. (Vernon)[29] is from Maine.
Good breeze—day warm.

COULTER. Nothing important. A pretty good sailing breeze. The upper deck seems more alive. The men affected with seasickness are on the way to recovery and taking an airing on deck. The lower deck has become almost intolerable with dirt during the late gale, the accumulation was great. We were greatly crowded, two-thirds unable to hold up their heads fifteen minutes without heaving and many doing worse as dysentery is

29. Different sources spell the name of the captain of the *James N. Cooper* as Vernon, Varney, or Barney.

prevalent. So that especially in the midst of a gale it was impossible for a set of land lubbers to scrub and drench a deck properly which was in such a state that we could not stand without holding fast to the berths.

February 6
BARCLAY. Calm.

COULTER. Not making much speed and very unfavorable to our course.

February 7
BARCLAY. Calm. The captain caught a young shark. This little incident gave us something to talk about and broke for a while the dull monotony of sea life. At night a light seen towards shore.

COULTER. Almost a dead calm. Unable to remain below on account of stench and very [un]comfortable on deck in consequence of the extreme heat. Captain Varney, (our ship captain) caught a fine fish which some pronounced to be a small shark. Our provisions have been very bad for some days back. Crackers perfectly green with mould, pork rancid and almost solid fat, occasionally a slight streak of lean like a small cloud in a clear sky. It is such that the monsters of the deep feast on the greater part of it. This has caused some grumbling among the men, not from an un-willingness to use a soldier's fare, but being compelled to receive such rations when better might be provided at the same cost and labor, but with less profit to those entrusted by the Government with the providing of such stores.

February 8
BARCLAY. Slight breeze. Spoke [to] a schooner from Tampico. They wished to communicate something but our crew very senselessly set up cheering and drowned their voices.

COULTER. Our sails were again filled with a good breeze. Land in sight about 9 o'clock A.M., a piece of bluff coast some hundred miles north of Tampico. The seasick boys were greatly rejoiced at once more seeing something firmer than water. But to their disappointment soon tacked about and put to sea. Hailed a small schooner bound for New Orleans and received the following intelligence—that the ship "Ondiaka," carrying four companies of the First Pennsylvania Regiment, had been wrecked some forty miles south of Tampico. Our ship Captain places considerable confidence in the statement—at all events it has raised considerable ex-citement.

February 9
BARCLAY. Calm. Porpoises playing near the ship.

COULTER. Winds have been contrary. Our ship has been tacked and tacked again without making much headway. Towards evening caught a breeze directly to our course, the only breeze that has been favorable to our course since sailing. Unless something happens may expect to be off Tampico in the morning.

February 10

BARCLAY. Woke up and found ourselves in a storm from the N.E. which veered and became a regular "norther" much more violent than the gale of the 2nd. The waves several times dashed over the deck. It was impossible to cook. Crackers and raw pork were greedily eaten, the latter article of food possessing at least the quality of novelty.

COULTER. Did not wake up this morning safely anchored in harbor, but on the contrary were roused from our sleep about 5 o'clock rocking in the midst of a heavy norther. The gale blew towards the shore which made it much more dangerous and we headed against it under reefed main top sail. Waves were large and strained the ship considerably. About noon were within 28 miles of Tampico, but the gale was too strong to venture in. Unable to do any cooking. Our fare, raw flitch [bacon] principally fat, the rank taste killed with vinegar and crackers with scarcely sufficient water to wash it down, the sea being too high to get any from the hold. Towards evening the gale increased.

February 11

BARCLAY. Still stormy. Supposed to be but a short distance from Tampico. Some doubts among the men whether the captain knew exactly where we were.

COULTER. Passed a very uncomfortable night with very little sleep, it requiring a tight hold to prevent falling out of the berths. Towards evening yesterday the men began to sicken again and last night the heaving was as general as during the previous gale. Last night met with rather a ludicrous mishap. Not being sick myself had been on deck. After dark came down and was making my way to my quarters holding to the range of berths on both sides the gangway. The whole way on either side was a lot of boys parting with their last meal so that the passage was beginning to run with undigested rations. Several told me to keep from their berths as they wished to heave. So I imprudently let go and trusted to my legs to carry me safe. Just on reaching my berth a heavy lurch threw the ship on her beam ends. My heels went up and down I came full length in a glorious mass of puke. It rather disturbed the equilibrium of my feelings. A poor fellow who had been praying and puking alternately for the previous three hours, hearing me, said "Hush, hush, we will all be at the bottom of the gulf before day." The fellow's fears and tone of his voice brought forth a burst of laughter at his expense and he quietly returned to his prayers. There was neither water nor light nor could I have cleaned myself at that time if I had them. So with the consolation that I was not alone in my dirty breeches, was compelled to pass the night with anything but a pleasant smell about my person. Today has been a repetition of yesterday. The gale has reached its height and towards evening was rather abating. In the edibles fared as yesterday.

February 12

BARCLAY. Sea becomes calmer. Make but little headway.

COULTER. Last night had another restless time of it. This morning the wind had fallen but the waves remained high during the entire day. This gale lasted about forty-four hours and was much more severe than the previous. Frequently the old craft was tossed completely on her beam ends, at one time a heavy sea struck her bows and dashed everything loose and movable across the decks. Breakfasted as during the last two days. Towards evening managed to boil some coffee. Such we called it, but by the time it was boiled, by numerous spillings and consequent fillings up it was reduced to little better than warm water slightly colored. Can expect something like sleep tonight.

February 13

BARCLAY. The orders were to report at Tampico and proceed immediately to the Island of Lobos. Finding that he was south of Tampico, the Captain steered for Lobos. The shipping at that Island were visible in the forenoon. At 1 P.M. a pilot steered us to anchorage off Lobos.

COULTER. This morning to our no small satisfaction again hove in sight of land, which proved to be the Island of Lobos, our place of destination. There was a large quantity of shipping lying off at anchor. Were piloted in and cast anchor about 11 o'clock A.M. The main land is in sight, the island being only about 7 miles distant from it. The island is small, covered with underbrush and studded along the shore with the camps of the troops who arrived before us.

February 14

BARCLAY. Early in the morning a small party was sent ashore to clear ground for tents. The balance of the company followed during the forenoon. Conveyed to shore in boats from the Brig of War "St. Mary," worked until evening and pitched tents. This Island is 60 miles south of Tampico and 7 miles distant from the mainland. The soil is sandy and over the greater portion of the Island there is a thick growth of underbrush. The lumber is small and of unknown species. The greatest curiosity on the Island is a tree something like the Bamian [banyan] tree of India.

The branches shoot into the ground and take root. There are "morning glories" here in full bloom. The Island is about a mile in circumference. On the [south] side there is a good open harbour, one of the few safe anchorages in the Gulf. On the eastern side there are breakers and the waves in breaking over them cause a continued roar. The Island is of coral formation.

COULTER. This morning the "St. Mary's," a sloop of war lying here for the protection of the transport ships, sent several surf boats alongside our ship for the purpose of landing us. A squad from each company was detailed to go ahead and clean a place for encampment. About noon the remainder with all our baggage were disembarked. Here found the following regiments and parts. A part of the First Pennsylvania Regiment. The Mississippi Regiment. A part of the Louisiana Regiment and the South Carolina Regiment, which disembarked yesterday. Found that it was a part of the Louisiana instead of the First Pennsylvania Regiment that was wrecked; that the men got safely ashore and were threatened by a Mexican force who gave them 24 hours to surrender, but they decamped during the night and arrived safely at Tampico, where they now are.[30] The "St. Mary" went up and burned the wreck and fired upon the enemy who retaliated. Pitched our tents and gathered a quantity of cane break for bedding. Three Mexicans were taken today as spies. They came as fishermen selling fruit and were connected with a small Mexican sloop lying near the Main land. A boats crew from the St. Mary's crossed and burned this sloop.

February 15
BARCLAY. Day pleasant. The company were divided into the following messes on board the ship.

No. 1	No. 2	No. 3	No. 4
Mechling	McWilliams, I.	Carpenter	Johnston
Bonnin	McWilliams, W.	McClain	Byerly
Gordon	Becker	Hansberry	May
Allshouse	Haines	Milner	Campbell
Brady	Kuhn	Cloud	Shields
Bigelow	Kegarize	Rexroad	Wentz
Kettering	Martz	Wise	McGarvey
McIntire	Rager	Grow	Waters
Forney	Shaw	Gorgas	Bills
Uncapher	Kerr	McCredin	Simms
Hartford	McClaran	Elliott	McClelland
Thomas	Heasley	Kelly	McCutcheon

30. The Louisiana troops were cast ashore about forty miles south of Tampico. Despite the presence of a superior Mexican force nearby, they evaded capture and made their way to safety.

No. 5	No. 6	No. 7
Kuhns, D.	Coulter	Carney
McCabe	McLaughlin	Hoffer
Carson	Ross	Underwood
Keslar	Kuhns, H.	Hays
Linsenbigler	Barclay	Fishel
Landon	Aikens	McGinley
Huston	Bates	Sargent
Geesyn	Steck	Melville
Miller	Marchand	Kuhns, P.
Stickle	Moorhead	Myers
Dougherty	McCollum	Spears
Hagerty	Smith	Hartman

A party detailed to clear ground back of the tents. Another detailed for well digging. By digging for between 3 and 4 feet through the sand water is obtained. The water is warm and of a slight salt taste. It makes very good coffee.

COULTER. Last night was on camp guard. Had no muskets but cut sticks to supply the place. Whilst sitting or standing still felt a rocking sensation and the whole island appeared to be heaving. It was caused by being so long on water. Our guard corporal had no watch by which to relieve us but had to depend upon his own idea of time. Getting sleepy, he went to his tent and was soon enjoying a nap, having previously told us that we should wake him when we thought it was relief time. About half an hour after, it commenced a drizzling rain which we did not wish to receive and so waking the corporal told him that the two hours were up. He having been sound asleep could form no idea of the length of time which had elapsed and not suspecting us of deceiving him accordingly relieved us. So we returned and enjoyed a fine sleep for our first night on Mexican soil. There was an alarm and several regiments were under arms. I did not hear it myself. When once asleep I am not so easily wakened. Some of our regiment were up but were in a pretty condition for an attack, there not being a musket or cartridge in the regiment. It proved, however, to be hoax. Commenced grubbing a spot near the center of the island for our camp, the place where we were being intended for a regimental parade ground. Also dug a well and found water at a depth of about ten feet as good as any on the island, but rather brackish. The Island of Lobos is very small, being about a mile or a mile and a half in circumference and about three hundred yards in diameter, containing some 160 or 200 acres. It is a low spot founded on a coral reef. The soil has the appearance of white sand, but is for the greater part mouldered coral and shale. It is covered with very heavy underbrush and a considerable number of good sized trees, lemon and gum. On some parts there is considerable cane break. It is completely surrounded by a reef of rocks varying from a few yards to a quarter of a mile distance from the beach. This forms a beautiful line of breakers which rise to a great height with a roaring noise, especially when the sea is high. It is populated by many large rats, land crabs, lizards and ants which are troublesome at night. Also there were large numbers of Sea Gulls on it which have generally deserted it, many having been killed by the first regiments who came here. Drew a ration of flour today the first we have drawn since being in the service.

February 16
BARCLAY. Day hot. The company worked hard by reliefs at the clearing. Enjoyed a delightful bath. Coming from the cold regions of the north, this is a luxury which only those who enjoyed can appreciate. Along and at a short distance from the shore are numerous specimens of coral formation and shells of the most beautiful shapes and colors.

COULTER. Continued the grubbing. Heat extreme, only pleasant morning and evening.

February 17
BARCLAY. Day warm. Still worked at the clearing. Provisions and a barrel of water daily are brought from the ship. Bonnin who has been acting as Corporal vice Byerly since the 11th Jany is officially apptd. and will hereafter act as company commissary, being exempted from other duties. We have daily three roll calls, at Reveille, Repeat and Tattoo. For want of a drum, Forney the other morning beat on a camp kettle.

COULTER. Still at the cleaning. Inclosed a very large gum tree in our ground which will make quite an agreeable shade. Drew a small ration of Mississippi water today from the ship, but it was even worse than the island water, having been brought in an old sauer kraut barrel.

February 18
BARCLAY. Warm and slight rain. The sutler's store is opened and a great rush is made to purchase anything and everything. His prices are enormous but he has a ready sale for everything, particularly eatables. Each Sergeant has a book with the names of his squad entered and no one obtains credit unless accompanied by either a Sergeant or the Book.

COULTER. This morning finished cleaning. The heat was great and the smoke from the brush piles severe. Pleasant in the evening.

February 19
BARCLAY. Warm. Men still at work.

COULTER. Extremely warm. Nothing doing.

February 20

BARCLAY. Capt. Vernon and Capt. Johnston went out a fishing. Capt. Johnston brought home for his share 52 very fine fish of a reddish color. They were divided among the messes and anticipating a good meal everybody is in a good humour. Removed tents back some distance and built arbors in front of them. After night a heavy rain.

COULTER. After reveille recommenced the grubbing, not having cleaned the proper place, but made short work of it. Breakfast over, removed our camp to the rear, leaving a regimental drill ground next [to] the beach. Erected bowers around our tents and the camp presents quite a pleasant and picturesque appearance, but unluckily were thrown too far to the left to enjoy the benefits of the gum tree around which we cleaned the other day. Drew fresh rations and today again ate good crackers.

February 21

BARCLAY. Plenty of fresh fish for breakfast. Cleared off parade ground in front and sent a detail to assist in clearing off the ground occupied by the three companies still on board the Gen. Veazie.

COULTER. Last night had a very heavy rain which has made it cool and pleasant this morning. The Mississippi and Louisiana Regiments have been ordered to Tampico. The wind must have been high on the gulf as a number of the ships dragged anchor last night, among them the "General Veazie" carrying three companies of our regiment who have not been allowed to land, there being a case of small pox among them.

February 22

BARCLAY. Another blowing. Received arms and accoutrements. Dress Parade. Mess No. 6 in honor of the day had a "Dinner." As is frequently the case on such grand occasions, everything went off in the most harmonious manner. The principles of Temperance were strictly observed and we evinced our admiration of the "Father of his Country" by feasting upon dried apples and salt mackerel, the only luxuries to be obtained in the barren Island of Lobos. By the quantity consumed, we endeavored to make up for the deficiency in the quality.

COULTER. This morning arms and accoutrements were distributed to us. Being the anniversary of Washington's birth, our mess determined to have an extra dinner, and it was an extra one, both for the quality of the dishes and the cooking, namely, half dozen boiled mackerel. We thought them very nice, although they might have been a little tainted. Dried apples stewed. They were edible, though it was perhaps difficult to distinguish whether they were stewed apples or lumpy tar. Apple pies. They were made of the same kind of apples as those stewed, and taking into consideration our ability to cook, their quality may be imagined. Lastly, biscuits, made of flour and water, with a little salt fat for shortening, prepared by a soldier's hand and baked after a soldier's manner, that is, burned without and sad within. Such was our feast. It was the best Lobos Island could afford. Had a dress parade this evening, our first regimental parade.

February 23

BARCLAY. Warm. Drilled by Squad, Company and Regiment. Col. Scott, on account I believe of some difficulties with the officers, has left us since we arrived on the Island. He quarters with the 1st Pa. Regt.

COULTER. Our first regimental guard was mounted today. Detailed for that duty. Much more severe than company guard heretofore.

February 24

BARCLAY. Received information that our destination was Vera Cruz. We had expected this and were not surprised. For the first time a Regimental Guard posted.

COULTER. Have had a more severe turn of guard than usual. The guard tents were so crowded that when off post could not get much rest.

February 25

BARCLAY. Day warm. Drilled three hours Regt. Drill. The 1st Pa. Regt. went aboard. Ships with troops and provisions are arriving daily.

COULTER. The First Pennsylvania Regiment embarked on board their respective transports. Destination supposed to be Vera Cruz.

February 26

BARCLAY. Warm. The usual drills.

COULTER. There has been an unusual number of arrivals today, eight or ten schooners, two sail ships and a very large steamer, which last brought in General Twiggs.[31] Have been unusually troubled with dysentery today.

February 27

BARCLAY. Two Regt. Drills. To be mustered in tomorrow.

---

31. David Emanuel Twiggs of Georgia (1790–1862) was a striking figure of a man, nearly six-feet tall with a brick-red face surrounded by white hair and white whiskers. Admired by his men, who nicknamed him "The Horse" for his rough, unpolished energy, he feuded with his colleagues, especially General William J. Worth. At the outbreak of the Civil War, Twiggs was in command of the Department of Texas which he handed over to the Confederacy, the only regular army officer to so betray his country and his command. Rewarded for this action by being appointed a major general in the Confederate army, he was too old and too feeble to exercise command in the field.

COULTER. Am mess cook today. As in the case with all cooks, cross and crabbed. Smoked, sweated and burned nearly to death. Several times got my water almost to a boil when away would go a burned stick and upset my kettle and put out my fire. Have had a great deal of tribulation today.

February 28

BARCLAY. Day warm. Regt. turned out formed in column by companies, opened ranks and unstrung knapsacks. The officers accompanied by Col. Roberts passed each company calling the rolls and examining the arms and appearance of the men. 4 rolls are made out with the names of the company, which are signed by the Company Officers and Mustering Officers. Each roll has such remarks as will satisfy the Pay. Dept. and show the War Dept. the state of the Company. [Lt. Fowler H. Sterne] was our mustering officer. This ceremony it is necessary to repeat every two months. Taken by the St. Mary's boats on board the Cooper.

COULTER. Received orders today for a general inspection and mustering into the service. Turned out eighty six officers and men, being the entire company except three sick, two (Taylor and Pease) left sick in the hospital at New Orleans and one (McDermott) deserted at same place. Our regiment make quite a respectable appearance when they are all out. Passed inspection and returned to camp with orders to be ready to move. At one o'clock struck our tents and re-embarked on board the "J. N. Cooper." The old ship is just as dirty as ever, and the lower deck, if anything, smells worse from our having had two weeks of pure sea breeze on the island. We have not received any official information, but there is no doubt that our destination is Vera Cruz. It is amusing to see the different sensations produced by this embarking in different persons. Some pleased at leaving the island and some willing to accept anything as a change for the monotony of camp. Some frightened at the idea of another trip on the gulf, having been very sick before and some terrified at the name of Vera Cruz.

March 1

BARCLAY. Rained. Nothing of importance occurred.

COULTER. Understood that General Worth[32] arrived this morning. The three companies of our regiment (B.C.G.) detained on board the "General

32. William Jenkins Worth (1794–1849). Although raised as a Quaker and untutored in war, the New York–born Worth entered the army during the War of 1812, where he served as Winfield Scott's aide-de-camp and comrade in arms, even naming his son Winfield Scott Worth. Between wars he served an eight-year stint as commandant of West Point. Brevetted a brigadier general for service in the Seminole Wars, he joined Zachary Taylor's army at the outbreak of the Mexican War and was largely responsible for Taylor's victory at Monterey, earning himself a major-general's brevet in the process before being transferred to Scott's army. Jealous of his military perogatives and politically ambitious (he even allowed himself

66 VOLUNTEERS

Veazie" on account of small pox are to be landed on the island when all
the other troops have embarked, under charge of Lt. Col. Geary, there to
remain until all their sick are well.

March 2

BARCLAY. Warm. In attempting to weigh anchor, our sailors have failed.
It has twice slipped. The mates and most of the sailors are drunk. Two
steamers, having on board Gen'l Scott,[33] Worth and other distinguished
officers, have started. Almost all the fleet are under sail bearing towards
Vera Cruz. Great preparations have been made. Nothing is more beautiful
than a ship under sail, unless it is a fleet. Some 30 or 40 vessels are now
under spread of canvass. It is a sight not often seen. It recalls to our minds
the Grand Armada which bore towards the shores of England the Chivalry of Spain. "The ocean" says a Spanish writer, "groaned beneath the
load."[34] No one here ever dreams that the same fate that befell the Armada
will ever befall this gallant fleet. *Failure, defeat,* are words never spoken.

COULTER. This morning shortened [sail] preparatory to weighing anchor. All during the forenoon was almost a dead calm and unusually
warm. About 11 o'clock a United States brig of war anchored some fifty
yards to our starboard. It is a beautiful little craft carrying six guns and
danced like a duck on the water. The sails were reefed and anchor cast,
and after lying an hour or so its sails were unfurled, anchor weighed and

---

to dream of the presidency), Worth was susceptible to the contentiousness that seemed to
afflict career officers of his generation. Turning even against his old friend and commanding
officer, he joined in the cabal leading to Scott's arrest and removal from command.

33. America's preeminent soldier in the years between the Revolution and the Civil War,
Winfield Scott (1786–1866) was the man most responsible for the professionalization of the
United States Army. During the Mexican War, he was commanding general of the army and
at the height of his powers after a dazzling military, diplomatic, and political career already
spanning forty years. Although the Vera Cruz expedition had been Scott's conception, President Polk had been reluctant to reward him with the command, in part because of fear of
Scott's Whiggish political ambition and, in part, because the vain, pompous general had
seemed insufficiently respectful of his commander in chief's administration. For lack of an
alternative, Polk was eventually compelled to give Scott command of the campaign but the
president's support was half-hearted and he would vindictively suspend Scott from command once the campaign had succeeded.

Scott ran for president in 1852 as the Whig candidate, only to be so soundly defeated by
Franklin Pierce that his party never recovered. Consoled by promotion to the rank of lieutenant general (by brevet), the first since George Washington to hold that rank, Scott continued in command of the army through the first year of the Civil War until he resigned, late
in 1861, too old and too feeble to mount a horse without the aid of a stepladder.

34. Barclay's memory of the quotation is reasonably correct ("The ships appeared like so
many floating castles, and the ocean seemed to groan under the weight of their heavy
burden."), but his recollection of the authorship is faulty. It was not by a Spanish writer but
by an Englishman: Thomas Lediard (1648–1743), author of *The Naval History of England,*
2 vols. (London, 1735).

it was off with the same expedition, although there was not enough air going to stretch the sails of our lubberly old craft, but they hung lazily against the masts. About 2 o'clock there sprang up a pleasant breeze and our crew undertook to weigh anchor and be off. But it slipped again and again and although they worked hard all afternoon at night it was thirty fathoms deeper than in the morning. So we had the bore of lying another night off Lobos. The majority of the vessels have left the anchorage; those remaining are under the protection of the "St. Mary."

March 3

BARCLAY. Set sail but did not this day move out of sight of land. Orders from Gen. Scott read. Lieut. [John] Sturgeon read the Articles of War, much to the amusement of his audience who consider them entirely unapplicable to their case.

COULTER. After much labor this morning weighed anchor and again unfurled our sails, but up until 1 o'clock it was a dead calm and most intolerably hot. In the afternoon made some speed, but at night were still in sight of Lobos.

March 4

BARCLAY. Fair wind. Making good progress. Numbers of flying fish seen.

COULTER. About 12 o'clock last night it blew up a stiff breeze and we have averaged seven knots ever since. Had plenty of Company today; counted sixteen sails in sight in the evening.

March 5

BARCLAY. Saw land in the morning. Later anchored off Anton Lizardo at 4 P.M. among the American fleet. This anchorage is 15 miles south of Vera Cruz.

COULTER. Have made but little progress today. A mere breath of air blowing. About noon hove in sight of San Antonio Lizardo and towards evening anchored a mile or perhaps two from the shore. The shore is apparently covered with a heavy undergrowth similar to the Island of Lobos and in one place there is what appears to be the ruins of some large building. There is a very large quantity of shipping here and many vessels coming in.

March 6

BARCLAY. Intensely warm. Drew 40 rounds of buckshot and ball.

COULTER. At reveille company mustered on deck. Roll call for the purpose of ascertaining the number of effective men. Only four reported unfit to carry a musket. Has been very pleasant today. City and castle of

Vera Cruz visible. This afternoon forty rounds of ball and buckshot cartridges were distributed to us. Learned that General Taylor had met and flogged Santa Anna.[35] Our loss set down at one and that of the enemy at four thousand.[36] General Scott sailed up to Vera Cruz to reconnoiter. Approached within range of the castle and was fired on several times.

March 7

BARCLAY. Cooked three days rations. Arms and accoutrements inspected. Drew 20 rounds additional cartridges.

COULTER. The late calm has changed into all the noise, bustle and active preparations for the landing. Twenty rounds more of ammunition dealt out and extra flints distributed. Ordered to prepare three days rations and hold ourselves in readiness to land at Sacrificios, three miles from Vera Cruz, after dark. Camp kettles and pans were in requisition all afternoon. In the bustle supper was forgotten and we had the pleasure of supping on raw bacon and crackers. When all was in readiness and some knapsacks slung, orders countermanded until 3 o'clock A.M.

March 8

BARCLAY. Day warm. Made all necessary preparations for leaving the ship. The delay landing is occasioned through fear of a norther, which the knowing ones smell at a great distance.

35. Antonio López de Santa Anna (1795?–1876), the self-styled "Napoleon of the West," whose flamboyant career dominated Mexican politics for a quarter century, during which he managed to be on virtually every side and an advocate of every party. First emerging as a supporter of the imperial pretensions of Agustín de Iturbide, he then led a revolt deposing him. After successfully turning back a would-be Spanish invasion at Tampico, Santa Anna supported Vincente Guerro's presidential claims; shortly thereafter he joined Anastasio Bustamente in overthrowing Guerro and installing Bustamente, then he overthrew Bustamente. He was chosen president in 1833 as a Federalist but switched sides and became leader of the Centralists. In 1835 he abolished the Republic and declared himself dictator.

That same year Texas revolted from Mexican rule. After initial success (the Alamo), Santa Anna was defeated and captured at San Jacinto. Despite Texans' anger at his cold-blooded slaughter of over three hundred prisoners at Goliad, Santa Anna was let free after being forced to recognize Texas independence. After a short stay in the United States, he returned to Mexico and turned back a French invasion attempt at Vera Cruz, losing a leg but regaining his popularity. Reelected as president, he ruled as dictator from 1841 to 1844, when he was overthrown and banished, only to be recalled and reinstated to meet the American threat.

After the Mexican War, he would again go into exile until 1853, when he was once more recalled, but his despotic rule scarcely lasted a year until he was overthrown and forced out of power, this time for good.

36. Learning that General Zachary Taylor's army in northern Mexico had been drained of over half of its forces to aid Scott's Vera Cruz expedition, Santa Anna seized his opportunity to attack the depleted American army of less than five thousand with fifteen thousand of his Mexican soldiers. The battle was fully joined near the hacienda of Buena Vista on

COULTER. Our deck was alive before the time ordered and we were once more ready to move when orders were again countermanded. Understand that the reason for countermanding this morning's orders was the fear of a norther. Last night was very uncomfortable. Were crowded into the lower deck where the heat was extreme and the smell from the boiled meat (of which each of us had a good portion in his haversack) and sweat which was running in streams from all, was intolerable. Could sleep but little and was compelled to go on deck early to get fresh air. About noon the frigate "Potomac"[37] sent a boat's crew with six muskets ashore to examine the old ruins (mentioned in note of Friday last) where a number of horsemen have been seen for some time back and supposed to be keeping communication between this place and Vera Cruz. On approaching within one or two hundred yards of the place were fired upon several times and compelled to retreat to the boat.

March 9

BARCLAY. The Company are generally in good health. Kerr, Spears, McClain, Heasley will remain, being sick. Huston remains as their attendant. Left the Cooper and were conveyed by a steamboat to the Man of War Potomac. It was a great relief to get out of the Cooper, which was a filthy hole. Nothing can exceed the cleanliness and order observed on board of the Potomac. Both the Penna. Regts. are on board. (The 2nd Penna Regt. at present consists of only seven companies. The small pox broke out among Companies B, H and G on board the Genl. Veazie and they were ordered to remain on Lobos Island under Lt. Col. Geary. James Johnston is with them.) The sailors on board the Potomac are exceedingly kind, offering us portions of their rations. We had the honor of dining on board. A large ration of the fattest kind of pork was issued and duly disposed of. Sergt. Marchand here met an acquaintance of John B's who treated him very kindly. The Potomac carried us to the anchorage, Sacrificios, 3 miles distant from Vera Cruz. The Castle and spires of the City are full in view. We are out of reach of their guns and the greatest activity is displayed throughout the fleet. Boats passing to and from all directions conveying orders, etc. The "Musquito Fleet"[38] consisting of two or three very small vessels each carrying a heavy piece, boldly approach the castle and open a fire. The Castle replies. Some of the shot fall very close to the venturesome little barks. About 4 P.M., the surf boats (large boats of light

---

23 February 1847. After a seesaw contest, the Mexicans withdrew with losses of about two thousand men. American casualties were perhaps one-third that number.

37. A first-class frigate of 1,708 tons, carrying eight 8-inch guns and forty-three 32-pounders, the *Potomac* was built in 1831. The captain was John H. Aulick.

38. The so-called Mosquito Fleet consisted of the steamers *Spitfire* and *Vixen* and the gunboats *Bonita*, *Petrel*, *Falcon*, and *Tampico*.

draught each carrying near 100 men) form in line filled with Worth's troops. Two vessels of the Musquito Fleet approach shore to protect them landing. The surf boats move toward shore in a line. Upon nearing the land the men leap into the water near waist deep and forming rapidly their ranks rush to the shore. About 5000 men are thus landed and their rapid formation was admirable. Moving along the sands, they ascend the first sand hills and display the Stars and Stripes. Three loud, long and hearty cheers from the fleet, a reply to the unfurling of our Country's Banner. The surf boats return in haste and more troops are landed. This continues until night. About 10 o'clock at night our Company was landed. Encamped within twenty feet of the water and lay down wrapped in our blankets with arms in hand. About 3 P.M. the enemy fired a few shot at the pickets on our right. The Regt. was called to arms. We got but little rest.

COULTER. Last night was as uncomfortable as the previous. Up before day and at 8 o'clock a lighter came along side to carry us to one of the Men of War, it being intended to leave the transports here. Went on board to the number of eighty-five officers and men, being our entire company except Montgomery and James Johnston, promoted to the Quartermaster's Department at Pittsburgh, and Taylor and Pease, left sick at New Orleans, McDermott, deserted at same place, and Heasley, Huston, Kerr, McClain and Spears to be left on the "J. N. Cooper" as too sick to land. Were carried to frigate "Potomac" which was to carry the two Pennsylvania Regiments. This is a beautiful vessel carrying forty-four guns and we were extremely well treated by the sailors. By 10 o'clock set sail and about noon appeared off Vera Cruz. The first view of the castle was magnificent; an immense white pile with numerous batteries covering a great space. The domes and spires of the city were beautiful. By four o'clock the first division under General Worth were in the surf boats ready to advance upon the shore. It was an exciting time. Every one had conceded that our landing must be opposed and the beach was covered with chaparral admirably adapted to conceal an enemy. But after half an hour's anxious suspense the shore was gained and our colors were planted without firing a shot. Loud, long and enthusiastic were the cheers that went up from the ships at this sight. Possession once taken, the remainder of the forces were loaded with all speed taking until 11 o'clock P.M. We were landed in the second division about 7 o'clock. The surf boats could only come within twenty yards of the beach and we waded out waist deep. Slept on our arms on the beach.

2

Up Hill and Down Hill
The Siege of Vera Cruz

The landing at Vera Cruz—the largest combined operation the United States army and navy had yet engaged in—went off without a hitch. Escorted by almost a hundred transports and men-of-war, Scott's army of twelve thousand men began to disembark at 4 P.M. Loaded into surfboats, specially designed flat-bottomed landing craft, they were rapidly rowed from their transports to the beach, the last wave arriving on shore about midnight. Not a single accident marred the landing, in contrast to a tactically similar French invasion of Algeria, seventeen years earlier, which had suffered about forty drownings.

Had the Mexicans chosen to meet the Yanqui invaders at the beach, American casualties could have been severe. Instead, the Mexicans sought safety behind the seemingly impregnable defenses of Vera Cruz. These defenses were impressive. The city was protected from attack from the sea by the castle of San Juan de Ulua, generally described by American journalists as "the Gibraltar of the West." Heavily fortified walls protected the city from assaults by land.

Such an assault, Scott estimated, would cost between two and three thousand American casualties, not to mention the heavy losses to Mexican civilians in the indiscriminate fighting inevitable in night attacks. Consequently, even though his generals eagerly volunteered to lead a storming party and Scott himself ruefully admitted that his countrymen would not be impressed by a victory unaccompanied by a lengthy "butcher's bill" of killed and wounded, he determined to reduce Vera Cruz by siege.[1]

This seemingly cautious strategy contained perils of its own. Siegecraft was generally slow, meticulous work, but speed was essential to Scott's success. From Washington he was being prodded by an impatient President Polk, undoubtedly eager to seize upon any setback as an excuse to replace Scott with a more politically congenial commander. Delay could also give Santa Anna time to rebuild his shattered army and attempt to break the siege. Most pressing of all, the Americans had to finish the business at Vera Cruz before the onset of the "vomito," or yellow fever season.

---

1. Winfield Scott, *Memoirs of Lieut.-General Scott, LL.D., Written by Himself,* 2 vols. (New York, 1864), 2:423–25.

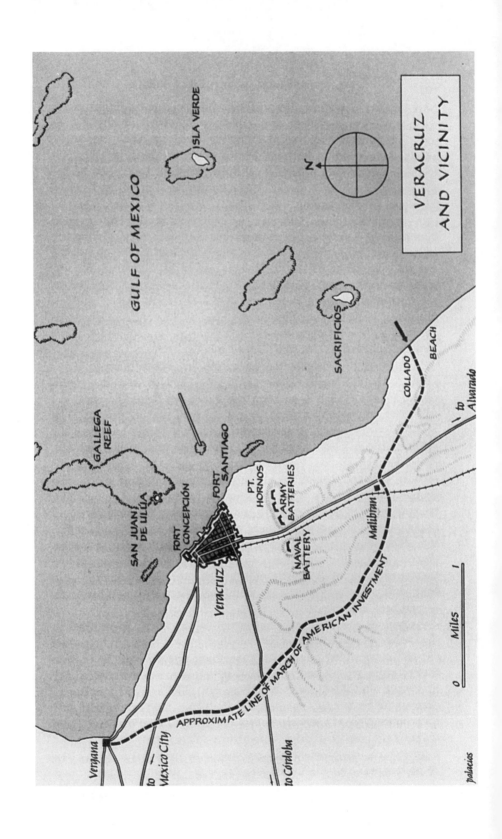

GULF OF MEXICO

ISLA VERDE

SACRIFICIOS

GALLEGA REEF

SAN JUAN DE ULÚA

FORT CONCEPCIÓN

FORT SANTIAGO

Veracruz

PT. HORNOS

ARMY BATTERIES

NAVAL BATTERY

Malibran

COLLADO BEACH

to Alvarado

APPROXIMATE LINE OF MARCH OF AMERICAN INVESTMENT

Vergara

to Mexico City

to Córdoba

0   1

Miles

palacios

N

VERACRUZ
AND VICINITY

March 10

BARCLAY. The sun rose clear and betokened another warm day. From the fleet innumerable boats are plying, conveying provisions, ammunition, cannon, etc. The army is scattered along the Beach. After a hasty breakfast from our haversacks, Gen. Patterson's[2] Division of Volunteers were formed in line about 8 A.M. and moved towards the hills. A steamer approaching very close opened a fire upon the Castle. With a great deal of labor a piece of artillery was planted on a sand hill and opened upon the City. The shots were mere fancy touches to ascertain distance and attract attention of the enemy. While mounting the hill the cry ran down the ranks that there was an attack in front. Immediately knapsacks were thrown off and the 2nd Penna. Regt. advanced at a run. The alarm proved false and several knapsacks were lost in our Company. Marching was extremely toilsome. From long confinement on the ships the men were weak. The sand was deep, being so loose that every step the foot sunk several inches. A heavy load and a hot day were additional annoyances. Preceded by the Tennessee Regt. and the 1st Pa. Regt., we marched on. The direction was towards the west of the City in order to surround it and cut off communications with the interior. To effect this it was necessary to march either out of reach of the enemy's guns or else under cover of the sand hills which encompass the City. Arrive about 10 o'clock at the second bench of the hills. Water is here obtained and the men rested. The gun from the hill on our right has been firing all morning. The enemy replying both from the Castle and City. About 3 P.M. arrive at the highest ridge of the bluffs on this side of the City and immediately descend along a road running through thick chapperal. A light engagement takes place between the advance and a party of Mexicans. The balls fall thick among the rear of Co. E. Proceed sometimes in single file along the path. Heavy chapperal on either side. The country appears expressly laid out for ambuscade. No enemy appear. Arrive tired at the ruins of old Monastery directly in the rear and in view of the City and being on the same plain. Good water. About 3 miles in rear of the City and 1/___ mile from the ruins there is a large building occupied as a magazine. A few shells from our artillery dispersed the Mexicans who occupied it and were engaged in removing the ammunition. The 1st Pa. Regt. took possession of the magazine this evening. The 1st Penna. and Tennessee Regts. moved on and occupied a height which overlooks the City. Some 600 lancers and infantry made resistance. They were quickly routed losing 6 men. No loss on

2. Born in Ireland and reared in Pennsylvania, Robert Patterson (1792–1881) served as an officer in the War of 1812, after which he became a prominent Pennsylvania politician and industrialist. At the outbreak of the Civil War he was appointed major general of volunteers. Given command of the Shenandoah Valley, he was assigned the task of preventing reinforcements from reaching the Confederate army at Bull Run, a task he signally failed to perform.

our side. The advantages gained today are very great. The City is nearly surrounded. It requires, however, the greatest labor to operate on this ground. There are no roads. The whole country is either thick chapperal or loose drifting sand. About dark, Lt. Col. Black[3] demanded an escort. Col. Roberts ordered 25 men from Co. E to escort him. Lt. Coulter and myself with 25 men had the honor to be detailed. Being already much fatigued, a rapid march of 2 miles along a path after dark was not very agreeable. In many places it was necessary to make use of the bushes to pull ourselves up the hills. Finally arrived at the quarters of the 1st. Col. Black left us without any orders and we returned again to our own camp. Arrived there late, perfectly worn out. During the night the enemy threw balls and shells. Twice aroused by alarms.

COULTER. About 2 o'clock A.M. called to arms, an advance party of the enemy having fired on the right of our line. The cause of the alarm soon retreated and we again lay down to await daylight. Again under arms as soon as it was light. About same time a small steamer called the "Spitfire" ran down under cover of a jutting point of land and exchanged a number of shots with the castle. About 7 o'clock our regiment moved. Extremely hot and very tiresome marching in the sand in which we sometimes sunk nearly over boot tops. Wound our way among the sand bluffs for a half a mile when there was a commotion on the right of the line and word came back that the enemy were in sight forward in considerable force. Knapsacks were cast away and we advanced at double quick. After proceeding at some distance at this rapid gait entered a small grassy bottom containing a couple of huts and surrounded by high sand bluffs covered in some places with chaparral. The Mexicans, if there were any number, had disappeared. A few were seen on the distant hills. Here occurred a scene not most creditable to our Captain. When word came back that the enemy were in front, order was in a measure broken and each company advanced as fast as possible without regard to regimental position and in fact we were found in the bottoms before some other companies whose positions were on our right. Our Captain who had just got up, walking to the head of the company remarked loud enough to be heard by many "Well, you did get up at last although you are a pack of God damned cowards." This was not very encouraging to a set of raw men who thought themselves on the eve of a battle. We did not come up as fast as we might have done on good ground. Having just come off the vessels the soft sand weakened us. All were tired, even older troops. Here halted for a short time that the men might regain their knapsacks and again moved on at a rapid pace for

3. Lieutenant Colonel Samuel W. Black of the 1st Pennsylvania Infantry. During the Civil War, he was colonel of the 62nd Pennsylvania Volunteer Infantry and fell at the head of his regiment at the battle of Gaines Mill, Virginia.

about three quarters of a mile when we entered another bottom covered in some places with scanty grass and watered by a small brackish stream. Here they were compelled to halt, the men just coming off ship board were broken down by the first rapid march and required rest and water. The heat was intense. Men were lying in every scanty shade exhausted and panting for water. The road was strewed with knapsacks, haversacks, canteens and loose articles of clothing which the men, unable to carry, had abandoned. Here we first came within range of the city batteries and several balls were thrown into our columns but without any injury. Ascending a small hill there lay before us an extreme and dense chaparral bottom through which we were to pass. Beyond this and to our left on an eminence lay a large white building which proved to be a magazine or at least had considerable ammunition in it. There was a considerable force in its neighborhood, both horse and foot and many horsemen were seen on all the distant hills. A field piece was dragged to an eminence commanding this building and with a few well directed shots soon dispersed its occupants. The two Louisiana and two Pennsylvania Regiments entered the chaparral together, the first by a left hand road to capture the magazine (which was, however, deserted before they arrived) and the latter by another leading to the right, to take possession of a height about a mile and a half in advance. The chaparral was dense and intersected by mere cow paths so that we were compelled to march single file and in a stooping position to avoid the overhanging bushes. By the time the first regiment and a portion of ours had entered they were fired upon, or thought so, and the right companies returning it, in consequence of the winding nature of the path, sent their volley among the companies next in rear, who mistaking it, answered and soon the firing became general. So that a large portion of the balls thrown among us were by our comrades, though I think mixed with some Mexican pills. Passed through this thicket without the loss of a man, which was singular from the amount of firing and carelessness with which they fired upon one another. Entered another valley leading directly to the city in which there was a large lagoon which we forded and halted in the neighborhood of an old monastery near which was a dwelling apparently but lately deserted. Here found a well of water and enjoyed a lunch from our haversacks. The First Pennsylvania with the Louisiana Regiment continued their march and shortly after the firing recommenced and continued for about an hour at intervals, when an officer riding past informed us that the heights were taken. During this time several lancers would ride down the drift from the city towards us and by way of bravado, fire their escopetas [muskets] and retreat with a yell. This they tried once or twice. A rifleman ventured up under cover of the bushes and when they came out again returned their fire. His ball passed too close for their fancy and they did not again repeat the experiment. Bivouacked here all night and slept on the hillside. A detail of twenty men was taken from our company to escort Colonel Black to his regiment. Were under arms several times during the night, but the alarms were either false, or the enemy finding us always on the alert, retreated.

March 11

BARCLAY. Co. E. detailed as "sappers & miners" to cut roads for the cannon and cavalry. The boys worked with good will. The enemy threw bombs and balls all day and judging of the movements of our troops they fired with great accuracy. An engagement took place between part of Genl. Quitman's[4] command and the enemy and missiles of every size fell among the working party, one shot in particular striking very close to Dr. Ross.[5] A round shot took off the head of Capt. [William] Alburtis, a regular officer. Two or three were wounded on the *heights*. The Alabama and South Carolina Regts. are now on the heights and Riflemen have taken possession of the ground between the Heights and the Gulf after a brush skirmish. Report says 16 Mexicans killed and 6 Americans wounded. The City is now completely surrounded, the investment extending from Gulf to Gulf. Three pieces of cannon after great labor have been mounted on the heights and three more arrived at the "ruins." Towards evening after a hard day's work the 2nd Regt. were removed from the ruins and posted at the railroad (this railroad runs some 6 miles from the City towards the interior) in order to prevent all entrance into the City. It having been ascertained that a large body of Mexican troops were without the lines and would likely attempt to communicate with the City, at first the Regt. were posted in two lines opposite to each other on both sides of the road. This was the most dangerous position our Company had been placed in, not that we feared the Mexicans but being directly opposite, we were in range of the "revolvers" of Co. A, every member of that Company being armed with that amiable weapon. Much to our satisfaction, about 10 P.M. the position of the companies were changed, all being placed on one side of the road to prevent accidents. Company E was now on the extreme left towards the City. The men were formed into two files which watched alternately. About 12 at night the picket guard ran towards camp crying "Fire, Fire, Raise the alarm," at the same time snapping his gun. The gun

4. Though born and educated in New York, John Anthony Quitman (1798–1858) became an ardent champion of Southern rights after he relocated to Mississippi in the 1820s. Although a man of scholarly tastes (he had once taught English in college) and polished manners, he adapted well to military life, becoming (along with James Shields) the most successful of Polk's political generals. After the Mexican War, he immersed himself in politics, being elected governor of Mississippi and, later, a congressman from that state, but dying before the secession of the Confederacy, a movement he would, no doubt, have heartily endorsed.

5. As there was no surgeon named *Dr.* Ross in the U.S. Army in Mexico, this is probably a misprint for *Lt.* Andrew Ross, who recently had been promoted from corporal in the Westmoreland Guards. Sent home on account of illness, he died at sea in May of 1847.

finally went off. Upon investigation it was discovered that two horsemen were the cause of the alarm, who turned back towards the City upon the discharge of the piece. Several alarms were raised during the night behind our encampment.

COULTER. Company E was detailed as axe men under cover of Company F to cut an artillery road around the hill from our camp until we came to a railroad supposed to lead to Alvarado, but as we afterwards discovered only finished a few miles from the city. It is a very good piece of workmanship, but the nature of the soil is too yielding to form any support. The wind in many places had laid the timbers entirely bare. From the top of the hill beyond, commenced our work. Passed a number of ranches and during our whole course balls and bombs thrown from the city at the heights fell among us and in our immediate neighborhood. Cut up hill and down hill, having to take considerable of a circuit to gain a practicable route which I think must have made three miles of road. Reached the heights and here found the First Pennsylvania Regiment who had been engaged at intervals all day. They had killed a number and captured several mustangs. A number of our men were wounded just when we came to the top. Saw a rifleman killed by a cannon shot. Returning, passed General Twiggs and his division with two field pieces. Our party escaped without loss, although several of General Twiggs' men were killed and wounded; on our road one of them, Captain Alburtis, was killed. Towards evening returned to camp and remained on arms. Shortly after, slung knapsacks and took up our line of march. Halted at the railroad where we crossed it in the morning. Were formed on each side of the road under cover of a fence and bushes, one half of each company to stand to their arms while the other half slept. As soon as night would completely conceal the work, three pieces of artillery were placed so as to reach the road in both directions. By the way, this was a poor position and showed but little generalship in our commander (General Pillow)[6] and in

6. Gideon Johnson Pillow (1806–1878) had been the Tennessee law partner of James Knox Polk, whose presidential nomination he helped secure. This seems to have constituted his chief qualification for military command. As a soldier, he has been described as "ambitious, quarrelsome, and, though personally courageous, exceedingly inept" (Charles Winslow Elliott, *Winfield Scott: The Soldier and the Man* [New York: Macmillan, 1937], 454). An accomplished intriguer, he helped inflame Polk's suspicions regarding Winfield Scott, and, indeed, it was Pillow's self-adulatory newspaper dispatches that precipitated the events leading to Scott's dismissal. During the Civil War, Pillow was a brigadier general in the Confederate army, in which capacity he was largely responsible for the ignominious abandonment of Fort Donelson in February of 1862, the last important command with which he was entrusted.

The episode complained of by Coulter was not the first of Pillow's military gaffes. Earlier, in northern Mexico, he had ordered an entrenching party to pile the dirt on the forward side of a ditch, thus protecting any would-be attackers. Nor, as the Pennsylvania volunteers would discover at Cerro Gordo, would it be his last.

case there had been an attack, we must inevitably have killed as many of our own men as the enemy. About 10 o'clock he discovered this and to prevent any cross firing, ordered the companies on our side of the road to the left of those on the other. Were under arms during the night in consequence of sallies from the city. One of these alarms was the cause of some amusement. A sentinel seeing a Mexican approaching at a short distance, attempted to shoot him, but finding his gun would not go off called to the officer that there was a Mexican man. He replied "Shoot him, God damn you, why don't you shoot him." The fellow said that his flint would not strike fire. "Shoot him, God damn you, shoot him" again replied the officer. The sentinel again attempted it, but could not. Another sentinel fired his gun to rouse the camp and the Mexican vamosed.

March 12

BARCLAY. Still continued to guard the railroad. Two 12 pounders arrived last night from the ruins and now in position to sweep the railroad. The sappers and miners are endeavoring to find the pipes which supply the City with water. They have succeeded in stopping one stream of about 10 inches. Sergt. McLaughlin and myself slip off to the beach some 3 miles distant in order to find a sutler store and get something to eat. Return without getting any eatables. The Mexicans towards evening having erected a small battery in front of the City fire two round shot. The second shot passes a few feet above Genl. Patterson's tent which is near the road. The General moves his quarters double quick time. At night our Company was placed on the road running near the railroad. Left (being on the extreme left towards the City) for a few hours solitary and alone. About 10 P.M. Col. Campbell[7] joined us with his Regt. [the 1st Tennessee Infantry.] As usual an alarm and all called to arms. As we are new troops there is always considerable noise and confusion at these alarms. A rattling of tins and canteens, awkward men hunting their places in line, etc., we here observed the quietness and order of old troops. The Tennesseans rose as one man and their Regt. made less noise than our Company. Considerable firing on our right. Towards morning, two cannon shot from the City.

COULTER. Before daylight this morning the artillery was dragged to our side of the road that it might not be seen from the city. Were allowed to rest this day. Had tolerably good water. The men have been helping them-

---

7. William Bowen Campbell (1807–1867) fought as a volunteer in the Seminole Wars and served for three terms in the U.S. Congress as a Whig, representing Andrew Jackson's home district in Tennessee before the outbreak of the Mexican War. After the war he returned to Tennessee and was elected governor in 1851. A strong Unionist, he opposed secession and turned down offers of military command from the Confederacy, accepting instead a brigadier-generalship in the Union army. Returned to Congress in 1865, he supported the policies of President Andrew Johnson in the brief time his failing health permitted.

selves from a garden across the way. The source from which the city receives a part of its water has been discovered. Tanks situate along the road. The sappers were engaged today cutting off this supply, which is rather a difficult job, as the pipes are very thick and made of Roman cement. Feeling a disposition for some venison or Mexican beef, a party of us determined to try our luck at shooting a cow. Traveled about a mile and a half down the road towards Alvarado where we fell in with several other parties on the same errand. Were in the act of pulling down a fine looking bull when the alarm was given that lancers were approaching. Some of the others gave us half a beef which they were unable to carry. There were a party of horsemen in sight but did not come within musket shot and we were allowed to carry off our spoil without further molestation. There was a grand roasting of beef when we returned. Cut a fine piece of steak which I roasted very nicely over the fire on a stub. Turned around to get a piece of cracker when some hungry devil nabbed my supper. This disturbed the equanimity of my temper and so I retired without cooking any more. A shot was fired this evening from the city which ranged full length of our camp but without doing any damage more than requiring us to move under the protection of the banks. During the night had an alarm, but it was of no consequence.

March 13

BARCLAY. Moved from our position to a road running at right angles with the railroad. Yesterday evening our lads got a half beef. This morning it was cooked. At 10 A.M. Company E were moved to the magazine. Lay in the sun all day. After night were again placed in our old position at the railroad.

COULTER. Before daylight knapsacks were slung for march. Halted about midway on the road to the old monastery in a place secure from the enemy's shot, who, having discovered us yesterday evening, it was supposed would open their fire as soon as it was light. Have breakfasted on the beef captured yesterday, and to my shame must admit that without the least inconvenience I had what would have provisioned a family and two small dogs. About 10 o'clock again on the march and halted at the magazine mentioned some days ago. Several of us went out to try our luck at capturing a donkey to pack provisions. Discovered two some distance down a drift of meadow which we pursued and soon found ourselves entangled in a deep marsh. Stuck fast several times and after continuing the chase for about half a mile returned to camp without any. Shortly after again went out for beef. Went about two miles down the railroad and by that time had been joined by several other parties so that we then numbered about thirty muskets under Lt. [Isaac] Hare, of Company F. Here left the road and entered the hills to the right. Marched about a mile, passing a number of ranches when we were halted by an extensive lagoon. While here a number of Mexican flints were found, which a Mexican from a neighboring ranch gave us to understand were lost by a party of lancers who, on seeing us come up the opposite hill, had retreated across the lagoon. For the first time considered that we were further out than any party had been before us and in the neighborhood of a supposed Mexican camp. Struck into a path which we thought ran parallel to the railroad and started for camp. After following this for about two miles fell in with a detachment of the New York Regiment who informed us that they had had a skirmish with a party of lancers near the lagoon we had just left. Found that the path which we had followed instead of running parallel to the railroad had led us into the hills and that we were now even farther from camp than before. Being put right, after a tedious march over several ugly hills and though brush, arrived at the magazine in fit condition to stow away beef, but without any. About 8 o'clock returned to our old position on the railroad and during the night were several times under arms on account of small parties sallying from the city, who, as usual, retreated on being discovered.

March 14

BARCLAY. Sunday morning, Co. E. marched to the magazine where we lay until evening with part of the 2nd Regt. The effect of removing us each day from the railroad appears to be to entice the Mexicans to attempt an entrance as they would only do this at night. There is every night an ambuscade laid for them which is removed in daylight. Saml. Montgomery visited us today. He brought me a couple of papers from Greensburgh. After leaving Orleans his business called him to the Brazos and he only landed a few days ago. Some of our boys shot and brought in another beef. It was cooked in a large tin vessel which had been captured and some excellent soup cooked. In the evening marched about three miles to a point N.W. of the City. The march was very fatiguing being thru deep sand and lay as usual all night under arms. Formed with the 1st Penna. and New York Regt. a strong picket guard. Co. E alarmed about 3 A.M. by our sentry Shields firing. Alarm false. We are now within about a mile and a half of the City. Prisoners taken in the country are brought in daily.

COULTER. At daybreak again returned to the magazine. The object of this changing of position is to prevent reinforcements or supplies from entering the city at night and to be out of range of their guns during the day. Rained for a couple of hours, which detained us, as some of the party were compelled to dry their wet loads. Stopped at a ranch where we ate some corn cakes, coffee and roast beef head. Here first learned the manner of making these corn cakes which are called "Tortillas." The corn is boiled in an earthen jar. Smashed on a stone with a stone roller, patted into cakes with the hand and baked on a hot stove. They taste of the cob and are very flat, no salt being used. The coffee (cafe it was called) had something of a taste like ours, but I understand it was made of a kind of a bean which grows here, coffee itself being too expensive for this class of people. The beef head was roasted on the coals with the hair on, but like the tortillas, without salt. While engaged at this feast, were disturbed by heavy firing in the neighboring chaparral, which we found to be a party amusing themselves by practicing platoon firing at such a distance from camp. After another short tramp through the bushes had the luck to shoot a couple of fine cows. On returning to camp had quite a feast. Some of the boys found an old tin vessel (I think the lining of a trunk) in which they made a company soup and we had quite a time roasting meat on the coals. About dusk marched and such a march as it was. Crossed the railroad below the magazine so as to conceal our force from the enemy. Traveled at a rapid pace over sand hill and through ravine for a distance of two or three miles—at the time I thought it ten—and halted on the extreme left of General Pillow's brigade and the right of General Shields.[8] Although short, this was a hard march, especially after having been out all day after beef. In climbing some of the hills were compelled to hold on to the bushes, which would sometimes pull out and away the chap would go rolling down the hill. Sand deep and towards the latter end dragged along without caring whether I went at all. Lay along the bank on the roadside under cover of the chaparral, with orders. In case of an attack, to fire into the road without showing ourselves. Were under arms but no enemy appeared. Were then ordered to turn out and sit along the roadside and if we slept, to sleep in that position as close to the bank as possible. Were not again alarmed during the night.

March 15

BARCLAY. Lay in our position of last night from which we have a close and beautiful view of the City. Heard distinctly the shouts of the Mexicans and their Bands playing in the morning. Were saluted as usual by several shot and shell. In the afternoon, Genl. Scott rode along the line and announced the glorious victory gained by Genl. Taylor at Buena Vista. This was the first time I have seen Genl. Scott. He is a very large, portly, kind looking man. I would judge about 55 years of age.[9] This evening moved

8. The Irish-born James Shields (1806–1879) could boast the unique distinction of having been elected to the U.S. Senate from three different states: Illinois, Minnesota, and Missouri. As a young man in Illinois, he had challenged Abraham Lincoln to a duel, but the two men made up the quarrel and became close friends despite their political differences. During the Civil War, Shields was a brigadier general of volunteers, serving most notably in the Shenandoah Valley.

9. Scott turned sixty-one on 13 June 1847.

about ½ mile to the right. The left of the Company twice formed to night on account of distant picket firing. Towards daylight commenced raining. No protection but our blankets which are completely soaked.

COULTER. Our position now is very near the middle of the line, the city lying rather between us and the castle and a mile and half distant. Have a beautiful view of the city and the batteries have been occasionally firing throughout the day, but with no effect as it is difficult for them to ascertain our exact position. General Scott rode along the line and confirmed the news received at San Antonio Lizardo of General Taylor's victory at Buena Vista. In the evening moved about half a mile to the right to the position lately occupied by the First Pennsylvania Regiment. Twice under arms during the night on account of distant firing.

March 16
BARCLAY. We have been living since we landed on biscuit and pork and a little fresh beef which the boys shot. Today coffee and rice arrived from the beach. Lay quiet all day. Several shot and shells fell near us. After night a brisk skirmish took place to our right. Report says at the railroad. Rained constantly for a long time. Very disagreeable. Corp. Bigelow and myself both being on the left made a bower of the chapperal and slept together.

COULTER. Towards daylight was a drizzling soaking rain. Got coffee, sugar and rice from the beach, the first we have been able to get. During the night there was brisk firing to our right; from the sound must have been in the neighborhood of the railroad. This night our blankets were again soaked with rain.

March 17
BARCLAY. A salute fired by the Navy in honor of Taylor's victory. Lieut. Armstrong with Mechling and Gordon sent to the ships for our tents, clothing, etc. Two details from the company at work cutting roads and assisting to haul cannon. The navy landing guns, ammunition, axes, spades, etc. A sailor killed by the Rancheros.

COULTER. There was a salute fired by the navy in honor of Taylor's victory. Lt. Armstrong and Mechling and Gordon were sent to the ship at San Antonio Lizardo for tents, clothing, camp utensils, etc. Tonight was on guard, but had no occasion to alarm the regiment. Was some firing in the direction of Twiggs' division, but none in our neighborhood. Tonight again rained on us.

March 18
BARCLAY. Bates sent to the hospital at the magazine. Received a mail which brought us letters and papers from home, the first since our depar-

ture. The joy is universal. Those who have at a great distance and after a long absence from home been placed in the same pleasant situation can appreciate our feelings.

COULTER. Received a mail today, the first since leaving New Orleans. The city and castle batteries have been firing at intervals, as they have done more or less ever since we landed, all day but without effect. During the night had the pleasure of another ducking.

March 19

BARCLAY. Moved to a new road running parallel to our present position and nearer the City. Made bowers to protect us from the sun and rain. 28 men detailed for duty at 2 A.M. under Lt. Coulter. 17 men under myself at 5 P.M. started to the beach where with 17 from each Co. in the Regt. they reported to the Commander in Chief. Under the direction of an Engineer officer dug a ditch (6 wide by 4 ft. deep) from the height near the beach towards the Cemetery. A line was extended along the ground and each man dug a certain distance. Worked hard all night and marched to camp after daylight.

COULTER. Breakfast over, again under arms for another change of camp. Marched across to a road cut some few days ago which cuts off a considerable bend in our line and is much nearer the city. Was engaged until noon clearing away the brush and making booths to sleep in. This done, went to the beach. Had a tiresome march of it. After passing the old monastery in part did not know the road, things were so much changed and the road so much shorter than when I had passed there, not having been down since the landing. Instead of a winding cow path through the chaparral bottom in which the firing happened on the first day, there was a good and straight waggon road. Instead of making the great circuit we did through the sand bluffs, the road was now direct and studded with the camps of Worth's division, who have tents, cooking utensils and all camp conveniences, while we poor devils roast our meat on the fire on sticks and are satisfied if we can get a spot clear of thorns to sleep in. The beach surpasses the levee of New Orleans. A number of rough board houses have been erected and for a great extent there are immense quantities of corn and provender, bags heaped, any quantity of barrels of provisions. Horses, mules, drays and carts without number and carpenters at work. A great deal of shipping off the bar and many vessels unloading their cargo. It appears more like the wharf of a mercantile city than the camp of an invading army. Here found Lt. Armstrong and Mechling and Gordon who have returned from San Antonio Lizardo with the three of our company left on the "J. N. Cooper" (McClain, Heasley and Huston). They reported that the other two were dead. Jno. Kerr died on the 11th inst. And Thos. Spears on the 16th inst. Our baggage was safely landed, but in our present migratory mode of life, it would only be a bother to us, and it was left at the beach in charge of Mechling and Gordon. Towards evening my stomach rather called for some nourishment, not having eaten anything since morning. Started for camp, where I arrived pretty well done out about 9 o'clock and compelled to lie down supperless. About 12 o'clock when I had gotten into a pretty good sleep, ordered under arms to assist in erecting a battery. Such a march as we had of it. The officer commanding us (Captain Loeser of Company A) was drunk and unacquainted with the road. He first marched us about two miles to the railroad and down that to very near the city. Finding his mistake, countermarched about a mile, then about three miles through the chapparal over a path in which we had to march single file in a stooping posture and dark as pitch. Again wrong and again countermarched about a mile in another direction. Then another countermarch and we might have continued it all night had we not been overtaken by a rider who conducted us to the battery where we arrived about an hour before daylight. Soon after under arms on account of an alarm. Heavy firing in our immediate neighborhood between a picket and a small portion of the enemy. But not wishing to disclose our position, we remained quiet and the firing soon after ceased.

March 20
BARCLAY. Nearly all the men having been on duty everybody is tired. The enemy are cannonading Worth who is erecting batteries near the Cemetery. A small foraging party was attacked and surrounded by a large body of Rancheros. Some of our men went to their rescue. No one killed. Heard of the death of John Kerr and Thomas Spears. The former died on the 11th, the latter on the 16th inst. Kerr was from near West Newton. He was an old school mate of mine, both being together at the Academy. He read law with Mr. Foster. I knew him well. He was of a quiet retired disposition, very amiable and well disposed to everybody. Spears was from Pittsburgh. When we left the ship no one supposed that he would die. The poor boy was only 18 years of age. He was of quiet turn and well liked in the Company. The rest of the sick and our stores are landed from the Cooper. A party sent today to the beach for provisions. 11 men detailed for extra duty, several of my seventeen boys among the number. The poor fellows, altho up all last night and almost worn out, obey without a murmer. They know that the work must be done and they will not back out. At dark orders from Col. Roberts for Co. E to move to the extreme right (our place in the Regt. is next to the left Co.) as there is some work to do, we have the post of honor. There has been considerable partiality shown of late in the Regt. and we are becoming tired of it. Night dark and gloomy. Wind high and clouds of sand drifting over us. The men are all in a very bad humor. Aroused to arms about midnight by a firing towards the City. Remained under arms for sometime.

COULTER. Worked on the battery until about 2 o'clock in the afternoon. It was a tedious job, half the time over the knees in sand and half of every shovelful darted back in one's face by the wind. Worked for a while on the top of the battery, which was very tiresome, being compelled to lie down flat to prevent being seen from the city and push the sand forward with our hands. Once raised up full length (but was ordered off the battery for it) and got a full view of the city. It being considerably below us and at no great distance from this work, which will certainly play the devil with it when it gets into operation. The city batteries kept up a brisk fire all day on General Worth, who has a position at an old cemetery considerably to our right. Our work lay rather between him and the extreme left battery of the city. The shot and shell from that continually passed near us and crashed through the chaparral in our neighborhood, but without doing any injury. When the relief did come in, Captain Loeser, still pretty tight, ordered us to remain until 4 o'clock, but, Lt. Coulter, taking the responsibility on himself, marched us to camp. Found the road, though long, much shorter than the night previous. Got some warm coffee which was refreshing after one day's total fast and the previous on dry crackers. Before we had been long in camp our company was again under arms and marched about half a mile to the summit of a sand hill some distance to the right of the regiment where we remained all night. Once under arms on account of an alarm, but as usual, Mexicans were scarce by that time. There was a heavy norther blowing all night and we were completely buried in sand, with ears, eyes, nose and mouth all full. This march caused some dissatisfaction in the company. Our Colonel wishes to include in his line an unguarded spot to the right of the regiment. Either from ignorance or partiality, instead of extending the regiment so as to throw the right on this ground ordered Company E, the company next to the extreme left, to the extreme right of the regiment.

March 21

BARCLAY. Going back to camp this morning, the sand was blown about so much that we could scarcely see our way. Several vessels were blown ashore. Learned that the firing last night was occasioned by a large party of Mexicans who came out from the City to ascertain where our fatigue parties were at work. They kept however at a respectful distance and fired at random. Our men did not reply, not wishing their position to be known. The batteries are advanced very near the City. This day is pleasant. Sergt. Marchand and myself ascended a hill in front of camp and for a couple of hours watched the Mexicans cannonading where they supposed Worth lay. In the evening our Regt. moved to the right to ground occupied by the 1st Pa. Regt.

COULTER. At daybreak again returned to our old camp at the left of the regiment. Were allowed to remain in camp all day to fish the sand out of our eyes. At dusk again changed in camp. The whole regiment were moved to the right and camped on the ground lately occupied by the First Pennsylvania. During the night were almost suffocated by the smell of carrion and beef bones left by its late occupants.

March 22

BARCLAY. A party from Co. E went out for beef. I went to the Ruins and the magazine to see the sick. At 2 P.M. Worth's batteries opened upon the City. Firing hot on both sides. Towards evening companies H & K ordered out as working parties, Companies F & E as their guard. March to the Seamen's battery.[10] This battery is somewhat to the left and nearer the City than Worth's. The enemy are yet entirely ignorant of its construction. The pieces about being mounted have been with great labor brought from the ships (they are 64's). Dense chapperal and a knob of the sand hill conceal the workmen. When the pieces are mounted the bushes will be cut away and the hill dug to a proper level. The guns are under the direction of navy officers. The men are filling sand bags, digging, carrying sand bags, etc. During the night a constant fire is kept up on both sides. Bombs are almost constantly in the air, sometimes two and three at a time. The bombs can be seen during their whole passage. It is a beautiful sight and the execution done in the City must be tremendous. Towards evening a steamer and some gunboats approach the Castle and open a brisk fire. During the night we obtained but little rest.

COULTER. Today were occupied in burying the carrion and in a manner purified the spot. About 4 o'clock a portion of the regiment were ordered for duty, Company E with the number. Marched to the old monastery. On the way there noticed that another battery had appeared, which from the direction could not be Mexicans. On arriving at the monastery discovered that General Worth had opened a battery, repaying with interest what he had been receiving for some days, and from the bombs I saw bursting in the city, with much more execution. Reported to General Pillow and ordered as a guard to the Sailor's battery at which we had been a few days ago. General Worth kept up a cannonade all night so as to draw the attention from our battery, which was not ready, and which, strange to say had not yet been discovered by the enemy, although a large number of men had been working there daily for some time back and within seven hundred yards from the city walls.

10. Because Scott lacked artillery heavy enough to breach the walls of Vera Cruz, he had to borrow guns from the navy. Commodore Matthew C. Perry obligingly lent him two 32-pounders from the *Potomac*, one from the *Raritan*, and three 8-inch shell guns from the *Mississippi*, the *Albany*, and *St. Mary's*, which were dismantled and hauled overland to the battery Barclay and Coulter were guarding. Because of interservice rivalry, Perry insisted that his guns had to be manned by naval personnel, hence the nickname "Seamen's Battery" for what was officially Battery Number Five.

March 23

BARCLAY. Yesterday Capt. Vinton[11] was killed at Worth's battery. The fire still continues with great activity. Nothing is heard but the continued roar of artillery. Altho the enemy fire with great accuracy, Genl. Worth has his men so well covered that only two or three have been injured. Some large pieces are being brought to the Sailors' Battery. It requires very great labor to haul the carriages through the sand. The sailors are the principal workmen. They are a jovial set and this land cruise is regarded in the light of a spree. They are so brisk and active and work with good will. It is amusing to see them at work. All orders are in sailors' jargon. About 100 of them were hauling up one of the carriages today. The officer in charge imagining himself on the Quarter Deck was away in the rear taking sight and giving orders. "Pull away on the ____board side." "Ay, Ay, Sir," answered the men at the ropes. "More men on the starboard." "Ay, Ay, Sir," was always the answer. The party who were out yesterday for beef arrived this morning at the battery with a very seasonable supply ready cooked. They were acceptable guests. Towards night we were relieved by some of the Illinois men. In marching past them the Illinois boys were much surprised at the size of our Company, the campaign having reduced their ranks. Marching to camp was very disagreeable on account of a high wind which blew the sand direct in our faces.

COULTER. This battery is a different looking affair from what we left it a few days ago. The breastwork is eight feet high and about ten feet deep. The work is about one hundred and twenty feet in length. It is the most secure and will be the most effective, being within blank shot of all parts of the city. It is intended for six guns, five sixty-eights and one thirty-two. When we left, the thirty-two was mounted and two others there and the rest expected during the night. Remained until 4 o'clock and then returned to camp. About 7 o'clock saw from our camp a great light in the direction of the city. It proved to be several buildings outside the walls fired by Worth's battery.

March 24

BARCLAY. This Sailor's Battery opened upon the City. The enemy had no suspicion of it until the guns opened. As the pieces are of the heaviest metal the destruction of life and property in the City must be very great. A detail from Co. E went to the beach for provisions. I read today 4 or 5 books of Telemachus[12] and wrote to W[illiam] F. J[ohnston].

11. Brevetted a major for gallantry at Monterey, John Rogers Vinton (West Point, 1817) of Rhode Island was praised by Winfield Scott as "perhaps the most accomplished officer in the army" (Scott, *Memoirs*, 2:429). He was killed, according to the official reports, "by the wind of a shell."

12. *The Adventures of Telemachus* by the French quietist bishop François Fenelon (1651–1715) was, in its English translation by Dr. Hawkesworth, available in many English

COULTER. The sailor's battery, at which we had been, opened on the city at 8 o'clock this morning. In the evening was detailed for guard. Stationed at an outpost on the summit of a high sand bluff. Had a beautiful view of the cannonade which was kept up at intervals during the whole night. The night was rather dark, but both the city batteries and ours could be distinguished by the flashing of the guns and the course of the bombs could be traced through the air by the burning fuses attached to them, until they lit with a terrible crashing in the heart of the city, bursting with a loud noise, lighting up the neighborhood. Was not disturbed on my post.

March 25

BARCLAY. Heavy cannonading until evening. A brisk skirmish took place about a mile from the magazine between Col. Harneys'[13] Dragoons and a party of Lancers. The latter retreated. A few prisoners and some thirty horses taken. Jack Gilchrist was in the fight. Lt. Coulter and myself were on guard tonight. The sentries were somewhat aguish and kept firing all night at imaginary Lancers. The consequence was I got no sleep having to visit each sentry as he fired. Two Mexicans, probably fugitives from the party defeated today, I believe were seen and gave cause for all the alarms.

COULTER. Cannonade kept up briskly all day. Heretofore we were not allowed to show ourselves on the tops of the bluffs to prevent drawing the fire of the enemy, but this caution is now thought unnecessary, and some of us took our station on a hill to see the effect of our batteries. This time

---

and American editions. An elevated work of "moral imagination," it utilized the adventures of the son of Ulysses as a framework to promote Fenelon's passive religiosity. After this diary entry, Barclay makes no further mention of the book.

13. A brilliant but chronically insubordinate officer, William Selby Harney (1800–1889) was the highest ranking cavalryman in Scott's army. Arrested and court-martialed for disobedience, Harney was restored to command in time to lead the decisive charge at the Battle of Cerro Gordo, for which he was brevetted brigadier general.

His post–Mexican War career was checkered, with brilliant episodes of Indian fighting alternating with political difficulties (usually self-induced). In 1855 he was responsible for the brutal Indian massacre at Ash Hollow, and in 1859 he almost precipitated a war with Great Britain. Ethan Allen Hitchcock described him as "a man without education, intelligence or humanity," and resigned his commission rather than serve under him. (Ethan Allen Hitchcock, *Fifty Years in Camp and Field. Diary of Major-General Ethan Allen Hitchcock, U.S.A.*, ed. W. A. Croffut [New York: G. P. Putnam, 1909], 418.)

During the Civil War, despite his Tennessee background, he remained loyal to the Union, but his services were not used due to suspicions of possible pro-Southern leaning.

In the episode at the Medellin Bridge mentioned by Barclay, Harney's impetuosity again superseded his judgment. Ordered to reconnoiter, Harney instead precipitated a skirmish with what he claimed was a force of two thousand Mexicans. Since the Mexican force actually numbered less than 150, Coulter's rumored estimate that they suffered from fifty to a hundred casualties (see entry of March 26) should be scaled down proportionately.

had a beautiful sight of a daylight cannonade as I before had of it by night. Had a complete view of all the batteries and the city, which lay considerably below us and about a mile and half distant. Saw some nautical shots made by the sailors in Patterson's battery. Every shot they either damaged the batteries or fired one of the domes or spires. Some of the boys with true Yankee impudence, ventured in around to within a few hundred yards of the city in order to obtain a better view. This evening a flag of truce was sent from the city requesting time to bury their dead. General Scott granted them six hours for that purpose. It afterwards proved to be only a ruse of theirs to gain time to repair their batteries. About 9 o'clock were under arms in consequence of several shots being fired. On examination, as has several times been the case, proved that the sentinels had been firing at jackasses.

March 26

BARCLAY. Batteries opened before daylight but ceased firing at daylight. The general report is that the enemy are about to surrender. Several flags have passed between Genl. Scott and the City. Four splendidly mounted horsemen have arrived from the Interior with a flag of Truce. The Ship of War, The Ohio, came to anchor yesterday. A most violent "norther" is raging today. The loose sand is flying in all directions. The air is darkened and objects at a very short distance cannot be seen. The Camp presents a most desolate appearance. Without tents the men lay rolled up in their blankets. The sand falls like snow. Indeed the storm forcibly recalls to our minds the violent snow storms of the north. Cooking is out of the question in camp and we retreat and build fires in the thick chapparal. Even there the sand follows us and we are forced to take a greater quantity of that article than our fastidious friends in the north would fancy.

COULTER. Cannonade continued very briskly until about 8 or 9 o'clock when it ceased altogether. It is now blowing a heavy norther. Sand blowing in all directions, blinding everything. H. B. Kuhns, who has been rather sick for some days back, was sent to the coast in company with two of the company. Wishing to see him fixed, followed. Had quite a time of it. Compelled to tie up my face to prevent being completely blinded. Reached the top of one of the sand bluffs where the sand, being yielding, was twice blown over and rolled to the very bottom. Lost my way and did not discover my mistake until in the neighborhood of General Worth's battery. My cap blew over one of the bluffs into the chapparal below. Going after it struck a path which I followed for about an hour, when I struck the main road, pretty well used up. Shortly after reached the beach. Not much doing there. Unable to land stores or ammunition, the sea being in a perfect foam. This norther is said to be the severest felt this season. Sand blowing here as badly as back among the hills. Roads drifting up and changing hourly which makes it difficult to find one's way. Heard that Colonel Harney, with a party of dragoons, some volunteers and a few artillerymen with two field pieces routed a Mexican force yesterday evening some ten miles south of this at a village called Medellin. Several of our men killed and wounded. Mexican loss from fifty to one hundred. Heard also that a capitulation is going on, which was confirmed by circumstances, all hostilities having ceased this morning. This night felt the cold more severe than since we landed. During the night General Worth mounted a number more mortars and is actively preparing to give them a worse drubbing in case they will not surrender.

March 27

BARCLAY. I went to the magazine to see Bates and McIntire and thence to the beach for provisions. The firing has ceased and it is generally believed that the Castle and City are about surrendering. A great many of our men are close to the walls, viewing the cemetery, buying liquor, etc.

COULTER. Cannonade has not recommenced. General Worth is treating relative to a capitulation. They still wish to get some terms, but General Scott will accept nothing but an unconditional surrender of the city and castle. This evening our company was detailed for camp guard. A new plan was adopted in posting the men. The entire three relays were posted in the evening, allowing two to sleep on post while the other stood his turn. This is of considerable advantage to the men, as they will not lose half their rest in trotting around every relief. Had no occasion for an alarm, although there were plenty of asses (the usual cause of alarm) running about.

March 28

BARCLAY. The Articles of Capitulation signed. Our fatigue party returned to camp for the first time without any beef. Cattle are becoming scarce. These excursions for beef are attended with great labor and considerable danger. Coulter, McLaughlin, Steck, Carney and Forney are the principal hunters. Sometimes they venture as far as 6 and 8 miles from Camp, kill their beef and carry it home on their shoulders over hills through marshes and chapperal. Arriving in camp almost exhausted, a supper of hot coffee, crackers and their beef restores them and in the morning they are ready for another hunt. Letters and papers received from the States. Dates up to the 12th Febry, 1847.

COULTER. Went out on a beef hunt today. Continued along the railroad to its termination and entered a meadow on the left where we soon discovered a number of cattle which were alarmed by our appearance. Quite a chase ensued and considerable waste of powder. Tried to shoot at one on the wing, but she only scampered off the faster with a bullet in her hind quarters as was evident from the gait and the blood in the track. This lot escaped us, but shortly after one of our boys pulled down a cow which proved to be rather old, and so we left her, choosing to hunt better game. Went on to a small village or rather a collection of some fifteen or twenty ranches about eight miles from camp. Visited the different huts and were civilly received merely on account of our force (being ten) or I believe the scoundrels would have cut all our throats had it been in their power. Towards evening returned to camp, tired, and on account of being so particular, without beef.

March 29

BARCLAY. Early roll call and breakfast. Arms and uniforms cleaned. At 9 A.M. the 2nd Pa. Regt. join Gen. Pillow's Brigade at the railroad. From thence march to the plain in front of the City. Gen. Patterson's Division form a line extending near a mile. At the distance of ¼ of a mile the Regulars form a parallel line. Through the interval the Mexican Army, numbering about 5,000 men, file, halt and stack arms. They are accompanied by a great many women citizens and hangers on. The Americans preserve a becoming silence during this humiliating ceremony. As the Mexicans leave the field, the Dragoons escorting the Genl. in _____ and a part of the regular infantry enter the City. At the same time the fleet moves towards the Castle. The day is beautiful. The gaudy colored clothing of the Mexicans scattered over the plain, the bright uniforms of the Regulars, the dark masses of volunteers, form a picture which can never be forgotten. _____ and the spires of Vera Cruz rise on our left and the ocean alive with moving vessels adds to the magnificence of the scene. The air is filled with martial music from the regular bands. Soon the "Stars and Stripes" rising from the Castle and the City tell their fate. The Mexican's power has passed away. Salutes having been fired by the fleet and flying artillery, the different regiments retire to their camps. General Scott has taken up his quarters in the Palace in the City.

COULTER. After an early breakfast marched to a large plain south of and near the city to witness the surrender which had been agreed upon. The whole army, saving camp and battery guards, were drawn up in line on each side of the plain, leaving the intervening space for the opposite army. The enemy to the number of about five thousand marched out of the city under arms, accompanied by bands of music and followed by men, women and children carrying off their goods and halted on the ground between our lines. At command, piled arms which were taken possession of by a guard. At the same time the Mexican colors were hauled down from the castle and different city batteries, and replaced by the stars and stripes amid salutes from the navy and our artillery. General Scott then entered the city in state at the head of his staff and the surrendering army were allowed to go where it suited them. They principally scattered off in the direction of Alvarado. There was more solemnity and grandeur in this scene than any I ever witnessed. So many leaving their houses and delivering up to a foreign enemy the strongest hold of the country, excited a feeling of sympathy and reminded one forcibly of the surrender of Granada by the Moors as described in history.[14] It was hard to see the degree of starvation to which many of them were reduced. Begging "pan" (meal) from us and many offering fifty cents for a single cracker. The number of arms piled on the field were nearly five thousand, but there is every reason to believe that many left the city in the disguise of citizens. After the surrender, the company returned to camp, except a small party of us who went to the beach for provisions. Returned by way of the cemetery where Worth's battery was placed. The ground is torn up in many places by the enemy's shot, each bomb sinking to the depth of five or six feet and by its explosion tearing up a hole from six to eight and even ten feet in diameter. The cemetery wall is considerably battered up and several vaults broken open. The small chapel in the center of this enclosure is completely riddled. A circumstance occurred here that will be looked upon by the more superstitious Mexicans as miraculous. The altar in the chapel was very nearly destroyed by the shot, and a veil of light gauze which covered the cross was torn by a ball. Yet, although almost every other part was damaged, neither the cross nor the image of Christ upon it was touched. All this damage to their own property was done by the Mexican batteries, and in part was the principal damage done by them. General Worth lay just before this cemetery in a deep ditch protected by a hill and heavy embankment in front, so that their shot either fell short or passed over him. His distance was about seven hundred yards from the city and considering the calibre of his guns and mortars, he must have done considerable execution.

March 30

BARCLAY. The 1st and 2nd Penna. Regts. marched from their camps on the sand hills to the plain in front of the City. Remained marching and under arms the greater part of the day. Tents arrived towards evening. Weather continues very warm. Pitched tents for the first time since we landed. This Camp is called Camp Washington.

COULTER. This morning packed up and returned to the place of surrender, where we found a portion of the army encamped. Brought our baggage from the beach, pitched our tents, and are once more in a manner

14. The fall of Granada in 1492 was the final step in the Christian reconquest of Spain, leading to the extermination and expulsion of the defeated Moors. Coulter most likely had in mind Washington Irving's *A Chronicle of the Conquest of Granada* (1829).

under roof. Went to the beach to see Bide Kuhns, who appears to be worse. The captain got a certificate of disability from the surgeon for him and Wm. McIntire.

March 31

BARCLAY. Orders to clean up. Camp quiet. Most lovely scene at night. The extensive plain covered with innumerable tents pitched in perfect order. The moon full and clear, rendering the most distant object on the plain visible. The brass bands of the regulars play during the whole evening until Tattoo. Our company are not so healthy as we could wish. The fatigues and hardships we have been exposed [to] have made their marks and many are complaining.

COULTER. Upon the surgeon's certificate discharges were granted today to H. B. Kuhns and Wm. McIntire. Went to the beach to see them off, but found that Kuhns had embarked without papers of discharge, pay or anything else. This afternoon overhauled my knapsack, washed all my clothes and am now ready for the march inland. This I look upon as one of the ugliest jobs of the campaign, to bend over a half barrel wash tub in the hot sun and rub at a lot of dirty shirts, socks and red drawers until one's hands are completely cramped and wilted by being so long in the water.

April 1

BARCLAY. Visited the City of Vera Cruz. Wandered about all day. The City is built in the moorish style of architecture. The houses are of brick and stone, faced with a plaster, which for hardness and durability resembles the famous Roman Cement. The roofs are flat, windows large and generally barred. Streets broad and running at right angles. Great preparations had been made to receive us in case we made an assault, a second Montery reception.[15] Many of the commanding buildings had sand bags on their roofs. The streets were strongly barricaded and in front of the walls ditches and circular holes dug. The City has suffered much from the bombardment. A great deal of property has been destroyed and many lives lost. It is to be lamented that children and unoffending citizens were the principal sufferers. No estimate can be made of the number of Mexican lives lost.[16] I am told the hospitals are crowded with their wounded. Besides cannon mounted to receive us in all directions there are two chief

15. The city of Monterey in northern Mexico had been so heavily fortified before its capture by Zachary Taylor on 24 September 1846 that one American officer termed it "the perfect Gibraltar." Over forty pieces of well-entrenched artillery guarded the approaches, and within the city the streets were barricaded and the houses loopholed for musket fire, resulting in perhaps a thousand American casualties during the city's capture.

16. Actually, these losses were not unduly severe. A leading authority estimates that out of a garrison of five thousand Mexican troops only eighty were killed or wounded, and of the

batteries (called Santiago and Conception) which were in admirable condition and are the principal defences of the City. Attended church and heard mass. This is much the richest church I have ever been in. The valuable ornaments of the altar are removed. Some fine statuary attracted general attention. I could not get to the Castle today.

COULTER. As a matter of course, all had a great desire to see the far famed city and castle which had just been taken. But our captain issued an order allowing none but such as had their belting cleaned to leave camp. For my part, I was in the dirty belt party, not from any particular laziness, but had employed my time in arranging more necessary articles, my clothing and musket, so that my belting, after sleeping in them for three weeks, were far from being white. The only effect of the order was that the dirty belt party got into the city first. We went down to the beach between the city and castle and enjoyed quite a fine bath, the bottom being good sandy. Entered the city at an unfrequented gate, the guard being good natured allowing us to enter without a pass. Once in, it does not present the inspiring appearance it did from the sand hills, nothing but the domes and spires being visible in the distance. It is built of coral and bricks, plastered, to which it owed its partial safety during the late bombardment, each shot only making a hole of its own size without otherwise damaging the building materially. The houses are generally old and many present quite a dilapidated appearance, the only buildings that had anything of a modern appearance being the custom house and some of the consular residences. The Governor's palace is a large, but very ancient building, surmounted by a tall spire. The streets are filthy, dead carcasses lying in many of them. The city wall in many places is in ruins. In a mercantile point of view it must have suffered greatly from the blockade, there being not the least sign of business and grass growing in the streets. They are undoubtedly harassed by the cannonade, but had they been anything of a resolute people, might have held out much longer. Every approach to it is covered by cannon, and had we even gotten in, must have suffered greatly, as every street was barricaded and raked by heavy artillery. Went into a cathedral. It is a large and stately building but much worn by time. It contained a number of specimens of marble statuary and many fine paintings. It was considerably damaged near the entrance by the bursting of a shell, but otherwise uninjured by our shot. At reasonable distances around the wall were placed batteries which defended every approach. On the beach at the north corner of the city wall was Fort Santiago which protected a great

three thousand civilians remaining in Vera Cruz about one hundred were killed and an unknown number wounded. The American army lost fourteen killed and fifty-nine wounded during the siege. (Justin H. Smith, *The War With Mexico*, 2 vols. [New York: Macmillan, 1919], 2:33.)

portion of the land side, and by means of water batteries raked the surface of the harbor to the castle walls. On the beach on the south corner was another, similar to the former, with water batteries called Fort Conception. This fort did the greatest execution during the siege, causing most of the damage sustained by our batteries. Crossed in a small boat to the castle of San Juan de Ulua. It consists of a number of batteries connected by bridges and built on an extensive reef. It mounts a number of beautiful Spanish long thirty-two's and Paixhans guns[17] of the largest caliber. It not only covers every approach, but the principal battery commands the others and every passage is raked by artillery. Cannot attempt anything like a minute description nor hazard an opinion as to its size. It is built of coral and in some places it is complete of rock. It is well supplied with ammunition and with a resolute garrison may be considered impregnable. It has a reservoir of water which is the best I have drank since landing. Don't know how this reservoir is supplied; some say by the rain water collected off the castle during the rainy season; others that it is supplied by pipes from the city. After rambling through it for a couple of hours returned to the city and to camp.

April 2

BARCLAY. Felt very unwell in the morning. In the evening took a sea bath—very refreshing. Co. E on Brigade Guard.

COULTER. This morning Company E was detailed for Brigade guard. This is the second time within a week that we, as a company, have been detached for guard and excepting company F (who were once detached) not a company in the regiment has been on guard even once. Orders to seize all liquor brought by Mexicans to camp. Had not been long on duty when one of the sentinels captured a demijohn of wine which was soon emptied by the guard, Colonel Cummins of the Second Louisiana,[18] officer of the day, leading off with a stiff horn. Played rather a robbing game with the Mexicans. Some of the guard would go up towards the city and entice a Mexican, with liquor, down to the camp. He would no sooner come within the line of posts when he was nabbed by a sentinel, his liquor taken from him and himself started off empty. A number of captures were made during the day. Liquor was abundant with the guard but scarce in camp. At night lay out, there being no guard tents. The dew is much heavier here in the bottoms than it was on the sand hills and I felt the want of a blanket considerably. Went on guard with a bright musket but it was considerably bronzed, such is the effect of dew here in a single night.

17. Named after their designer, Henri Joseph Paixhans of France, who introduced them in 1824, Paixhans guns were intended primarily for naval use. They threw conical projectiles rather than the traditional spherical balls.

18. Confused with Lieutenant Colonel David H. Cummings, of the 2d Tennessee Infantry.

April 3
BARCLAY. Regular drill.

COULTER. On dress parade. Several orders were read. One from General Scott lamenting recent outrages committed on Mexican persons and property, and called upon all good Americans to assist in discovering the perpetrators. Based upon this, another from General Pillow, ordering that no soldier should pass the guard without a permit from his captain, and that each regiment, after drill, should stack arms on the color line, there to remain till night unless requisite for duty. Also another from Colonel Roberts ordering daily regimental drills.

April 4, Easter Sunday
BARCLAY. Day very hot. Drill at 6 A.M. Dress Parade at 8 A.M. Visited the City, heard mass and hurried to the pier to get across to the Castle. The Castle is about ¼ of a mile from the City. I was there for near two hours but could not see more than half of the works and curiosities. The building stands upon a coral reef. The main building, the Castle itself, commands the City and mounts a great many pieces which face in all directions. Two separate and distinct defences called Water Batteries are on that side of the Castle farthest from the City and towards the Gulf. In case the Castle were stormed from the Gulf it would first be necessary to carry the Water Batteries. The assailants would here be exposed to the fire from the main building. And if the main building itself were entered, so intricate and curious are the works that the defenders could make resistance and slaughter the attacking party without exposing themselves. In open boats on the Gulf the stormers would suffer greatly. Once in the works their situation would still be worse. Defended by an American garrison I cannot conceive how this fortress could be taken. There are many admirable cannon mounted on the Castle. My attention was more particularly directed to some old Spanish brass pieces with quaint Latin mottoes. One very venerable gentleman had for his motto (in Latin) *"The last argument of Kings."* It must have been very disgusting to this royal old piece to lend his energies in a contest between two dirty republics. As the Castle was erected some 300 years ago it begins to show signs of decay. Time did not permit me to examine the works so thoroughly as I would have wished.

Same day. Five dollars was distributed to each man out of the fund raised in Westmoreland County for the Guards.

COULTER. Went for wood this morning, everything burnable near camp being consumed. Compelled to go a considerable distance and had quite a job of it. Did not return until noon. Got a pass and went to the city. Arrived too late to see what I wanted, their church service, and so, wandering through the streets for a while, returned to camp. Received five dollars as a portion of my share of a fund raised for the company upon leaving Greensburg. Rumored that we leave the Jalapa in a few days.

April 5
BARCLAY. I went to the hospital and paid Martz, Myers, May and Forney $5 each. Found Forney and Martz very unwell.

COULTER. This morning instead of turning out on drill went to the beach and enjoyed a fine bathing. Waded in until the waves passed entirely over me. It is, I think, the healthiest thing that can be done in this climate. Returned too late for drill, but did not give way to sorrow on account of it. Has been exceedingly warm. Orders from General Scott were read on dress parade this morning that the regiment should be in readiness to march at a moment's notice; men should lighten their knapsacks as much as possible. Officers should leave behind all extra baggage; only three tents allowed to a company for those who might get sick on the march and to secure the arms in, during wet weather.

April 6
COULTER. Had the usual drill this morning. Again made an overhaul of my knapsack and washing of dirty clothing preparatory to march. Made a purchase of a blanket which was very opportunate as I found I should have to march without one.

April 7
BARCLAY. Orders to prepare to march. Kept very busy in making descriptive Rolls for the sick who are to be left behind and in preparing for the march. Cooked necessary provisions, struck tents. Kept three for the brass. The rest of the tents, two trunks, three musket boxes and two barrells of the men's clothing, the extra camp kettles, etc., left in charge of the Quartermaster. Everything is ready for an early start. The following men are sent to the hospital: Ross, Forney, Brady, Elliott, Grow, Hartford, Kelly, Martz, McCredin, McCutcheon, McGarvey, Myers, Wise, May. On the 31st of March, Kuhns, H. B. and McIntire were discharged on account of sickness. Huston is left behind as an attendant to the sick.

COULTER. Mess cook today and had quite a time sweating over the fire. Experienced all the trouble and vexations incident to cooks.

April 8
COULTER. Ordered to prepare four days rations and report all our sick unable to march. The following sick were reported: Corporal Ross, Drummer Forney and Private Brady, Elliott, Grow, Hartford, Kelly, Martz, McCutcheon, McGarvey, May, Myers, McCredin and Wise with Huston as hospital attendant. Struck our tents and pushed wagons, but slept in camp.

3

Some of You Will Get Your God Damned Heads Blown Off
The Battle of Cerro Gordo

April 9

BARCLAY. Took up line of march first to the City then along the Gulf. The sand deep and loads heavy. About a mile from the City Sergt. Marchand who was previously unwell gave out and was compelled to return. I accompanied him back part of the way and was very sorry to bid the Sergt. good bye. We had passed many pleasant hours together and I had hoped we would spend many more. After following the beach some two miles the road took to the left and became more easily travelled. The Regt. was much scattered. Unaccustomed to march it was very fatiguing to carry a big knapsack thru the sand. Towards evening the water in our canteens was exhausted and I suppose for the first time in their lives our boys suffered from thirst. After night we crossed an extensive prairie, but still no camp. The Regt. by this time were scattered in parties of threes and fours and the majority of them already stretched along the road for the night. About 8 o'clock at night entirely used up I threw myself down on the road side in company with a party of Illinois boys. Suffered much from want of water.

COULTER. Up and breakfast over by four o'clock. Marched about nine o'clock. Before we had gone a great way our orderly, Sergeant H. C. Marchand, finding that he was unable to stand the fatigue, returned to Vera Cruz, making sixteen we have left there. This was the most difficult day's duty I have yet seen. The sun was high when we started and by the rapid march through the deep sand half the men were exhausted and began to look for shade when I was compelled to leave the ranks—ranks they were called, although half the men had already fallen out. Kept along with the many who straggled for about ten miles, when we began to think seriously of camp. Inquired of several Mexicans who passed us in the opposite direction the distance to camp, but it appeared to recede in proportion as we advanced. By dark, although a straggler, had left over half the division behind. Continued for a while longer, when I came to a party of one of the Illinois regiments camped under a shade. Determined to remain here for a night. Shortly one of the company _____ passed and I agreed to go on, but after a half mile march further we were compelled to halt and made our bed among some prickly pears. Soon after hailed two more, Corporals Carpenter and Bonnin, who agreed to camp with us. The country through which we passed was for the first eight miles a deep sandy chaparral country in which there was one small stream intersecting the portion called Rio del Medio. There a prairie of considerable size in which there was a small village called Santa Fe, about ten or twelve miles from Vera Cruz. This prairie was covered with thousands of cattle. We then again entered the chaparral country where we now camped. For the last two miles it appeared like a continuous camp. Men lying under every shade completely exhausted and reckless of the danger they ran. Three hundred resolute men could with ease have destroyed the whole division. Had not had a drop of water. Some of the men's feet were [sore?] and blistered and were so overworked that when they did lie down were unable to sleep. Men and wagons were passing all night.

April 10

BARCLAY. Started at daylight and after an hour's march arrived in Camp. Only three or four of our men got in last night to camp. Distance from Vera Cruz 22 miles. As I was approaching camp almost dead with thirst, I passed some wagoners cooking. Their camp kettles were on the fire and water about milk warm. Giving me permission I took a long draught and notwithstanding the warmth must confess I never enjoyed a drink so much. Left camp at 8 A.M. and after a march of 8 miles arrived at a stream and encamped. The road was good and country poor. I have been sick all day.

COULTER. Off before day so as to have the cool of the morning, but our condition may be imagined without any water since noon yesterday. So stiff and sore as to be almost unable to march and loaded with knapsack, musket, four days rations (what was left of them) and forty rounds of cartridges. Shortly overhauled Jack Gilchrist, one of our old company, who came out in Company K, First Pennsylvania, who had been in the same predicament as us, unable to reach camp. Marched about two miles where we overtook one of our company (Shaw) who gave us some water, which greatly refreshed us and we shortly after reached camp. About the last mile or so rather descended into a valley with tolerable sized timber. The camp was near a large bridge on a very fine stream called La Perote,[1] about twenty miles distant from Vera Cruz. Only about half dozen of our company reached this place yesterday. Here got some coffee and enjoyed a good wade in the stream. My feet were then in large blisters. After being in camp a short time the column was ordered to get ready for march. Profiting

1. Possibly a misreading of Río del Potero.

by yesterday's experience, several of us started before the regiment and made about six miles when we halted in a beautiful shade near a large bridge over a dry ravine, to rest and examine haversacks. While here the regiment passed us and I did not see it again until evening. My feet were worse and knapsack unusually heavy. Going up a rugged hill was completely exhausted and compelled to lie down in the sun, but this made me worse, and mustering up resolution, managed to reach a shade where I remained until a waggon passing, I threw my knapsack into it and getting on the feed trough, rode to camp, a distance of almost two miles, where I arrived an hour before sunset. This camp is situated on a fine stream called Tolome with magnificent shade, distant about ten miles from last camp. Although I left Vera Cruz with four day's rations of bread, had eaten the last cracker before reaching this camp, and made my supper on some beef, one of the mess having cut a portion off a cow lying along the roadside, which had been killed for the heart and liver and left. This we boiled, eating the broth and saving the meat for next day's meal. It tasted very fresh and was in part unwholesome without salt, of which we had none.

April 11

BARCLAY. Early start. Marched over a rough hilly country 9 miles and arrived at the National Bridge. This splendid bridge spans the Rio Antigua, a clear rapid mountain stream. This is a strong military position. The scenery along the stream is exceedingly romantic and the stream reminds us of the Loyalhanna. Santa Anna owns a hacienda here which is said to be his favorite country residence. It proves that the modern Napoleon has a good eye for the picturesque. During today's march we passed very large droves of cattle feeding and roaming at large. The Mexicans say they are the property of Santa Anna and that he owns the land which adjoins the road for some 50 or 60 miles.

COULTER. This morning completely done out carrying knapsacks two days, declared that we would carry them no longer and packed them in the baggage waggon (a few having done so yesterday) where they were allowed to remain, and in fact were hauled for the remainder of this march. Started before the brigade moved. Was greatly relieved by not having my knapsack, and with greater ease than either of the previous days made a good portion of the march in the cool of the morning. Had no provisions but the boiled beef of last night, without salt, which began to taste noxious, and so I tried some prickly pears, but after getting my lips and tongue full of the beard with which they are covered, gave it up. About ten o'clock reached camp, Puente Nacional, or as it is called, National Bridge, distant about ten miles from last camp. It is a magnificent bridge of solid masonry and of great length, crossing the Rio Monti in one of the mountain gorges. This is a fine cold stream and I enjoyed a pleasant bathing in it before the brigade came up. The country through which we passed today is rather barren and covered with cactus (Prickly pear) without much shade. It was a gradual ascent until within about one or two miles from camp, where it descended again into the gorge. This is a strong pass and in our hands would be impregnable, but was deserted by the enemy on the approach of General Twiggs. It is narrow, bounded by abrupt cliffs of considerable height on which are built batteries of some age and a line of breast works lately erected. Just beyond the bridge is a fine hacienda belonging to Santa Anna. By the negligence of our commissary, did not draw any beef and it was not until night that he issued a ration of bacon. Our General ordered today that no beef should be killed by the men and we would have had quite a famine had not one of our mess purchased a piece of salt pork. After dark I bribed a waggoner with half a dollar to steal me a basket of crackers, which I distributed to some of the company, retaining a good day's ration for myself, but shortly after, some fellow thinking he had a better right to them, stole my portion, and so I retired without any bread after all.

April 12

BARCLAY. Early start and rapid march. The road dusty. Country rough. Encamped at Plan del Rio. Distance today 15 miles. A very ancient fortress commands the road here. Two rapid mountain streams here cross the road, each spanned by very substantial bridges. Water pure and pleasant. Heard while on march cannon in advance and upon our arrival found Twiggs' Division encamped here awaiting reinforcement. The enemy are 3 miles in advance strongly entrenched on a mountain pass which commands the road. The ranches we have passed these last two days have been deserted and there have been many reports of the strength and determination of the enemy. Santa Anna is at the head of the army and has made most extravagant threats of defeating and driving the invader into the sea.

COULTER. As yesterday, started before the division. Determined this time not to sit down at all to rest, the only effect of that being to stiffen one and make him the more indisposed to move again. Had gone about twelve miles and was trudging all alone, being in advance of the entire division, except perhaps half a dozen, when I heard the report of a cannon some distance ahead. Was completely taken by surprise at this and quickened my pace and before I had gone far heard some twenty reports. Overtook an Irishman with a loaded jackass. "Och" said he, ["]they're at it. I hear the cannins." His ass did not relish fast walking and I soon left him. Shortly after met an express who told me that General Twiggs had engaged the enemy and that I should go no further than a ranch a mile or so ahead, as the hill was full of lancers. Reached this ranch where I found four others of our division who had also been stopped by the express. Our number soon increased to a dozen and we concluded to push ahead. On our way down the hill met a lieutenant and about twenty dragoons. Told him the express's story about the lancers, at which he laughed and said that his party were the lancers he had seen; that he had chased the express about a mile to tell him his mistake, but he only ran the faster. Two miles from the ranch we came to the stream of Plan del Rio,[2] where there was a portion of Twiggs' division, the rest having gone up to the pass to reconnoiter. The reports which we had heard was the firing on these. Captain Johnston[3] of the Topographical Engineers was badly wounded in this reconnoiter. While here a dragoon picket placed at the further bridge was killed. When we had been here about an hour Twiggs' men came down the hill and sometime after, our division arrived and camped on this stream. It proved to be General Santa Anna with about fifteen thousand men who had fortified himself in the pass of Cerro Gordo about five miles ahead. Plan del Rio, our present camp, is about eighteen miles distant from Puente Nacional. The country through which we passed today was poor, without a drop of water on the entire march. From the ranch on top of the hill where we had been stopped by the express it descends rapidly into the valley watered by Plan del Rio. Along the descent are many evidences of fortifications. A large quantity of small brush was cut and made into bundles called facins [fascines] for making breast works. There are two large bridges within a hundred yards of each other crossing the river which divides at this point. Between these bridges on the left hand side is an abrupt hill which rises to a great height, crowned by an old Spanish fort. Ascending this ridge and going some distance around the fortifications of Cerro Gordo, were visible on a corresponding ridge across the ravine through which the river flows. Plan del Rio is a small mountain stream, running in many places through deep and rugged banks and over a rocky bed, generally shallow, but in places reasonably deep.

General Twiggs, in his innocence, almost blundered into a Mexican trap. Unbeknownst to the American command, Santa Anna had managed to reconstruct his shattered army after its defeat at Buena Vista and had as-

---

2. Coulter is understandably confused. The river was known as Río del Plan, and Plan del Río was the name of the adjacent village.

3. This was the first of five wounds suffered in the Mexican War by Joseph Eggleston Johnston (1807–1891, West Point 1829). During the Civil War, Johnston held the rank of general in the Confederate army. A dour and contentious officer, slow to attack and quick to make excuses, he won no major victories but did conduct a number of highly successful retreats, most notably that before Atlanta when confronted with the overwhelming Union force led by William T. Sherman. After the war he served a term in the U.S. Congress representing Virginia and died from pneumonia contracted while attending the funeral of his old nemesis, Sherman.

sembled a force of twelve thousand to block Scott's advance into the interior. Had the Mexican dragoons not attacked prematurely, Twiggs would surely have walked into an ambush.

Failing to draw the proper lesson from his narrow escape, Twiggs, who was not known for excessive caution, prepared to make a frontal attack on the Mexican works with his division of less than three thousand men. Only the timely arrival of his superior, General Patterson, not known for excessive boldness, caused the attack to be delayed until Scott could arrive with the rest of the army.

Upon his arrival, Scott, unlike Twiggs, carefully reconnoitered the enemy's position and discovered how formidable it was. Santa Anna had fortified three hills commanding the right of the National Road, while on the other side of the road there was a sheer five-hundred-foot drop to the river below. To the north, the fortifications were protected by a hilly, tangled overgrowth that Santa Anna thought not even a rabbit could penetrate. Captain Robert E. Lee of the Engineers, however, was able to find a trail through this wilderness that could lead around the enemy's flank. While it was being secretly improved, the rest of the army marked time, within sight of Santa Anna's fortifications.

April 13

BARCLAY. Remained in camp. Provisions run short, wagons returned to Vera Cruz for provisions. I sent by a wagon master H. C. Marchand's descriptive Roll. Most delightful bathing here. Orders received to start at 3 A.M. tomorrow morning to the enemy's batteries with two days provisions in haversacks. Great fuss. The flour is sour and no crackers. Everybody hungry and in a bad humor. I am very unwell myself being much weakened by a constant diarrhea which has annoyed me since leaving Vera Cruz. At 10 o'clock P.M. orders of marching countermanded. Gen. Patterson being in chief command will not risk a battle until Gen. Scott and the rest of the troops arrive.

COULTER. Reconnoitering continued and firing occasionally heard. Small parties of the enemy infest the road and a soldier was shot while walking behind a waggon a short distance from camp. Provisions are scarce. A small party of us went down the creek to a banana grove a mile from camp. This grove is beautiful, the long large leaves of the banana forming a fine shade. Saw some of the leaves from eight to ten feet in length and about a foot in width. There is a fine cold, stream issuing from the side of the hill out of a small cave or grotto which is quite a romantic place, being entirely of crystaline formation. Late in the evening ordered to prepare two day's rations and hold ourselves in readiness to advance upon the enemy at three o'clock A.M. It was a difficult matter for us to prepare two day's rations when nothing in the shape of edibles were issued to us. As a last resort parched the full of my haversack of corn, a quantity of which having been captured in the neighborhood. Orders were countermanded, it is believed in consequence of the scarcity of provisions. We might have had plenty of beef, but our general, in his omnipotence, ordered that none should be killed unless it had been bought from the owners and properly issued to the men. In this way we get poor beef, short rations of it, and having no other rations as bread, etc., we could not manage to make a single meal out of the day's rations. It appears to me at least, very silly to regard the rights of property of an enemy so strictly, and purchase from them the necessaries of life, when at the same time they were within a short distance of us, strongly fortified to dispute our passage, when we might have obtained the same by force.

April 14

BARCLAY. Although it is expressly against orders a party from Co. E went out for beef. It is better to disobey orders than to starve. After a long and toilsome tramp they return loaded. We have plenty of beef now, but neither salt or bread.

COULTER. Notwithstanding our General's orders, being completely starved out, a party from our company went out for beef. Dropped out of camp singly so as not to be observed and entered a deep gorge about two miles off in which there was another banana grove. Were about to give up the hunt when two of our party luckily killed a couple of cows. These were soon skinned and quartered, and each quarter being strung on a musket, two of us carrying one, being thirteen in number, managed to carry six quarters. Had a laborious time of it making camp. Dared not go by the road for fear of the General. So, entering the chaparral, dragged our meat up several hills through the dirt and then rolled it down the other side. Had to ford both branches of the creek and carry our loads up its steep banks. However, all arrived safe at camp and then we made quite a feast on boiled beef, though without salt, but we were too hungry to mind that. In the evening again ordered to prepare two day's rations and be ready for the attack, but no rations were issued. Added some boiled beef to my store of parched corn. During the night orders were again countermanded.

April 15

BARCLAY. A Regt. party went out today for beef. Killed 14 and returned late to camp. Crackers and flour drawn. Gen. Scott has arrived. Two or three prisoners taken. Many stories as to the plan of attack.

COULTER. In the morning, finding that the attack would not be made this day, and the regiment being almost starved, depending on a negligent quartermaster, our adjutant with a volunteer party of four from each

company, went for beef. We followed the road back towards Puente Nacional for about ten miles before seeing any cattle. Here discovered a herd
which we followed down a range of cliffs into a deep ravine and it soon
resembled a light infantry skirmish, so much powder was burned. I followed a couple about two miles down the ravine and had the luck of
shooting both, but was alone and could not bleed them. Soon I found two
of my comrades. By this time the Mexicans could be heard on all the hills
calling in their cattle, but all did not go at their bidding. Killed eighteen
head in all and loaded our waggon to the cover. This ravine is very deep
and dark, the sun being shut out by the trees. It can only be entered by cow
paths over steep and rugged rocks. About a mile from the road it is watered
by a cold stream. We had left camp with very little breakfast and I had eaten
nothing through this day, so that I was almost famished with hunger. On
our return we found a tree loaded with a fruit something like our wild
plum, of which I ate a great many. They operated on me in the shape of a
sudden and violent dysentery, which so sickened and weakened me that it
was with the greatest difficulty I reached camp by tatoo, which I would not
have done had it not been for the assistance of a comrade (Jim McLaughlin).
For the last few miles I was so weakened that I staggered in walking, and
when near camp vomited very freely, which greatly relieved me.

April 16
BARCLAY. Three additional sick men in Co. E. Slight rain. The camp is
dull and tiresome. A Tennessean found mortally wounded. Buried with
military honors.

COULTER. Got up this morning very weak, but much better from the
thorough cleansing my stomach received yesterday and with an appetite
like a horse. Today have been engaged boiling and jerking our beef. Scott
and Worth came up today and a portion of Worth's division[;] reconnoitering still continued. Occasionally have a few shots from the enemy's batteries and sometimes a volley of musketry fired at our advance parties, but
the ball proper has not yet commenced. A Tennesseean was killed and I
believe one or two wounded today on a beef expedition.

April 17
BARCLAY. Fresh beef and diarrhea the order of the day. Orders to hold
ourselves to march tomorrow morning at 3 A.M. Worth's Division with
some heavy guns have arrived. For the last few days the Guerillas have
managed to shoot 3 or 4 of our men daily while out foraging. A severe engagement took place today between Twiggs and the enemy. Twiggs had
advanced to his position preparatory to tomorrow's work. The enemy attempted to dislodge him and in great force made three attacks. They were
repulsed with loss. On our side 11 men killed and 40 wounded. In our

camp the men are attending to their own affairs with as much indifference as if tomorrow was to be a festival day instead of a day of blood shed. After night, Lieut. Armstrong, Shields, Aikens, Kettering, Hartman, Carson, and McClain detailed to report to an Engineer Officer for duty. Sargent, Milner, *Dougherty, Rager* & Philip Kuhns are sick. They will remain in camp tomorrow.

COULTER. This morning received orders to be ready to move at a moment's notice. General Twiggs with a part of his division and the Howitzer Battery advanced this morning, after a sharp action and the loss of about sixty men, carried his position. Crackers were issued and with our beef, our haversacks now have the appearance of plenty again. Within the last few days a number of our men have been killed on forage parties. Today a party of the Tennessee Regiment, one of our company was also along (Gordon), went for beef and entered the ravine, where our party had gotten so much beef a few days ago. All the cattle had now been driven in here and none were to be seen near the road. Before they had entered a mile into the gorge, were fired upon from every rock and compelled to fall back with the loss of one killed and two severely wounded. It was not discovered that there was a lancer camp in this ravine and they had driven in the cattle and collected the forage there for the purpose of starving us out of our position. I don't understand how our party, scattered as it was, and so far into the ravine, escaped last Tuesday. A detail was made from our company to carry ammunition for a gun that had been planted on top of the ridge to the left of the road—Lt. Armstrong and Kettering, Aikens, Carson, Hartman, McClain, McClelland and Shields. During the night Aikens and McClelland returned to camp. In the morning the company was formed for same purpose, when the Captain made the following remark: "Now men, we are going up the hill tomorrow, and I want you all to stand up to it, although I expect some of you will get your God damned heads blown off." While other officers were encouraging their men for the coming fight, such was the language of our leader.

In the ensuing battle of 18 April, Pillow's Brigade, of which the 2d Pennsylvania Infantry was a part, played a minor supporting role. The main action was intended to be at the western end of the Mexican position as the Americans were supposed to steal around Santa Anna's works via Lee's path and burst upon their flanks while cutting off their retreat. Pillow's Brigade was to demonstrate against the easternmost Mexican battery in something between a feint and a diversion. Neither part of the plan was executed as Scott intended, but the main attack did succeed in driving off the enemy in panic (though not in blocking his escape). Pillow's contribution was bungled from start to finish, being saved from disaster only by the collapse of the Mexican army elsewhere on the field.

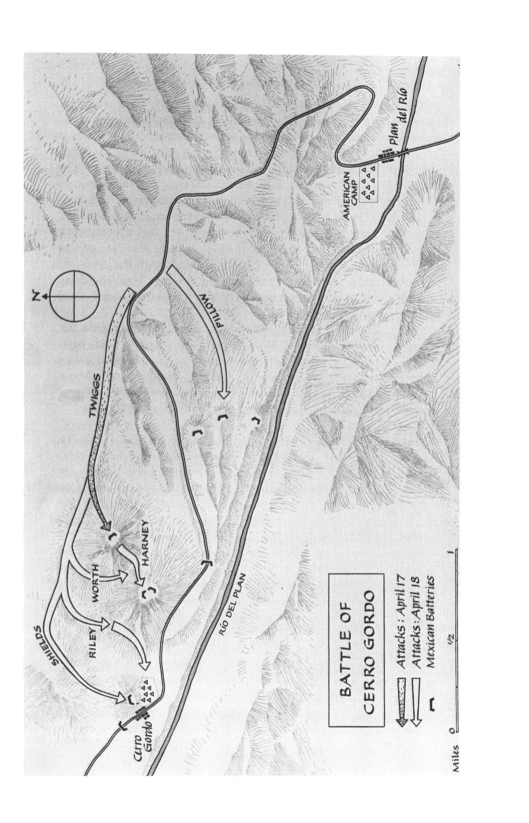

BATTLE OF
CERRO GORDO

Attacks : April 17
Attacks : April 18
Mexican Batteries

Miles   0   ½   1

N

PLAN del Río

AMERICAN CAMP

RÍO DEL PLAN

PILLOW

TWIGGS

HARNEY

WORTH

RILEY

SHIELDS

Cerro Gordo

April 18

BARCLAY. Was fought the Battle of Cerro Gordo. Twiggs from his position gained yesterday attacked the left of the enemy and assisted by Shield's Brigade turned that part of the Mexican line. This was accomplished with heavy loss on our side. Pillow's Brigade in the meantime (consisting of the 1st and 2nd Tenn. & the 1st and 2nd Penna. Regts.) moved along the main road for near 3 miles, filed to the left and were intended to operate in the enemy's right. The 1st Penn. and 2nd Tenn. Regts. were to storm supported by the 2nd Pa. and 1st Tenn. Regts. On account of the difficulties of the ground no accurate survey had been made of the enemy's works on this side. The number and position of their guns were unknown and Genl. Pillow will always be censured for leading men against a battery which had not been properly examined in the first place. The orders were for the assaulting regts. to charge at the sound of the bugle. By some strange and unfortunate mistake the charge was sounded before the 1st Pa. was in position. Indeed Col. [William T.] Haskell's [2nd] Tenn. Regt. was the only Regt. in the Brigade in position when the charge was sounded. They dashed most gallantly forward and were received by a murderous fire of cannon and musketry. The ground in front of the enemy's batteries for near 200 yds. was covered with thick chapperal. Immediately in front of their batteries were piles of bushes cut and placed so as entirely to impede the advance of the stormers. After doing all that men could do, the Tennesseans were forced to retire leaving a large number of their regt. killed and wounded. The 2nd Pa. Regt. were marching by the flank to get their position. So narrow was the path that it was often necessary to move single file. When the charge sounded, the Regt. moved as rapidly as possible and when they had arrived on the ground they were intended to occupy the Tennesseans were broken and retreating. They pushed through and in places broke our ranks. Thus we were exposed to the same heavy fire that cut down so many Tennesseans and the only way I can account for our comparatively small loss is that we were protected by the chapperal from the aim of the infantry and the Mexicans as usual elevated their cannon too much. The grape and musket balls whistled above and about us and the veterans of Monterey admitted that they had never heard so heavy a fire. After filing past the enemy's batteries, the regiment was halted. Campbell's Regt. (the 1st Tenn.) was halted in our rear. The 1st Pa. was on our left and Haskell's was everywhere and nowhere. Pillow had received a wound in the arm and Col. Campbell was in command. The Col. was in a most furious humor, perfectly rampant. He was mad and did not know exactly whom to blame or what to be mad about. Col. Roberts, who may be personally a brave man but who has not the slightest presence of mind, is running about perfectly bewildered. Campbell orders the Pa. Regt. to charge. As he does not designate either the 1st or 2nd neither obey him. So he damns the Pennsylvanians for a set of cowards. He next inquired who commanded our Regt. Being informed that it is Col. Roberts, he now orders Col. Roberts to advance with his Regt. Roberts, who is on the right, does not hear him and there is no movement. Campbell jumps about, damns the Pennsylvanians, damns Col. Roberts for a coward that he will expose him, etc. While Campbell is leaping about someone informs him that Roberts' Regt. is the supporting and not the charging Regt. and that Col. [Francis M.] Wyncoop commands the 1st Pa. This throws the honest Colonel into a new dilemma and while he is scratching his head the orders arrive to suspend operations that the works are covered by Twiggs and that the enemy have surrendered. Four batteries mounting 21 guns and defended by 7000 infantry commanded by Gen. La Vega,[4] defended the heights where we moved towards. After the Battle was over Gen. La Vega stated that no 10,000 men could have carried the Heights on which he was posted by an assault in front, but he was forced to surrender when Twiggs carried the main height and gained his rear. After receiving these orders the Brigade was countermarched and formed on the road while the Mexican *prisoners* were marched past. Our loss in the Battle is near 500 killed and wounded. No correct estimate can be made of the Mexican loss. The efforts they made to defend the pass were very great. After Santa Anna was repulsed by Gen. Taylor at Buena Vista, he immediately began preparations to receive Scott, well knowing that Gen. Taylor could not advance with his small force. Cerro Gordo is a pass running through the chain of mountains which border the Plan del Rio. (Cerro is a Spanish word applying to elevations not high enough for mountains and too lofty for ordinary hills). So rough are these mountains that it is impossible to cross them anywhere except through this pass, nor can any passable road be opened. It is therefore a very important military position. The mountains rising high on each side of the pass give every advantage to the defenders, whose flanks are protected by the steep banks of the peaks. Santa Anna had here assembled near 26000 men and had by ditches and entrenchments added much to the natural advantages of the position. But nothing could resist the advance of Twiggs' men and the Mexicans, their entrenchments entered, fled in all directions. In the flight and pursuit near 2000 were killed and wounded. About 5000, among whom were a great many officers, were taken prisoners and an equal amount deserted. Santa Anna, with a large body of Lancers, fled early. Worth's Division, which remained inactive during the Battle, immediately advanced and Col. Harney, with his Dragoons, pursued the enemy in the most rigorous

---

4. An able soldier, General Rómulo Díaz de la Vega (1804–1877) was captured by Zachary Taylor at the battle of Resaca de la Palma and exchanged. As the chief of the Division of the East, he was again captured at Cerro Gordo but this time refused to give his parole. He later served as acting president of Mexico for three weeks in the fall of 1855, after which he would be exiled for a time for backing the wrong side in his country's endemic civil wars.

manner. This victory will bear comparison with any battle won by Gen. Taylor. At Buena Vista Taylor, in a position of his own selecting, resisted and baffled Santa Anna with a much larger force. At Cerro Gordo, Gen. Scott with a force not much larger than Taylor's acted on the aggressive and stormed and carried the works of Santa Anna, notwithstanding the number of the defenders, and strong natural and artificial defences. Had we been defeated or repulsed at Cerro Gordo, the army would be forced back to Vera Cruz at the sickly season. Nothing could have been accomplished until the arrival of reinforcements from the States. Much time would have been consumed and the Mexican nation roused from a long series of defeats by a single victory would have collected her resources and presented a firm unbroken front to the invader. As it is the advantages are immense. Santa Anna defeated and as may be reasonably expected, his influence gone, that band of robbers y-clept an army, whose power and influence have heretofore kept down everything like a peace party, are now dispersed and dishonoured. A plentiful and healthy country is now in our possession and the road is open to the City of Mexico. The Mexicans having passed, we marched to camp, having given three cheers for Gen. Worth, who with his staff rode by. The old fellow took off his beaver and appeared pleased with the compliment. He is a man under the middle size, compactly built, a good horseman. His hair is turning grey. His face is animated and prepossessing. He is a very great favorite with the rank and file. He owes his popularity to his great military talents and his well known regard for the comfort and lives of those under him. Both in quarters and on the field of battle, Gen. Worth's chief object is to save his soldiers.[5]

COULTER. Up. Breakfast over and everything packed for the advance by four o'clock. The train was collected in a circle on one of the camp grounds so as to form a protection for the guard. About six o'clock the brigade moved. The road was full of men moving to the hill and we met many wounded of yesterday's fight coming down. After making about three miles our brigade entered the chaparral to the left of the road. At this time the battle had commenced at the other points and the sound of musketry was general. We had moved about a mile further when the right of the brigade came under the enemy's fire. Our regiment formed the left. Moving up a hill by a narrow cow path where several men were shot and lying across the path, a portion of the men stepped over the bodies, but this was too slow a way, and some ran around a small clump of rocks and bushes and joined the line on the other side. This is what General Pillow afterwards, in his report, called the wavering[6] of the Second Pennsylvania

5. Barclay's appraisal is overly generous. At Monterey and, later on, at Molino del Rey, Worth demonstrated a reckless disregard for the safety of the troops under his command.
6. In his supplemental report on the Battle of Cerro Gordo, dated 29 May 1847, Pillow said that, according to Colonel Roberts, "his regiment was exposed to such a galling fire

and their movement around the hill. We were now completely into the fire and moved on single file and in some places double file, as the nature of the path would admit. Colonel Roberts moved the regiment on until he met Colonel Campbell, of the First Tennessee who, mistaking him for Colonel Wyncoop, of the First Pennsylvania, ordered him to charge or he would expose him. This caused some words and we remained during that time standing under the fire. The forces were then all marched forward out of range of the enemy's guns and rested on our arms. The hail of grape, canister and musketry was terrific. We were placed in a thick chaparral where could hardly march, unable to see from whence the shot came. Men were falling at every step and enduring a fire which we could not attack. As we marched, got a glimpse of the enemy's works, hombres heads above the breastworks. A temporary halt was made and before again moving, an express came up with the intelligence that the other batteries had been taken, the one at which we were had surrendered (this we did not know, not being able to see for the chaparral) and Santa Anna was in full retreat closely pursued by Colonel Harney and General Shield's brigade of volunteers. The loss of the Second Tennessee was severe. General Pillow was slightly wounded in the arm.[7] The loss of our regiment was twenty-one wounded. Our company lost one wounded (Jacob Miller) severely in the leg by a musket ball. We then marched to the main road. Shortly after took charge of the prisoners, some 6,000, and returned to camp. Our whole loss in these two days fight was 425. That of the enemy some 2,000. It was only intended to make a feint and draw off a portion of the enemy's force, but our General was ambitious and wished to carry the works with his Tennessee men without the Pennsylvania regiments, but the works were too strong, mounting some fifteen guns. The following is the disposition of Company E on ths day: Camp guard Kuhns (Philip), Dougherty, Milner, Rager and Sargent. Kuhn started up the hill, but after several fruitless attempts, being sick, was compelled to remain behind. Detailed for extra duty, Lt. Armstrong and Kettering, Carson, Hartman, McClain and Shields. Aikens and McClelland went with this party yesterday, but returned same night. Entered the fight with the company: Captain Johnston, Lieutenants Murry and Coulter; Sergeants Barclay, McLaughlin and Mechling; Corporals Carpenter, Bigelow and Bonnin; Privates Aikens, Allshouse, Bates, Bills, Byerly, Campbell, Carney, Cloud, Coulter, Decker, Fishel, Geesyn, Johnston, R. & H. L., Kegarize, Keslar, D. Kuhns, Landon,

---

from the grape and cannister which swept down the hill as he was ascending, and enfiladed his line (marching as it was obliged to do by the flank), that his line waved out of the path around the brow of the hill."

7. In the three minutes or so in which they were exposed to Mexican fire, almost eighty members of the 2d Tennessee Infantry were killed or wounded, including every field officer other than the colonel; Pillow claimed he was "shot all to pieces" and retired forthwith from the field to nurse his wound.

Linsenbigler, McCabe, McClaran, McCollum, McGinley, McWilliams, J. McWilliams, W. Marchand, Melville, Simms, Smith, Uncapher, Underwood, Waters, Thomas and Wentz.

April 19

BARCLAY. Beautiful day. The 2nd Regt. guard the Mexican prisoners. They are a miserable looking set. The greater part new levies, tho there are among them many moustached veterans, the men of Monterey and Buena Vista, soldiers who have been in all the contests of the different parties of the Republic. A great many women accompany the army and are now busy in attending to their lords and masters. They all appear unconcerned, trading swords, horses, etc. The officers appear to be as great scamps as the men. The Commissary Dept. has issued to them a ration of bread and pork. As it is likely the only meal they have had for some time, they enjoy it very much. Their guns are being broken up. The stock is knocked off and the barrel broken or bent. The prisoners are all to be released in *parole*. Gen. Scott considers it easier to take them prisoners again than to lead and guard them. Orders to march tomorrow. During today the mournful death march has sounded from morning to night. The gallant dead have been conveyed to their long homes. Requiescat in pace.

COULTER. This morning our regiment was detailed as a guard for the prisoners. They were quite a promiscuous crowd huddled in one of the camp grounds and surrounded by a line of sentinels. A large quantity of Mexican muskets and ammunition were destroyed today, being useless to us and our means of transportation is limited. In the afternoon the mass of prisoners were released on verbal parole and the officers, such as would give it, on written parole of honor. General La Vega and some few others would not accept this and were sent as prisoners to Vera Cruz. Remained in our old camp this night.

April 20

BARCLAY. This morning I felt so weak and worn down from the effects of the diarrhea that I remained with the wagon intending to ride as much of the way as possible. The company is rear guard and are late in starting. Jacob P. Miller, who received a severe wound from a musket in the leg at Cerro Gordo, is left behind. March 4 miles through the pass commanded the entire length by the enemy's batteries. Near the head of the pass a great many Mexicans are lying unburied—the smell very disagreeable. The road today is good. At very close intervals we pass dead mules and horses. Pass a hut crowded with wounded Mexicans. Many of Harney's fine horses are killed in the pursuit—rode to death. Great quantities of Mexican provisions captured, also ammunition. In the pursuit the Mexicans occasionally made stands, but were almost immediately routed again, the place of

contest always marked with dead animals. After a march of 22 miles encamped at St. Barbara near Encero and near a country seat of Santa Anna.
The boys bring into camp plenty of beef. The country is much improving.

COULTER. This morning off for Jalapa. As usual managed to get in advance of the brigade. As we passed along the scene of the late action saw
the extensive fortifications of the enemy. Here got a partial glimpse of a
portion of the works against which our brigade had operated. An extensive breastwork on the left hand ridge. The battery could not be seen from
the road. For several miles along the road the timber was felled so as to
give a clear range for their artillery and prevent an approach without being seen. Ascended the sugar loaf hill which General Twiggs carried. This
is Cerro Gordo proper. It is the most difficult of ascent and crowned by a
large battery. On the side which General Twiggs charged there was quite
a quantity of dead hombres, they having left their works and advanced
upon our men. On the summit there was a battery surrounded by a breastwork completely encircling the hill. There were many wounded Mexicans
lying here, who had been collected in the neighborhood, among them several women. Descended the opposite side where the enemy retreated. Here
was an ugly sight; men shot in every position, some spread out in the act
of running. About three quarters of a mile further on was the battery in
the road with a breastwork and ditch running a great distance to the left.
Here were large quantities of ammunition and muskets. A short distance
further, near some ranches, were large quantities of provisions, stores and
arms as well as shoes, boxes of clothing, rice and red peppers, which are
an indispensable article of a Mexican's diet. There were also many wounded
Mexicans here. The whole road during today's march was strewed with
dead and horses and mules shot in the retreat. In one place I saw a whole
team of eight mules dead in the harness and a number of dead Mexicans in
the waggon and around it. Although only the second day after the battle,
the bodies were already putrid and the smell intolerable. Camped near a
fine hacienda, said to belong to Santa Anna at the juncture of two streams
called Los dos Rios. This day's march at the time I supposed to be about
twelve miles. But the distances given by travelers make it six miles from
Cerro Gordo to Encero, a place within a few hundred yards of where we
are encamped, making our day's march twenty-two miles. This I think
too much, but perhaps, finding so much to interest us, did not perceive the
distance. The country through which we passed today was for the first five
miles through the scene of the late fight, wild, rough and romantic, then a
barren chaparrel until near camp, where it was a clear grazing country
and enclosed by stone walls, the first line enclosures we have seen on this
march. Two of us arriving at camp long before the company and wishing
to discharge the loads which we had put into our muskets on Sunday
morning with the expectation of shooting a greaser, went for beef. Chased

a fine bull, and besides a number of shots fired by my comrade, I put six balls into his hide before bringing him down. Returned to camp for assistance and brought in half of the beef. But several of the boys, remembering the starvation at Plan del Rio, also shot cattle and brought in quarters, so that beef was unusually plentiful in camp, a hind quarter to each mess. A glorious feast ensued. The meat was of the finest quality. Detailed for guard tonight for leaving the company on march. Much more annoyed by Mexican dogs than by Mexicans, the hombres being unusually scarce for the last two days.

April 21

BARCLAY. The snow covered peak of Orizaba visible. Left camp early—road fine—the men refreshed. Reached Jalapa[8] at noon. Halted for a considerable time at the outskirts of the City. Marched through the City without halting and encamped three miles beyond in a large meadow. The water is plenty and cool. There is a cotton factory here owned by an old Spaniard said to be the god-father of Santa Anna. His establishment is managed by a yankee from Connecticut.

COULTER. This morning for the first time saw the snow mountains of Orizaba. Managed again to get ahead of the brigade. Reached the suburbs of Jalapa about 10 o'clock. Shortly after, the brigade arrived and we marched through the city in column and encamped beyond the town. The country through which we passed today shows much more signs of civilization than any previous, and as one approaches Jalapa the view is magnificent. Jalapa is a beautiful place; streets and buildings are clean and white. As is the case with all Mexican towns, built principally of plastered stone and tiles. Beyond the city the country is rich and cultivated. Ate some blackberries on the road side. Our camp, called "Camp Patterson," is situate in a beautiful meadow, which is watered by a fine stream of cold water. There is a cotton factory near, owned by Englishmen. Our day's march is nine miles to Jalapa and three miles from that place to camp, making the whole distance twelve miles. During the night for the first time suffered from cold and my blanket was completely wet with dew.

April 22

BARCLAY. Having only three tents a majority of the company sleep without any covering. Lieut. Murry was appointed by Col. Roberts Regt. Commissary at Plan del Rio. He is acting at present in that capacity.

---

8. A city of perhaps ten thousand inhabitants, Jalapa was universally praised for the mildness of its climate and the beauty of its women. A delighted soldier, John Kreitzer of the 1st Pennsylvania Infantry, remarked on the "cluster of Orange Groves, which fills the air with their sweet flagrance [sic], making the entry to Jalapa like the Garden of Eden more

COULTER. Commenced building bowers to sleep in. Learned that General Worth entered the castle of Perote without firing a shot. During the night again felt the cold. Was completely exposed, not having my bower finished. It is very hot here during the day and as cold at night. The men will suffer who threw away their blankets on the march as useless.

April 23

BARCLAY. Beautiful day. I am unwell. Boys engaged in building bowers. There is a tolerable market—oranges, bananas, fine apples, blackberries, etc. The three Lobos companies join us, having come up under Quitman. James Johnston looks remarkably well. Heard of our sick at Vera Cruz. Myers and Hartford are dead. With the former I had but slight acquaintance. He appeared to be a fine fellow. Poor Hartford was from near Jacksonville, Westmd Co. He was a young man of delicate constitution and most excellent qualities. Worn down by the fatigues and hardships at Vera Cruz, he struggled to perform his duties to the last moment, anxious to go on guard when he was not detailed on account of his weakness. The company were very desirous of having him discharged before they left Vera Cruz. The Surgeon at first refused because he was not low enough and when he was far gone he again refused because if he was discharged he would never get home. Hartford was a victim to either the ignorance of Dr. M. [Frederick W. Miller] or to the influence which Col. Roberts exerted over the Doctor. Heard today that Gen. Worth had taken posession of Perote Castle without firing a gun, the Mexicans being completely thunderstruck at the results of Cerro Gordo.

COULTER. General Quitman with his brigade arrived today and encamped near us. Lt. Colonel Geary with the three companies of our regiment left at Lobos Island came up with this brigade. Although left on account of small pox and many of them had that disease, not a man has yet died in any of these companies. Learned of the death of two of our sick left at Vera Cruz, James Hartford and Lewis Myers. Slept more comfortably during the night.

April 24

BARCLAY. Regt. Parade. A part of our company in town. Made out additional descriptive rolls for the sick at Vera Cruz, learning that there was some difficulty in regard to those left. Wrote to S. M. Montgomery and made the rolls into a package.

---

than any thing I can compare it to" (cited in John P. Bloom, "With the American Army in Mexico, 1848–1849" [Ph.D. diss., Emory University, 1956], 98).

COULTER. Had a dress parade this evening and for the first time turned out a full regiment. Orders from General Pillow were read requiring three hours daily drill. A poor chance of having this obeyed.

April 25

BARCLAY. Company E on guard. Received letters from Foster, Keslar and Eichar.[9] Wrote several letters. As everyone has received news from home the Company are in good humor. Dick Johnston has received a commission as 2nd Lieut. in the 11th Regt. Gave descriptive rolls to Capt. [John] Herron [1st Pa. Inf.] who will send them by a friend to Vera Cruz. Rained constantly all night.

COULTER. This morning our company was detailed for brigade guard, which I escaped by having previously gone to Jalapa. Attended mass at a cathederal in the plaza. The first in the shape of religious service I have heard since leaving Greensburg. Strolled through the town and returned to camp in the evening. Today received a mail lately arrived. Dick Johnston received in it a commission as 2nd Lt. in the 11th Infantry, a new regular regiment lately organized. Passed an unpleasant night; rained greater part of the time and my blanket was completely soaked.

April 26

BARCLAY. Went with Dick and Lt. Coulter to the City. Saw Capt. Drum[10] and he instructed Dick how to proceed and gave him the address of Gen. Jones.[11] While tramping around saw several beautiful women, who will compare favorably with the lasses in the States, although as a matter of course they are not so handsome as the girls we've left behind us. The people are better dressed and much more respectable looking than the inhabitants of Vera Cruz. The City is built on the side of a hill, the houses of the same material and the same fashion as the buildings in Vera Cruz. The market is the best we have yet seen and the stranger is favorably impressed with the cleanliness of the City, the appearance of the people and the beautiful scenery of the surrounding country.

9. Three active Westmoreland Democrats. Foster is probably H. R. Foster of Greensburg, the Democratic nominee for Congress; "Keslar" is probably a misprint for Henry or Daniel Kistler, the former active in militia affairs, the latter the Democratic candidate for sheriff; "Eichar" is John Eicher, mentioned in Barclay's journal entry of 30 December 1846. Considering these correspondents, it is likely that Barclay was more deeply involved in local political matters than his diary indicates.

10. Simon Henry Drum, U.S. Military Academy, class of 1830, was captain of the 4th Artillery. A Greensburg native, he was the son of the local postmaster and the brother of Richard Coulter Drum. He was killed at his post on 13 September 1847 at the Belen Gate during the storming of Mexico City.

11. Brigadier General (by brevet) Roger Jones, the adjutant general. His address, of course, was The War Department, Washington, D.C.

COULTER. Suffered no further inconvenience from last night's wetting than the trouble of drying my clothes. Have been engaged this afternoon answering some letters received yesterday.

April 27
COULTER. Put through a general washing today and cleaned my musket which began to look the worse of the wear. Report in camp that Santa Anna is lying between us and Worth with a heavy force. No reliance is placed in it however.

April 28
BARCLAY. Went to the City today again with Dick and remained there 4 or 5 hours waiting for Col. Roberts. Capt. Drum had directed Dick to report himself in company with his Colonel to Gen. Scott and he would be ordered to some duty. It rained today in torrents. Col. Roberts finally was ready and we went up to Scott's Quarters. Gen. Scott was busy. H. L. Scott,[12] A.A.A.G. directed Dick for the present to remain with his Company. Dick and I took two or three rounds of brandy principally for medical purposes.

COULTER. Mess cook today and had a most glorious time of it. Rained heavy greater part of the day. Had flour rations to bake and wet wood to bake them. Attempted to make pan cakes or rather slap jacks and by the time I had a few baked my batter was reduced almost to the consistency of water by the rain. Did not get through until nine o'clock at night and then they were little better than so much lead. After which slept in wet blankets in a drizzling rain.

April 29
BARCLAY. The constant rains to which the men have been exposed lying on the cold ground without tents or shelter of any kind is producing a great deal of sickness. The water tho cool and pleasant to the taste is strongly impregnated with a mineral substance and the surgeon recommends that it be drank very sparingly or else after it has been warmed. As a matter of course men will not take this precaution. Sent Carpenter and Rexroad to town to the hospital today. Rager and Miller are already there.

COULTER. Quite pleasant in the morning. General cleaning up of muskets for the coming inspection and mustering in of the regiment. About

12. Captain Henry Lee Scott, a West Point graduate (class of 1833) from North Carolina, was Winfield Scott's aide-de-camp. Despite their names, the two men were not related until 1846, when H. L. Scott married Winfield's daughter, Cornelia. The younger Scott's army career was mainly spent on his father-in-law's staff, culminating with a stint as colonel and inspector general in 1861. He retired from the service (along with Winfield Scott) later that year. The initials Barclay appends to his name stand for Acting Assistant Adjutant General.

noon commenced raining which continued until near evening. Supped on coffee without bread or meat and again slept in a soaking rain.

April 30

BARCLAY. Raining today. Many sick. Only 43 of Co. E for duty. Provisions are issued irregularly. Instead of crackers, flour is issued. The only mode of cooking the flour is into "Slap Jacks," a heavy greasy cake which would give an ostrich dyspepsia.

COULTER. Rained all day and in consequence inspection was postponed. Had another wet night.

April 31[13]

BARCLAY. Wrote several letters, one to George Larimer informing of the death of poor Hartford.

May 1

BARCLAY. Inspection and mustering in. Only 48 men of Co. E in ranks. Their arms in fine order. In the forenoon, day warm. In the afternoon, heavy rain. A little mutiny in Camp. A crowd of the soldiers went to the Colonel in a body demanding food. The Colonel gave them no satisfaction. A charge was immediately made upon all the market greasers. I was busy at the muster rolls. Was the mustering officer this time.

COULTER. This morning detailed as guard to a General Court-martial now sitting. Relieved about two o'clock. This afternoon were inspected and mustered into the service, numbering fifty-six officers and men fit for duty. Threatened all afternoon but did not rain and we passed a more comfortable night in consequence.

May 2

BARCLAY. Forenoon warm, afternoon rain accompanied with thunder and lightning. Dress Parade orders from Gen. Scott. There are great complaints and very just ones among the men. While Gen. Scott is watching with a paternal eye the interests of the Mexicans, issuing the most severe orders against any interference, he is suffering his own soldiers, the volunteer portion of them, to be exposed without tents in a season when it rains daily. What makes it more provoking, in the City of Jalapa only three miles distant, plenty of good quarters can be obtained, both public and private. The American paper published in Jalapa daily announces that "they are cheered with most refreshing showers." I finished the muster

---

13. As April of 1847 had the customary thirty days, Barclay has clearly lost count. More than likely he skipped his entry for 27 April, and then pushed the next four entries one day ahead of their proper position.

rolls today. Volunteers sent to the guard house for robbing Mexicans. A court martial is in session with business it is said for three months. The principal depredations committed by the soldiers are taking the fences and roofs of old huts for fire wood and stealing chickens and other eatables. For such offences they are placed under guard, court martialed and punished. The mournful dead march again today—a sound frequently heard. Finding that there is no sign of being removed, our boys are building bowers, etc., to shield them as much as possible from the rain.

COULTER. With Jim McLaughlin and Keslar, volunteered to go to Vera Cruz and return as guard to a train, but on examination, found that instead of a guard, we were wanted for waggoners and mule drivers; in consequence, took back our volunteering. Orders were read to us this evening to hold ourselves in readiness to march on the return of the train from Vera Cruz. As usual, rained the greater part of the afternoon and fell in torrents. During the night, waking up, found that I was lying in a great puddle of water.

May 3
BARCLAY. Made out monthly return. Rain as usual.

COULTER. Today drew two days provisions and ordered to march tomorrow morning. Busy all day preparing, when towards evening orders were countermanded. Had another rainy night.

May 4
BARCLAY. James Johnston and Shields sent to the hospital today, the former very unwell. Orders which we had to march countermanded. Dead march again. Sickness of the camp very great and increasing. Yesterday two or three wagon loads of Mexican clothing captured at Cerro Gordo brought in and duly distributed.

COULTER. The year volunteers[14] received orders to march to Vera Cruz en route for New Orleans, there to be disbanded, viz: Georgia, Alabama, two Illinois and two Tennessee regiments and also another Tennessee regiment now at Plan del Rio. The remaining regiments, the South Carolina, New York and two Pennsylvania are formed into a brigade under General Quitman. Had rained all day and we have not been able to dry our blankets. We have a number of sick who occupy the tents, but they are very damp and the men cannot get into the hospital, it being full. Our company has

14. The terms of enlistment of the seven regiments and two companies of volunteers who had signed up for one year's service expired around mid-June. Despite all of Scott's inducements to reenlist, scarcely enough of them remained to fill one company, and the rest departed for home, leaving Scott in the middle of a hostile country with an army of only about seven thousand men at his disposal.

eight there now. In fact, between the wet ground and slap jacks we will all soon be in condition for the hospital.

May 5

BARCLAY. Took a walk. Day pleasant. Being very unwell I thought a little exercise would do me good. The country most lovely—vegetation green. Met with many flowers and plants which flourish in Penna. The rose, pinks, sturgeons [nasturtiums?] and morning glories recall a June day at home. Alas the sickness which is carrying off many and will break down the constitutions of many more reminds me that we are far away from the land of plenty, comfort and health and are *basking* in the *sunny* South.

COULTER. The company was detailed for guard today. After some difficulty mustered twenty-five, which with seven left as cooks, is our whole duty force. The night was pleasant which happened very opportune for us on guard.

May 6

BARCLAY. The orders having been countermanded the 2nd Regt. today march for Jalapa. The field officers being desirous of immortalizing themselves and handing down their names to posterity as heroes and warriors of renown pretend to be in a bad humor and are making a great fuss at being forced to remain in garrison. The men weak and sick, having a prospect of comfortable quarters, are satisfied to remain until their strength is recruited and their sick comrades restored to health. The quarters allotted to us are barracks formerly occupied by Mexican troops, public property, and strange to say were entirely unoccupied during all the time that we lay exposed. The camp which has just been broken up was called "Camp Patterson." It might with more propriety have been named "Camp Desolation." So weak was I when we marched to the City that I was compelled to fall out of ranks and did not reach quarters for some time after the company. Tonight very near being put in the guard house.

COULTER. Was put on post at five o'clock this morning, and by some mistake or negligence in relieving, allowed to remain until near noon. Rather a long tour. The regiments about to be disbanded left today. Learned that our regiment has been detailed as the volunteer force to garrison Jalapa. Today our mess made a purchase of a fine large skillet or dutch pan oven from one of the Illinois regiments. About noon waggoners arrived to haul our baggage and shortly after we marched to the city. General Quitman with the remainder of his brigade marched today for Perote. Jack Gilchrist was by some mismanagement left sick on the camp ground without assistance and was taken with our company to the city. A part of the regiment, Company E included, were quartered in the Cuartel de la Guardia Nacional which has heretofore been used as a hospital, and there were yet in it a number of sick Carolinians. The smell from the inner yard is filthy. Two other companies are in the same room with us and we have not more than sufficient room to stack arms. As expected, went to bed supperless, and on account of our confined quarters, a large number of the men slept in the open court. For my part I tried it in the room on the brick tiles, the first time I have slept under roof since landing.

4

The Filth of the Regt. is Disgraceful
Jalapa

In the first flush after Cerro Gordo, Scott gloated: "Mexico has no longer an army!"[1] As it happened, it was Scott himself who was in danger of losing his army. Over seven regiments of his volunteers had been enlisted for only one year, a term which would soon expire. When virtually all of these volunteers chose to return home rather than reenlist, Scott's army, never large, was stripped to less than six thousand men, too few to continue offensive operations. Fresh troops were on the way, but until they arrived, the American invaders had to mark time.

Short of medicine, salt, clothing, transportation, and ammunition, depleted by illness, with its precarious supply line to Vera Cruz harassed by Mexican guerrillas, Scott's recently victorious army was wasting away in "protracted and irksome" garrison duty deep within a hostile country.[2] In the meantime, the indefatigable Santa Anna had somehow managed to raise yet another large, if poorly trained, army to defend his capital.

By early July, the first reinforcements reached Scott's forward position at Puebla, and a month later a second detachment under Brigadier General Franklin Pierce arrived. With this fresh infusion, Scott could resume his long-delayed march to the interior, although he still lacked the resources to protect his ever-lengthening supply line.

Leaving behind only a small garrison at Puebla under Colonel Thomas Childs to guard the many sick and wounded, Scott concentrated the remainder of his army, about ten thousand in all, for the advance. In a gesture reminiscent of Cortes, who had burned his boats behind him, Scott abandoned the route to Vera Cruz, giving up his line of supply and of retreat. "We had to throw away the scabbard," he said, "and to advance with the naked blade in hand."[3]

The audacity of this move was not appreciated by President Polk, who was now confirmed in his determination to remove his independent-minded commanding general at the first opportunity. Opposition from

---

1. Winfield Scott to Zachary Taylor, 24 April 1847. *Senate Executive Document No. 60*, 30th Cong., 1st sess., 1171–72.

2. Scott, *Memoirs*, 2:453.

3. Ibid., 460.

*Polk could be expected; he had been suspicious of Scott from the very
start. But in far-off London, a greater military authority, the aging duke
of Wellington, was equally pessimistic. "Scott is lost," Wellington declared. "He can't take the city [of Mexico] and he can't fall back upon his
base."*[4]

May 7

BARCLAY. The surgeon at the hospital gave a dose of Glauber's salt.[5] I
thought it was a rather singular medicine for the diarrhea. Our men who
are at the hospital are much better. A private in Co. B died—a case of neglect on the part of the physicians.

COULTER. Was mess cook today, but made a poor account of my cook-
ship. Had but very little to cook and no place to cook it. Passed the night
as the previous, on the bricks.

May 8

BARCLAY. Co. E on guard. I went to church. It far surpassed the church
at Vera Cruz.

COULTER. By good luck got something to eat today. Moved from our
quarters in the room to the portico in the yard. Slept under the portico
this night. The smell from the hospital was almost suffocating.

May 9

BARCLAY. Attended church and heard mass. The greater part of the Devotees are women. A good many catholic soldiers of our army take part in
the ceremonies. Sunday is a great market day. There is ten times as much
fruit and vegetables for sale today as on any other day in the week. On
Saturday evening a civil officer has lines drawn across the plaza (of lime or
chalk) and the market people are regulated by these lines. In general a certain part of the plaza is assigned to certain descriptions of vegetables and
articles of sale. Rexroad, a man we were so unfortunate as to enlist in
Pittsburgh, was discharged today much to the satisfaction of the whole company. This afternoon took a walk towards a stream which runs at the foot
of the City. There is an orange grove here which is a most delightful place
to promenade in. The stream supplies an extensive cotton mill which is
owned or managed by Englishmen. Met Englishmen who appear very
friendly. They damn the Mexicans for a set of robbers and cutthroats. Had
a splendid bath, the water very pleasant.

4. Ibid., 466n.
5. A type of epsom salts, used most commonly as a purgative.

COULTER. This afternoon took a walk to a height northwest of the city. A mountain battery had been erected on it to command the town, but from some cause was deserted. Had a tiresome walk, but was repaid by the magnificent view on reaching it. There is a small building on the summit of the hill in which are written the names of many travelers who have been there. This night slept in the commissary's room. The smell not quite so strong there, but the difference is supplied by the quantity of fleas.

May 10

BARCLAY. Washed clothes and loafed today in the beautiful shade about the bridge. The wash house is a long open building with some fifty holes. A dam in the creek supplies it with water and the stones to wash on are of a convenient height and all the arrangements are convenient. There are two or three large buildings of this kind in different parts of the City and they are generally thronged with Mexican women. Orders today that no private should leave quarters without a pass. This order is villanous. It takes away the only pleasure we have, viz., of spending a few hours in the heat of the day in the groves in the suburbs of the City and thus we will be confined day and night to our filthy barracks.

COULTER. Complaints have been made to the officers relative to the quarters. They say "we will see to it" and there it ends. A police party have been engaged today cleaning up the rear of the quarters and burning the straw in the hospital. Had another night on the portico; still very unpleasant, principally from the smoke of the straw.

May 11

BARCLAY. The day is clear. Orizaba appears nearer and if possible more magnificent than ever. Writing a pass for myself I slip off to the grove and for hours watch the fashionables promenading and the poor devils of Indians passing with their immense loads. No one can form an idea of the load of wood, charcoal and vegetables these poor beings carry. The load on their back is made steady by a band around the forehead. When they return from the City their gait is a little trot. They appear more like brutes than human beings.

COULTER. Had a dress parade this evening.

May 12

BARCLAY. The funeral of a Mexican officer took place today. He died in consequence of wounds received at the Battle of Cerro Gordo. The ceremony was imposing. The body was first conveyed to the Church and after the rites of the Catholic religion on such occasions had been performed, it was taken to the grave. A band of the regulars and a regular escort were in attendance. Genls. Scott, Twiggs and many of the American officers were also present. A train is looked for from Vera Cruz.

COULTER. This was ordered as a general washing day in the regiment. Made an overhaul of my knapsack. Our town seems to anticipate an attack from the fact of numbers of the citizens leaving the place and some other circumstances. The train from Vera Cruz is looked for and with some anxiety, as it is a day or so late, and more particularly as it brings money to pay the men.

May 13
BARCLAY. After lying so long and cruelly exposed at Camp Patterson we were glad to get into any quarters. Nothing, however, can well be conceived more filthy than the barracks where the men now lay. Our company are crowded on an open porch. We manage to keep it clean and everything well arranged, but the filth of the Regt. is disgraceful and will, unless remedied, create a disease. An officer is daily appointed to see that quarters are policed but they pay but little attention to it.

COULTER. This morning attended the funeral of a Mexican Colonel wounded at Cerro Gordo. The body was first taken to the Cathedral, where some ceremonies were performed and then covered with honors of war by a company of our soldiers. Generals Scott and Twiggs, with their respective staffs and the officers of the state attended, apparently much to the satisfaction of the people.

May 14
BARCLAY. A train with a mail came in today from Vera Cruz. Altho Guerillas were heard of along the road they gave them no trouble. A bull-fight came off today.

COULTER. The train from Vera Cruz came in today, having had a difficult trip, but without molestation. There was a Spanish bull fight this afternoon.

May 15
BARCLAY. This is said to be the day for an election of President of the Mexican Republic. We are all in favor of Herrera as he is said to be in favor of peace.[6] One of our comrades died today, William Wentz of Hempfield Twp., Westmd County. He was a man of great physical strength and

6. Although the Mexican Congress was scheduled to select a president on 15 May, the vote was postponed due to the prevailing state of chaos compounded by the return of Santa Anna and the remnants of his army to the capital. At first threatening to resign his command, he was persuaded to take over the presidency and continue the war on a more vigorous basis. José Joaquín Herrera (1792–1854), the president of the supreme court, whom

vigorous constitution. His disease was the diarrhea which was rendered fatal by the exposure at Camp Patterson. Many of our company are suffering from the same cause. Wentz was buried with military honors near a small church in the suburbs of the city. I wrote to his father informing him of the death of his son.

COULTER. Today is said to be the day of election for a president of the Republic at the City of Mexico. William Wentz, a private of our company, died in quarters today and was buried with honors of war.

May 16
BARCLAY. Another bull fight. I have been at the hospital. It presents a bad sight. Crowded with sick whose wants are not as well provided for as they should be. There are not enough of surgeons in the first place and the majority of surgeons in the army that I have met with are insolent ruffians. A man in the States would be ashamed to speak to his dog in the way these men address the sick. Numbers are dying daily. The dead are now not carried but hauled away in wagons. It is sad to see men who left home full of high hopes, young, gallant and patriotic, pining away in a hospital, exposed to the carelessness of nurses and attendants and daily insulted by ruffians who, their inferiors in moral and intellectual worth, are for the time their superiors in rank.

COULTER. This afternoon attended a bull fight at the Plaza de Toros. Five bulls were fought and killed in succession. It was the first performance of the kind I have ever seen and therefore a novelty, but at the same time, from my ideas of a Spanish bull fight I think it must have been rather a small performance.

May 17
BARCLAY. The men are in a bad humor about their pay. It was reported and believed that the train which came in a few days ago had money for the army. There is however no sight of pay day yet. Uncle Sam owes us near six months wages and why don't he pay up, etc., is the question.

COULTER. As a large quantity of money is said to have arrived with the train, the men very naturally expected to be paid, but as yet there is no sight of it, which causes some growling.

Barclay correctly identified with the cause of peace, was not even considered for leadership in the supercharged, defiant atmosphere of that day. He would, however, be given the opportunity to occupy the presidential chair on three separate occasions from 1848 to 1851, including the period that saw the final withdrawal of American troops from Mexico.

May 18

BARCLAY. Nothing of interest occurred. The weather which was extremely inclement when we were exposed has since our arrival in the City become fair and pleasant. The guard duty is heavy. A number of the men are unfit for duty. The remainder are frequently on guard, a portion of them being today on at the picket.

COULTER. Mounted guard today on the piquet near the Plaza de Constitution Mexicano.

May 19

BARCLAY. Garrison life presents but few incidents worthy of note. This afternoon the troops in the City were formed and marched to the plaza. Four soldiers had been court martialed and found guilty of robbery. They were to be punished today and whipping was part of the punishment. The culprits were three regulars and Drummer [Don F.] Revelon of Co. B of the 2nd Pa. Vols. Three muskets were stacked and the prisoners stripped to the pants and tightly tied to the stack. A regular Drum was ordered to take the whip. An officer was present to count the lashes and Gen. Childs[7] on horseback to superintend generally. The Drum who appeared a good natured fellow laid on the first three strokes very gently. Childs ordered him immediately to the guard house. This had the desired effect and amid much writhing the prisoner received 39 well and slowly laid on. He was then taken from the stack and the same ceremony was gone through with the rest. They were then taken back to the guard house. The object of assembling the troops was that they might profit by the example. There was among all however a general feeling of disgust. The men no doubt were scoundrels who deserved punishment, but everyone regretted that such a punishment could be inflicted under the laws of our country. Barbarous and cruel is such a punishment. Instead of reforming, culprits by the exposure are hardened. Spectators forget the crime in sympathy for the sufferers and our country is lowered in the eyes of all her children when she forgets the principles of humanity and modern government and permits a punishment which is only known in cruel savage nations or in most barbarous times. Two thousand years ago a Roman citizen was protected from such a disgrace. In the nineteenth century an American citizen is subjected to the dishonour of being publicly whipped.[8]

7. A career officer in the regular army, Thomas Childs (1796–1853) of Massachusetts went straight from his classes at the U.S. Military Academy (1814) to the battlefields of the War of 1812. There, as well as in the Seminole Wars and the Mexican War that followed, he distinguished himself by his reckless personal bravery, finally leading to a brevet as brigadier general for his successful defense of Puebla in the siege of 1847.

8. The outrage expressed by Barclay and Coulter over corporal punishment was shared by many of their countrymen, leading to a movement for its abolition. In 1850 Congress

COULTER. Today all the forces in the place were mustered in the main plaza to witness the whipping of four soldiers convicted of robbery. Three of them were regulars and one a volunteer belonging to Company B, of our regiment. The performance was, I thought, cruel and had a bad effect upon the Mexicans, many of whom saw it. It is the first instance of a volunteer being whipped during the war and has raised considerable excitement and caused the uttering of many hard expressions against the officers of the Court Martial.

May 20

BARCLAY. The three regulars who were whipped yesterday were this morning drummed through the streets to the tune of the "Rogues March." Their heads were shaved, a large placard pinned to their backs and a file of men marched behind them at charge bayonets. I do not know why the volunteer was not subjected to the same drumming. Probably the court martial thought that for a volunteer the whipping was sufficient.

COULTER. This morning the persons who were whipped yesterday, had their heads shaved, and except the volunteer, drummed through the streets to the tune of the rogue's march with a platoon of soldiers behind them following at a charge bayonet and the word "robber" in large letters upon their backs. The volunteer's head was shaved by mistake, that not being a part of his sentence. Another small train came up in charge of Captain Walker[9] of the Mounted Rifles. Had a heavy rain this afternoon which makes our quarters rather uncomfortable.

May 21

BARCLAY. Heavy rain. Quarters particularly disagreeable. Lice and fleas, fleas and lice, and so on to the end of the chapter.

COULTER. Had another general washing up of my clothing and enjoyed a good bath in the creek. It is almost impossible to keep clean or comfortable in our present quarters. Fleas are superabundant and body lice are becoming plenty. In some of the rooms are seen crawling on the floor.

---

compelled the navy to ban flogging and the army followed suit early in 1861. The whipping post lingered in some states well into the twentieth century. It was last used in Delaware in 1952 and was not banned altogether until twenty years thereafter.

9. Samuel H. Walker, born in Maryland sometime around 1810, fought in the Florida Indian Wars before joining up with the Texas Rangers under John C. Hays. Upon Walker's advice, Samuel Colt modified his newly invented revolving pistol to make it better adapted for use by mounted men and named this first practical revolver the Walker Colt in his honor. Walker was one of the Texans captured by the Mexicans at Mier and was held prisoner at Perote until his spectacular escape. He returned to Mexico as a captain in the U.S. Army and became known as a relentless scourge of his former tormentors until his death in action at Huamantla on 9 October 1847.

Caught three in one of my shirts today, the first I have seen about me. They appeared to be stragglers as I could find no signs of a settlement.

May 22

COULTER. Today General Twiggs and division marched to Puebla.

May 23

BARCLAY. So numerous and industrious are the fleas that many of the men cannot sleep at all at night. They take an occasional nap in the day time. These vermin which are mere matter of amusement in the States are here a subject of very serious consideration. One of our men killed and another wounded badly today. Several Mexicans were arrested on suspicion and sent to the guard house. Yesterday Gen. Twiggs started for Puebla with his Division. Gen. Scott left today.

COULTER. General Scott left for Puebla. Detailed for guard and again on the piquet. All passed off quietly until about 9 o'clock P.M., when a man covered with blood and having several severe wounds on his head and arms came running into one of the pickets and reported that himself and a companion had been attacked near the suburbs of the city by a party of Mexicans and that he supposed his comrade was killed; that he only saved himself by breaking from their hold and running into the piquet. Went with the patrol in pursuit of the perpetrators. Scoured that whole portion of the city and suburbs from which he came and found no traces of his companion. Captured two Mexicans who afterward proved to be in the service of the United States. One of them speaking English informed us that he had been attacked, but the Mexican, though armed with a musket, ran on his presenting a pistol. Using him as a guide captured the Mexican in a bye-path among some bushes, who was identified by our guide and confessed that he had been guilty and said his musket was concealed in the bushes, but he would not get it. Took them all to the guard house. First two were released afterward. The last was detained. While on guard slept on the street without a blanket. The Pebble stones were not as soft as feathers.

May 24

BARCLAY. Today Mess No. 6 had a dinner of roast pork, an event very important and interesting. The weather continues pleasant. Men are on guard every third day. The guard duty is severe. Gen. Childs is strict. He has an important post. The garrison is small and the enemy's forces in the neighborhood are supposed to be numerous. He is therefore always on the alert, requires all ceremonies to be gone through and every man to do his duty. The ceremony of guard mounting is neat and beautiful. The details from the different companies are marched on the ground by the 1st

Sergeant of the guard. The Adjt. Genl. orders the commissioned and non-commissioned officers to the front, assigns them their posts and orders them to inspect arms. Arms are inspected, ranks closed, guard wheeled into column and marched in review before the officer of the day. Previous to this however the music beats of a splendid brass band belonging to the artillery is in attendance each morning. The new guard marches past the old guard who are under arms and from whose officers the officer of the new guard receives his orders. Some of the Regular officers are unnecessarily strict. They keep the guard standing under arms in the sun for hours. Among the volunteers these regular officers are very unpopular.

COULTER. Mess No. 6 had a roast of fresh pork today. It was not hard to take, but caused some dysentery.

May 25

BARCLAY. There are in all catholic countries processions of a religious kind to which the natives pay great attention. As the war party in this country have during the war appealed to the religious prejudices of their countrymen and represented the Americans as carrying on a war against their religion, it has always been the policy of our army to remove these prejudices as much as possible. This policy was tonight carried too far and a most gross outrage committed upon the feelings of the privates of the army. Gov. Childs issued an order that the guard should be turned out when the procession approached, take off their caps, ground arms and kneel while the procession was passing. These orders were carried into effect, the officers of the guard showing the example and the privates following through fear of punishment. Such a performance might have been very appropriate for Napoleon and his men who were all avowed infidels and who embraced the Mohammedan religion merely for ambitious purposes. But the American army is composed of a different material. The men are not infidels, a majority of them belonging to religious and pious families, and a large majority of them are of the Protestant persuasion. A man's religious opinion should be respected and held sacred and the forcing men of Puritan principles to kneel to a procession of this kind is about as just as it would be to require Catholics to trample upon the holy cross. Protestants consider such ceremonies as idolatrous and altho Gov. Childs may think differently he should still respect the prejudices of a large majority of his command. Such an act of tyranny should not be passed over and altho he is a brave and skilled officer the State could far better dispense with his services than suffer American soldiers to be insulted in such a manner. There is a great excitement among the privates. Many swear that they will undergo every punishment before they will obey such orders. From the general expression I think it will be very difficult for the _____ to find a guard as complaisant and obedient as were the guard of tonight.

COULTER. Tonight occurred a scene which reflected but little credit upon Governor Childs. There was a torch light procession of the citizens with the Bishop at their head. Governor Childs himself entered the procession with a lighted candle in his hand. The guard at the main guardhouse were ordered to kneel, reverse arms and take off their caps to the Bishop. Some of the guard at first refused, but the officer of the guard, Captain Winder,[10] of the First Artillery, compelled all to kneel, striking several with his sword. It has raised some excitement.

May 26

BARCLAY. A small train left today for Vera Cruz. Lieut. Murry of our Company, Corp. Carpenter and James Johnston have been discharged and all start for home. Lieut. Murry has leave of absence until the 15th of June when he is honorably discharged. He resigned on account of sickness, being much worn down at Camp Patterson. Johnston and Carpenter also suffered much. They were both for a considerable time in hospital. Their diseases were contracted from exposure at the same fatal camp. It is unnecessary to add that they all bear them our best wishes for their safe and speedy return to their homes.

COULTER. A small train left today. Three of the Westmoreland Guards, Lieutenant Murry, Corporal James Carpenter and Quartermaster's Sergeant James Johnston, lately discharged, left with it for Vera Cruz.

May 27

BARCLAY. Weather continues pleasant, but the boys are becoming tired of a garrison life and the strict rules of Gov. Childs. It heretofore has been our custom in the evenings after supper to loaf on the steps of the Cathedral and have a sociable chat over the stories and rumors of the day. As we talk about such nonsense and about scenes at home and of our absent friends, time rapidly slips by—and time is one of the greatest enemies of the soldier. For some cause or other the Governor has issued an order to the guard to prevent all persons from being about the steps. As there is no convenient comfortable loafing place about we are deprived of the luxury of these chats. But we must submit for Childs don't do his business by halfs. We are generally more successful with our own officers and come off better in our contests with them. Col. Roberts a few days ago issued an order that commanders of companies should immediately have the hair of

10. John Henry Winder (1800–1865) of Maryland was a West Point graduate (1820) brevetted lieutenant colonel during the Mexican War. His greatest fame, however, came during the Civil War when he served the Confederacy as provost marshal and commander of prisons. In that capacity he was responsible for the notorious Andersonville Prison, and had he not died shortly before the war's end very likely would have been tried, and possibly hanged, for the atrocities committed there.

all their men cut short according to the regulations. This caused a great hubbub. Men swore that altho they had intended to have their hair cut it now should remain long, that Col. Roberts need not attempt to act Childs, that he could not make regulars of us. The only consequence of the order was that many determined to wear their hair uncomfortably long and they did so.

May 28

BARCLAY. There was another Catholic procession tonight. The Governor who has doubtless heard of the universal dissatisfaction among the men on account of the performance a few nights ago, had sense enough not to renew his orders. All that is required of the guard is that if they are near when the procession passes they shall take off their hats. This is right. Every gentleman can willingly pay such a mark of respect.

COULTER. Yesterday unusually dry, nothing worth mentioning happened. Mounted guard this morning. Stationed at the main guard house on the patrol. Got but little sleep, having to patrol the whole city at different hours of the night to prevent any disturbance. During the evening there was another Catholic procession similar to that of Tuesday evening last, but finding some dissatisfaction among the men in consequence of that performance, the officers of the guard did not require us to kneel, but only requested that those who did not wish to take off their hats might remain within the portico. Governor Childs was in the procession also with a lighted candle.

May 29

BARCLAY. Heard of the death of Ross and May. Ross received a commission of 2nd Lieut. at the same time Johnston was appointed. Being then sick at Vera Cruz, he made application for a furlough and started for home in company with Montgomery, Marchand, Keenan and Forney, the latter three discharged soldiers. He became worse during the voyage and died off Tampico. Ross was a good man in every sense of the word. He was born in Westmoreland County and educated at Schenectady College, N.Y. He studied law with Jas. H. Kuhns, was admitted and when he left home was doing a fine business which was rapidly increasing. Being a man of talent, of most sterling honesty and of a happy, merry disposition, he had many warm friends. He was the life of a party and his death has left a blank in the circles of the young in Greensburgh which can never be filled. May was from Youngstown. When we left Pittsburgh he was one of the most robust men in the company. He died in hospital at Vera Cruz on the 19th of May. He had been discharged on the day previous. He was a very witty fellow and the jokes of poor Buck May will long be remembered about Youngstown.

COULTER. When I came off guard this morning found that by some means or other I had gotten a number of big grey backs (body lice) upon my person. Heard of the deaths of two more Westmoreland Guards, Corporal Andrew Ross, who had received an appointment as 2nd Lt. in 11th Infantry, and returning home on furlough, died on the Gulf. George May, private, was discharged on account of disability at Vera Cruz and died before leaving that place.

June 1

BARCLAY. The company now numbers 4 Sergts., 3 Capts. and 50 privates for duty. There are four sick in quarters. During the last month McCredin, Kelly, Forney, Rexroad and Carpenter were discharged, the three former from Vera Cruz.

June 2

BARCLAY. The Regt. are being paid off. Our turn will come soon.

COULTER. Find no notice in my original notes of Sunday, Monday or Tuesday last. This morning again mounted guard on the piquet on patrol. Had considerable sport during the night while patrolling. Went some distance to a remote part of the town where patrols were not in the habit of going. Came across a party of Mexicans on a spree with a guitar and plenty of Aguardiente noisily enjoying themselves in a Fonda [an inn]. They were completely taken by surprise on seeing a patrol enter, but after making them dance a couple of polkas, left without disturbing them. Met several other parties of the same nature but did not molest them more than frightening them with "calabosa" [jail].

June 3

BARCLAY. Received from Major Burns,[11] Paymaster, two months pay. The market is good and the eatables have to take it at all the stores liquors are kept. The Temperance pledges are in many instances forgotten. Aguardiente, Mexican brandy and egg nogs are all the go. The latter is a tolerable good drink. The aguardiente and brandy is terrible stuff. The former is a clear whitish liquor distilled from the sugar cane. It is very cheap and very fiery. The Greasers drink it like milk. The brandy is a mixture of aguardiente and different drugs.

COULTER. After being relieved this morning the company was marched to the paymaster and received two months pay. My pay was fourteen dollars out of which I paid a sutler's account of near five dollars contracted at

11. Archibald W. Burns of New Jersey, an additional paymaster, played a bit part in the cabal against Winfield Scott by pretending to be the author of the "Leonidas" letter in an attempt to divert punishment from its true author, Gideon Pillow.

Lobos and Vera Cruz when money was scarce. We are now in the heart of the country where we can buy cheaper from the Mexicans and I wish him a happy time with the next bill he gets from me. Four of our mess left today, much to the satisfaction of the remainder, leaving us a snug mess of six. In consequence of being paid so lately the boys are in great spirits, some enjoying the benefit of the large market which is always here and many testing the quality of Mexican liquors.

June 4

BARCLAY. Mess No. 6 dissolved partnership by mutual consent. Bates left the mess a few days ago and Aikens, Smith & McCollum left today. There is now 6 of us left, Coulter, McLaughlin, Marchand, Steck, Moorhead and myself. We were so fortunate as to get a skillet from the Illinois men who were discharged and today we bought a very good coffee pot from the sutler.

COULTER. Colonel Roberts, seeing the comparative freedom in which we have lived, has given orders for four hours daily drill. There is a poor chance of its being obeyed, as neither officers nor men feel disposed to mount guard every third or fourth and some every other day and then drill in this manner for the remainder of the time.

June 5

BARCLAY. Nothing doing. As the men all have money they are not living altogether on Government rations.

COULTER. An unusually dull and lazy day.

June 6

BARCLAY. Five Mexicans brought in charged with robbing a traveller. Patrols at all the gates ordered to suffer no one to pass in or out. It is reported that there is a force of Mexicans armed in the City and the Governor is anxious to cut them off from the country and take them if possible.

COULTER. This morning mounted guard at the main guard house on patrol. Five Mexicans were captured, part of a gang of robbers who infest this neighborhood for the purpose of plundering trains, discharged soldiers and Mexican citizens indiscriminately. Today they had wounded and robbed a traveler near the city. Soon after dark the whole patrol were marched to the suburbs of the city and posted on a piquet at a large gate, the main entrance to the city from this direction. The piquets were posted at the other roads leading from the town for the purpose of capturing these plunderers, a large number of whom, it was said, were at this very time in the city. Compelled to remain on post all night without relief. It was very cold without a blanket, especially as were not allowed to walk about, but had to conceal ourselves among some old buildings and permit no one to enter or leave the city. In one of the neighboring houses there was a "fandango" at which the dance was continued until near day. An old woman, by whose door I had concealed myself, perhaps fearing the armed Quites[12] (watchers) who were near her dwelling, prayed very loud all night. No disturbance during the night and we were relieved about daybreak.

June 7

BARCLAY. It is generally rumored and believed that the garrison of this City will be broken up and the troops will march on. As the men are all sick and tired of a garrison life they are all in hopes that the rumor may prove true.

COULTER. Have slept near all day to compensate for last night's loss. There are many rumors afloat about this garrison evacuating Jalapa and marching to Puebla.

June 8

BARCLAY. One of the picket guard stabbed last night on post. A train came today from Puebla. Every appearance of marching shortly, but no orders yet. Campbell and Miller discharged and started for home, the former very low.

COULTER. This morning a dead soldier was brought in from the piquet, having been stabbed while on post. A train came in from Puebla and by the accounts it brings, we will soon leave Jalapa. A train left this place today for Perote with the sick and hospital stores. Escorted by three companies of the First Pennsylvania Regiment who have been here for some time.

June 9

COULTER. A small train left today for Vera Cruz. Adjutant Dutton and Lieutenants Williams and [Peter H.] McWilliams returned with it on the road to the States on recruiting service, although all believe this to be a mere excuse to get out of the service. Three Westmoreland Guards lately discharged, Campbell and Rexroad, on account of sickness, and Miller in consequence of wound received at Cerro Gordo, left with this train for Vera Cruz.

June 10

COULTER. This morning detailed for guard again. Again on patrol at the main guard house. This tour of guard was the easiest I have struck at this place, not being once called upon.

12. Coulter may be trying to say *cuides*, "guardians" or "chaperones."

June 11

BARCLAY. Marching orders have been received to start on the 14th inst. The train has returned to Perote with the sick of our Regt. McCollum sent up. The detachment of the 1st Penna. Regt. which was in garrison here escorted the train up. Friend Carney has been so fortunate as to get a fiddle. He is in his glory and since the arrival of the stranger, the quarters have presented many merry scenes.

COULTER. Since Tuesday last have received marching orders for Monday the 14th inst. One of our company made a purchase of a violin the other day and our quarters have been quite lively ever since.

June 12

COULTER. Spent this night most miserably. Expecting to leave daily, our quarters have been neglected. The collection of dirt is great and the stench intolerable.

June 13

BARCLAY. For the few last days times have been lively. Gen. Cadwalader[13] is looked for this evening and active preparations have been made to take up the line of march immediately upon his arrival. But little attention is paid to police duties and the Quarters are now filthy beyond description. A party from our company are on wagon guard tonight.

COULTER. Spirits of the men are lively with the expectation of shortly evacuating this place. General Cadwalader with a large train and some reinforcements is daily expected from Vera Cruz. This evening detailed for guard and picketed at the waggon yard to protect the train now there. Felt like old times to get out into the chaparral again and stand guard after the good old volunteer fashion. Dew very heavy in the bottom and our blankets were completely wet, but yet it is a relief from garrison duty.

June 14

BARCLAY. Cadwalader is not here yet. Great anxiety is felt on account of the train. The orders to march are still in force and have not been countermanded, tho as a matter of course we will not move until the train arrives. Companies D, G, & K ordered to hold themselves in readiness to

13. A well-connected, well-to-do Philadelphia lawyer, George Cadwalader (1804–1879) was appointed a brigadier general of volunteers in 1846 and was breveted major general for gallantry at Chapultepec. At the outbreak of the Civil War, he was appointed major general of volunteers and in May of 1861 put in charge of Baltimore, then seething with pro-Confederate sentiment. The next month he was placed under Patterson as second in command of the ill-fated Shenandoah campaign that opened the way to the Union defeat at Bull Run. In 1862 he was shunted aside to a board, charged with revising U.S. military laws and regulations, on which he served until the war's end.

march to the National Bridge where it is supposed Cadwalader is detained by the opposition of the Guerillas. Provisions are issued to those companies and they are about starting when an express arrived and announced the train to be near Jalapa.

COULTER. Our marching orders were not countermanded, yet we did not leave today and will not until General Cadwalader arrives. This evening three companies of our regiment (D. G. & K.) together with some dragoons and an artillery force, were ordered to prepare to march to Puento Nacionale to the relief of General Cadwalader, whom it was thought could not force his way through. But before they had started news was received that he was encamped at Encero and would be in tomorrow. Heavy rain this afternoon.

June 15
BARCLAY. The anxiously expected train arrived today. The force is about 2000 which escorts it. Quarter Master Montgomery and Hugh Brady came up with it. The rest of our sick at Vera Cruz were either unable to travel or detained in the hospital as cooks and attendants. The Guerillas were very troublesome, particularly at the National Bridge. They were there assembled in force and it was with some difficulty that they were dislodged from their covers. Many of our men were killed and wounded. A great many mules killed and some 34 wagons it was necessary to burn with their contents in order to prevent them from falling in the hands of the enemy. The first attack and most severe was made before the train reached the National Bridge.

COULTER. This morning the train came in. It had been attacked several times on the route and had lost a number of waggons and some men. Captain S. H. Montgomery, formerly belonging to our company, and H. J. Brady, one of our sick left at Vera Cruz, came up with this train.

June 16
COULTER. Tonight detailed for guard. Again posted at the train camp. During the night it rained in torrents, but we had luckily taken possession of a ranch for a guard house.

June 17
BARCLAY. Tomorrow we march for certain and no mistake.

5

Seven Months in the Service and 4,000 Miles from Home
Jalapa to Puebla

June 18

BARCLAY. At 4 P.M. the garrison of Jalapa took up line of march. Rained in the evening. Arrived at Camp Patterson—pitched tents. A few days ago we drew a full complement of tents and the company are well supplied. The tents we drew were old ones which had been turned over by the 1 year volunteers. We have been fortunate in getting them.

COULTER. Yesterday and today had a busy time preparing to leave. By noon all the waggoners had left and all United States property had been removed, when we took up our line of march evacuating Jalapa. Encamped at the old ground "Camp Patterson." We had drawn tents, sufficient being left by the disbanded regiments to supply us. Rained during the night, but we were pretty well sheltered by our tents, although old.

June 19

BARCLAY. Left camp at 6 A.M. The advance moved much earlier. Our Regt. is about the middle of the train. The march is slow and tedious. There are about 400 wagons and 3000 men. The train contains a large amount of money and valuable military stores. The Mexicans are aware of the value of the train and are extremely anxious to finger some of the cash. Attacks are therefore expected and the command moves with the greatest caution. A strong party are in advance. Scouting parties are thrown out and sentinels placed on high prominent points near the road on the lookout. The country for the first six miles is level and rich, the soil deep and tolerably well cultivated. The road then ascends the mountain and for the next six miles is steep. The scenery in ascending the mountain is wild and romantic. The mountains are timbered with pine. Several beautiful cascades are in view, the water falling an immense distance. After a slow march of 12 miles, arrived and encamped in a valley among the mountains near the village of La Hoya. The village is deserted and the houses and fences are considered lawful spoil for fire wood. One of our mess shot a pig here upon which we made a hearty supper. Tomorrow we march through the famous Black Pass where a fight and considerable difficulty is expected.

108

COULTER. This morning our regiment moved about six o'clock. The advance had started some time before, but such is the size of the train that our movements are slow and tedious. Our regiment was divided into two battalions. Ours, under Colonel Roberts was placed about the middle of the train. There are some 360 or 400 waggons and the force about 2,500 or 3,000 under Brigadier General Cadwalader. An attack was expected on account of our having a large amount of money and stores. Encamped in a meadow near the village of La Hoya, distant eleven miles from Camp Patterson. Scouts had been thrown out in all directions who discovered some signs of an enemy, but no attack was made. The country through which we passed today was hilly and woody, in some places good sized timber. It was one continuous ascent and our present camp is elevated considerably above Jalapa. On the right hand side of the road as we marched saw a most beautiful cascade issuing from a ravine and falling to a great distance. At one point of our march the view was most extensive and magnificent. Some say that from the same point the Gulf of Mexico is visible, but the distance was so great that I could distinguish nothing but what appeared to be the blue of the sky. The village of La Hoya is small and lies at the entrance of La Olla pass. The ranches are built of wood with high peaked shingle roofs, the shingles fastened with wooden pins. At this time it was totally deserted, the inhabitants having gone up into the pass to assist in the next day's attack upon our train. Had the cause of this desertion been known at the time, the village would have shared a different fate. It has the reputation of being a most villainous hole,—a perfect settlement of ladrones [thieves]. One of our mess (Steck) caught a pig here and we had quite a feast of fresh pork.

June 20
BARCLAY. Train put in motion at an early hour. The road is ascending and winding round the mountains, in places very steep. The country is rough and barren. It appears to have been thrown up by some volcanic eruption. The surface and probably to a great depth is composed of a hard reddish colored substance somewhat resembling iron ore. The scenery is remarkably wild and romantic. At times we were travelling in the mist and again above clouds which hung upon the sides of the mountains. Occasionally so dense was the cloud that it was impossible to see 30 paces. The Black Pass is a narrow rough road running some 6 or 8 miles through the mountain. It is a formidable military position and a handful of brave men might here for days make a successful resistance against a much superior force. The heights which rise almost perpendicular completely command the road, and it was not without a feeling of dread that we entered the dark pass and saw the mountains towering as it were directly over us and which it would be utter madness to attempt to scale. As we entered the pass the height on the left appeared to be fortified. A kind of

rough breastwork was thrown up but for some reason or other no resistance was here made. The road being steep and rough the progress was necessarily slow. Flankers and scouters were thrown out on both sides and every precaution was used. Towards noon and when the advance were nearly through the pass a body of the enemy were discovered. A few shots were fired at them from the mountain howitzer[1] and the advance dispersed them without difficulty. The opposition would likely have been much more vigorous on the part of the Mexicans had they not found themselves between two fires. Capt. Walker with his Company and a detachment of the 1st Penna. Regt. marched from Perote to cooperate with Cadwalader and if necessary assist him thru the pass. Coming upon a force of Guerillas he charged them in his usual manner and dispersed them, killing some 19 and wounding many others. This lively and unexpected attack disarranged the plans of the Guerillas and saved Cadwalader considerable trouble. In the skirmish one of Walker's Dragoons was killed and the Capt. had his own horse shot under him. After leaving the pass entered a little valley, fertile and well cultivated. As the Ranches were all deserted they were fired. Being composed strictly of pine, they burnt freely. Arrived at Las Vigas, a town of some size. It was completely deserted. The inhabitants have a bad reputation. They are said to be robbers who plunder indiscriminately both their own countrymen and foreigners. As they are now all joined the Guerillas for the purpose of plundering the train, their houses are fired. It looks as if we were departing from our general rule when property is thus destroyed and the smoke arising from all directions in this beautiful valley does not produce in my mind very pleasant feelings. But Capt. Walker has an inveterate hatred against the Mexicans and when he has the power he carries on the war according to his own peculiar feelings. I do not think it is very good policy to permit the gallant captain to thus exasperate the whole people, for every man of common sense knows that we should conciliate as well as fight and prevent by every possible means the arousing of the Mexican nation. Against the government and war party we must be successful, but if the whole people are once aroused either by an attack upon their religion or property, a resistance will be made similar to the Spanish campaigns of 1813 & '14.[2] The United States may pour army after army into this country. Nothing will be gained and the bones of thousands of the men of the north will whiten and bleach upon the plains of Mexico. Passing Las Vigas we halted about 4 P.M. at a small stream 12 miles from La Hoya near a still house. During the last two miles it rained and after we arrived in camp the rain came down thick

1. Light artillery designed for rough terrain. The parts were easily disassembled and each piece was light enough to be carried by a pack animal.
2. The stubborn resistance of the Spanish people to Napoleon's occupation from 1808 to 1814 gave guerrilla warfare its name.

and heavy. We had no shelter, not even a bush. However, building large fires we counteracted the effect of the rain as much as possible. The Regt. wagons our Quartermaster has very sensibly placed in the rear. The train is detained by the roughness and steepness of the mountains and it is 10 P.M. when our wagons arrive in camp. Hastily pitching our tents we crawl into *bed,* wet, cold, tired and supperless, damning the weather, the quartermaster and the road.

COULTER. On route by sunrise. Just after leaving the village saw a number of pieces of heavy artillery dismantled lying on the ground. Spiked and otherwise unfitted for use. It is said they were captured and destroyed by General Worth when he passed here. As we were just entering a long and dangerous pass, and the march was slow, flanking parties were thrown out in all directions. Several alarms were given and at length it was found necessary to fire several shots from the mountain howitzer to dislodge them from a ravine. Shortly after the flanking parties became engaged. At the same time, having heard of the anticipated attack and coming to our assistance from Perote, a detachment of the First Pennsylvania Regiment, under Colonel Wyncoop and Captain Walker's company of Mounted Rifles, attacked the enemy in the rear and routed them, pursuing them for a distance of several miles. Captain [Presley N.] Guthrie, of one of the new regiments [the 11th Inf.], the rear guard of the train, was severely wounded in the leg, which was our entire loss, except some eight or ten of Captain Walker's horses which were killed or crippled. Early in the morning Walker's men fired all the ranches within a reasonable distance of the road. Shortly after leaving the pass made a temporary halt in the village of Las Vigas, which was deserted and was accordingly fired by our regiment on leaving. About dark arrived at Molino Blanco, where we encamped twelve miles distant from La Hoya. All the ranches on this march were deserted. It was taken for granted that the inhabitants had been engaged in the late attack and all were burned to the ground. It commenced raining about an hour before reaching camp and continued until near midnight. There was an old building near which appeared to be a still house. There was a large quantity of dry pine wood in it which happened very opportune. By some accident our baggage waggon containing our tents, blankets, knapsacks and cooking utensils and provisions was detained until about ten o'clock, and we were compelled to sit during this time in the rain. When it did arrive, pitched our tents and slept in the mud supperless. The country through which we passed today was for the first five miles through the strong pass of La Olla. There were many signs of preparation in this pass and it was evidently intended to make a stand here had not General Worth followed too closely in their rear. There were several batteries built across different places in the road and numerous breastworks along the hillsides. It was a rough, rocky piece of country, covered with large timber, principally pine. After leaving this pass we entered an open cultivated country. From this place commences the table land of Mexico. Las Vigas was a pretty little village built principally like La Hoya, of wood, and six miles from that place. The houses were many of them quite commodious and of good size. There was a very neat little chapel in it, but it was considerably injured by some of our soldiers quartering in it.

June 21

BARCLAY. Early start and the men who lay down last night in the worst kind of a humor are now cheerful and refreshed. After marching about 3 miles came in sight of Perote Castle, which rises upon a large plain. Passed through a level, fertile country. Large fields of wheat, barley and corn, the corn knee high. About 12 M. arrived at Perote, a dull disagreeable looking place said to contain about 6000 of a population.[3] It is distant 36 miles from Jalapa. As we are now on the top of the mountains and at a great elevation above the sea, the weather is quite cool. Marching through the town we encamped on the plain near the Castle. Pitched tents and by the time we had got something to eat we were too tired and it was too late to visit the Castle. Tomorrow I will take a look at it.

COULTER. Made an early start and shortly after came in sight of the town and castle of Perote. The castle presents a beautiful appearance in the distance, situate in a most extensive plane. About 10 o'clock reached it and encamped near the walls. Our day's march was ten miles, but did not appear so long, the road not being hilly. The castle of Perote is a beautiful and masterly piece of work. The main work is a square with bastions at the four corners. It is surrounded by a ditch fifteen feet deep by about twenty feet wide, outside of this by a strong palisade and is entered by a draw bridge. This ditch it is said can be filled with water in ten hours by pipe leading to a neighboring stream. The inner court is clean and quite handsome. It now mounts between forty and fifty guns, none I believe larger than twelve pounders, all the heavy pieces having been taken to Cerro Gordo. There are two mortars in it of the most beautiful workmanship, old Spanish pieces and intended for twenty-two inch bombs. There is an extensive corn and bean patch on the plane near the castle. The town of Perote contains at present some six thousand inhabitants. It is a very old and dilapidated place and has a most rascally reputation. There are some religious buildings in it, but they are very ancient and the bells in

3. According to a Tennessee volunteer: "The city of Perote is just a little the filthiest, most smoky, dusty or murky place that I ever saw, or that I ever want to see again" (cited in George Winston Smith and Charles Judah, *Chronicles of the Gringos: The U.S. Army in the Mexican War, 1846–1848: Accounts of Eyewitnesses and Combatants* [Albuquerque: University of New Mexico Press, 1968], 225).

the belfrys perfectly green with time. Our company was detailed as camp guard this evening. Built a large fire and had quite a comfortable time of it.

June 22

BARCLAY. Visited the Castle of Perote. This building was erected during the days of Spanish power and was principally used as a prison for State criminals. When a great man became troublesome in Spain he was shipped off to Mexico and once within the walls of Perote his opposition and intrigues were harmless. It is however a strong military work. The works cover about 40 acres and are surrounded by a ditch 90 feet wide which can be filled with water to the depth of near 20 feet. At the time the castle was taken it mounted 72 guns besides several very large mortars. Perote being erected at a later date did not show as many signs of decay as Ulua. The works are all in fine order. Viewed as a military position the Castle of Perote does not possess one tenth of the importance of Ulua. The latter is the key to Mexico City. An invading army would suffer no inconvenience from Perote except that of leaving a garrison in the rear. Rising in the midst of a dry large plain the Castle does not command any road or pass. Thanks to the panic occasioned by the Battle of Cerro Gordo and the activity of Gen. Worth this Castle surrendered without firing a gun. Had resistance been made the Castle would have been taken, but it would have required time and labor. As there is no elevation commanding the Castle, the approaches would have been made by ditches running parallel to and zigzag with the Castle. In one part of the ditch stands a cross upon which criminals were shot. The Castle possesses a melancholy interest to our army. It was here that the [Mier] prisoners[4] after having been marched in triumph over the greater part of Mexico were confined. Here is showed the hole from which Capt. Walker and a part of his companions escaped. And when we consider the sufferings to which these men were exposed, abused in the grossest manner, a number of their party murdered while prisoners in cold blood, the feeling of retaliation which influences the survivors is in a great degree palliated and cannot be violently condemned. An American prisoner while here confined was obliged to repair or rig a flag staff.

---

4. In October of 1842 about 750 Texans launched an expedition into Mexico. Appalled at the lack of discipline in his command, the leader decided to abandon the invasion, but three hundred or so Texans, including Samuel H. Walker, decided to push ahead on their own. Surrounded at the isolated village of Mier, they surrendered and were marched into the interior. Escaping, they headed for Texas but became lost in the desert, reduced to eating snakes and grasshoppers and drinking their own urine. Recaptured, they were forced to take part in a macabre lottery, drawing beans from a jar, with the losers (one out of ten) who drew black beans to be shot. Walker and the other survivors were imprisoned in the Castle at Perote where they were brutally mistreated.

While at the job it is said he deposited a coin under the staff and hoped he might see the day when he could remove it and see the American flag waving over the fortress. He has had his wishes gratified. The Castle is now used as a general hospital. The sick men of Jalapa are all here and numbers are daily dying. Orders are to leave all the sick here of Cadwaladers force. The Doctor has designated several of our company to remain. The 1st Penna Regt. remain to garrison Perote.

June 24

BARCLAY. Regt. drills twice a day. This is the most unpleasant place we have yet been in Mexico. There is no market. A cold bleak wind sweeps over the plain raising clouds of dust which recall the sand hills of Vera Cruz to our minds. The same men who in February lay almost naked outside of their tents on account of heat are now in June shivering in their blankets. Such is the difference which an elevation of a few thousand feet makes in the climate.

June 25

BARCLAY. A part of Gen. Pillow's command arrived here today. They are troops raised under the Ten Regiment Bill.[5] As they have no tents, they must suffer much from the cold.

June 26

BARCLAY. Besides those in hospital there are many sick in camp and the sickness is increasing. It is no wonder. The merriest and most healthy man here gets the Blues. I sincerely hope that we will soon get off. The dead march was the music which welcomed us to the Castle and is heard all hours of the day. It is a sad sight to see 4 or 5 coffins carried in a row. It is a sight seen here.

June 27

BARCLAY. Preparing to march again—three days provisions issued. Our sick men, frightened at the number of deaths here, refuse to remain with the exception of McCollum and Dougherty. Their descriptive rolls are duly made out and they remain behind. A great many lives might no doubt be saved if communications with Vera Cruz were open and a train could go down with discharged soldiers. But this cannot now be done.

5. A bill authorizing the addition of ten new regiments to the regular army was introduced in the House of Representatives on 29 December 1846, was passed on 11 January 1847, but was held up in the Senate until 10 February. Enlistments under the act were not begun until mid-April and the new troops did not reach Mexico until June.

Several discharged men from the 1st Regt. came to Jalapa before we left. They were obliged to return with us to Perote. Among them was Andrew Mosgrove of Kittanning.

COULTER. This is the only date that I find in my original notes for camp of Perote, nothing worth note having occurred. One incident of importance to our mess: Made a purchase of some corn meal and had a breakfast of mush, Captain Montgomery having kindly given us a bottle of molasses, supped on a fine mess of corn cakes and molasses. The weather is unusually cold here in consequence of our now being on the table land and our elevation much greater than formerly. While walking one day in the castle ditch saw a large cross with a quantity of human skulls and bones lying around. Learned that it is what is called the "criminal's cross," a person condemned to death being first tied to it and allowed to starve, or is shot, as his sentence may be. The body is then allowed to rot upon the cross and the bones to lie about without the rites of burial as a terror to others. Saw the room in which the Mier prisoners were confined. It is a dark dungeonlike place, lighted by a very small window. This castle appears to be something of the nature of a national prison, all criminals having been sent here, and as a great military depot. It cannot certainly be intended as a defense against invasion, being easily gotten around. There is an interesting incident told of Captain Walker, one of the Mier prisoners, when he was confined in this castle. The prisoners made and planted the present flagstaff of the castle. Whilst making this staff, Walker predicted that the stars and stripes would float from it before five years were past. He placed an American dime or ten cent piece under the foot of the staff and desired that he might live to take it out. His prediction was verified and he did live to get his dime again. The hospital in the castle is now crowded and the deaths are unusual, averaging from eight to ten per day, often being as high as fifteen in a single day. Boards are unusually scarce here and the men are buried in their blankets around the castle outside of the ditch. The town of Perote is a most dismal place. It was with the utmost difficulty that any bread could be bought in it. Market very poor. No business doing. Gambling appears to be the only occupation of the inhabitants and I suppose its accompanying crime, robbery. There has been rumors in camp ever since being here of a Mexican force of some six thousand with twelve pieces of artillery having fortified themselves between this and Puebla for the purpose of cutting off the train. In consequence we have had daily battalion drills and our colonel appears very anxious to make us perfect in the formation of hollow squares so as to resist any attack on the open plains, as though a lot of Mexicans could muster sufficient courage to attack a force because small on open ground. Therefore we have had the pleasure of tramping around the castle to the tune of "form division," "form square," "march," "reduce square," etc., etc. We have received marching orders for tomorrow morning and are preparing three days' provisions for that. Our company leaves two sick in the hospital of Perote, McCollum and Dougherty.

June 28

BARCLAY. It was with a feeling of joy that we took up our line of march this morning a little after daylight. Our old commander, Col. Childs is at our head. The march today was across a level barren plain with scarce a sign of vegetation. Indeed it has the appearance of being at times overflowed with water. Day hot—ground hard and of a whitish color which is severe on the eyes. Water very scarce. Arrived in the afternoon at the village of Tepeyahualco a distance of 22 miles from Perote. As the road was a perfect level, marching was very tiresome. We had frequently the occasion to observe the judgment of Col. Childs. He is an old soldier and understands how to march men. He halts frequently and for a short time. The train has thus time to close up and the command is kept compact. In the first days march from Vera Cruz Pillow's Brigade were scattered over a line of ten miles. Col. Childs is one of the best officers in the army. And notwithstanding he was always strict and at times tyrannical at Jalapa, yet he is a favorite among the volunteers. He is a man above the middle size of stout lusty appearance, black eyes and a black mustache. He is a splendid horseman. He distinguished himself at Monterey and Gen. Scott noticed him in a very flattering manner for his courage at Cerro Gordo.[6] One of the Colonel's failings is that he is a little too fond of his liquor. This however rather raises him in the opinion of the men.

COULTER. Our brigade, composed of the First Artillery and the Second Pennsylvania Regiments, under Colonel Childs, marched about daylight. Encamped at the village of Tepeyahualco, distant about twenty-one miles from Perote. This was a long and tedious march on a perfect plane. From camp to Perote an abrupt mountain rising from the midst of the plain, called Pizarra was visible, apparently only a few miles distant, yet, although we have marched twenty-one miles since that, the mountain is still almost two miles in our advance. Water was very scarce on this march. All we had was the little we carried in our canteens and that was very warm. There was water at the hacienda of Santa Gertrudis, twelve miles distant from Perote. It was drawn from a deep well by means of a large wheel, but was so bad that the officers would not allow the men to drink it. The appearances on this plain are very deceiving and one imagines that he can see a lake of water continually before him a mile or two

6. Although Scott did commend "the often distinguished Brevet Colonel Childs" in his official report on Cerro Gordo, he did not single him out for special praise in significantly greater measure than that doled out to the other officers engaged in the battle.

distant. One of our men (Shields) getting very sick on the road, I gave him the water in my canteen, intending to cross to the lake to fill it again. I saw what I was perfectly convinced was a fine body of water a short distance from the road and a man on horseback approaching, standing in it and the horse drinking. After walking about a mile in the direction of the water, I perceived the illusion, the water receding as I advanced and the horseman who had not moved was now plainly visible standing on dry ground. Our company with one or two others are now encamped on the plain in front of the village, the rest being quartered in some buildings. The water here is like that of Santa Gertrudis—very bad and drawn from deep wells. It is the worst I have seen on the route, having a taste something similar to the water of Lobos Island. While here I did not drink a quart of it, having tried for the first time the celebrated Mexican drink called "Pulque," extracted from a plant which is now becoming abundant known as the Great American Aloe or Century Plant. The village of Tepeyahualco is small, dirty, old and dilapidated, with apparently as little business doing as at Perote.

June 29

BARCLAY. Remained today in camp. The water here is bad. It tastes something like the Lobos water. The bread which we purchase at a Mexican store is very good, being much the best we have yet met with in Mexico. Co. E is on guard today.

COULTER. Remained in camp today. Bought some warm bread here which was the best I had eaten since being in Mexico. Our company was detailed for guard this evening. Stationed as a picket on the left of the village. Had some sport with one of our company (Rager). He was wakened during the night to go on post, but being afraid to stand out alone, declared that it was not his turn and he would "die first" before going on post. He went at length and as a punishment was allowed to remain on duty four hours. This brought some ludicrous expressions out of him much to the amusement of the rest.

June 30

BARCLAY. Still in camp. The Regt. was inspected and mustered in, except Co E and Co C which were on guard. A ration of fresh mutton issued today for the first time. Orders issued to Company E to start at daylight on a forage expedition.

COULTER. This is the last day of June and we have now been just six months in the service. In consequence, the regiment was inspected and mustered into the service, except ours and Company C, who were on guard. For the first time drew a ration of fresh mutton today. Our company received orders this evening to be ready to go out on a foraging expedition tomorrow.

July 1

BARCLAY. The Company left early. Rode in wagons to Soto, a village 7 miles distant, where the wagons were loaded with corn and barley. Returned in the evening and got ducked in a shower of rain. I did not accompany the party being busily writing at the muster rolls. After supper, Lt. Col. Geary inspected and mustered us into the service. Melville is very unwell with the Rheumatism.

COULTER. Four companies of our regiment and a company of dragoons were off by daylight with the forage waggoners. They being empty, we rode out to a hacienda called Soto, distant seven miles from camp. While here several of us went in quest of water; found a deep well and with much difficulty, by means of a large wheel and revolving buckets, drew water and filled our canteens. It was very bad and deeply impregnated with lime. The rope, buckets and wheel, by being long in the water, had a complete coating of lime. Soon filled our waggons with corn and barley. The proprietor sold to us willingly but at extravagant prices. On our march back were overtaken by a heavy rain and considerable hail. After supper, ours and Company C, having been on guard when the regiment was mustered, were mustered and inspected by Lt. Colonel Geary.

July 2

BARCLAY. Regt. drill. An inspection of cartridge boxes and marching orders read. Magruder's Battery of Flying Artillery[7] exercised today. Their movements were very rapid.

COULTER. Today four companies came in from Perote with some waggons. Here again I noticed the deceiving appearance of the plane. When at a distance these waggons appeared to be moving through deep water. Had a battalion drill at ten o'clock under Colonel Geary, who made considerable of a fool of himself, insulting several officers and charging up very fiercely to the base drummer and snatching a drum stick from him which he threw away. The regiment was again ordered out in the afternoon and

7. John Bankhead Magruder (1810–1871), a West Point (1830) trained artillerist. Hot-tempered in battle, he displayed, in social pursuits, such courtly manners that he won the nickname "Prince John." Appointed a brevet lieutenant colonel for gallantry at Chapultepec, he resigned his commission in 1861 to join the Confederate cause. After spectacular early successes that led to a major-general's stars, his fortunes faded after an inept performance during The Seven Days. He was then shunted off to minor commands. After the Civil War, he returned to Mexico as a major general under the ill-starred Emperor Maximillian.

after (as Major Brindle says) "a very particular inspection of cartridge boses" (the Colonel could not trust to the inspection of company officers but examined all himself) marching orders and a number of extra remarks and items were read to the regiment.

July 3

BARCLAY. Off by 4 A.M. We are in the advance. Encamped at a small hacienda 12 miles today. Nathaniel Thomas who was unwell, while attempting to get into a wagon, slipped and fell. The wagon passed over his breast and injured him very much. Shields is also very sick. Provisions are scarce and only two days rations are issued. The crackers are very bad being full of weavils. A board of officers condemned the first barrels, but as no other provision can be had we must take what we can get. Neither coffee or salt are issued.

COULTER. Off by daylight in the advance. The First Artillery, one battalion of our regiment with two field pieces and mountain howitzer and squad of dragoons found the advance encamped about noon at a small hacienda called Virreyes, distant about twelve miles from our last camp. Our march today was through a level plane well cultivated and our camp is in an old corn field. The water here is good. One of our company, N. Thomas, was severely injured today—attempting to get into a wagon, fell under and was run over, hurting his breast and side dangerously. Drew provisions here and were put on rather short rations. The bread which we did get was mouldy and full of weevils and was condemned by a board of officers. Got very little meat—not sufficient to make one supper. Got no coffee and very little salt, two articles indispensable to a march. One of company G of our regiment died and was buried here. Our fuel at this camp was principally dry corn stalks. The water here was drawn from a deep well.

July 4

BARCLAY. Day sacred to the hearts of every American citizen, whether enjoying the comforts of home or roving amid the snows of the polar or the sands of the torrid zone. Now gladly would we celebrate the anniversary of our Country's independence in a proper and becoming manner. How patriotically would we imbibe a pint of old Monongahela in drinking toasts to the men of '76 and with what a glorious spirit would we enter into the merits of the dinner and heartily cheer the orator of the day. But alas! humiliating as it is, the confession must be made that we free and independent citizens had neither dinner to eat, toast to drink, orator to cheer or liquor to enliven the day. Upon musty crackers and cold water we made our breakfast and upon cold water and musty crackers we made our dinner. Left camp at 6 A.M. Marched across a level plain 10 miles and encamped at the "Ojo De Agua" (Eye of Water). The spring is very large, the water clear and beautiful. Much to our disappointment it was quite warm. The weather cool in the morning and noon. Rain at night. Being left in canteens, the water becomes cool.

COULTER. Fourth of July. Breakfasted on mouldy crackers and water and off early again in the advance. Encamped at a hacienda called "Ojo de Agua," distant about ten miles from Virreyes. Our march today was through a fine fertile plane with extensive corn fields on each side of the road. Encamped near a small stream on a fine piece of ground with very high grass which made us a soft bed. There is a large spring here, known among many as the boiling spring, which gushes up from the ground. The water has a good taste, but it is rather warm. Wood was very scarce here, being nothing but brush. For twenty-five cents managed to buy almost half a pound of very poor coffee from a neighboring fonda. Rained heavy greater part of the night.

July 5

BARCLAY. As there was no orders last night and no sign of a march this morning, we thought we would lay here all day. But about 9 A.M. the music struck up "Strike your tents and march away" and in a few minutes everything was in the wagons. It is astonishing how quickly soldiers can have all ready to move, particularly after they have been sometime in the service. A camp may be perfectly quiet, men eating or sleeping. Suddenly the drum beats. Knapsacks are packed in an instant and while one part of a mess are striking the tent the others are tying or packing the cooking utensils in the wagon. And where but a few moments before there was a town of tents, the inhabitants comfortable and quiet, there is now a dozen of wagons packed and soldiers formed ready to march. Passed today through a rich fertile country, well cultivated. Corn is the principal article raised. We pass fields which must contain at least 1000 acres. Indeed so extensive are they that no estimate can be correctly made of their size. The corn is well worked and looks well. The rows are as straight as an arrow. It would do some of our old Westmoreland farmers good to see some of these big fields. Marched today 3 miles. Encamped near the road. Wood and water plenty—water good. Since leaving Perote we have moved very slow waiting for Gen. Pillow. The Mexicans disappointed heretofore it is supposed will make another attempt on this train which they know to be very valuable. Day after tomorrow we pass through the celebrated Pinal, where large bodies of the Mexicans have assembled. Strengthened by Pillow's force there is nothing to fear. Company E on guard tonight.

COULTER. Expecting to remain in camp today, we were enjoying a fashionable breakfast of beef broth and crackers about nine o'clock when the drum beat to strike our tents and march. Encamped at a place three miles distance from "Ojo de Agua" where we had better water and more wood.

Marched today through a fine country waving with corn. The water here is good and is drawn from a deep well. We are encamped on a hard sandy road. Had no sooner stacked arms when, our regiment, fearing another scarcity of wood, charged upon some old long buildings, and in spite of Colonel Childs, secured quite a lot of fine dry pine logs. Our company was detailed for guard this evening. General Pillow, with a part of his advance, who had been a day's march behind, came up with the remainder of his force at "Ojo de Agua."

July 6
BARCLAY. 3 A.M. camp roused by the long roll. The pickets have fired. The troops are formed. After remaining under arms some time discover that the alarm is false. The pickets have mistaken some corn hoers for Guerillas. The messes set to cooking breakfast and at 5 A.M. left camp. Passed through a very fine country and after a march of 12 miles arrived near the entrance of the Pinal where we encamped. The Dragoons who have been out scouting have dispersed two or three parties of Guerillas and succeeded in taking a few prisoners. Pillow encamped with us tonight.

COULTER. Coming off post at two o'clock this morning and expecting to make an early start, commenced cooking. Was just getting my coffee to a boil when bang, bang, bang went some dozen carbines fired by the picket. The regiment was soon under arms, and some of the boys being roused up, crowded around my fire and upset my pot, spilling my coffee. The alarm soon subsided. Some say that the picket fired upon a party of corn hoers, but if it was so, they were early risers. About daylight marched again in the advance and encamped at the entrance of Pinal Pass on a small stream distant twelve miles from last camp. We passed through a fertile and cultivated country. Camped in a meadow. Water tolerably good and wood plentiful. Just before marching this morning there occurred an amusing scene. It has been customary to allow any sick men on march to have their muskets and cartridge boxes hauled in the baggage waggon. One of the company (Rager), being a little terrified by the firing of the picket, and wishing to avoid a brush if there was any, attempted to put his musket into the waggon. Lt. Coulter, who had been watching him, took him by the cuff of the neck and marched him forward into the ranks. "Now, now, now, Coulter," said Rager, "Let go my neck." "Well, go on and join the company then," said the lieutenant. "There is nothing the matter with you but your infernal cowardice." "Now, now, Coulter!" said Jim, "just take me into the field and I will fight as well as any of them." "That may be," said the lieutenant, "but the devil is, to get you there." Rager joined the company and during the whole march kept a little in advance, much to the amusement of the rest, who were continually inquiring if he wished to have the first shot at the Mexicans. Since coming to camp the dragoons have been out and captured several Mexicans and some mustangs. They report heavy bodies of the enemy in the neighborhood. It is said that the pass is fortified some distance ahead and this evening the impression is that we will have a brush tomorrow.

July 7

BARCLAY. Left camp at sunrise, Gen. Pillow being in command. After a march of near 3 miles entered the Pass. The road is narrow and on the left very steep and high hills rise abruptly. The hills are thickly covered with pines. For about 4 miles the road is commanded or rather overtopped by these heights. The Mexicans had made preparations to give us some difficulty. With great labor they had collected large stones or rocks. The handspikes were under them and in a moment the train for a great distance could have been overwhelmed with rocks. However, when Pillow joined us the combined forces amounted to about 6000 men. A strong advance was thrown out who scaled the height and on whose approach the enemy dispersed. The activity of the Dragoons yesterday was also of service. During the passage strong flanking parties were thrown out at short intervals. Our company remained for over an hour as a flank guard and it required rapid marching to overtake the Regiment. Passed at noon a small village (Acajete) where we were all struck with the tasteful architecture of a small church. Arrived about 3 P.M. at Amozoc a pretty little town. Days march 18 miles. The last few miles was very fatiguing, the road being heavy with sand. In places the road today was very narrow being dug thru the hills. The banks on each side rise perpendicular to the height of from 10 to 20 feet. The road is cut with gullies which in the rainy season must contain great bulk of water. They are now dry. These places are famous for being the haunts of robbers and I can conceive of no place which would be more convenient to rob a stage coach. The business of highway robbery it is said was carried on to a great extent in the *palmy peaceful* days of Mexico. Two or three highwaymen were always enough to rob a coach full of passengers and there are frequent instances of 8 or 9 military gentlemen yielding without a struggle to two or three determined freebooters.

COULTER. Under arms by four o'clock. Our battalion was placed some fifty waggons from the advance. The advance was made very heavy, our force being now some five thousand men, having been joined by Pillow's force. Marched some eighteen miles and encamped in the village of Amozoc. Much to the surprise of all, not a shot was fired on this day's march. When we entered the pass the First Pennsylvania Regiment were ordered to climb the hill on the left hand side and dislodge any force that might be there. At this point every preparation for attack was visible, although the enemy were gone, having evidently been there early this morning. For half a mile along the summit of the ridge great masses of rock were piled with freshly cut hand spikes under them ready to be tumbled down on the train when it came in proper position. Our company was placed in several nooks on the right hand side to hold them until the train passed, which gave us quite a rapid march to regain the regiment. The country through which we passed today was varied. La Pinal Pass, the left hand side was a bluff hill rising to a great height, in many places almost perpendicular. Covered with large jutting rocks and a heavy growth of pine trees. On the right hand side there are in some places banks some ten feet high but generally descend gently into the plain. Passed through a village called "Acajete" and are now encamped in the Plaza of "Amozoc." This appears to be more of a thriving business place than any we have seen on this entire march. Purchased the cheapest bread here that I have yet seen in Mexico. We were met here by Colonel Harney with several regiments, he having been sent from Puebla to assist us through the Pinal Pass.

July 8

BARCLAY. Left Amozoc early, our Regt. in the advance. Day most beautiful. Soon came in sight of the tall spires of Puebla and of two snow mountains (of which we had a peep at Perote) Popocatepetl and Ixtaccihuatl. After a short halt at the Bridge entered the City at 1 P.M. Struck with the fine hearty appearance of our men and their animals who have been here some time. We look hard, tired and dirty. The march has been long and many days toilsome. Puebla, the City of the Angels, is a splendid city.[8] The streets are wide, well paved and clean. The houses are large and we have become reconciled to the style of architecture. We now see thousands of Mexicans to where we only saw hundreds before. The City contains a population of 80,000 inhabitants. Whether to show us the City or show us to the citizens we were marched for over an hour through different streets. At the far part of the city from which we entered there is a beautiful garden laid out in walks, the beds tastefully arranged. After filing us round and showing us the beauties of nature touched up by art, we were again marched for a half a mile and placed in an old church. This is the quarters of the Regt. Several of the companies are on the porch below. The rest are on the porch above. Our company have about the best quarters. The courtyard like in many of the Mexican buildings is square and a fountain in the midst. As we were all tired I did not run around today. Towards evening I mounted the Captain's horse and went in search of Shields who was in the sick wagon. Found him at the quarters of the 1st Penna. Regt. He is very low and after a good deal of trouble I succeeded in getting him into a wagon and conveyed to quarters. It rained very heavily.

8. Puebla de los Angelos, the second largest city of Mexico, with eighty thousand inhabitants.

COULTER. On route by daylight. After marching some three miles, came in sight of the city of Angels. The domes and spires of Puebla present a most beautiful appearance in the distance. Also came in sight of two snow mountains. The volcano "Popocatepetl," and another, the name of which I will not attempt to pronounce, but it is written thus: "Jetaccihutal" so Grenow [?] spells it. Madame Calderon[9] writes it thus "Jxtaccihuatl." The Mexican mode of spelling it is "Ixtaccihuatl." On this day's march is the first I remember of having seen the Aloe in bloom. It is said that it blooms but once a century, but won't vouch for that. There is a stem something like a sunflower stalk which shoots up from the heart of the plant often to the height of twenty feet or even more, about four feet of which is beautifully ornamental with large branches of orange colored plumes. Arrived at the suburbs of Puebla about one o'clock, distant ten miles from Amozoc. The city of Puebla, when one is in it, has more of a modern appearance, than any town or city I have yet seen in Mexico. The houses mostly appear new and the streets well paved and clean. Were marched through the city and halted in a beautiful public garden in which we expected to encamp, but were disappointed, being soon marched out. After some more tramping, our regiment was quartered in an old monastery, now used as a Mexican hospital, belonging, I believe, to an order called the "Monks of St. John." In the courtyard is a fine fountain of water and four magnificent cedar trees. We are quartered in the porticoes around the yard, one half in the lower and the other half, our company included, in the upper portico. The walls around the building are hung with large and ancient paintings. The Mexican hospital which occupies a part of this building is the best I have seen. Kept in perfect order, everything clean and it has not the disagreeable smell incident to all hospitals.

July 9

BARCLAY. The great curiosity of Puebla is the Cathedral. In all countries the Catholics spend large sums of money in building fine churches and ornamenting them. Even the poorest congregations affect a splendour in their places of worship. In Mexico, one of the richest countries in the world and one which has been governed for 300 years by the most bigoted of the Catholic race, the Spanish priesthood, this splendour is carried to a great excess. I can form no idea of the amount of money which must have been expended in erecting and ornamenting this building. The spires rise to the height of 216 feet. They are full of bells, some of which are of an enormous size. One is seven feet in diameter at the mouth and the metal is thick in proportion. The gilding, carving and ornamental work inside is truly magnificent. This Cathedral forms one side of the Plaza which is

9. Madame Calderón de la Barca, author of *Life in Mexico During a Residence of Two Years in that Country*, 2 vols. (Boston, 1843).

large and has always a good market. The principal stores of the City are in
the plaza and adjoining streets. The amount of business carried on is very
trifling in comparison to the population. A large proportion of the inhabitants are poor and lazy. They only work enough to keep themselves from
starving. Shields is very unwell, so far gone was he this evening that the
Doctor gave him up and for a time we thought the breath had left him. By
the exertions of Steward Holmes and the Steward of the Mexican hospital
he was brought to. I have detailed two men to attend him tonight. No
hopes are entertained of his recovery.

COULTER. After a long nap, not being waked up to strike tents at four
o'clock, took a walk through the city. The market in the main plaza presents a great and rich variety. Saw some large peaches and some noble
pears, apples, etc., were kept in abundance. Entered the Grand Cathedral,
which is a large and stately building. Inside, it is a most splendid affair,
composed of a number of arches and domes supported by massive stone
pillars of great heighth, many of them covered with crimson velvet. The
main altar is supported by twenty pillars some fifteen feet high and about
the thickness of a man's body, completely plated with gold. There are
many candlesticks of gold and silver. There are two large organs in the
center of the building. The walls and ceiling are covered with rich and
costly paintings and gilding. Left after hearing some of their mummery
and dropped into a Mexican eating house and called for dishes. After going nearly through their whole bill of fare and having received a negative
answer to every call, managed to get a dish of veal cutlet, such they called
it, but it had more the appearance and consistency of tough bull's beef and
very strong with onions. However, it tasted more like civilization than anything we had eaten for some time, so imagining it cutlet, we accordingly
devoured it. This evening one of our company (Shields) was taken very
sick, and in fact, given up [by the] regimental surgeon. The old doctor of
the Mexican hospital took him in charge, and after having gone through
some religious ceremony, and placing a string of beads and cross around
his neck, rubbed him with several balsams and ointments, and to tell the
truth, eventually saved his life. Kuhn and I were detailed to attend him,
and during the night he was perfectly insensible and in severe convulsions
and several times we were compelled to throw our whole weight upon
him to prevent his getting his blankets off and becoming chilled.

July 10
BARCLAY. The Colonel has issued orders that no man shall leave quarters without a pass and without having his side arms on, and that each
company shall appoint two cooks who shall cook the rations of all together, and that no man shall eat between meals which are ordered at certain hours. The men are all in a bad humor about this latter order, the

appointment of company cooks. If they perform their drilling and guard duties I do not think that Col. Roberts ought to interfere with the mess arrangements. We are all now provided with the proper cooking utensils and get along well as we are and why the necessity of a change. The most of the men swear that they won't stand it. I have appointed Moorhead and Keslar cooks.

COULTER. This evening orders were read not to allow any of the men to pass out of the quarters without sidearms and a pass signed by the officer of the guard. Also another ordering all messes to be dissolved and requiring each company to cook in common. This latter order has raised some excitement among the men. Our gallant colonel has very suddenly discovered that all the sickness results from small messes. Don't know, but it appears to me that we have the most contemptible staff in the army. Our Colonel, it is true is cool under fire, but otherwise he is an ignorant jackass and allows himself to be imposed on and is completely under the thumb of Colonel Childs. The other two are a pair of vain, ignorant tyrants and cowardly as sheep.

July 11

BARCLAY. The cooks got breakfast and so did the different messes. The company officers order me to dismiss the cooks and prepare our meals as usual.

COULTER. This morning the new mode of cooking was tried, but the old messes cooked their own breakfasts also and none were left to eat the common meal but a few too lazy to cook their own rations. Attended mass in the Grand Cathedral. Went up a set of winding stairs to the dome on the top of the spire. Had a most magnificent view of the city and surrounding plain and mountains. Looking down on it, the city presents an odd appearance. The flat tile roofs, in many places covered with green moss, appear most desolate, like the deserted ruins of a great city. In the belfry there are some twenty bells, many of them very large, two of them in particular being almost 8 feet high, seven and a half feet across the mouth and about a foot in thickness. There are two very lofty spires to this church, but one only (the one which I ascended) has any bells, and although it contains twenty, it is not more than half full. The company mess fell through before night and we had supper after the good old system.

July 14

BARCLAY. Nothing new these last few days. Guard duty is light. We run where we please about the city. I have been up on the spires of the Cathedral, the view is grand. The country around is level and the scenery picturesque. The streets of the city running at right angles and teeming with the dense population. The dwelling houses are flat roofed. Some 60 churches and religious houses rise in different parts and their domes and spires add much to the beauty of the City. Besides the fine garden I have already mentioned, there is a park or grove called the Paseo. It is a favorite place of resort and is filled with flowers, fountains, etc. Orders to drill four hours each day. There is daily two roll calls at revellie and tattoo. At Jalapa we had three. The Regiment was reviewed today by Brig. Gen. Shields. The turnout was large and the men look well.

COULTER. Nothing new within these last few days. The Colonel's orders for company cooking, four hours daily drill and leaving quarters were reinstated and the old granny swore "By God" they should be obeyed. Nevertheless, we still wag along in the good old way, regardless of the threats of our gallant staff. Our regiment is transferred to General Quitman's division, much to the satisfaction of the men who are tired of Colonel Childs' dynasty. Colonel Childs, I may say, is one of the best officers in the army on march. He always has his men well provided when it can be done, and he can make longer marches with less fatigue to the men than any other. But we were unlucky to have been in a garrison under him and then he was rather strict for a set of volunteers. General Quitman's division is now composed of the South Carolinians, New York and First Pennsylvania Regiments in one brigade under General Shields, and the Second Pennsylvania Regiment forming a detached fragment of another brigade. Today our divisions were reviewed by Generals Quitman and Shields. Had a good turnout.

July 16

BARCLAY. Reviewed today by Genls. Quitman and Scott. I was unwell and did not turn out. The Division it is said looked well. The New York and South Carolina Regts. compose a Brigade under Shields. The 2nd Penna. Regt. is the fraction of a brigade. Quitman commands the Division.

COULTER. Today the army was reviewed by General Scott. It was a grand affair to look at, but not to we poor devils who were kept out so long in a hot sun. The colonel, like a calf, gave up without a struggle, and has allowed the men to cook as they thought proper (his drill and leaving quarters orders have also been gotten around) saying like a sulky school boy "I don't care a God damn how you cook." He shows nothing but irresolution, after issuing orders, to let them be set at defiance with so little effort to maintain his authority. Under such a colonel there is no danger that we will ever stand high as a regiment.

July 25

COULTER. For the last eight days have endured the monotony of garrison. We were once ordered to hold ourselves in readiness to march, but those orders were countermanded and there is now no knowing when we will move. As is generally the case in an idle garrison, having heard many rumors of peace and war; about marching, some say to Mexico City and others to Vera Cruz; that Mexican ministers have arrived. You can have their arrival any day of the week, and I have heard a number say that they actually saw them arrive in this city with a body guard. (The idea of ministers of peace bringing guards.) There are reports of negotiations going on in this city and we have had peace declared and even ratified by our Congress at least a dozen times. Yet all such rumors are closely followed by others of immense fortifications at Rio Frio and the City of Mexico and the great army under Anna's famous generals marching against Puebla. These reports gain little credit among the older regiments, but it is amusing to see how they are picked up and greedily swallowed by those lately from Vera Cruz.

July 26

BARCLAY. For the last fortnight nothing has occured worthy of note. Our sick are now in the Mexican hospital. The building we occupy is an old church, a monastery belonging to the order of Saint John. Like all the religious houses the walls are covered with paintings. None of them however possess any great merit. The officers are quartered near a mile from us. After revellie I generally take a tramp to the Colonel's Quarters and make my morning report. After breakfast there is generally a Regt. drill. The Regt. are marched some two miles out of the City and drilled a couple of hours by Geary generally. This is dull and tiresome. After drill we amuse ourselves by funning about. Melville and myself usually adjourn to a Pulque shop and pass an hour or so in drinking pulque and talking to the old shop keeper. After dinner go to the officers quarters or Montgomery's or to the plaza. We have nothing to read and not enough to do. The City is full of eating houses, both American and Mexican. Their rates are too high for our funds. In the company there is but little change. The Captain and several of the men are unwell. Shields is getting better slowly. McGinley is writing for the adjutant. The men are amazed one day by the most flattering rumors from Mexico. Flags of truce have arrived and there is a speedy prospect of peace. The next day their pleasant hopes are dissipated by accounts of the fortifications which the Mexicans are erecting to defend their Capitol. The volunteers lend a greedy ear to all rumors of peace. Their anxiety to get home is very great. On a march in active service they are contented, but they become very impatient in garrison. Today a Division Drill by Major Gen. Quitman. The Regt. were under arms for six hours.

COULTER. Today had a division drill under General Quitman. Were six hours on the field under a boiling sun. In the evening it was proposed to go to Cholula in order to see how many would volunteer for that excursion.

July 27

BARCLAY. Being unwell today I was not able to accompany part of our company who visited the ruins of the City of Cholula.[10] The distance from Puebla is eight miles. The party that went out were about 200 and the tramp must have been very pleasant. This city possesses a melancholy interest to those who sympathise with the sufferings of the ancient people of the country. In the days of the montezumas it contained 300,000 inhabitants and was one of the first cities of Mexico. When the Spaniards invaded the country a meeting took place in the grand plaza of Cholula between Cortez and the Mexican chiefs for the avowed purpose of entering into a treaty and league of amity. Cortez learning from his Mexican mistress that her countrymen meditated treachery here upbraided them with it and gave orders for his troops to fall upon them. This was done. A most terrible massacre followed and some 100,000 of the natives paid the penalty of their treachery. Such is the Spanish version of the affair. The ancient city is in ruins. In the days of its prosperity it covered a space of ground equal in extent to Philadelphia. The population is now about 6,000. In the center of the City rises the celebrated pyramid of Cholula whose base covers fifty acres. Height fifteen hundred feet. The pyramid is built of stone and unburned brick. The sides are covered with vegetation, bushes and even trees of considerable size. The ancient people erected this immense pyramid in honor of their Deity. Upon the summit was a temple to the sun. There is now a neat Catholic church in the top from which there is an extensive and beautiful view of the surrounding country. The church is called Santa Maria. There is also a nunnery (the San Francisco) which contains 300 nuns. The party returned in the evening tired with their long tramp but amply repaid for their toil.

COULTER. This morning two hundred of the regiment turned out under Captain Loeser for the expedition to the pyramid of Cholula. It is an ancient city of the old Montezuma race now principally in ruins. It once contained three hundred thousand inhabitants but now contains about six thousand. The ruins are for the greater part visible and the city appears to have covered a space much greater than Puebla. The plaza is still visible in which Cortes killed a hundred thousand Indians and marched by a column, erected, the inhabitants say, by Santa Anna. In the center of the city is the pyramid of Cholula, its base covering about forty or fifty

---

10. A pre-Columbian structure substantially larger but, at 210 feet (not the 1500 feet claimed by the diarists), not so high as the great pyramids of Egypt, the pyramid at Cholula was, as Barclay relates, the scene of a vast Indian massacre perpetrated by Cortes. By the nineteenth century it was so overgrown with vegetation that it appeared to be a natural hill rather than a man-made structure. It was, nevertheless, a popular attraction for American soldiers, including Winfield Scott, whose visit may have been inspired by Napoleon's famous tour of the Egyptian pyramids.

acres and fifteen hundred feet high. It is now covered with undergrowth. The summit is paved and a paved way up to it on which was once built a temple to the sun, but is now replaced by an ancient Spanish chapel called "Santa Maria." Near the pyramid is the remains of an old Indian mound. There is in this city a convent called "San Francisco" containing at present about three hundred nuns. There are also several large churches here. The city of Cholula is distant seven miles from Puebla, making one day's journey fourteen miles. It was quite a frolic, a day of general spree. All were determined to celebrate it as the 4th of July, we having been on march that day. Many put on, what is called here, the "big drunk." On our return all regimental order was destroyed and every one went where he pleased, many of the stragglers not getting in until dark.

July 28
 BARCLAY. Regt. Drill.

 COULTER. Had a division drill under General Quitman. A day or so ago our ration of meat was condemned as unfit for use. At this time we received more in lieu of it. In consequence, today received two days' rations and bull beef is now plentiful. This evening there was a scarcity in the bread line.

July 30
 BARCLAY. Samuel Gorgas died today and was buried with due honors. This young man was born in Centre Co. Shortly before he joined the company he had worked for the Telegraph Company. He was unwell when we left Perote, but refused to remain. For a long time no hopes have been entertained for his recovery. He bore his suffering like a man.

 COULTER. No account kept of yesterday. This morning one of our company (Samuel Gorgas) died in the hospital and was buried today with the usual honors. Our mess had a very nice mutton pot pie today.

July 31
 BARCLAY. We have for duty one 2nd Lieut., 4 Sergts., 3 Capts., 1 music and 41 privates. Sick—1 Capt., 1 Corp., 7 privates. Extra duty 1 1st Lieut. Lieut. Armstrong was ordered some days ago to the command of Company H. A most excellent pot pie in No. 6 is worthy of note. Besides other good qualities it had the effect of restoring Old Livers to his usual good health and appetite.

 COULTER. Just seven months in the service and 4,000 miles from home.

August 1
 BARCLAY. Lieut. Coulter and the company are on guard today at the prison and Gen. Quitman's Quarters.

COULTER. Company E with Lt. Coulter, were detailed for guard today. Placed at the city prison and Governor's quarters. Here one can see the condition of prisoners in a Spanish prison. The prison allowance is small and they have generally to depend upon the charity of friends for food. At certain hours prison is open and it is hard to see the crowd of beings, many half naked, standing at the grating, anxiously expecting some friend with provisions and, what appears to be of equal importance to them, "Segaros." Guard duty is much lighter here than we have been accustomed to, this being only the third time I have been on since coming to Puebla. The force here is large and the duty is apportioned among them all.

August 2
COULTER. Are still in doubt as to our future movement. Many and contradictory are the reports current in quarters.

August 3
BARCLAY. For the few last days nothing worthy of remark has occurred. A garrison life presents but few varieties. We go the grand round of drilling, guarding, eating and sleeping. Today an unusual excitement was produced by the arrival of a mail. I received letters from Ed and W. A. Johnston, also a letter from Alec at Annapolis. The latter, as it was the first I ever received from him and as it was well written, gave me great satisfaction. By different letters heard of the deaths of Lieut. Murry on the Ohio, of Forney at Louisville, and of Andy Huston at Vera Cruz. Three more of our little band gone to their long homes. Lt. Murry first became sick at Jalapa and finding that he could not live if he remained in Mexico he reluctantly resigned. When he started for home he was reduced to a skeleton. He bore up patiently and manfully and as we learn was mending until after the boat left New Orleans. He then grew worse and died on the river near Wheeling. His remains were taken home and buried at the Long Run grave yard. Lt. Murry was engaged in merchandizing when the Regt. was called out. He was a man of good business habits and of fine natural talents. He was a gay cheerful disposition and he was a great favorite among the young folks about Greensburgh. A. J. Forney was born in Fayette County but raised in Greensburgh. He learnt the coopering business but was remarkably skilled in all mechanical pursuits. He had a genius for inventions. Had he been permitted to live it is likely that he would have added improvements to many of the branches of mechanics. He was a quiet, studious, persevering young man and it was often regretted that he did not receive a good education, for his natural talents were certainly very great. Andrew R. Huston was a citizen of Greensburgh for some 8 or 10 years. He had been among us and when the company was accepted he bid farewell to wife and several children and shouldered his musket. Poor Andy, he was liked by everybody. He was a kind, generous,

good hearted fellow and he fell a victim to his very amiable qualities. It was necessary to detail a nurse for our sick and Andy was the man selected. Altho he would have preferred accompanying the company he still cheerfully obeyed and remained behind. He was a good tender nurse and sacrificed his life in attending to the sickness and suffering of his companions. However glorious may be the death of the soldier who falls on the field of battle supporting the flag of his country, the fate of our old friend was equally noble. He fell where his duty called him, administering to the wants of the sick and the dying.

August 6

COULTER. Have received marching orders for Sunday the 8th. A train came up today from Vera Cruz under General Pierce,[11] bringing a mail by which we learned the deaths of three more Westmoreland Guards. Lt. Murry, discharged at Jalapa, died en route home; A. Jackson Forney, drummer, discharged at Vera Cruz and died en route home; Andrew R. Huston, died in the Hospital at Vera Cruz.

August 7

BARCLAY. Two independent companies have arrived from Pennsylvania. They are commanded by Capts. [James] Caldwell and [Samuel M.] Taylor.[12] The former Co. were raised principally in Mifflin County, the latter in Bedford County. They are attached to our regiment and are known as companies M & L. Orders to march tomorrow for Mexico City. Gen. Twiggs left today, on the 9th Gen'l Pillow and on the 10th Gen. Worth will take up the hue of march. Gov. Childs will remain as Governor of Puebla. The 1st Penna. Regt. to be the *chief* garrison force. All those who are unable to stand a vigorous march of 4 days are ordered to remain. I have been kept very busy in making out descriptive rolls of our company. Capt. Johnston, Corp. Shields, Aikens, Hagerty, Heasley, Kuhns, P., Landon, McClaran, Rager, Simms, Smith, Stickle, Thomas, Underwood and Waters will remain. Hoffer and Fishel are ordered to remain but refuse—say they can stand it. The sick are sent this evening to the hospital and everything is ready for an early start tomorrow morning.

11. Brigadier General Franklin Pierce (1804–1869), son of a governor of New Hampshire and a Democratic party political figure in his own right. His brief military career climaxed at the battle of Contreras, where he fell from his horse and fainted from the pain of a wrenched knee. He parlayed these Mexican War exploits into the Democratic party's nomination for president in 1852, easily defeating, in the subsequent campaign, his old commander Winfield Scott, the Whig nominee. Pierce's unfortunate presidency was marred by the controversy over the Kansas-Nebraska Act and the suspicion that he was too solicitous of Southern interests.

12. Caldwell died of wounds received while storming Mexico City, and Taylor died of illness later in 1847.

So all hopes of peace at present over and all those agreeable rumours about white flags, commissioners meetings, etc., which we have for so long hugged to our breasts are fled. I do not think that Gen. Scott has been deceived by these appearances of peace. While we have been laying here there has been several heavy rains. It is said that these rains were the cause of the delay, as the roads in the neighborhood were inundated. But I judge the chief cause of the delay was the waiting for reinforcements. They have now arrived under Brig. Gen. Pierce who also brot up a heavy battering train and a large supply of provisions. Captain Drum, who has every opportunity of knowing, informs us that Gen. Scott's effective force will not number over 11,000 men, notwithstanding the reinforcements. There are a great many sick left behind.

COULTER. General Twiggs and division left this morning for Mexico City. Two more Pennsylvania companies lately called, under Captains Taylor and Caldwell, came up with this train and are attached to our regiment, the former as Company L and the latter as Company M. The detachment of the First Pennsylvania Regiment here under Colonel Black, remain as a part of the garrison of this place. Company E leaves fifteen sick here in the hospital as follows: Captain Johnston, Corporal Shields, Privates Aikens, Hagerty, Heasley, Kuhns, P., Landon, McClaran, Rager, Stickle, Simms, Smith, Thomas, Underwood and Waters. On guard again tonight.

6

As a Matter of Course We Will Be Victorious
Puebla to the Outskirts of Mexico City

August 8

BARCLAY. Up at daylight. In line by 6 A.M. The Regt. with the two additional companies numbers about 600 men. Lt. Armstrong is in command of Company H. Lt. Coulter commands us. About 8 A.M. bid farewell to Puebla. Day very warm. Gen. Quitman is our commander and all have the greatest confidence in him. There will be fighting before we get into the City of Mexico but as a matter of course we will be victorious. Arrived at noon at Rio Prieto, a low damp encampment. Distance today 10 miles. The messes cooked supper this evening with charcoal.

COULTER. Reveille beat this morning at three o'clock and we were en route by six. The following is the roll of Company E as it left Puebla this morning and subsequently entered the valley of Mexico: Lieutenants Armstrong and Coulter; Sergeants Barclay, McLaughlin, Mechling and Byerly; Corporals McGinley, Bigelow and Bonnin; Fifer Kettering; Privates Allshouse, Bates, Bills, Brady, Carney, Carson, Cloud, Coulter, Decker, Gordon, Haines, Hansberry, Hartman, Hays, Hoffer, Kegarize, Kuhn, D. Kuhns, Fishel, Geesyn, Linsenbigler, McCabe, McClelland, McClain, McWilliams, J., McWilliams, W., Marchand, Melville, Milner, Moorhead, Sargent, Shaw, Steck and Uncapher, making forty-five officers and men. Encamped at Rio Prieto, distant ten miles from Puebla. We have a very disagreeable camp in a marshy meadow near a small stream. No wood here and we drew charcoal to cook with. Having no furnace nor the proper means of using this kind of fuel, had quite a time boiling coffee.

August 9

BARCLAY. Left camp late. Marched over a sandy well cultivated country. Quartered tonight in a building at San Martin, a small village. Distance today 11 miles.

COULTER. Going to the stream this morning before daylight for water, stepped too close and went into some three feet of mud and water. Not having time to dry myself or wash the mud and gravel out of my shoes, had quite a disagreeable march. Halted at the town of San Martin, distant eleven miles from Rio Prieto. The country through which we have passed these last two days is rich and cultivated. We are quartered in some vacant buildings, much better than a camp, and our water is supplied from a deep well. San Martin is a neat village for Mexico, but many of the inhabitants have at this time left.

August 10

BARCLAY. On march early. The Regt. in advance, Co. E the advance of the Regt. The road ascending. Considerable delay in getting the train along. Before reaching camp the rear was attacked by a party of Lancers who fired at a distance. One man wounded. The Dragoons charged to the rear at full gallop. There was a great excitement, but more cry than wolf. At noon arrived at Rio Frio a small stream which would be called a Rivulet in our country. March today very tiresome, being about 22 miles from our encampment of last night. The water of the Rio Frio coming directly from the snow mountains is very cold and is said to run to the Pacific. We had just got our tents pitched when it commenced raining. The rain poured in torrents until midnight. Our mess with great difficulty cooked in the marque.[1] This night was extremely unpleasant.

COULTER. On march early, our regiment in the advance and company E on the right of the regiment. Encamped at Rio Frio, distant twenty-two miles from San Martin. This was a most uncomfortable march for me. Completely stuffed up with cold and unable to perspire freely without which, any march, however short, is extremely fatiguing. The rear of our train was attacked by a party of lancers, but they only succeeded in wounding one sick man who had lagged about a hundred yards behind the rear guard. The country on this march was cultivated until you enter the pass of Rio Frio, where it becomes wild and abrupt, covered with pines and rocky. They had evidently been preparing this pass for our reception. There were many signs of fortification. The timber was cut so as to give a free range to their artillery and a line of breastworks built along the summit of the ridge on both sides of the road. Rio Frio is a very small stream, in fact a mere rivulet, but is the best and coldest water I have yet drank in Mexico. Had just gotten our tents pitched when it commenced to rain. Our lieutenants and our mess have joined for mutual convenience on this march. The rain was so heavy that a fire could not be kindled and we cooked our supper in the markee. Had a disagreeable time cooking it and then I had quite a task eating it, having by this time a very sore throat. It rained in torrents during the greater part of the night.

August 11

BARCLAY. Being the rear guard the Regt. left camp late today. It was after 9 A.M. when we were in the road. Lt. Armstrong resumed command of

---

1. Barclay means to say "marquee," a large field tent. Coulter calls it "markee."

Co. E, Sergt. Hambright having been appointed to the 1st Lieutenancy of Co. H. The road for the first 6 or 8 miles is ascending and we marched through the defiles of the Rio Frio, where an engagement was expected and where the good people of the States dreaded that we would meet another Cerro Gordo. But no enemy were seen. They had made some slight fortifications but on our approach fell back to the surer defences on the causeways. The mountains here are not so steep or rugged as at any of the former great passes. The woods are pine and look beautiful. Lt. Coulter, who is an old hunter, pronounces them full of deer. However, we have not time to make an excursion through them. The march today is tiresome. Being in the rear the least delay of the train requires a halt and then to make up we are marched at double quick time. About midday arrived on the summit of the mountains and had descended but a short distance when the valley of Mexico burst upon the view. The air at that great elevation is pure to a degree that the dwellers in lower countries have no idea of. Objects at a very great distance are distinctly visible. In a moment all cares, toils and hardships are forgotten and every one is silently beholding the great valley which lies at his feet. A plain of near 200 miles in length and 60 in breadth lies before us. This valley or plain is surrounded by chains of lofty mountains, which extend to the right and left as far as the eye can reach. Popocatepetl and Ixtaccihuatl tower high above the clouds, two heavy headed giants, the guardians of this enchanted valley. The plain itself is dotted with lakes shining in the sun. Huge bluffs and pyramids formed by nature rise abruptly in all directions. Several towns buried amid the groves that surround them and innumerable haciendas give an appearance of life to the scene, their white walls in beautiful contrast with the surrounding green, their spires and domes visible from the mountains. Afar to the west we see, or imagine we see the dim outline of the City of Mexico itself, the goal of all our wishes, the termination of our pilgrimage. This idea adds to the feeling which the magnificent scene has created and in imagination we revel in the Halls of the Montezumas. After a long march arrived at Camp. Distance today 23 miles. During the last 5 miles marched thru a rain. Gen. Quitman and the principal parts of the Division are at Buena Vista. Our regiment is about a mile in advance and are very badly encamped at a deserted hacienda on the border of the lake. The ground is wet. As we are in a woodyard we will not want for that article. We are on the main road to the Capitol. Gen. Twiggs' Division is in advance of us at Ayotla about 2 miles. The enemy are strongly fortified at the Penon[2] about 3 miles from Twiggs. The engineers have been reconnoitering Penon.

---

2. El Peñón Viejo—a well-fortified rocky hill, rising steeply to about 450 feet, which commanded the route to the eastern gate of Mexico, the San Làzaro Garita, about seven miles away.

COULTER. Our regiment being rear guard today, did not leave camp until late. Last Night's rain used me up entirely. This morning was very stiff; the cold had settled in my bones and I was anything but fit for march, especially as rear guard, the difficulties of which are known to any one who has done any marching. The last seven miles of today's march were through a rain. The advance of our division halted at a hacienda called "Buena Vista." Our regiment was marched almost two miles further making our day's journey twenty miles. The country through which we passed today was a rapid ascent for the first seven miles, then a descent for about ten miles, when we found ourselves at length in the valley of Mexico. This mountain is covered with a heavy growth of timber. We are encamped in the court-yard of an old hacienda built of sun burnt bricks. One or two of the companies are quartered in the building, but we are in our tents. Cattle have been kept here, and between the mud and cow dung, we have quite a pleasant mess to walk through and sleep in. There is a large quantity of wood in this yard from which is received the appellation of "woodyard" as which it is best known in the regiment. There is a branch of a canal which terminates in the building, which leads directly to the city of Mexico and is the source of considerable market to that city. After a late supper, very little of which I could eat, however, slept in my wet clothes on this muddy ground.

August 12
BARCLAY. Lay in camp today. It is said that Penon is almost impregnable. Detailed 4 men to assist in taking flats from the woodyard to Twiggs' Quarters. This evening Pillow's column descended the mountain and instead of moving along the main road inclined to the left and halted at Chalco a town on the lake of the same name.

COULTER. Last night has made my cold considerably worse. Throat so sore that I am unable to eat the rations; it is very painful even to drink coffee. My mouth and gums are very sore also and my teeth loose. However, we will have a day or so of rest and then I will be fit for march again. General Twiggs is about five miles in advance of us and reports the enemy fortified at Penon, about ten miles from Mexico. The road between here and the enemy's works is covered with water and we cannot make a nearer approach. Today muskets are being cleaned and cartridges dried preparatory to the brush. Had a dress parade this evening and the regimental position of the companies were altered. We were formerly next to the extreme left; we are now the sixth company, the right color company on right of center.

August 13
BARCLAY. Still in the woodyard. It is a filthy place, wet and damp. Several of our company are experiencing the bad effects of lying upon the

damp ground. Severe colds and pains in the limbs. McGinley who has been unwell since we left Puebla is much worse. He sleeps now in the Colonel's room. The Mexicans have killed one of Co. H. It is supposed he was on a plundering expedition. Severe orders are issued against the men leaving quarters. Worth's Division instead of following Twiggs and Quitman follows Pillow.

COULTER. Today detail was made from our regiment to take a number of boats lying here down the canal to General Twiggs' camp. I understand to build a bridge. A party of the regiment were out plundering some houses today, but were attacked by the owners who killed one belonging to Company H.

August 14
BARCLAY. Regiment reorganized. Co. E which has heretofore been the 2nd company from the left is now the right of the left wing. Orders to march tomorrow at 5 A.M.

COULTER. Are still quartered in the wood-yard. This is a filthy place and hard on me. I am still affected with a cold. We have marching orders for five o'clock tomorrow morning.

Up to this point the advance of the American army, though not without peril, had at least been relatively straightforward. All that was required was to follow the National Road west from Vera Cruz. As the outskirts of Mexico City were approached, hard choices had to be made.

That city was a natural fortress, made even stronger by the frantic defenses recently erected by Santa Anna. Surrounded by lakes, swamps, and, at the south, a vast and supposedly impenetrable lava bed, the Pedregal, the city could be approached only by long, narrow causeways, each of which led to a garita, *or "gate." Designed as customs houses, these* garitas *could do double duty as effective barriers to an invading army.*

To continue along the National Road to the San Lázaro Garita, or eastern gateway, would require passing directly under the thirty cannon mounted on the hill of El Peñón. Yet each of the other approaches had drawbacks of its own. Only one path could be taken; which should it be?

After making a personal reconnaissance of the ground, Scott decided to turn Santa Anna's position by a difficult march around the southern shores of Lakes Chalco and Xochimilco.

By 18 August the American army had concentrated at San Agustín, a village due south of the capital city, but its strategic problem had not been resolved, merely transferred to another location. Mexican troops and guns were moved swiftly from El Peñón to the southern approaches and again barred Scott's path. Ethan Allen Hitchcock, Scott's scholarly aide, realized the practical force of what had hitherto seemed only an academic maxim:

the value of interior lines. "We now begin to see," he said, "that while we move over the arc of a circle surrounding the city, the enemy moves over a chord, and can concentrate at any point before we can reach it."

To make matters worse, forage for horses and rations for men were running low and Scott himself (as even Barclay observed) appeared distracted and discouraged. "Our prospects darken every moment," Hitchcock confided to his diary. "Now is the time for the General to keep cool!"[3]

August 15

BARCLAY. Expect a fight today. Strike tents and at 6 A.M. march towards Twiggs' encampment. Passing the encampment about a half a mile the road became much worse and about the time we were looking for a fire the Division was halted and countermarched. Passing the woodyard and Buena Vista we moved to the right and followed the road taken by Pillow and Worth. Halted about 2 P.M. in the church yard in Chalco. Worth left Chalco this afternoon moving along the left of Lake Chalco. This large lake is one of that chain which surround the City of Mexico. Protected by lakes and marshes the City can only be approached by traversing narrow causeways which have been raised from the water. Like Venice, Mexico City rises from the midst of lakes and marshes. The Penon defends the main road from Puebla. After several careful reconnaissances it is considered inexpedient to attack it. Gen. Scott says it would [not] be carried without the loss of 1500 men. I do not understand the movement of our division. This morning probably there was a misunderstanding of orders but I rather am inclined to believe that the object was to attract the enemy's attention by our advance, the number of men and wagons making a somewhat formidable appearance, while in the meantime Pillow and Worth would move along to the left of the lake and thus gain one day's march before the real object was known. While laying in Chalco Gen. Scott and staff galloped past on the route taken by Pillow and Worth. The old General's face looks careworn. March today about 10 miles.

COULTER. According to orders, this morning we struck our tents and marched down to Colonel Riley's[4] camp, about three miles from ours. Here our orders were countermanded and we marched back again a short distance beyond our old camp, and taking a left hand road, after a march of about six miles, encamped at a town called "Chalco" near a lake of the same name. It had been intended to storm the fortifications from Twiggs' position, but after consideration, it was thought fit to desert this course and march around the enemy's works. Such is the cause of our strange

---

3. Hitchcock, *Fifty Years*, 275–76.

4. Bennet Riley of Maryland entered the army as an ensign in 1813. Rising patiently through the ranks he was brevetted major general for his conduct at the battle of Contreras. He died 9 June 1853. Fort Riley, Kansas, is named in his honor.

movements today. By this movement the order of march has been completely revised. General Worth, who had the rear division, is now the advance, then General Pillow next, our division, under General Quitman, and General Twiggs brings up the rear. We are encamped in a church yard, but were not allowed to pitch our tents for some time, expecting we might be ordered off suddenly. In the afternoon it drizzled a little and finding that there was no likelihood of our being called out, pitched our tents. Some of the boys had quite a time plundering a neighborhood pear orchard and some bee hives.

August 16

BARCLAY. Left Chalco early. Marched today 9 miles. The road runs through corn fields the greater part of the distance. The corn is in prime eating order and roasting ears are all the go. Encamped after many halts on the bank of the canal. Twiggs today abandoned his camp and moved toward Chalco. The Mexicans in great force thought to cut him off, but a few rounds of artillery altered their intentions.

COULTER. Moved this morning at a reasonable hour and after many halts encamped on the bank of the canal, distant about nine miles from Chalco. Marched today over a very dusty road through a continuous corn field and are encamped on an open grassy spot. Many of the boys were eating raw corn all day, and a large quantity both roasted and boiled has been devoured since reaching camp. The consequence is that dysentery is becoming prevalent.

August 17

BARCLAY. Today march was very slow. Pillow and Worth who are in advance are obliged to feel their way. The army is now moving in the reverse order from what they were in when we left Puebla. Worth in the advance and Twiggs in the rear. The road is narrow and very bad. Encamped in a beautiful grove. Distance 5 miles.

COULTER. After a march of about six miles, principally through corn fields, encamped in an olive grove. Baked some corn dodgers [cornmeal cakes] and got some honey from our waggoners which had been plundered at Chalco. Was on guard here. Sent to the train some distance from our camp. While there heard what we thought was heavy firing. After standing relief (we divided the guard so as to have only one tour) I cleared off and returned to camp so as to get a sleep in a tent.

August 18

BARCLAY. The Division in motion at an early hour. Our Regt. is the rear guard. The road today runs along the border of the lake. In the rainy season, and indeed but a few weeks ago when Major Gaines[5] made his escape it is overflowed from the lake. The Mexicans never imagined that we would take this course or they would have made the road entirely impassable. As it is the wagons and artillery are got along with great difficulty. After it was evident that the attack of Penon was abandoned the enemy did obstruct the road some by rolling rocks into it. But our advance were soon upon them and removed the obstructions quickly. A wagon breaking down caused the delay of a couple of hours. Worth and Pillow had a slight skirmish driving before them the enemy's cavalry. The firing we distinctly heard. Old Twiggs came up in a most terrible rage, cursing and swearing at the delay. It was amusing to see the rage the old gentleman worked himself to. His face was as red as a turkey cocks and he roared out a tremendous volley of oaths. He swore that Gen. Scott had sent word for him to hurry up and he couldn't do it, that he never was in such a predicament in his life before and detained too by a _____ wagon. Finally got on the road again and marched very fast. Gen. Worth had driven the enemy from San Agustin. Toward evening a rain came up and completely soaked us. After a march of 10 miles encamped in a corn field near San Agustin. Camp ground wet. From a ridge close by had a beautiful view of the country, of San Agustin now occupied by Pillow and of San Antonio a hacienda where Worth lays and the enemy in a selected position near him. A dragoon on guard tonight wounded himself in the arm, it is supposed intentionally.

COULTER. Our regiment was rear guard today. Had a most tedious march. The road was unusually bad, in many places filled with rocks, in others hub deep with mud. The train moved very slowly sometimes requiring an hour or so to get the waggons over a rocky or muddy spot. A waggon broke down and we were halted until it could be fixed. While halted, General Twiggs came up to us; for some time there had been firing ahead and old Bully was in quite a pet because he could not get along faster. "Here I am" said he "lying in the road, firing ahead and me unable to go on—all for a God damned old waggon not worth two dollars. Why the hell don't you throw it into the ditch?" We moved on and shortly after,

5. John Pollard Gaines (1795–1857), a veteran of the War of 1812, was a Kentucky lawyer and politician when, on the outbreak of the Mexican War, he was commissioned lieutenant colonel in the 1st Kentucky Cavalry. In January 1847 he, along with Major Solon Borland, carelessly allowed their commands to be surrounded by overwhelming Mexican forces at the hacienda of Encarnación, deep within enemy-held territory in northern Mexico. Surrendering without firing a shot, Gaines and his men were marched into the interior, undergoing severe cruelty and deprivation. Gaines escaped and was placed on General Scott's staff as a member of his inner circle of advisors.

Gaines was elected to Congress while still in captivity and after his term was appointed territorial governor of Oregon where his high-handed, turbulent administration managed to alienate almost all parties and factions.

General Twiggs taking another road marched around us. Towards evening commenced raining and we got quite a ducking. After a march of almost eight miles, encamped late in a cornfield. Another devouring of corn in all shapes ensued. Not being near recovered from my cold yet and the ground being very muddy, slept in the markee on a cot bottom with Lt. Armstrong. Today General Worth entered the town of San Agustin and Captain Thornton[6] of the [2d] Dragoons was killed while reconnoitering, being cut almost in two by a cannon shot.

August 19

BARCLAY. Early start and soon arrived in San Agustin a small village deserted in a great measure by the inhabitants. Remained over an hour under arms in the plaza. In the meantime Pillow marched out, his Division to act as a strong covering force to the reconnoitering parties and also for the purpose of cutting roads. Quitman's Division moved into Pillow's Quarters. We pitched tents in the yard in front of the church and orders that no man leave. Pillow moving some 5 or 6 miles in a N.W. direction unexpectedly comes upon a large body of the enemy in a chosen position and protected by several pieces of heavy artillery. Twiggs' Division is hurried up to the support of Pillow and about 3 P.M. the cannonading opens. The light batteries of the flying artillery, hastily got into position, for a long time maintain a fire with the heavy advance of the enemy. From the steeple of the church at San Agustin the firing is plainly seen. The greatest excitement prevails among the volunteers. The long roll beats and in an instant the 2nd Regt. is formed. But as it is necessary to leave a force in reserve at San Agustin, the 2nd Penna. Vol. and the marines are left behind and the New York and South Carolina Volunteers composing Shields' Brigade are ordered onwards. There was a feeling of gloom and despondency in our Regt. which is indescribable. At Cerro Gordo the Pennsylvanians were blamed for *waving* and all feel the necessity of wiping off the imputation of anything like backwardness. A volunteer Regt. like the Roman's wife should be above even suspicion. Here is an opportunity and for some reason or other we must stay back. This evening was spent in watching the firing which continued until dark. The reports brought in are that no impression has been made upon the enemy and that our loss is considerable. The night sets up dark and gloomy and is in unison with our feelings. A heavy rain commences and pours down during the entire night. Sheltered by our tents we pity our brethren who are exposed to the storm. But gladly would we exchange situations and endure all the horrors of the _____ storm. They are in the path to honor. We are lying here idle in the honorable post of wagon guards. In today's fight it is dis-

6. This was the same Captain Seth Thornton whose capture near the Rio Grande on 25 April 1846 had given President Polk his justification for war with Mexico.

covered that the Dragoons cannot act on account of the roughness of the ground. The Mexican force is composed of over 6,000 men from the army of the North. They are under command of Gen. Valencia.[7]

COULTER. This morning early, marched into San Agustin, distant about a mile from our camp. General Pillow's division was here, but moved on when we entered. Our regiment is encamped in a church yard just vacated by some of Pillow's men. General Pillow had not been gone many hours when heavy firing was heard which continued without much alteration until night. Our loss this day was not very heavy, but little damage was done, however, to the enemy's works, having Magruder's light battery firing upon them, which suffered severely. At night both parties lay in their positions, no advantage having been gained by either. Our division was under arms the greater part of the day in readiness to go to his assistance if necessary. Towards night the South Carolina and New York Regiments, under General Shields, were ordered to march. The Second Pennsylvania Regiment was left to guard the train. During the whole day up until towards night (and once we were actually formed every one thought to march) not one of our regimental officers were with the regiment. Colonel Geary was, I understood, officer of the day (he might, however, still have shown himself) but the other two were both fit for duty and were not at their posts. This has been urged as a reason why the Second Pennsylvania was not taken.[8] General Shields arrived at the scene of action and took up his position during the night.

While the Westmorelanders were ingloriously guarding the wagon train at San Agustin, the fortunes of the army whipsawed from the brink of disaster on 19 August to the verge of triumph on the 20th.

Outnumbered two to one, the Americans faced a well-entrenched foe who blocked all the roads to Mexico City. Between their position and that of the Mexicans lay the Pedregal, an old lava bed approximately five miles by three. A trackless lunar landscape of volcanic rock sharp enough to rip apart a horse's hooves, crisscrossed by a labyrinth of gullies and ravines, it

7. General Gabriel Valencia probably had no more than four thousand men at his disposal.

8. Although Coulter blamed the dereliction of his officers for the regiment's ignominious assignment of guarding a storage depot rather than sharing in the glory and death of the battle of Contreras, General Scott put a better face upon this duty. In his report of the battle Scott explained: "I regret having been obliged . . . to leave the fine 2nd Pennsylvania volunteers and the veteran detachment of United States marines—at our important depot, San Agustin. It was there that I had placed our sick and wounded, the siege, supply and baggage trains. If these had been lost our army would have been driven almost to despair; and considering the enemy's very great excess of numbers and the many approaches to the depot, it might well have become, emphatically, the post of honor" (report of Major General Scott No. 32, 28 August 1847).

seemed so impassable that the Mexican advance guard near Contreras under General Gabriel Valencia paid it only desultory attention.

However, an American reconnaissance party led by Captain Robert E. Lee of the engineers with the assistance of Lieutenants P. G. T. Beauregard and Zealous B. Tower, discovered a pathway through the Pedregal that, if improved, could lead men and artillery to a point behind the Mexican lines. Road work was commenced on the 19th of August. When the progress of the work party was barred by Valencia's troops, Gideon Pillow, on his own initiative, decided to sweep them from the field. Instead, he bungled the attack and managed to place a substantial part of his own army in grave peril, sandwiched between Valencia and Santa Anna (at San Angel) and with his command, as Beauregard exclaimed, "in the d----dest scatteration"[9] imaginable. Only nightfall spared them from possible annihilation.

Convinced that he had already won a great victory, Valencia allowed his men to get roaring drunk while he handed out commemorative medals and promotions. Refusing Santa Anna's order to pull back to San Angel, Valencia insisted that "the miserable remnant of the North Americans was shut up in the Pedregal" and could easily be dealt with the next day.[10]

But the American forces were stealthily regrouping under General Persifor Smith. Having discovered a ravine leading through the Pedregal to Valencia's rear, Smith's men gathered through the dark, ready to pounce at dawn. The "gallant and indefatigable Captain Lee"[11] was sent back to headquarters through the rocky maze in order to explain the plan to Scott and to ask that a simultaneous attack be launched on the enemy's front.

All went according to plan. At daylight, while the Mexicans were still half-asleep, Smith's men rose from the mist to appear in their rear, just as other Americans attacked front and flank. In seventeen minutes, as timed by Smith's pocket watch, the battle of Padierna (officially called, through some confusion, the Battle of Contreras) was over. At a cost of only sixty American casualties, some seven hundred Mexicans were dead or wounded and eight hundred more made prisoners, including four generals. The rest were in wild flight towards Mexico City, running straight through Santa Anna's army at San Angel, which joined them in their panicky rout. Scott flogged his men on in hot pursuit. "Make haste, my sons!" he jubilantly urged.[12]

In the meantime, on the eastern side of the Pedregal, General Worth launched toward the Mexicans at San Antonio. With the fall of San Angel that position was untenable, and the Mexicans abandoned it in haste.

9. P. G. T. Beauregard, *With Beauregard in Mexico: The Mexican War Reminiscences of P.G.T. Beauregard*, ed. T. Harry Williams (New York: DaCapo Press, 1969), 48.

10. Elliott, *Winfield Scott*, 508.

11. Scott, *Memoirs*, 2:474.

12. Geoffrey Perrett, *A Country Made By War* (New York: Random House, 1989), 166.

Two defeated Mexican armies streamed north seeking safety. Their paths converged near the village of Churubusco. At this point Santa Anna pulled his troops together for a last stand. It was a well-chosen defensive position, featuring a fortified bridgehead to guard the river crossing and a thick-walled convent to shield the defenders. It should have been turned rather than stormed, but Scott's army had been swept along so quickly by its victories that Scott had temporarily lost control of its movements. For two-and-a-half hours the Americans battered against the convent's walls until it fell, losing momentum as well as nearly a thousand killed or wounded. The Mexican army lost ten times that number, but the Mexican capital was, for the time being, saved.

Rather than run the risks of house-to-house fighting, Scott halted his troops outside the city gates and was persuaded to agree to a truce, during which he hoped an honorable peace could be negotiated. It took over two weeks for him to realize that he had been duped and that Santa Anna was merely using the negotiations to buy time to rebuild his shattered defenses. The war had to be resumed.

August 20

BARCLAY. Last night during the rain and storm our troops were not idle. Covered by the darkness of the night plans were carried into execution which could not be done in day time and by daylight the different corps were in the desired positions. Making a joint attack in front which attracted the enemy's attention, Riley's Brigade made a furious onset in their rear. Covered by the nature of the ground, the enemy were ignorant of the advance of the Brigade, who suddenly rising from the ground as it were within a few hundred yards of their rear rushed furiously forward yelling and cheering. Completely panic struck, the enemy fled in all directions. But so skillfully was the American force posted that a great many were killed and many taken prisoners. Those that escaped were hotly pursued. A large force sent out by Santa Anna to the relief of Valencia and a heavy body of Lancers who were hovering around could give no assistance. The 2nd Penna. Regt. had early this morning been formed and moved towards the battle ground. All was joyous and full of hopes but after a march of about 2 miles information arrived that the work was already done and we were marched back disappointed to our quarters. The results of the Battle of Padierna or Contreras were great. This position was the key of all the enemy's fortifications on the western and s. western part of the City. Nor could any of their other works have been approached until this was carried. Altho their works were defended by 24 pieces of heavy artillery, 6,000 veteran troops and chiefly by the volcanic formation and roughness of the ground in their front and flanks, yet the action lasted only 17 minutes from the time Riley charged until all was over. A great many of the Mexicans were killed in their retreat. Ninety four officers and

near 800 privates were taken prisoners, together with all the artillery am-
munition and a great number of small arms. The pieces taken from General
Taylor at Buena Vista were here recaptured and our old townsman, Capt.
Simon Drum, was so fortunate as to be the first man who laid hands on
them. Both Lieut. Johnston and Drum were engaged in this fight. It is to
Brig. Gen. Smith[13] that the army attributes the honor of the plan of the attack in the rear and a more brilliant and decisive charge was never made.
Part of the retreating Mexicans, hotly pursued by a small party of our
troops, flying thru San Angel never stopped until they reached the City
distant from Contreras over 12 miles. The chief body of them, however,
fell back upon their fortifications at Churubusco where lay Santa Anna
with the main army. About 1 P.M. the fight again commenced. Scott taking advantage of their panic advanced with Pillow, Twiggs' and Shields
Brigade to Churubusco. Worth in the meantime drove the enemy from
San Antonio and rapidly approached to form in the grand battle. From
the roofs of San Agustin we were for a long time the anxious spectators of
this conflict. For hours nothing was heard but the continued roar of cannon and the sharp rattle of musketry. All were in doubt. No one dreaded
defeat but all mourned the long continued conflict which foretold the
deaths of many of our brave men. About 4 P.M. an express arrived and announced that victory had again perched upon our _____, that the enemy
had lost all, their artillery, ammunition and defences and that the City
now lay open to the advance of the army. Santa Anna has escaped. As
usual he fled early. Among the many prisoners taken are some 40 deserters
from our army, the notorious San Patricio Legion[14] with the villanous

---

13. Persifor Frazer Smith (1798–1858), a Princeton graduate who settled in Louisiana
and became active in legal and militia affairs. He commanded a regiment of volunteers in
the Seminole Wars and received a colonel's commission in the regular army at the commencement of the war with Mexico. His rare combination of boldness and efficiency, most
notably at Contreras, the success of which was largely his responsibility, quickly won him a
general's stars. Unlike many of his brother officers, Smith never indulged in the backbiting
and jealousy so endemic in the army, and he won the respect and even affection of all ranks.
There are hints that Scott was grooming him as his successor when Smith's sudden death in
1858, on the eve of the troubles with the Mormons, put an end to that project.

14. The San Patricio (St. Patrick) Battalion consisted of about 260 deserters from the
American army who had been induced to switch sides. Though most were Catholic, they
were not all Irish, as was generally assumed. Of 103 whose origins are known, only forty
were from Ireland, while twenty-two were American born; the rest being from Germany,
Scotland, Canada, France, Poland, and elsewhere. (Robert Ryal Miller, *Shamrock and Sword:
The Saint Patrick's Battalion in the U.S.-Mexican War* [Norman: University of Oklahoma
Press, 1989], 175.) Estimates from other sources differ somewhat.

Although the San Patricio deserters compounded their offense by taking up arms against
their country, desertion itself was a common practice during the Mexican War. The army
lost 9,207 men through desertion (5,331 regulars and 3,876 volunteers), a total substantially
larger than the authorized size of the entire army shortly before the war's commencement.

Riley[15] at their head. Their position was in a church and their resistance now desperate. Three times the Mexican troops in the Church hoisted the white flag and three times did these desperadoes tear it down, most of them knowing and all fearing that death would be their portion if taken fought until all was lost. It was their cursed fire which mowed down so many of our brave men and which prolonged the contest. The Dragoons hitherto from the nature of the ground prevented from participating in the battles, now were hurled upon the retreating foe and right freely did their sabres fall. The road from the City to the works at Churubusco was filled with wagons going and returning, loaded with ammunition, provisions, etc. A wagon which broke down near the City caused a delay which gave our Dragoons time to overtake and capture the whole train and many prisoners who were detained by the blockading of the road. So impetuous was the pursuit that a company of Dragoons advanced to the gates of the City whereupon the enemy opened a fire indiscriminately upon our men and their own masses. It was in this pursuit that Major [Frederick D.] Mills of the 15th Inf. was killed. Our loss in the Bloody Battle of Churubusco was very great numbering near 1,000 men killed and wounded.[16] It was necessary to carry the enemy's works at the point of the bayonet and there being no cover the charging columns were all exposed to a terrible fire of grape and musketry. Almost every Reg. in the army were engaged and all suffered severely, particularly Shields' Brigade. The brave Col. Butler[17] fell at the head of his Regt. Lt. Col. [James P.] Dickinson was badly wounded as was Col. [Ward B.] Burnett of the N.Y. Vols. Over 100 men in each of these regiments were killed and wounded.

COULTER. This morning the firing recommenced and our regiment was at last ordered to join General Pillow. Before reaching the place of action we heard three loud, long cheers from our men and shortly after, we were ordered back, the fight was over. Such was the battle of Contreras. We were on the verge of getting into it, but the enemy knuckled under too soon. In this fight Captain Drum, of the 4th Artillery, re-took the two pieces taken from Lt. [John P. J.] O'Brien of the same regiment, at the battle of Buena Vista. The enemy, who were under General Valencia, retreated across to

15. Sergeant John Riley had earlier deserted from the British army before enlisting with the United States. Sent to Mexico, he deserted again, helping to form the notorious San Patricio Battalion. Despite his offense, General Scott commuted Riley's sentence from death by hanging to whipping and branding on the grounds that his desertion had occurred before the formal American declaration of war.

16. A close estimate. In all the fighting of the day, of which the engagement at Churubusco was by far the bloodiest, American forces suffered 1038 casualties. The Mexican losses were perhaps ten times that number.

17. Pierce Mason Butler (1798–1847) was a captain in the regular army in the 1820s but resigned his commission for civilian pursuits. In 1836 he was elected governor of South Carolina.

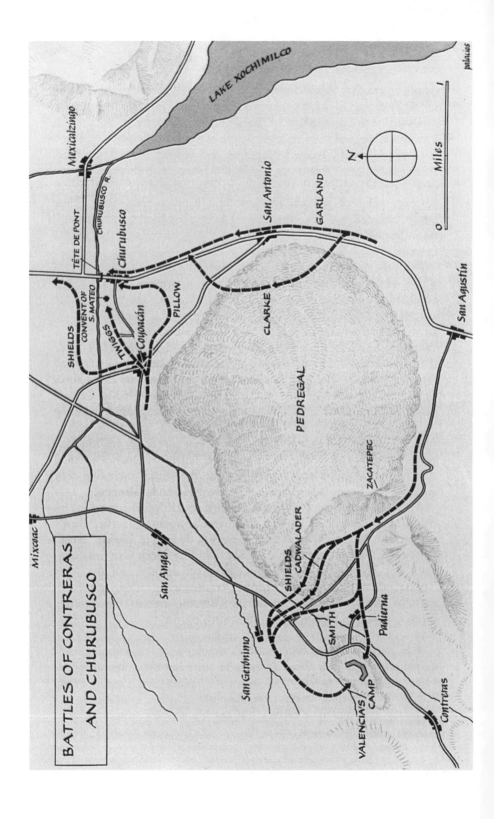

BATTLES OF CONTRERAS
AND CHURUBUSCO

LAKE XOCHIMILCO

Mexicalzingo

CHURUBUSCO R.

TÊTE DE PONT

Churubusco

San Antonio

GARLAND

SHIELDS

CONVENT OF S. MATEO

Coyoacán

PILLOW

TWIGGS

CLARKE

San Agustín

PEDREGAL

Mixcoac

ZACATEPEC

San Angel

SHIELDS

CADWALADER

San Gerónimo

SMITH

Padierna

VALENCIA'S CAMP

Contreras

N

Miles

0   1

palacios

Churubusco. They were pursued by General Twiggs through San Angel. General Shields followed across a very rough and rocky piece of country. They would have made a stand at San Antonio, but General Worth entered the works with them. They made a stand at the convent of Churubusco and the battle of that name was fought this afternoon. They were again routed and pursued by our dragoons to the very gate of the City of Mexico. The two volunteer regiments of our division, who were in this fight, suffered severely. Colonel Butler of the South Carolina Regiment was killed here and Lt. Colonel Dickinson, of the same regiment, received a wound of which he has since died. Colonel Burnett, of the New York Regiment, was severely wounded. We could plainly hear the firing at this fight but were left still as a train guard at San Agustin. General Quitman was also left with us, as only a part of his command was called out. We have been enjoying ourselves here with the fruit in which this country now abounds. Peaches and apples are over-abundant. It appears to be one continuous orchard around the town. Bread and marketing are rather scarce yet, as the greasers have not gotten over their fright at the noise of the cannons.

August 21

BARCLAY. This day is the anniversary of the entry of Cortes into the City of Mexico—326 years ago.[18] The bold and crafty Spaniard by arms and arts made an entrance into the magnificent City of the Montezumas. It would be a singular coincidence if the American army should enter today. The New York and South Carolina men return to San Agustin. Another batch of prisoners are brought in today. The officers are confined in the church in front of which our Regt. is encamped. Among the officers taken are Gen. Salas[19] of Guerilla memory and Gen. Anaya,[20] Ex-President of the Republic. The former was taken at Contreras, the latter at Churubusco. The officers confined in the church appear very indifferent as to their fate. Many of them are very young and none of them appear much to regard the death and slaughter of their friends or the downfall of their country.

COULTER. General Worth is now close to the city and the enemy are driven within their inner lines.

18. Mexico City fell to Hernando Cortes on 13 August 1521, not on 21 August.

19. Although José Mariano Salas (1797–1867) was responsible for organizing the so-called Guerrillas of Vengeance, he was not, as Barclay suggests, an irregular but a full-fledged general in the Mexican army who served as president of the republic, albeit as a figurehead for Santa Anna, whose return to power in 1846 Salas had facilitated.

20. Pedro María Anaya (1794–1854), a career soldier who served briefly as minister of war in the Herrera administration, also served as interim president in the absence of Santa Anna at the time of Cerro Gordo. Captured at Churubusco, he was paroled, and from 11 November 1847 to 7 January 1848 served again as interim president, in which capacity he appointed the commissioners to negotiate peace with the Americans.

August 22

BARCLAY. No movement made yet. It is said that negotiations are going on and that an armistice will likely be signed. This village is larger than I thought it was when we first entered. It is said to be quite a fashionable resort in the summer for the folks from the City.

COULTER. The whole army is now before the city, except the Second Pennsylvania, who are still engaged in the honorable employment of taking care of a ranch of sick, wounded and prisoners and a lot of waggons, mules and rascally waggoners. The New York and South Carolina Regiments have been ordered back to this place.

August 23

BARCLAY. As many of the houses have been deserted and their contents not removed several burglaries have been committed and guard duty is consequently pretty severe. This is always the case. The quiet and honorable soldier suffers for the crimes and misconduct of the scoundrels who disgrace the army and nation. Nothing of any interest occuring.

August 24

BARCLAY. The country in the neighborhood of this town is rich and well cultivated. Among the curiosities is a spring which bursts from the side of a hill about a half miles walk from Camp. Lt. Armstrong and myself have paid it a visit. The town itself is much scattered, gardens and orchards intervening between the houses. These orchards are now loaded with apples and peaches. The fruit is generally of an inferior quality, tho on some of the trees it is very good. Many of the orchards are guarded. We manage however to get as much fruit as we can well dispose of. It is the first time in Mexico we have met these favorite old acquaintances in such abundance. The Mexicans show great carelessness in regard to their orchards. The trees are suffered to grow up without pruning, the space between the trees is covered with shoots. The apples are small, generally of an oblong shape and always of a yellowish color. I have not seen a red apple. There is no difference between the peaches here and in the States. We also met for the first time the horse chestnuts, a large nut of the shape of the common chestnut and a taste like an acorn. When roasted they eat very good. But the greatest luxury we receive here is the milk. It is rich delicious milk. Heretofore the stuff the Mexicans called milk was a nasty mixture of asses or goats milk and water. Every morning there is a cartload of milk in pails sold here. It is brought from between this and the City.

August 26

BARCLAY. At Dress Parade today was read the Articles of an Armistice entered into between the American and Mexican Commissioners. The object of the Armistice is that the Commissioners of the two governments may meet and conclude a treaty of peace. No additional fortifications are to be thrown up and neither party to receive reinforcements. The Armistice to be ended by either party giving the other 48 hours notice. Gen. Scott could have entered the City on the evening of the 20th, but considering that the great object of the war, an honorable peace, might probably be better obtained from the foe before they were completely humiliated, he halted his victorious columns at the gates of the Capitol and agreed to the appointment of the Commissioners. All are now fully impressed with the belief that a treaty of peace will be signed by the Commissioners. The rumors confirm and strengthen this belief. The treaty signed, the question arises whether we volunteers will be sent home immediately on the signature or be detained here until the ratification of the instrument by the Congress of the two nations. That we will be sent home forthwith is the general impression and many fear we will be marched back without seeing the City. This will be hard and many schemes are laid as to how we will manage to see the City. Altho all are anxious to get home again, the unpleasant reflection forces itself upon our minds that if we return home *we* can claim but little glory in our Mexican campaign. It is true we have suffered sickness, endured hardships, but upon what battle field has the flag of Pennsylvania been unfurled? At Cerro Gordo it *waved,* not in victory but *from the line.* At least so Gen. Pillow said and Col. Roberts was not the man to contradict him. At Vera Cruz we were not mentioned and in the two great battles which have been fought in the valley we have not been engaged. Notwithstanding this disagreeable view of our actions we are on tiptoe expectation of returning home and will tell our friends there that it is opportunity, fair opportunity which makes heroes and that we never have had a fair opportunity.

COULTER. Our division is still quartered at San Agustin eating apples and guarding prisoners and train. We have about a hundred Mexican officers prisoners confined in the old church where we are quartered. For the present all hostilities have ceased, an armistice having been declared between the two armies. Had a dress parade this morning and the proceedings of the commissioners were read to us, as follows: An armistice to continue until terminated on the part of either army by forty-eight hours notice. Neither army to erect fortifications or receive any reinforcements of munitions of war except for subsistence. All hostilities to cease within twenty-seven leagues of the City of Mexico. And some other articles.

August 27
BARCLAY. A party of wagoners who were sent into the City today for provisions were most shamefully stoned by the citizens. A wagon master and several of the wagoners were badly injured. This is outrageous.

Santa Anna should have prevented or punished the mob. The wagons were sent in according to the terms of the armistice which has now been wantonly broken by the Mexicans.

COULTER. This evening had a very heavy rain which continued the greater part of the night, completely flooding our camp and making tents very uncomfortable to sleep in.

August 28

BARCLAY. All the companies of the Regt. having moved out of the church yard except our company we have now plenty of room. We prefer this encamping to going into dirty filthy quarters. Today moved our tents to a more comfortable part of the yard. The Mexican officers are generally released on parole.

COULTER. The entire regiment except our company have gone into quarters, leaving us alone and with plenty of room. So to prevent another casualty in case of rain like yesterday evening, moved our camp into the hard beat walk which runs through the middle of the yard and is somewhat raised above the remainder of the ground. So we have our tents pitched and securely ditched for the rain. Heard that a provision train, sent into the city by General Scott, was stoned and some waggoners hurt if not killed. It is said that some Mexican troops were ordered to quell this riot, it being merely a mob of the citizens.

August 29

BARCLAY. Whether because we are about starting home or for some other equally powerful reason, part of Co. E are quite merry today and have managed to become jolly on villanous Mexican aguardiente. The time once was that decent American whisky was on demand on such occasions, but now aguardiente is gladly substituted—bah—"sic transit gloria mundi."

COULTER. Company E was quite lively today; in fact completely broken loose. It was not perhaps a proper day, but aguardiente had completely the ascendency.

August 30

BARCLAY. Orders for inspection tomorrow. I was engaged in making out rolls.

August 31
BARCLAY. Division of volunteers inspected today by Lieut. Lovell,[21] A.A.G. of Major Gen. Quitman and mustered into the service. Orders received to hold ourselves in readiness to march at a moments warning.

COULTER. According to general orders issued some three days ago, today, General Quitman's division was inspected and mustered into the service at this place. This makes eight months in the service of the United States for Company E. Mounted guard today at the main guard house. Orders have been received by commanders of companies to hold themselves in readiness to march at a moment's notice. There appears to be some disturbance in the city.

September 2
BARCLAY. The muster rolls having been prepared and signed by the mustering officer were condemned by Paymaster [Albert G.] Bennett and it is necessary to fill them up again. As all the clothing that the company have heretofore received is included and charged in these rolls the job is heavy. Lieut. Armstrong has not been well lately. McGinley is still sick and lies at the Colonels quarters. Melville is also very unwell. The rest of the company are in good health.

September 3
BARCLAY. The reports heretofore promising gentle peace have given way to rumors of war, and the general impression now is that we will get a sight of the City of Mexico.

September 4
COULTER. Tonight was one of great noise and considerable sport in our camp on account of Geesyn becoming influenced with aguardiente and greatly troubled with ghosts and the devil, who was now disturbing him in consequence of his former sins. He had laid down in the markee when one of the boys drew a stick across his face. Thinking that all were asleep, he was greatly frightened at this, and springing up with a yell, ran down the camp. Here he saw something moving under a tree (it was one of the

---

21. Mansfield Lovell (1822–1884) was born into a military family, the son of the army's surgeon general and, inevitably, entered West Point, graduating just before (1842) the Mexican War, in which he was twice wounded. Leaving the service, he practiced engineering in New York City, where he was deputy street commissioner until the Civil War. Joining the Confederacy as a major general, he was unfortunately assigned to command the defenses of New Orleans, a position that was indefensible with the resources allotted him. After the war he resumed his engineering career, most notably in clearing New York's East River for maritime traffic.

company) and turning, he rushed back to the tent with a scream at every leap. This roused the whole company and all joined in the sport, keeping it up until midnight.

September 5

BARCLAY. W. H. Melville, who was taken a few days ago to the hospital, died this morning. His disease was at first the diarrhea, which changed into the dysentery. Melville had not been well since we left Perote. At Tepeyahualco he was attacked with something like the inflammatory rheumatism from which he suffered very much. His death was much regretted as he was one of the most cheerful and pleasant men in our company. He was buried with due honors on the green in the suburbs of the City.

COULTER. This morning one of Company E, (Wm. H. Melville) died in the hospital at this place and was buried today with the usual honors. The last few days of camp life have been as usual, dull, with nothing to break the monotony except the many reports relative to peace and war. Sometimes we have the treaty signed and the volunteers about to march to Vera Cruz. Next the armistice terminated and bombardment about to commence. Then an unexpected revolution in the city. Once we had the treaty signed and Santa Anna, Scott, Worth and Trist[22] on a spree together. Although we have all these rumors from which any one can be pleased, affairs still remain in uncertainty.

September 7

BARCLAY. Received today from Paymaster Bennett six months pay. Our accounts are now squared up with Uncle Sam until the 31st of August. This pay was very acceptable as most of the men were out of funds. As they are paid in silver the sum makes a considerable bulk. Lieut. Coulter has very kindly received the money not required for immediate use and deposited it in his trunk. He will hereafter act as Paymaster until the deposit is exhausted. Orders to march tomorrow morning. More fighting to do.

---

22. Nicholas Philip Trist (1800–1874) served, in his youth, as private secretary to both Andrew Jackson and Thomas Jefferson, whose granddaughter he married. Fluent in Spanish and conversant with international law, Trist was chosen by Polk to accompany Scott's army as a special agent to negotiate a peace treaty with the Mexicans. The touchy Scott, angered at being superseded by a man he disdainfully regarded as a mere clerk, at first refused to deal with, or even talk to, Trist, but eventually the general and the diplomat became close friends. Suspicious of that friendship and fearful that Trist might prove too lenient to the defeated foe, Polk recalled his envoy and ordered him back to the United States. Disregarding this order, Trist concluded the negotiations for the Treaty of Guadalupe Hidalgo on his own authority. Polk reluctantly accepted the essentials of the treaty but, in a final spiteful gesture, refused to pay Trist for his services.

COULTER. Today we received six months' pay—up to the last of August. This evening marching orders were read to us for tomorrow morning.

September 8

BARCLAY. Early under arms and the Division in line remained for two or three hours formed while the wagons with the stores and sick are getting under way. Marched towards the City. We have the Mexican prisoners in charge. Heard after marching a short distance that Worth had engaged and defeated the enemy. Soon the news arrived that altho we had been victorious our loss was very heavy. Having halted several times we did not arrive until the afternoon at Coyoacan, distant some 8 miles from San Agustin. A short time before entering the town, Lieut. Coulter told me that he had heard that the 11th Regt. were badly cut up and both of us expressed our fears in relation to Lieut. Johnston of that Regt. A few moments after arriving in Coyoacan Capt. Montgomery rode up and told me that poor Dick was no more. It was sometime before I could convince myself of the truth of this afflicting intelligence, that one whom I had seen but a few days before in all strength of vigorous manhood was now sleeping in the dull cold arms of death. But the sad news is too true. Taking advantage of the armistice to collect and reorganize his scattered forces, Santa Anna made the most active preparations for the defence of his Capitol. The military academy of Chapultepec, a commanding military position, was strongly garrisoned. Additional breastworks were thrown up at the different garr[itas], the artillery from Penon was removed and the terms of the armistice were broken in every respect by the perfidious enemy. Knowing that the fortress of Chapultepec would be assaulted and that the northern side of that fortress was most vulnerable, Santa Anna extended a line of defences on that side, the line terminating in the ruins of a hacienda on the right and in a building formerly a mill on the left. These fortifications were strongly defended by a large body of infantry and several pieces of artillery removed from Penon. Ignorant of the heavy force of the enemy on the evening of the 7th Worth with one of Pillow's Brigades was ordered to dislodge the enemy from this position and to destroy a foundry and the ordnance supposed to be there. The attack was intended to have been made at daylight but owing to some delay it was near 8 A.M. when the different columns moved to the assault. After ascending to the plain above Tacubaya the ground offered but little protection to our men. In front of the enemy's line is an open prairie and it was necessary to make the charge over it. The shot and shell from Chapultepec fell with fatal accuracy among the ranks of the assailants who were at the same time exposed to a raking fire from the Mexican troops immediately in front. Once or twice our columns mowed down in front wavered but rallying they again came up most gallantly to the work. The Mexican Lancers watching like vultures at a distance for our retreat came charging down upon the little band but a few rounds from the field artillery scattered them. After the loss of many of the most gallant officers in our army and the fall of near one third of the men engaged, a lodgment was effected and the right flanks of the enemy turned. They immediately gave way, a great number of officers and privates were taken prisoners and a most destructive fire opened upon the retreating masses. Pursuit however was out of the question. The Castle of Chapultepec opened upon the victors and covered the retreat of the vanquished. After blowing up an old foundry Worth marched back to Tacubaya and abandoned the field of battle where so many brave men fell and where nothing was gained except glory. The 11th Regt. of Infantry under command of Lt. Col. [William Montrose] Graham was ordered to the field as a supporting force. The severity of the conflict changed it into an assaulting Regt. Lt. Johnston was in command of his company. From all accounts he behaved in the most cool and intrepid manner. Col. Graham highly complimented him and swore that "he would make Majors of his 2nd Lieuts." But it was ordered otherwise. Neither Col. Graham or his Lieut. survived the conflict. Graham was shot and fell from his horse. Johnston received a severe wound in the thigh. Altho it disabled him he still cheered on his company and while encouraging his men onward a musket ball struck him and passed through the lower part of his abdomen. He fell and soon was speechless and death in a short time released him from all his sufferings. Thus died my earliest, my best friend. Raised together from childhood, a long friendship of the closest intimacy was never interrupted. He was frank and confiding, generous to a fault. He had many friends who were warmly attached to him, and in his own family among his own kindred he was the favorite of all. No event has occurred in Mexico which cast such a gloom over our company as the death of their old comrade. The survivors when they mourn his loss are comforted with the knowledge that he died at his post where duty and honor called him and where if the chance had been allowed him he would himself wished to have died. His soul passed away with the spirits of Scott, Graham, Merrill[23] and a host of brave men who thus sealed with their blood their devotion to our country. He was not doomed to pine, linger and die in an army hospital, but a battle field was the closing scene of his life. Glory, Honor, Duty waved him onwards. His country had entrusted him with a responsible post and he was surrounded by men who were the soul of chivalry. The sharp rattle of musketry and the dread roar of cannons was in his ears, the stars and stripes flashed before his eyes, and

23. Martin Scott, a major in the 5th Infantry, was born in Vermont, served as a lieutenant in the War of 1812, brevetted a lieutenant colonel for gallantry at Monterey, and fell at the battle of Molino del Rey; Moses Emory Merrill of Maine graduated from the U.S. Military Academy in 1826, was appointed captain of the 5th Infantry in 1837, and died at the battle of Molino del Rey.

where he fell the victorious cheers of his comrades told him all was well. The melancholy consolation of being with him during his last moments was denied us. What were his thoughts, what were his feelings none can tell. But while life remained his thoughts doubtless reverted to the scenes of home, of childhood and in the pangs of death the sorrows of surviving friends caused more generous grief in his generous bosom than all the sufferings which he himself endured. O may he in a brighter and better world again meet with those who loved him so tenderly in this. Capt. Montgomery after informing us of all he knew of the death of Richard left. He said that he expected that he would be obliged to move tonight and that Quitman's Division would also likely move tonight. We are quartered in a deserted hacienda. Co. B & E occupy one room and E has a small room to itself. The quarters are inconvenient. The battle fought today is called El Molino del Rey (The King's Mill) and long will it be remembered and mourned by those who cannot forget a departed friend.

COULTER. Marched this morning. Passed through a part of the fortifications of San Antonio. Made a temporary halt at a church yard where we left the prisoners who were brought with us from San Agustin. Some of the regiments were quartered near this, but we marched to the further end of Coyoacan and were quartered in a very large building about eight or nine miles from San Agustin and about half a mile from San Angel where General Twiggs' division now are. Here learned the particulars of a battle fought today at Molino del Rey, which confirmed what many of our men thought, that they had heard reports of artillery this morning before leaving San Agustin. Our loss is estimated at seven hundred and was fought by General Cadwalader's brigade and Worth's division. It is said to have been the bloodiest battle yet fought in the country for the numbers engaged and the loss in officers was unusually severe.[24] Among the killed were Lt. Richard H. L. Johnston of the 11th Infantry, formerly a private in our company. This battle was fought for the purpose of gaining possession of some mills where the enemy were casting cannon. The place was carried and the mills blown up. It was expected we would move on today, but an express brought orders from General Scott to remain. Our quarters are greatly crowded. We have not more than room just to lie down.

24. American losses at Molino del Rey were 124 killed and 582 wounded; the Mexicans lost perhaps 2,000, with 700 prisoners captured. This disparity in numbers cannot conceal the fact that the affair was a blunder by the Americans. The fault was Worth's but the responsibility was Scott's for permitting a battle that should not have been fought for a goal (the capture of a few cannon) that was not worth the effort. On the eve of the final assault on Mexico City, the Mexicans received an unexpected boost to their morale and the small American army lost men it could not replace.

September 9

BARCLAY. Early this morning Lt. Coulter called on Gen. Quitman and obtained permission to go in search of Lt. Johnston's body. We rode to the quarters of the 11th, a hacienda some 3 miles distant. The officers there informed us that after he fell his coat had been taken off and that in consequence thereof his body had not been recognized as an officer, nor had it yet been found. Lt. Tippin[25] accompanied us to Tacubaya. Capt. Montgomery overtook us on the road and went along. We rode to the quarters of the 9th Regt. Montgomery said that when he left the field, Lt. Drum was there and that he might know what had become of the body. When we arrived at the Camp, we learnt that on the night previous the 9th had been ordered to the South of the City and were now several miles distant. We next passed through Tacubaya intending to go to the battle field but upon arriving in sight found that it was in possession of the enemy. Returning to Tacubaya went to the hospital which was filled with the wounded and dead. Several dead officers will be buried today. Lt. Johnston is not among them. After a diligent search throughout the hospital the body cannot be found. At 1 P.M. the funeral of the dead officers took place. Again returned to the hospital in hopes of learning something which will direct us in our search but all is in vain. Returned in the evening disheartened to our Regiment.

COULTER. Mounted guard about noon today. The division are in hourly expectation of marching and in consequence we have our waggons packed which is very inconvenient as we cannot get our cooking utensils. We had a marine sergeant on guard and had some sport playing him the slip. He had no regular relief but called on any one to go on post. So when he called our names we did not answer which put him in quite a sweat.

September 10

BARCLAY. The deserters who were taken at Churubusco have been tried by a court martial. Sixteen were this morning hung by Twiggs at San Angel distant about a quarter of a mile from this.[26] I did not go to the execution. Sixteen who deserted previous to the Declaration of War were whipped and branded with the letter D on the cheek. Each received 49 lashes well laid on by a Mexican mule driver. These Wretches richly merited death. Those that were whipped will be confined during the war. The

25. Andrew Hart Tippin of Pennsylvania, lieutenant in the 11th Infantry during the Mexican War, was colonel of the 68th Pennsylvania Volunteer Infantry during the Civil War.

26. Although the San Patricio deserters had incurred the special wrath of the soldiers of the American army, General Scott insured that they were given a fair trial and invoked numerous legal technicalities to show mercy to those who from youth, prior service, or other reasons might be spared the death penalty. Fifty were sentenced to be hanged and the sentence was executed in batches, with sixteen hanged at San Angel on 9 September, four at Mixcoac the next day, and the remaining thirty on 13 September, during the battle of Chapultepec.

deserters with the exception of one were Irishmen. Had peace been made I do not think any of them would have been executed. The injuries they done us and their crimes would have been overlooked in the general rejoicing at the termination of hostilities. But the blood of our men shed at Molino del Rey still dampens the earth and a treacherous enemy and all their aiders and abettors must now learn that the strict rules of war hereafter will be followed to the letter and that the time has arrived when mercy and tender dealing must give way to sterner measures.

COULTER. This morning was posted upon a large building as a lookout. Had a most magnificent view of the City of Mexico. While on post here saw sixteen of the deserters taken in the late battles, hung near San Angel. Riley, their leader, and a number of others who had deserted before the war was declared were flogged and branded on the cheek with the letter "D." Those that were hung had deserted after the declaration of war. Drew flour rations today and were unable to take them, having to keep our waggon packed to move at a moment's warning. Managed to buy some bread from a baker who was trying to make a speculation off the wants of the men. Had to pay him a dollar, and many two dollars a loaf for his bread and it was only by a walk of two miles and hard crowding that one could get it at that price.

7

The American Army Has Enacted Miracles
The Battle of Chapultepec
and the Capture of Mexico City

On the morning of 11 September, Scott convened his generals and engineers in a council of war. The chief question was whether the City of Mexico should be attacked from its western or southern gates. Scott supported the latter option, but he was opposed by most of his subordinates and the bulk of the engineers, including Captain Robert E. Lee, who favored the southern approach (a view later seconded by Captain Ulysses S. Grant who was not, of course, invited to this meeting). The junior engineer present, Lieutenant P. G. T. Beauregard, who had personally reconnoitered the ground, argued so persuasively for the western approach that some of the generals changed their minds in its favor; General Riley on the grounds that it would entail "less work and more fighting." Scott then stood up to his full height of six feet four and one-half inches and announced: "Gentlemen, we will attack by the Western gates!"[1]

The principal barrier to that route was the hill of Chapultepec, a huge rock towering some 150 to 200 feet above the plain. On the flat summit of that hill stood an old Spanish fortress used as a military academy and, in fact, among the eight hundred or so defenders were over forty teenage cadets. Although their position seemed formidable to the Americans below, the Chapultepec garrison was really undermanned and ill equipped, considering its strategic position commanding two roads leading to the nearby capital city.

The American assault of 13 September came from two directions. The larger force, under command of Pillow, attacked from the west and south, across a swamp and over a Mexican minefield that, fortunately, did not explode. Quitman's somewhat smaller division, to which the Pennsylvanians were attached, attacked simultaneously from the southeast once the signal (a five-minute lull in the artillery bombardment) was given.

In the subsequent fighting it was Pillow's Division which first carried the citadel (though not Pillow himself, since he was again, as at Cerro Gordo, incapacitated by a minor wound). The Pennsylvanians, however,

1. Beauregard, *Mexican War Reminiscences*, 68–72.

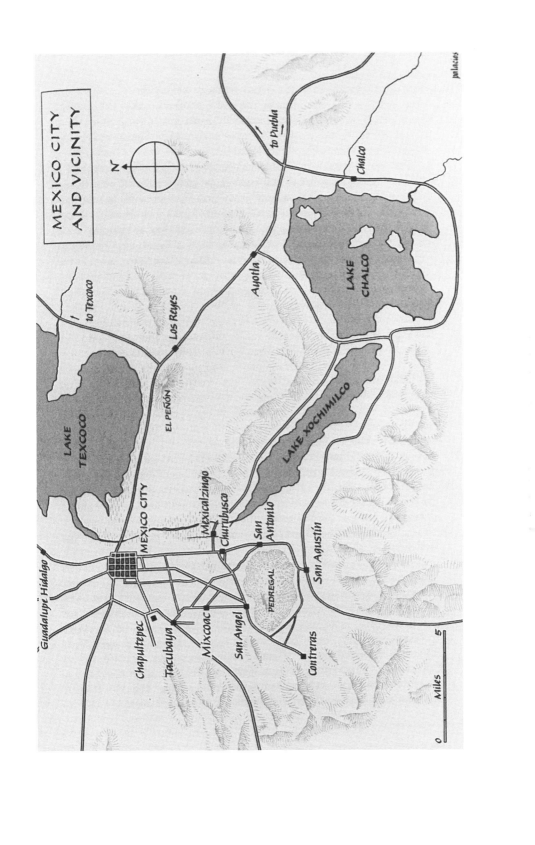

MEXICO CITY AND VICINITY

N

"Guadalupe Hidalgo"

to Texcoco

LAKE TEXCOCO

Los Reyes

EL PEÑÓN

MEXICO CITY

Chapultepec

Tacubaya

Mixcoac

San Angel

PEDREGAL

Mexicalzingo

Churubusco

San Antonio

San Agustín

Contreras

LAKE XOCHIMILCO

Ayotla

LAKE CHALCO

Chalco

to Puebla

0   5
Miles

palacios

approaching from another direction, amid scenes of indescribable confu-
sion, understandably considered their own contribution to the day's suc-
cess to have been more decisive than it actually was.

September 11

BARCLAY. Today we have orders to pack up and be ready to move. The same orders were given yesterday and afterwards when all was ready the orders were countermanded. A storming party from the Regt. was formed today. Each company was ordered to send three men, one or two of whom would be selected. Co. E having met, several volunteered. Hagan Carney, Lebbeus Allshouse and Jacob Kuhn were sent to the Colonel's quarters. Of those three Carney was selected. Altho in the coming fight we all may be exposed to danger, still our comrade Carney runs a greater risk than any of us. This may be our last meeting. Whatever feeling is thus excited in our breasts, it is carefully concealed and we part with him joking and apparently confident of meeting again. The honor of our Company will be safe in his hands and in the darkest hour of battle may the God of Battles shield and protect him. This afternoon several rounds were fired at our reconnoitering parties. About an hour before dark the Division formed moved towards the south of the City. After marching about 2 hours suddenly turned and as it were countermarched on the road running parallel to the one we have been hitherto marching on. About midnight halted with orders to take a nap. Lieut. Coulter lying his head on what he supposed was a stone and smelling something very disagreeable, upon examination discovered that his pillow was a skull. While lying here in a half drowsy state, a singular panic was created by a horse which galloped past on the road. The men imagined that the horse was running over them and some cried that the Lancers were coming. As we were all half asleep the effect was very amusing. The whole regiment were roused and there was the greatest scrambling for arms ever I saw. Edward Hansberry who had been detailed as a guard here met with an unfortunate accident. He was in the advance and when the Division halted the guard were ordered to lay down. The heavy artillery was passing and one of the teams veering somewhat out of the road drew the wagon directly over his feet mashing them very severely. Sergt. McLaughlin with six men were ordered to carry him to the hospital at Tacubaya.

COULTER. Our waggons were packed all day ready for a move. There was a call made for three men (volunteers) from each company from which fifteen men were to be selected as our portion of a storming party to form the advance in the attack upon the enemy's works. Allshouse, Carney and Kuhn volunteered from our company of whom Carney was chosen as one of the party. The Pennsylvania detail is to be commanded by Lt. Hare, of Company F. This evening we were ordered to march. Our blankets were taken out of our knapsacks and carried by the men. The rest of the baggage was packed in the waggons. March about dusk. Our progress was slow, having a large train, and we had several naps on the roadside. All the train, baggage and sick were left at the village of Mixcoac. Company E left sick, Corporal McGinley and Privates Linsenbigler and Shaw. Marchand, who was also unwell and unfit for severe duty, was left here as a waggon guard. We marched some distance further and there lay down to rest until it would get light. While here a horse broke loose from the person having it in charge and galloped among the men, rousing them up and causing considerable disturbance.

September 12

BARCLAY. About daylight arrived at Tacubaya, the headquarters of our army. Here the regiment was divided. An Engineer officer guided Maj. Brindle with Companies E, I, L, M to the left of Tacubaya. After proceeding a short distance we halted and loaded. The garrison of Chapultepec were being waked from their slumbers by the Revellie on a Mexican trumpet. This shrill music reminded us of Vera Cruz and Cerro Gordo and is the harbinger of another fight. After marching about ¾ of a mile to the north[2] of the Castle and in direction of Molino del Rey we were halted in among a pulque field and ordered to conceal ourselves as much as possible. Co. I had been detached from us and the 3 remaining companies are to guard and support Lieut. Hagner's[3] Battery No. 2. At daylight the cannonading commenced. The day was warm and beautiful. Far to our right and towards the gate of San Antonio, Twiggs opened upon the enemy. At sunrise, Drum's and Hagner's Batteries No. 1 and 2 opened a brisk fire upon the Castle. It was sometime before the exact range was obtained, but soon the effect of the fire was visible. Every ball and bomb fell with the greatest accuracy and clouds of dust told where they had taken effect. Nor was the Castle idle in the meantime. They replied shot for shot but their fire done but little execution. Several shots fell among and flew past the pulque stocks where we lay concealed. Our position was dangerous as we lay directly in the rear of Hagner's Battery and were consequently in point blank range of every ball fired at this battery. It being necessary to do some work there, about one half of our Company were detailed, who worked near 2 hours. The fire between the skirmishing parties of both armies has been very briskly kept up all day. Our skirmishes are advanced very close

2. Barclay's position was actually somewhat to the southeast of the castle rather than to the north, but he was in no position to consult a compass at the time.

3. Peter Valentine Hagner would be brevetted to the rank of major for his work that day at Chapultepec. Continuing in the army until 1881, he served in the Ordnance Department, commanding the Watervliet Arsenal during the Civil War. He was rewarded before his retirement with a brevet as brigadier general and died in March of 1893.

to the fortress. We suffer today for want of provisions. The cannonading continues all day. At night a heavy guard is posted. The night is cold.

COULTER. While still resting on the roadside before day this morning, one of the teams attached to a heavy piece of siege artillery, became frightened and ran among the men, dragging the waggon and gun after them. One of our company (E. Hansberry) who had been one of the advance guard of the division, and at this time sleeping near was run over by the waggon, smashing one foot and injuring the other leg. Several others escaped the same by being dragged away by their comrades. Sergeant McLaughlin with Carson, Gordon, McClelland, James McWilliams, Haines and Sargent, was sent to carry Hansberry to the nearest hospital. Just before daybreak we entered the village of Tacubaya. Here four companies (E.G.L. & M.) were detached under Major Brindle, for extra Duty. We took a cross road and went up a hill, passed a large building with the Spanish colors flying over it and a sentinel on the roof at the time. It being too dark to tell exactly what the flag was, we thought we were on the point of storming the enemy's works. We marched about midway between Tacubaya and Molina del Rey and took our position on a hill among some aloes immediately in the rear of Lt. Hagner's battery for the purpose of protecting it. As soon as it was perfectly day the battery opened, but being poorly constructed, without platforms, they could not damage the enemy's work, it being the Castle of Chapultepec upon which we were operating. A detail was sent from our force to repair the battery. We carried timber from a neighboring ranch and made a platform upon which the guns might rest. This battery is composed of two pieces, a long twenty-four pound siege gun and a ten inch howitzer. After this they were able to get the range and did most terrible execution, every round shot boring through the building and our shells bursting immediately over their guns. The Castle was considerably elevated above our battery and they could not range their guns upon it, but many of their shot and shell passed over and raked through the plants in which we were concealed, and strange to say, not a man of our party and only two at the battery were wounded during the entire day. Lt. Hagner made some brag shots during this day's bombardment. During the day a mortar was planted over at Molino del Rey which did great execution, throwing every shell into the very center of the works. We have also a fine view of the operations of another battery under Captain Drum of the 4th Artillery, planted just at the end of the village of Tacubaya. He made some most magnificent shots upon his side of the works and dismounted several of the enemy's guns. Captain Drum's battery also mounted two guns, a long twenty-four and a howitzer. We remained here all day and slept on our arms at night. It was extremely cold and our blankets saturated with dew.

September 13

BARCLAY. Monday. At daylight Drum and Hagner open again upon the Castle. The firing on the extreme right was also renewed. The companies under command of Maj. Brindle marched to Tacubaya where all the regiment was assembled with the exception of Co. I which remained on guard at a Battery. The men who had been detailed to assist Hansberry, not being able to find the company yesterday, rejoined us this morning. Company E, that is the valley men, were again together with the exception of Hansberry, McGinley, Linsenbigler and Shaw who were in hospital, Haines who was left to attend on Hansberry and Marchand who being unwell when we marched from Coyoacan was detailed to remain with the wagons. While Gen. Quitman's Division was forming the firing between the Batteries and the Castle was kept up with great spirit. The Castle of Chapultepec is built upon a knob or mound which rises high and abrupt from the plain. The Castle is approached by a road which winds around the mound. On all sides the hill is steep and in many places inaccessible. The main building intended for an Academy is converted into a regular fortress which formidable by its position is rendered still more so by the defences and outworks which surround it. Pillow's Division advanced on the side toward Molino del Rey while at the same time Quitman's column charged on the S.W. side toward Tacubaya. On the left of the Castle and in the main road the enemy had erected a battery which besides sweeping the road itself also could be turned upon any forces advancing toward the Castle from Tacubaya. All being ready Maj. Twiggs of the Marines[4] in command of the storming party moved toward the battery on the road. Pillow's skirmishers became busily engaged on our left and our Division moved in file along the road. The road here was low and concealed by pulque bushes. The New York and South Carolina Regts. were ahead of us. After marching slowly for about a half a mile in this manner the head of the column wheeled to the left and the order to charge was given. We were now in full view of the Castle and exposed to their fire, besides being in a convenient range of the cannon and musketry of the battery on the road. When our company came to the turning point the ground about us was covered with the wounded and dead. Quitman and Shields protected by a old ranch were there cheering and encouraging the men on. Major Brindle stood in the field waving his sword and doing all a man could to cheer us forward. The sight was not very encouraging but we rushed

---

4. A brother of General David Twiggs, Major Levi Twiggs was one of the handful of marines (less than three hundred in all) attached to Scott's army whose presence would give validity to their boast of having served at "the Halls of Montezuma." Unfortunately for the corps' proud tradition, one unsentimental historian has concluded that "except [for] thirty to fifty under Captain Terrett the Marines did not distinguish themselves" at Chapultepec. (Smith, *War With Mexico*, 2:410.)

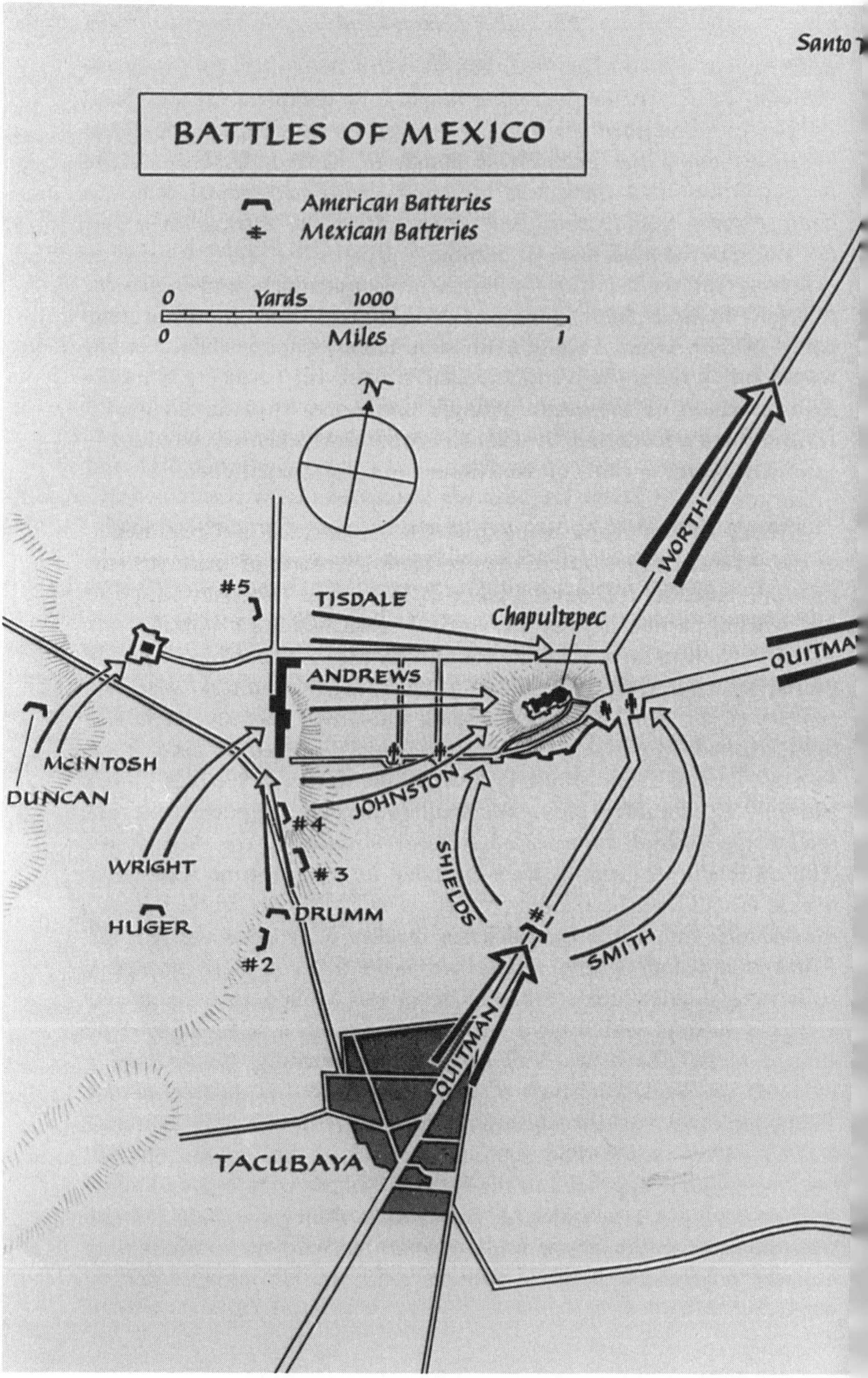

BATTLES OF MEXICO

⌐ American Batteries
✦ Mexican Batteries

0   Yards   1000
0   Miles   1

N

#5

TISDALE

Chapultepec

WORTH

QUITMAN

ANDREWS

McINTOSH

DUNCAN

JOHNSTON

#4

SHIELDS

WRIGHT

#3

SMITH

HUGER

DRUMM

#1

#2

QUITMAN

TACUBAYA

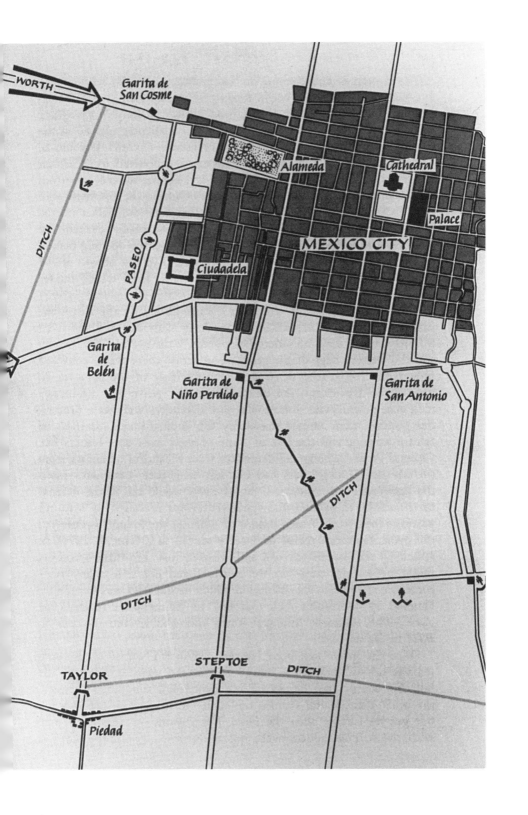

WORTH

Garita de
San Cosme

Alameda

Cathedral

Palace

MEXICO CITY

DITCH

PASEO

Ciudadela

Garita
de
Belén

Garita de
Niño Perdido

Garita de
San Antonio

DITCH

DITCH

DITCH

TAYLOR

STEPTOE

DITCH

Piedad

forward. A wall at the base of the mound upon which the Castle is erected was distant about 300 yards. For near 50 yards we ran through a corn field and then entered a meadow of high tangled grass. Through the meadow and cornfield run 7 or 8 ditches parallel with the wall and one or two at right angles with it. The most of these ditches were from 10 to 12 feet wide. One or two we managed to leap, but being weighed down with our arms and exhausted with running we waded through the majority of them. The water was waist deep and mud to the depth of one or two feet in the bottom. It was very difficult to get thro those ditches. What rendered our charge less rapid was the tall grass. A narrow and not a direct path led from the road at the point where we wheeled to the wall. How this path came there I do not know. Thinking to get along faster I once jumped into the grass but soon discovered my mistake and returned to the path. By this time companies and regiments were mixed up, the strong and active having the advantage over the weak. All things must have an end and so had this somewhat amusing race. We finally reached the wall and a more completely exhausted and used up set of fellows never before were seen. We lay here about 10 minutes.

COULTER. This morning about daylight I was sent out on picket. In an hour or so after the pickets were called in and we returned to Tacubaya. One of the companies (G) with us were down in some old ranches and did not get the word to move and in consequence did not reach Tacubaya in time for the charge. The remainder of our regiment were here, having been all day yesterday covering Captain Drum's battery. Here we were joined by Sargeant McLaughlin and his squad who had been sent yesterday morning to carry Hansberry to the hospital. When they had performed that duty the company was gone (they knew not where) and they found the remainder of Captain Drum's battery. Haines was detailed to remain with Hansberry and in consequence was not in the charge. Our division was shortly after formed in line of battle. We advanced along the Tacubaya road for a distance of more than a quarter of a mile. As soon as we left the village the enemy opened a considerable fire and we had several men killed on this road. We next turned off the road at an old ranch near which was Generals Quitman and Shields, cheering the men on, and entered what had been a cornfield. At this point the fire was most terrific and here was our principal loss. From this spot we entered a large meadow intersected with some eight or nine ditches about six or eight feet wide and waist deep with mud and water. Here many of the Yorkers ditched it to avoid the fire, and a few steps from where we left the cornfield I saw Colonel Geary in a ditch dodging grape shot most faithfully. Farther on, as I was getting out of a ditch, I saw Lt. Armstrong fall heavily against the bank with a groan. At the time I thought he was killed, but in jumping the ditch he had fallen short and struck with his breast on the bank, injuring himself considerable. The Castle of Chapultepec is situate on a rocky knob which rises abruptly from the plain. Around the base of this knob was a wall which we wished to gain. Although our regiment were the left of the division and the last to enter the fire, we were the first found under this wall. On the road about a quarter of a mile above, where we turned off, was a battery. At the same time that we entered the meadow, the storming party charged this battery so as to gain a position beyond and cut off the retreat of the enemy. It was from the fire of this road battery and the infantry along the breastwork at the foot of the hill that we sustained our greatest loss. The fire from the castle itself was inconsiderable. In crossing this bottom our company lost three men wounded: A. G. Bates, severely, shot through both thighs; C. F. Sargent, severely, shot through left thigh and slightly in left wrist; G. Decker, slightly, struck in the eye by a spent ball, the force of which was stopped by the rim of his wool hat. While under this wall we were joined by Colonel Geary, who came up limping. He said he was not wounded, but had only sprained his leg.

BARCLAY. [*Continued*] Having recovered our breaths, the regiment filed to the left along the wall, passed thro a breach which had been made in it by cannon and rushed toward the hill or mound. In this flat at the base of the hill are many cypress trees and behind each of those trees were as many of the New York Regt. as could crowd. The fight was now going on bravely. On the right the storming party under Twiggs were engaged with the battery on the road and on the left Pillow was driving in the enemy from their out works. Passing the New Yorkers who Lieut. Lovell A.D.C. of Quitman was cursing and beating with his sword, that part of the 2nd Pa. Regt. which had kept together formed at the base of the hill, Maj. Brindle being in command. Lt. Coulter was now in command of our Company. In passing thro the meadow Lt. Armstrong had made the same mistake as myself. Thinking to gain the wall sooner by running thro the grass he lost ground and stuck in a ditch from which as there was no one near him to lend assistance he extricated himself after great difficulty. The regiment being formed there was some conflicting orders. Maj. Brindle ordered us to move to the right, thinking to enter the Castle by the main road. At the same time an A.D.C. ordered us to ascend the hill by the left. Lt. Coulter took the responsibility of disobeying both. He wheeled our company and we rushed directly up the hill which was here very steep. Capt. [John] Humphreys [Company B, 2d Pennsylvania Infantry] followed us. By this means Company E was the first company of the Volunteer Division in the Castle. Indeed they were the first full company in either of the Divisions in, for altho Pillow's men had driven in the outposts there were but few of the men into the main building and they were without any company organization. Our company kept well together. L. Allshouse was the first man of the Company which entered and he was closely followed by the rest. H. Keslar assisted in hoisting the first flag which went up.[5] The battle was now over. Chapultepec was won. The scene was now grand. From the top of the walls could be seen the Mexican army in full retreat and endeavoring to gain the City by the two causeways which form a junction at Chapultepec. They retreated in confusion and without attempting to check the pursuers. The fun was now on our side. No longer under cover the enemy presented a fine mark. The rifles and the 3rd Infy joined in the pursuit along the De Belen causeway. A mountain howitzer was brot to bear and done some execution. And a great many were shot from the walls of the Castle. Had there been Dragoons the enemy's loss would have been much greater. As it was a great number were killed, wounded and taken prisoner. Among the latter is Gen. Bravo,[6] a General of Division and one of the great men of Mexico. The Castle now presented a singular appearance. Besides storming parties organized from Worth and Twiggs Divisions, Pillows Division and Quitmans were all jammed pell mell together. Some were firing upon the enemy retreating across the fields. Others watching the chase. Some bread and a barrel of aguardiente attracted the attention of others. The building and library were also ransacked. Indeed the charge at Chapultepec was a real militia charge and the same may be said of most of the battles in Mexico. The tactics of the service may be useful in fighting against the soldiers of Europe but they cannot be applied in this country. As at Chapultepec every one fights on his own hook. While such general confusion was prevailing among the troops in the Castle, Gen. Cadwalader appeared upon a balcony and made a very appropriate little speech. He exhorted the men immediately to join the colors. He called upon the Company and Field Officers to organize their commands and not delay in pressing upon the enemy, that all had witnessed the fatal consequences of a delay after a previous battle, etc. These few remarks were plain and every man was struck with the propriety of them. Order was established and all hastened to rejoin their respective Regiments.

COULTER. [*Continued*] The division then filed around the wall and entered the enclosure near the west end of the works. Here again a number of Yorkers, both officers and men, treed behind the large trees that were here.

5. This was the death warrant for the remaining thirty condemned San Patricio deserters. They were kept standing at the gallows, with a noose around their necks, for two hours under the blazing sun waiting for this moment. When the flag indicating the capture of Chapultepec was raised, the trap was sprung, so that the deserters' last sight would be the victorious Stars and Stripes.

6. A legendary partisan leader in the Mexican war for independence, Nicholás Bravo (1776–1854) was the first vice-president of the Mexican Republic and the last survivor of the original revolutionary leaders, most of the rest having devoured each other. During the storming of Chapultepec, he was in charge of the Mexican garrison.

Wading through a muddy ditch, we were under protection of the rocks and bluffs. Here Major Brindle (Colonel Geary had remained at the wall, being too cowardly to advance) attempted to form the regiment in line and there were a number of conflicting orders given. Major Brindle ordered the men to form in line. An aide was directing the left companies around the hill at the same time. General Cadwalader appearing on the top of the hill, ordered the men directly up over the bluffs. Lt. Coulter, on seeing Cadwalader, called on the company to follow and marched directly up the hill, followed by Company B, Captain Humphreys'. By this means, Company E was first company of the regiment, and in fact of the division, into the castle. Allshouse was the first of our company across the gateway. When we entered there were between fifty and a hundred of General Pillow's men in the works, and the enemy still made a show of resistance, although the majority had retreated down towards the city. In the meantime General Smith and brigade had followed the storming party and was in position to cut off at least part of the retreat. The grove at the base of the hill was full of hombres, and for the first time we had the pleasure of returning the peppering they had given us both here and at Cerro Gordo. After we had entered the lower wall, there was but one of our company hurt, Sergeant Mechling, slightly wounded in the knee by a spent ball. One of our company, Keslar, assisted in raising the first flag that waved over the castle proper. The volunteers colors were first on the outworks. After we had been here a short time were rejoined by Lt. Armstrong, who had recovered from his fall. For Lt. Coulter, I must say that he behaved most gallantly and deserves a more particular mention than he gets in the reports. Some of the boys got considerable plunder in the shape of bread and whisky in the castle. After the works were entered but little quarter was shown. General Bravo and some officers were taken prisoners, but few others were taken alive. The regiment then moved down the hill and formed as soon as collected on the road leading to the city. Here we were rejoined by Carney who had been in the storming party. While here, General Scott rode up and addressed a few words of soft solder (about wives, sweethearts, etc.) to the Pennsylvanians, us he said in particular. It would have done very well had he not afterward addressed the same to the other volunteers successively. Here also our most gallant colonel joined us. I know not why it is, but in the reports of this fight both the New York and South Carolina Regiments get great praise, and the Pennsylvania Regiment is barely mentioned, although they were first at the lower wall and first of the division into the castle proper. The blame must rest somehow with our field officers, one of whom at least did act most cowardly, and afterward in his report falsely asserted that he "resumed the command of his regiment at the summit of the hill" and who also says "he was wounded in the groin" although at the time he said that he was "not wounded" but only had his "leg sprained." The following is the roll of

Company E as engaged in this charge: Lieutenants Armstrong and Coulter; Sergeants Barclay, McLaughlin, Mechling and Byerly; Corporals Bigelow and Bonnin; Fifer Kettering; Privates Allshouse, Bates, Bills, Brady, Carson, Cloud, Coulter, Decker, Fishel, Geesyn, Gordon, Hartman, Hays, Hoffer, Kegarize, Keslar, Kuhn, Kuhns D., McCabe, McClelland, McClain, McWilliams J., McWilliams W., Moorhead, Milner, Sargent, Steck, and Uncapher, and also Carney in the storming party. After returning to the road Sergeant Byerly and Kettering and Brady were sent to carry off the wounded to the hospital.

BARCLAY. [*Continued*] While Worth followed the retreating foe along the Cosme Causeway, Quitman's Division moved along the De Belen Causeway. Previous to leaving the fortress Lt. Armstrong rejoined us. His sword had been shot from his hand and he was wet to the chin. We were all rejoiced to see him as we had feared he was either killed or wounded. We had also the pleasure of meeting Capt. Montgomery and Maj. McMiken[7] in the Castle, two Pennsylvanians who were among the first that entered Chapultepec. While marching from the Castle Gen. Scott rode up. The cheering was tremendous. The old fellow looked the very personification of happiness. Hagan Carney again rejoined us. The gallant stormers had suffered severely. Much to our joy he was permitted to rejoin us. The regiment halted and the roll call called it was discovered that Sargent and Bates were missing. As they had been wounded a party was sent out to hunt them up and convey them to the hospital. It was here that Lt. Col. Jno. W. Geary rejoined the regiment. He was in command when the regiment left Tacubaya, but was not in command when the regiment was formed to make as was supposed the last desperate charge. At that very important and critical moment the Colonel was safe and snug behind the wall where we had halted. He accounts for his remaining there by a sprain, wound or contusion which he received while crossing one of the ditches. It will always remain on record as a remarkable instance of activity and physical energy that the gallant colonel managed to reach the wall as soon as he did considering the impediments offered by the ditches (the Colonel actually reaching a place of safety in advance of some our Company) and it will always be regretted that the same energy did not carry him at the head of his regiment into the fortress of Chapultepec. Gen. Scott now had two routes to enter the Capitol. After the termination of the armistice, the outer line of Mexican defences having been broken through, they fell back upon another line equally as strong and much nearer the

7. Not a member of the army, McMiken was, in Geary's words, "a gentleman from my own State, accompanying the army, who by his appeals to the State and National pride of the men, contributed much to the enthusiasm of the regiment" (*Pennsylvania Argus*, 24 December 1847).

City. For the purpose of their dividing their forces and concealing his real intention, Scott made a feint attack with Twiggs' Division upon the gate of San Antonio. A great many troops had been marched and counter-marched towards that point. A heavy cannonading for three or four days had been there kept up and everything indicated that [on] that road we intended to make the grand attack. But this was open, commanded by the heavy artillery of the enemy and no cover of any kind was there to protect a storming party. The highways which lead from Chapultepec to the City are broad and level. On each side is a waist. Along the midst of the highways runs the two celebrated aqueducts which supply the City with water and whose broad arches afforded protection to the advancing columns of our army. Along the Cosme road Worth moved and as this road was considered less strongly defended than the De Belen road by it the City is to be entered. Gen. Quitman's Division with the Rifles and a portion of Twiggs' are received by a heavy fire from a Battery on the road. This however is quickly carried, the pursuers from the Castle entering it with the fugitives. The second battery of the enemy on this road is about 2 miles from the Castle and is at the gates of the City. The fire from this battery is very heavy. The Artillery on Battery No. 1 is turned upon the enemy and we approach the Garita slowly but gradually by taking advantage of the arches. The fire from the enemy is incessant. The trees along the causeway are shorn of their limbs and balls of all sizes fly like hail past us. The road is deserted, save here [and] there a straggler may be seen. Small parties carrying back the wounded or aid-de-camps conveying orders. A great many of our men are killed or wounded by this incessant fire. Capt. Caldwell is badly wounded in the foot and carried off. The fight on the left continues and a constant roar of cannon and musketry announce that Worth is warmly engaged. However the advance are nearing the Garita. The different regts. are mixed up. Under the same arch is seen men from all the different regts. About 1 P.M. the rush is made and the Garita Battery carried. The enemy now fell back to the Citadel a very strong building built on the verge of the City, and kept up a terrible fire. The guns at the Garita were turned upon the Citadel and a heavy fire was opened. Genls. Quitman and Smith both were present and behaved with the greatest coolness. When we entered the Garita Gen. Quitman taking a drink of water invited some of his friends to take a drink saying that we were now in the City. Three cheers were given for Gen. Quitman, three for the S. Carolina and three for the Pennsylvania Regts. From 1 o'clock until dark the fire from the citadel swept the road on both sides of the aquaduct. Capt. Drum turned a six pounder of the enemy upon the Citadel. His company have been all killed or wounded except 5 or 6. The piece was in the middle of the road and much exposed. The Capt. behaved with as much calmness as if he had been on a dress parade. After firing all the round shot he informed Gen. Quitman of the fact. Quitman ordered him to load the piece with grape and advance it and in case the enemy should make a charge he might fire upon them. This was accordingly done about an hour afterwards. The enemy made a feint of charging, Drum opened upon them with grape, the Citadel replied and a round shot struck Capt. Drum taking off one foot and breaking the leg immediately above the other. This took place directly beside us. At one time having occasion to move his piece he called upon his "Westmoreland friends" to give him a lift. They done so. He was carried back to Chapultepec (Uncapher and Geesyn assisting). Gen. Scott met the party and expressed his sorrow at the loss of one who he said was among his most able officers. The Capt. was from pain and loss of blood insensible. He imagined that the battle was still raging and that he was at his piece. He died a few hours after he reached the Castle. Thus fell in the prime of life and vigor of intellect one of the most _____ officers of the line. As he on all occasions showed his kindness to our company we regret his loss. He was a most amicable man and a good Christian.

COULTER. [*Continued*] Shortly after we were supplied with more cartridges and our division took up the march towards the city. The retreat had been closely pursued and many of the enemy had been killed on the causeway in attempting to escape through the ditches and swamps on either side. The road on which we now were was an artificial causeway built through a watery ground. Along the center of this road was a large aquaduct which supplied the city with water, the arches of which were the main protection to our men in this advance. There were several batteries commanding this road, the first of which was entered with the retreat. At the second, which was at the city gate, about two miles from the castle, they made a stand and opened a heavy fire upon our advance. This cannonade was returned from the first battery with the guns and ammunition taken there. During this time our division lay in the arches of the aquaduct ready to support our artillerymen. The cannonade continued some time during which time the shot and shell came whistling the whole length of the aquaduct. One shell lit immediately in front of our company, but entirely buried itself in the mud and when it exploded only covered us with dirt, without doing any further damage. It was here that Captain Caldwell of Company [M] received the wound of which he afterwards died. He very probably exposed himself and was struck in the foot by a piece of a bomb. At length the riflemen, by means of the aquaduct, had gotten near the enemy's battery, and were ordered to charge, and supported by our division, carried it. This was at the gate of the city and thus was the City of Mexico first entered by the volunteers' division at twenty minutes past one o'clock P.M. on the 13th of September, 1847. The fight was not yet over however. About three hundred yards in our advance was a large building called the citadel, which had a battery and extensive breastwork. Here the enemy again made a stand. We also received an occasional cross fire from the San Cosme and San Antonio batteries. Shortly after taking position here Captain Drum came up and opened a fire on them with one of their guns supplied with captured ammunition. Captain Drum behaved most gallantly and raked the entire road and street with his piece. No place of shelter could be found here. The cross fire from the other gates passed through the arches and the battery and infantry at the citadel fired at an angle, the shot striking one side and glancing through the arches. Many of our men were killed by these glancing shots. An old building behind which we had also taken shelter, was bored entirely through by enemy cannon shot. They also used what are called wall or parapet guns. Captain Drum soon expended his round shot and was unable to use grape and canister for fear of killing some of our own men along the arches. So he ran his gun down the road to meet the enemy in case they would attempt to charge, but unfortunately exposed himself to the cross fire and was mortally wounded, both legs being taken almost off by a round shot. The loss of men at this time was severe. The riflemen did considerable execution picking men off their breastworks, but we were unable to do anything with our muskets and were compelled to bear the fire during this whole day. During the day there occurred an incident which I understand has in the report been unjustly credited to the New York Regiment. When Captain Drum first came up he had no men with him and no assistance to plant his gun. Our company were all at the gate at the time, and the Captain seeing us, called on his Westmoreland friends to assist him. The company immediately manned the drag ropes and soon placed the gun in battery. But we unluckily all wore the dark blue jackets (the particular uniform of the New York Regiment) and were mistaken for Yorkers. (God forbid.) At dark, the firing ceased on both sides and we marched to one side of the gate in an open piece of ground (being exposed it would not be occupied during the day) to rest for the night.

BARCLAY. [*Continued*] About dark a cheer from Worth's men announced that on that quarter all is well. This night is very cold. A bleak wind whistles over the lakes which appears to sigh at the approaching downfall of the proud City. Our haversacks are in vain examined. Not the slightest article in the shape of food rewards the research. Hungry and cold, our clothing wet from the waistbands down from crossing the ditches, we throw ourselves upon the margin of the marsh without blankets. The party who were sent back for the wounded had orders to bring our blankets from Tacubaya. They have not done so. It is in vain to try to sleep notwithstanding the fatigues of the past few days. We lie shivering, the cold benumbing every limb. About 3 A.M. we are roused to work. This is a glad summons. During the night working parties have been busy, heavy cannon have been brought up and batteries of sand bags erected. Two 24's are mounted already. We work until daylight in digging ditches, carrying sand bags, etc.

COULTER. [*Continued*] Before charging the castle in the morning we had left our blankets at Tacubaya and now we severely felt the want of them. The ground was wet and swampy and the night extremely cold; in fact I believe it was the coldest night I have experienced in Mexico. Three or four of us lay down together and tried to spoon it to keep warm. Every five minutes we had to change the spoon so as to warm the upper side. Being on the outside, it was exceedingly cold, so I went to another party, forced myself between them and had a short nap tolerably comfortable. Our company were unusually fortunate today. Our loss at the gate was two wounded, McClelland, severely in the foot by a musket ball and Fishel, slightly, struck at the same time by several spent balls on thigh and breast. The following is the roll of Company E at the Garita De Belen today: Lieutenants Armstrong and Coulter; Sergeants Barclay and McLaughlin; Corporals Bigelow and Bonnin; Privates Allshouse, Bills, Carney, Carson, Coulter, Decker, Fishel, Gordon, Hartman, Hays, Hoffer, Kegarize, Keslar, Kuhn, McCabe, McClelland, McClain, James McWilliams, Milner, Steck and Uncapher. Corporal Bonnin returned to Tacubaya at night. Geesyn, D. Kuhns and Cloud started and lingered in the road and never came to the gate. Moorhead and W. McWilliams for some reason, remained at Tacubaya, and the party sent to carry off the wounded never returned. As soon as night concealed the operations, a battery and breast works were commenced. After midnight our regiment was called on to relieve those at the work. One thing that speaks badly for some of our officers was that when the regiment was called on for this purpose Captain Naylor, of Company F, was the senior officer present and took command of the party. Colonel Geary, Major Brindle, Captain Loeser and Captain Murray all fit for duty senior officers were not there. A portion of the men placed several guns in battery, while the remainder filled and carried sand bags and built a breast work principally for infantry. I think there has been considerable injustice done to the Second Pennsylvania Regiment in the report of this night's operations. In General Quitman's report the New York Regiment receive the principal, and in fact the only one's who receive any credit for building this battery and breastwork and placing the guns in position. General Quitman is, I think, not to be blamed for this, as many of our regiment wearing the dark blue uniforms could be easily mistaken for New York men. But for my part, although I was on this work half the night, I did not see any but Pennsylvanians engaged on it. The conduct of Generals Quitman and Shields on this day is worthy of note. General Shields was wounded near the castle and not able to participate at the gate. General Quitman was as cool as any one could have been quietly sitting in a drawing room. He walked almost regardless of the danger he ran, seeing all the operations and directing the men. He appeared more like a father to his men than a commander, telling all in a kindly tone to obey his orders and he would take care of them. He did not leave the gate at any time during the day or night, except to approach and examine the enemy's works. But Lt. Colonel Geary did behave most contemptibly again at the gate. When we marched into the gate he did come up, but soon made excuse to fall back and did not again make his appearance that far up, but remained some distance down under the arch, carefully keeping himself out of harm's way, and at night when we were called up to work on the battery, although repeatedly called and inquired for, did not make his appearance. To him and him alone must be attributed the cause of why the Second Pennsylvania Regiment is not more particularly mentioned in the reports of this day's operations. His name is mentioned, but as slightly as possible and the regiment are only mentioned as just being there, but all that might have been done by them is attributed to other regiments. General Quitman is a soldier and an honorable man and cannot be accused of partiality. Jno. Geary has made such a contemptible report and his conduct was so evidently not that of a soldier, that the General must have been completely disgusted with him. Our two lieutenants were both at the gate during the whole time and Lt. Coulter was on guard during the night. The South Carolina and New York Regiments, although neither of them as large as ours, each lost more men than the Second Pennsylvania. This, by some who were not present, is looked upon as rather discreditable to our regiment. But we were in every post of danger that they were, and the only way it can be accounted for is, at the castle, we being the left of the division, were the last to enter the fire and were then first under the wall, thereby being not more than half the time under fire that the others were. At the gate, our regiment were there from the time the place was carried until we marched into the city, but the men during the day not being able to do any execution, sheltered themselves as much as possible. While at the gate our company had only one man severely wounded, although several were struck by spent balls, while in the other regiments the loss was much greater. At one time seven men belonging to the same company of the South Carolina Regiment, were killed by a single shot. There were several other cases of this kind. Yet during the whole day our regiment had only seven men killed. While our division were engaged at this gate the remainder of the enemy were operating at the others. General Twiggs, with his division and Steptoe's[8] light battery made a feint attack on the

8. Edward Jenner Steptoe of Virginia graduated from the U.S. Military Academy in 1837. For his performance at Chapultepec he was brevetted lieutenant colonel. In the early months of the Civil War he was appointed lieutenant colonel of the 10th Infantry, a position he resigned after holding for only a few weeks. He died in April of 1865.

gate of San Antonio Abad. General Worth, supported by General Pillow, made an attack on the San Cosme gate and entered the city about midnight.

September 14[9]

BARCLAY. As daylight breaks a good many anxious eyes are turned toward the Citadel from which every moment we expect to see issuing a fire of cannon. Daylight has been fairly broken and a white flag is seen coming from the City. During the night Santa Anna and his army fled and a Deputation from the City authorities announced that Mexico had surrendered. The Division was immediately formed and marched toward the City. In passing by our work of last night and seeing our 24's in such a good position to batter the City it was with a feeling of regret that the opportunity had not been allowed us. Notwithstanding the general satisfaction that the fighting was over, it still would have been very pleasant to have given the greasers a few round from our heavy artillery. As we moved on we saw many of our men lying in the arches in the cold embrace of Death. It was a sad sight. When about entering the City one of our men was lying stript naked, his heart cut out. Even this sight did not shock us, to such a degree do men become hardened in war. The 2nd Penna. Regt. halted at the Citadel a large building covering near 10 acres of ground. The enemy's cannon here are spiked and the building rifled of everything that the Mexican soldiers could carry away. There still remains an immense number of different kinds of arms in the ordnance dept. and ammunition. Our quarters are comfortable. We now look round to see the casualties of the last three days. Hansberry run over by the cannon wagon is still in hospital. Bates and Sargent wounded at Chapultepec and McClelland wounded at the Garita are also there. Bates received a musket ball thro the upper part of the thigh. Unmindful of the pain he hurried on through the field with the company. Another ball struck him through the other thigh near the same place and inflicted a much deeper wound. He was obliged to halt. Sargent was struck by a musket ball in the wrist and almost immediately afterwards by a piece of a cannister ring in the hip. McClelland was wounded very severely in the foot while near an arch by a musket ball. A spent ball at Chapultepec struck Sergt. Mechling near the knee. It made no wound. He was lamed and did not come up to the Garita. A spent ball struck Decker near the eye and blackened it for him. Keslar and Fishel received glances of balls in the legs, Bonnin one through his canteen and haversack, Coulter one thro his hat. There were two or three other members of the company who were shot through the clothing. We should all be very thankful to a kind Providence who has preserved our lives and when we sympathize and sorrow for our wounded comrades

---

9. In the excitement of the capture of Mexico City, Barclay ran two days' activities together and neglected to differentiate the entry for 14 September from that of the previous day.

we are consoled by the thoughts that their wounds are not dangerous and that they soon will be restored to their wonted usefulness. The 2nd Penna. Regt. lost some 9 men killed and near a hundred wounded. They behaved well and all felt that if any dark spot has heretofore rested upon the reputation of the Regt. it is now wiped away. When leaving the Castle Gen. Pillow inquired what troops are these? pointing to our Regt. "Sir," said Sergt. [Absolem] Guiler of Co. H, "this is the 2nd Pa. Regt., the men who you said waved at Cerro Gordo." Pillow answered that he always had the highest respect for the Pennsylvanians and after some delay "I think you have a damn sight of impudence for a sergeant."

COULTER. Continued working until after daylight. As it approached day it was expected they would re-open the fire and at every shovelfull that was thrown on the breastwork we took a glance at the enemy's works, expecting every minute to receive a fire. However it became a perfect day and no signs of them recommencing the fight and the works appeared deserted. It was not for us to open first, as we wanted the delay to finish our battery. After the work was nearly finished we were about to open fire with a long twenty-four, when it was stopped by a flag of truce coming down from the city. They unconditionally surrendered the city and stated that the enemy had retreated. The division was formed, marched in and took possession of the citadel. It was completely deserted. This is a very large building surrounded by a wall and ditch, the whole covering about ten acres. There were a number of pieces of artillery standing about, but all unfit for use, having been spiked by the enemy before leaving. Inside was a complete workshop and armory; cannon and small arms in large quantities in every stage of manufacture; ammunition in every state, loose and prepared for use; in fact there were all army stores in immense quanities, clothing, etc. There were a few mouldy crackers which we pounced down upon, being rather hungry. Our regiment was left to hold this work and the remainder of the division marched to the Grand Plaza, where they were afterward joined by General Worth's division. Today the Stars and Stripes were placed on the National Palace of Mexico. Although our men had possession of the Plaza, the enemy had not all left the city, and with the rabble and lepers of this city, still kept up the fight. Steptoe's battery was placed at four streets leading from the Plaza and raked them full length whenever they made any resistance. Mounted guard this afternoon. The fire was kept up all day and during the night. In some cases they approached very near our quarters and fired at the men. Some of our regiment went out to skirmish with them and there were a number wounded. During the night the fire was kept up continually. They would stand at the corners and fire at random up the streets so as to kill any who might be passing. Their loss was more severe than ours. Forgot to state that yesterday evening the South Carolina Regiment marched to Tacubaya and remained in quarters during the night and this morning when the division was marched to the city they were left as a guard at the gate.

While the Westmorelanders were left behind to guard the abandoned Citadel, General Quitman stole a march on his fellow officers and entered Mexico City. The silent, sullen Mexicans who lined the sidewalks and rooftops did not witness a particularly triumphant procession. The American soldiers were ragged and bloodstained, and Quitman himself, who had fallen into a canal on his way, was splattered with mud and shuffled along on foot, minus one shoe. At seven o'clock a tattered American flag was raised over the National Palace. An hour later, General Scott thundered into the Grand Plaza on a magnificent white horse, so resplendent in his plumes, epaulets, and full dress regalia that even the Mexicans burst into involuntary applause. After appointing Quitman military governor of Mexico City, Scott marched into the Halls of the Montezumas as the band played "Yankee Doodle." Although intermittent sniping and ambushes took a heavy toll of the Americans over the next few days, organized Mexican resistance in the capital had come to an end.

BARCLAY. [*Continued*] Being now at the supposed end of our journey we can look back and reflect upon the late stirring events through which we have passed. Within the last month the American army has enacted miracles, performed deeds which will live forever upon the pages of history. A period of three hundred years has not diminished but rather added to the brilliancy of the exploits of the Spaniard. But Mexico has again been conquered and the second invaders had to contend with difficulties to which Cortes was a stranger. Of the eleven thousand men who marched from Puebla, three thousand have fallen killed or wounded upon the field of battle. At least one thousand have been rendered ineffective by sickness and the army does not number more than 7000 men for duty.[10] This small force has entered like a wedge into the heart of the Mexican Republic, overcoming all opposition. Some day it may be withdrawn, but the fragments of this country will never again be all united. Rome in the days of her glory always advanced her eagles and never suffered the God of Boundaries to turn his face towards the Capitol. But Mexico torn by civil internal convulsions, pressed by a foreign war, the center of her territory invaded and in possession of the foe can only preserve her nationality by sacrificing territory to her affectionate sister of the north. By such sacrifices Mexico will for a time have a place on the map and be ranked among the nations of the world. But her downfall is inevitable. It will not take place at present but the time is approaching and the young of the present gener-

10. An accurate estimate. Justin H. Smith calculates that Scott had 7,180 men available for the final assault on Mexico City. (Smith, *War With Mexico*, 2:151.)

ation may see the day when the "Stars and Stripes" which now float in triumph over the City will be the banner under whose folds the inhabitants of all Mexico will find shelter and protection. The Anglo Saxon race, that land loving people are on the move. In an incredible short time they have overrun an immense territory in the north. Long since have wishful eyes been cast towards the fertile plains of Mexico. And the same people who have driven before them the various Indian tribes and have in Texas come in contact with the Spanish race will soon hang like a wave over the province of Mexico. No embankments, no treaties can prevent the inundation. A contest between the races will follow and the Anglo Saxons have never been conquered. If they once obtain a footing, entire possession will be the result. However great a calamity war may be and however much we may regret the sad consequences which follow in its train mankind will [have] no cause to mourn a change of things in this Country. Everything betokens ruin and decay. Other civilized countries strive to keep up with the spirit of the age. Those who rule Mexico endeavor to keep down every feeling of progress or improvement. Two great parties here divide all power and wealth—the Church and the Army. Without their support no government can stand and with a tacit understanding they wink at the tyranny and excesses of each other. The holy fathers who like the locusts of Egypt darken the land are content with vast possessions in real estate, with treasures amassed by a system of robberies for centuries and with palaces both as residences and places of worship which in gorgeous magnificence recalls the fairy palaces of Arabian tales. Clothed in silk they fare sumptuously every day and they require from all that submission and respect which they consider themselves entitled to as the vice [regents?] of Christ upon earth and woe to the Mexican who incurs their displeasure. As well might he resolve to endure all the tortures of the inquisition as to thwart one of the holy fathers. Crushed and broken down in fortune and fame his life would not be safe in a land where that religion prevails in all its purity whose maxim is that "the end justifies the means." The military men are in possession of the lucrative offices and to them belongs the peculiar perogative of robbing everyone except the church. Taxes are assessed without regularity, the favorites of government escaping. Loans are enforced. Congress, the so styled representatives of the people, are browbeaten or bribed. The rank and file of the army are maltreated and forced from agriculture and often after long services when pay is due them driven by the oppression of their chiefs to desert and take to robbery. The highways are infested with villains and neither person or property are safe in travelling even the great public roads. Neither commerce, manufactures or agriculture flourish. Large bodies of land are owned by individuals and worked by the Peons, the Indian race, the most degraded and ignorant of the human species. These poor _____ and unfortunate beings, the descendants of the lordly Montezumas, are made the beasts of burden, are sold and transferred from master to master and undergo a slavery far more abject than the negroes of the north. Education, which in all civilized countries is cherished carefully, by government is here entrusted to the clergy, who, far from wishing to tutor their puppets according to the liberal and enlightened principles of the present day confine their minds to the narrow contracted views suited to the designs of priestcraft. Nothing noble can be hoped from the rising generation. Law and justice are mere formalities. The Courts of the law are influenced in their Judgments by the power and influence of their suitors. As in all countries of the west which throw off the Spanish yoke the experiment of a Republic has been unsuccessful. Revolution has followed revolution in rapid succession and anarchy which is the worst species of despotism has often taken the place of legal government. At the present time, however, much [as] we would deplore such a retrograde movement, there is no doubt but that a monarchial government would be best suited for this country. A sovereign at the head of the army and the throne supported by the clergy would without difficulty suppress all the internal dissensions and in course of time by correcting abuses in the laws, encouraging the arts and protecting the property of all, Mexico would occupy that station which her fertility, her position and her great resources entitle her. A wise prince and congress in time, following the example of the ancient kings of England, would curb and break down the immense power of the church, which never can be done under the present form of government as the clergy are the great ruling estate. Two modes therefore suggest themselves for the bettering of the condition of the people of this country. 1st, the gradual absorbtion or annexation of the territory to the United States and 2nd, the establishment of a monarchy. The latter alternative, whatever advantages it may offer, will likely never be adopted, as it is contrary to the wishes of the people of the United States and is antagonistical to the spirit of their constitution. The time has arrived when the United States is the governing power on the Western Continent and if her rulers assume the proper firmness no European government will attempt to thwart her in the Western World. It is then probable that Mexico will unite her destinies with the Republic of the North. Whether a chain of states extending from the Atlantic to the Pacific and from the St. Lawrence to the Isthmus of Darien, all forming one great nation and represented in one Congress, can be kept together is a question which time alone can answer. A general system of education and a diffusion of knowledge among all classes are the great foundations upon which such a Republic alone can be built. If Providence in his wisdom has intended that the human family in the Western Continent shall enter into a confederation of this kind certainly no form of government is better suited to so grand an object than that system formed by the genius of the men of '76. A government which protects all and favors none, which will neither perpetrate or suffer a wrong and where the people themselves thro the ballot box select their rulers and thus are made responsible for the wisdom, justice and economy of those they choose. Many schemes might be suggested whereby the condition of Mexico would be improved and the philanthopist may rejoice that if any change whatever is made it must be for the better.

The United States in the present war has shown a forebearance and chivalrous spirit highly honorable. The injuries done to American citizens by the Mexican government, the refusal to satisfy claims arbitrated and awarded by commissioners chosen by both nations and the many insults offered to our flag were sufficient causes for a declaration of war. A brave people in Texas struggling for their freedom and treated in the most barbarous manner excited our sympathies and when threatened by another invasion they threw themselves into our arms and asked to be admitted into the Union, they were admitted. I have long been satisfied in my own mind that the annexation of Texas was not only politic but was right in every sense of the word. The tyranny of Mexico justified their rebellion. The great powers of Europe acknowledged their independence and it would have grieved the heart of every generous American citizen to have seen that gallant little band of their own blood crushed subdued and massacred by the armies of the Mexican Despot. But we had ample causes for commencing hostilities prior to the annexation of Texas and a feeling of friendship and compassion for a sister republic long *deferred* that last great argument. But time only added to our list of injuries and it was necessary to bring matters to a point. The annexation of Texas had the desired effect. If Mexico had always been true to her treaties and acted towards the United States in that honest manner which one nation should show to another, notwithstanding all the convincing arguments in favor of the annexing of Texas, I do not think that Congress would have received that country so long as Mexico laid any claim to it. The respect for a neighboring nation would have made us overlook our own interest. But the system of insult and injury adopted by Mexico towards the United States had long been felt. Old friendship and sympathy were forgotten. The cold blooded butchery of the Texians had excited our horror. All love, all respect [for] Mexico was gone and the time had arrived to look to her own interests. The annexation of Texas and the removal of the army toward the Rio Grande were the causes of Mexico commencing hostilities and the argument of party men that the occupation of the territory between the Neuces and the Rio Grande was the cause of the war is entirely fanciful.[11] Mexico was prepared to wage war as soon as Texas was admitted

11. One of the "party men" holding this position that so irritated Barclay was Abraham Lincoln, then serving his one and only term as a congressman. Shortly after the declaration of war, which President Polk had urged on the grounds that Mexico "had shed American blood upon American soil," Lincoln introduced a resolution asking on what "particular

and never made the plea of the Neuces line until she received the clue from her friends in the United States. Having failed after every plan had been tried to settle difficulties amicably, war became a matter of necessity on the part of the United States. The Battles of Palo Alto, Resaca de la Palma and the storming of Monterey,[12] while they displayed the prowess of American arms, impressed the people of the United States with the idea that Mexico having felt some of the evils of a war which threatened her would speedily come to terms and that all difficulties would be settled. They did not however understand the state of affairs in Mexico. The military men had now an excuse for demanding from Congress large appropriations to the army, which passing through their hands were a source of profit. It was therefore their policy to blow the flames of war for their own individual advantage. Satisfied that the center of the Republic would never be invaded from the Rio Grande, they swaggered in safety and rested upon the substance extorted for the avowed object of carrying on the war.

A long peace had unprepared the United States for as vigorous a prosecution of the war as might have been desired. But history will do honor to the enlarged and comprehensive schemes of the American Government. When all hopes of negotiation were terminated measures were adopted to take possession of the northern provinces of Mexico, which being far removed from the capitol would not be so strongly defended as more central provinces. The navy was ordered to cooperate with the land forces and the most perfect success followed this gigantic plan. At the same time it was necessary to make the large cities of the central provinces feel the weight of the war and an advance would probably be necesssary to the capitol itself. The base of operations on the Rio Grande which had heretofore been used was far distant from the Capitol and a barren tract of country intervened. It was therefore abandoned as a base and the City of Vera Cruz selected as the point from which an entrance might be effected into the heart of the country. General Taylor instead of acting on the aggressive was directed to take the defensive and under the command of Gen. Scott the main army made a successful descent upon the City of Vera Cruz. Lieut. Richey, the bearer of dispatches to Gen. Taylor, disclosing the plans of the campaign was robbed and the Mexican Government became possessed of our designs.[13] Taking advantage of his reduced numbers, Santa Anna

---

spot" that blood had been shed. The implication was that by sending Taylor's army south of the Nueces River to the Rio Grande, Polk had actually invaded Mexican territory and was, thereby, the aggressor. Lincoln's major speech of his brief congressional career, on 17 January 1848, was an expansion of this argument and, even though he was always careful never to vote against supplies for the army, it left the impression that he was opposed to the war, an impression which was partially responsible for his failure to win reelection.

12. Three battles in northern Mexico won by General Zachary Taylor.

13. When Winfield Scott was assembling his forces for the Vera Cruz expedition he attempted, near the end of 1847, to confer with Zachary Taylor, but Taylor, aware that Scott

thought to overwhelm Taylor, but the indomitable bravery of our troops turned the torrent at Buena Vista, saved Texas from an invasion and enabled the administration to carry out the original plan of the campaign. The preparations to secure success at Vera Cruz were on the most extensive scale. The Castle of Ulua had the reputation of being second only to Gibraltar. The northers which rage in the spring rendered the descent dangerous and a dread of the yellow fever required that the siege should be pressed with the greatest vigor. No expense was therefore spared in order that the troops might land with safety and that the enemy's works might be rapidly carried.

When Vera Cruz was taken the true policy would have been to have pressed on immediately to the interior. But the want of means of transportation prevented as rapid a movement as could have been wished. This was a great neglect and was the cause of the detaining [of] the army both at Vera Cruz and Jalapa. After the Battle of Cerro Gordo a vigorous rush should have been made upon the Capitol. The same panic which caused the Mexicans to surrender Perote and Puebla without a blow would have induced them to have yielded the City itself without a struggle. Whether it was want of transportation or the small number of troops or whether deceived by hopes of peace, the delay at Puebla was most unfortunate. Had the one year volunteers been retained until their time had expired, in my opinion Mexico City could have been taken a few days after Puebla was entered. Once in possession of it no Mexican force could have driven us out. But the long inactivity after the Battle of Cerro Gordo gave time to the enemy to organize their armies and surround their capitol with defences and when Gen. Scott left Puebla his force was but little larger that it would have been had he pressed on immediately after the Battle of Cerro Gordo. How much bloodshed would have been spared had Gen. Scott only had a little more of the go-ahead Napoleon spirit about him.

Besides the scarcity of transportation and the discharging so soon the one year volunteers, both to be regretted, the administration formed an erroneous idea as to the healthfulness of this country. They poured in troops but did not consider the amount of sickness. Gen. Scott should have been reinforced at Jalapa by as many men as could have been raised under the 50,000 act[14] and the President should have immediately called out all the troops that he was empowered to raise. Like all countries, Mexico has been described by many fanciful writers. Her climate, her people

---

intended to deplete his command of its best troops, avoided the meeting. Scott was compelled to explain his plans in writing. The officer entrusted to carry the dispatch to Taylor, Lieutenant John Alexander Richey, an 1845 West Point graduate from Ohio, was intercepted by Mexicans and killed on 13 January 1847, placing Scott's most confidential plans in Santa Anna's possession.

14. Referring to the number of volunteers authorized by the war bill of 13 May 1846.

and her peculiarities have filled many a book. The administration were no doubt induced to believe by the many writers on the subject that the health of the army would be good if they reached the table lands and that the only region to be feared was the "tierra caliente" [hot country] in the neighborhood of Vera Cruz. Experience has proved the falsity of this impression. The hospital at Vera Cruz has been rivaled by the hospitals at Jalapa, Perote, Puebla and Mexico City and thus notwithstanding the number of reinforcements he received Gen. Scott's ranks were continually thinned by disease and when he left Puebla his army was as I saw but little larger than after the engagement at Cerro Gordo.

But now Mexico City has been reached and the volunteers have a prospect that their pilgrimage is o'er, that our "dreadful marches will soon be turned to delightful measures."[15] Home with all its bright pleasures rises before the imagination, Home which we soon hope to reach.

The quarters in the Citadel are comfortable. Our boys amuse themselves in ransacking its many apartments and gathering swords, escopets, etc. A detail is on guard. The firing up street continues.

15. *Richard II*, act 1, sc. 1.

8

Revelling in the Halls
The Occupation of Mexico City

September 15

BARCLAY. A part of Santa Anna's troops have remained in the City and are fighting from the house tops and attacking stragglers. A good many of our men have been killed. The riflers and regular infantry thrown out as skirmishers are driving the Mexicans before them wherever they appear. All houses of business are closed. Daniel S. Kuhns while walking about a square from the Citadel was stabbed with a sword in the side by a Mexican horseman, two of whom seeing him alone and unarmed made a dastardly attack upon him. His wound was very severe and he was with difficulty assisted to quarters. I ran for Dr. McKainy (Surgeon McMillen[1] being absent) who after examining his wound pronounced the wound mortal. Dr. McMillen afterward arrived and said that he might recover. Lieut. [Ashton S.] Tourrison was severely wounded today in the street fighting in the leg. Fighting and plundering is going on today. A Dutch ale house near quarters is a place of common resort. Altho its accomodations are not very extensive, they are very comfortable in comparison with what we have been used to of late. A good glass of ale and a respectable beef steak are set up. Early this morning orders to move. The Citadel is to be occupied by the 1st Artillery and the 2nd Pa. Regt. must find some other quarters. After all things were packed and in the wagon detained until the afternoon, while the officers were searching for quarters. Day warm. The fighting in the streets has been stopped and all is quiet. Regiment formed and marched toward the Grand Plaza. The quarters intended for us were occupied and we halted at night and slept under the arches which form a side of the Plaza. No supper was cooked and we lay on the pavement. This was revelling in the halls with a vengeance. The night was beautiful. The moon shown clear and bright. The Bands of the army were playing in the Palace whose white walls shone in the moon light. The magnificent Cathedral was before us forming one side of the Plaza.

---

1. Dr. Robert McMillen, a civilian contract surgeon employed by the regiment at one hundred dollars a month.

COULTER. This morning while I was on post at the gate of the citadel, one of our company (D. Kuhns) was severely wounded. He was walking, unarmed not quite two squares from quarters but around the corner that he could not be seen from the citadel. He was attacked by three mounted men and stabbed with a small sword through the left breast, passing into his lungs. The wound is very severe. During the day managed to plunder, from the clothing here, a pair of red Mexican uniform pantaloons which happened very opportune, as the one's I have are completely worn out. This afternoon was sent as one of a guard to search a building for a quantity of money which had been stolen from a Frenchman. Made a complete search. The floors were taken up and all boxes, etc., examined, but no trace of either thief or money could be found. The portion of the city in which we now are is very poor; buildings scattered and inhabited by the lowest classes of Mexicans. The firing continued at intervals during the day and a number of shots were fired at night.

September 16

COULTER. This morning received orders to move to the heart of the city. This place is not proper quarters for infantry; it is an artillery post. About noon the First Artillery arrived to take our place and we marched to the Grand Plaza. As we entered it the city becomes much cleaner and is decidedly a handsome place. At present it looks dull. The stores and houses are shut and very few people in the streets. Nearly every house bears some flag to protect them from our soldiers. Foreigners all hang out the flags of their native countries and the Mexicans for the most part have the white flag at their windows or on the house tops. The city is considerably injured by the many revolutions which have occurred in it. The traces of their many civil wars are visible in all the houses. All are pierced by bullets and in some places whole squares are raked with cannon and grape shot. The Plaza is a very large square, but by no means as grand as I expected. There is in it the commencement of a very large column or monument. The appearance of the Plaza is considerably injured by a large board shanty standing near the center used as a workshop for the column. It is well lighted by many lamps and in fact the whole city can be lighted up. The Grand Cathedral is a magnificent affair on the outside; have not been in it. There are two tall white spires on it and belfrys for a large number of bells, but there are not many in them at present. The National Palace is a very large two story building covering about two squares but exceedingly plain. It was intended to have quartered us in a large building near the Inquisition, and it had been cleaned up for that purpose, but on account of the negligence of our Lieutenant Colonel, it was occupied before our arrival. In consequence we were compelled to lodge in the Plaza under the porticoes without any supper.

September 17

BARCLAY. Up early. Felt bad. Went to a French house for bitters. A guard at the door—couldn't get in because I was a roundabout.² Coulter and Armstrong returned with me and we had a round of brandy. How often have we experienced the pleasures and benefits of brandy since we left home. When worn down with fatigue, hungry, wet or cold, how often has a draught from the Bottle infused energy and comfort. Let reformers slander thee as will. Let the moral teachers both from the pulpit and lecture room denounce thee. Still, O King Alcohol, we must always hold thee in grateful remembrance. Too great intimacy with thee injures, but a slight and occasional acquaintance both improves and delights.

Made a good breakfast in this French tavern which is a splendid establishment. The guests call for what they want and pay in proportion to the number and quality of their dishes. The rates are high.

Moved today from the arches or Portals of the Plaza to the University. Quarters on the porches of the University. Our company are on the second story. The quarters are clean but open. In the courtyard of the building stands the celebrated bronze statue of Charles IV on horseback.³ It was presented by a Queen of Spain to the University. It is one of the wonders of the Western World. Never having seen any work of art of the kind before, I am not a very competent judge of its comparative merit, but it strikes the eye as a most perfect specimen of workmanship. The horse stands upon a plate raised some 4 feet. The height of the horse is said to be 10 feet high. The statue of the King 11 feet. I cannot vouch for the correctness of these dimensions. They are certainly not less. The horses of our officers in the yard appeared like mice beside their mammoth brother. Altho but rude critics, we all pronounced the work perfect save the want of *warts* on the legs. The officers have quarters about two squares from the Company in a private building. The houses in the City are built in the same style but at greater expense than in the other cities thro which we have passed. There are the same white plastered walls, large barred windows and flat roofs, but many of the buildings are much larger and have more taste about them. The places of business are still closed, the many doors barred and bolted in a manner which surprises us. The principal market is near the Grand Plaza and is said to be one of the finest in the world. There are any amount of fruits and vegetables. The market is well arranged—a bronze

---

2. Enlisted men, so called because of their characteristic "roundabout" jackets, cut short with a circular bottom, as opposed to the more elegantly tailored uniforms worn by officers.

3. Charles IV (1748–1819) was King of Spain from 1788 to 1808, when he abdicated his throne under pressure from Napoleon. The statue had originally stood in the Grand Plaza, opposite the cathedral, but after Mexico won its independence, Charles, not the most enlightened or popular of monarchs, was removed to a less conspicuous location in the university courtyard.

statue of Santa Anna mounted on a shaft stands in the center. The inscription on the base makes him out a very great man, but after seeing the work in the courtyard of the University, we did not much admire the taste of the Mexicans. The Hero of Tampico[4] looks very contemptible in his military suit. Among the curiosities of the city are the Cathedral and Palace, Theatre and the Museum in the University Building. These treats are all in store for us. At present we must keep about quarters as another move will be made.

COULTER. About noon today found quarters at the National University about a square from the Plaza. These are clean, fine quarters but open, being quartered as at Puebla in the porticoes around the court yard. In this establishment there is a very large museum, and in an enclosure at one side of the court are a number of relics of the Aztec race, a very large sacrificial stone covered with a number of hyrogliphics, several large stone images, priests robes made of bird skins, several belts of wampum and some skins of animals stuffed. Just in front of this building is the city market place. It is a large building covering a square with a very large court. The outside of this building is a number of shops and inside is the vegetable and fruit market. Here is the greatest variety that I have seen in any market. Vegetables are stacked up in the stalls in many fantastic and beautiful shapes. In the center of the market is a column with a statue of Santa Anna upon the summit. In the center of the court yard at our quarters is an immense equestrian statue of Charles the Fourth of Spain. The following is the history and description of it as translated from an old Spanish Almanac: "On the 9th of December, 1803, was exposed to the public in the Grand Plaza of this city the Equestrian statue of Charles the Fourth of Spain. It is one of the most magnificent monuments of art which the Republic possesses. It exceeds anything of the kind in Europe, except the statue of Marcus Aurelius at Rome. At present it is at the National University. It was erected at his own expense by the Marquis of Banciforte, who, being viceroy of Mexico, erected it in remembrance of his having on the 9th of December 1786, first set foot on the road leading from this city to Vera Cruz by way of Orizaba and Cordoba." The material of the statue is bronze. It was under the direction of Don Manuel Folsa, who sketched the design and formed the mould. He committed the fusion to Don Salvador de la Vega who soon carried the statue to the Plaza. The metal weighs 60,000 pounds and took from the afternoon of the 2nd until the morning of the 4th of August to melt it and fifteen minutes to pour into the mould. The whole height of the horse and rider is seventeen feet and the cavity of the belly is sufficient to contain five men. I will not vouch

4. In 1829 Santa Anna defeated a Spanish army near the Mexican seaport town of Tampico, thereby preserving Mexico's newly won independence.

for the truth of all this, but it is decidedly a magnificent piece of workmanship. The street fighting completely ceased after Thursday. There has been some sentinels since killed however.

September 18
BARCLAY. The shops and stores are beginning to be opened. As all is now quiet confidence will soon be restored and business go on as usual.

September 19
BARCLAY. A party sent from each company in the Regt. to bring the wounded from the hospital at Tacubaya into the City. It was hard work but cheerfully performed.

COULTER. Went to Tacubaya as part of a detail to bring in our wounded, the hospital being moved to the city. Had quite a job of it. Several of the men were too severely wounded to bear being hauled in waggons and we were compelled to carry them in litters on our shoulders for a distance of four miles.

September 20
BARCLAY. The Regt. is again formed for another move. As has been frequently remarked by all, we are generally accomodated after everybody else and must give way until everybody is accomodated. Marched about a mile from the Plaza and took up quarters in a house formerly used as a tobacco warehouse, a manufactory. The South Carolina Regt. occupy part of it. Our company have good quarters in a room in a wing of the building. There is a large yard in front of us and no other company is near to annoy us. We are by ourselves. The room which we cleaned out had plenty of wood in it and there are over 1,000 pine boxes piled up in a shed near by. So there will be no scarcity of mess chests or fire wood. Water is also convenient and a good place to cook and if we get plenty to eat what more do soldiers want. There is a great quantity of tobacco material in different parts of the house, bales of stems and snuff, also bagging, boxes, benches, etc., all of which are lawful prey. Tobacco being a government monopoly farmed out to companies, certain districts are allowed to raise and certain companies to manufacture tobacco. Heavy duties are paid for these privileges. The manufacture of this article is a source of considerable revenue and the consumer pays a burdensome tax. From all appearances we are likely to have a long rest.

COULTER. Today the regiment moved quarters to the very suburbs of the city. Barring the situation, they are very good quarters, called the "Escuela Normal" (Normal School) last used as a tobacco house and at present there is a considerable portion of tobacco in the building. The whole building is impregnated with a strong tobacco smell, which will have the effect of banishing fleas and lice, a matter of great importance in this country. There is a fine fountain of water here, but it is supplied from the aquaduct which is supplied from one of the neighboring lakes and is, in consequence, rather warm. The neighborhood is very poor, the streets filthy, houses poor and inhabited by the poorest classes, padrones [?], ladrones, etc., are in abundance. The South Carolina Regiment are also quartered in this building.

September 21

BARCLAY. Nothing doing. The men amusing themselves in running about and seeing the City. One very important discovery has been made, that our quarters are free from vermin owing I judge to the great quantity of tobacco stems and snuff which are not very agreeable to these interesting little animals.

COULTER. Today we have been engaged in fixing up matters about quarters and I suppose we are destined again to endure the vexations and troubles of a garrison. The city is now completely settled. Many of the stores and houses are opened. Inhabitants have again ventured upon the streets. After a short acquaintance they are better pleased with the Yankees, or at their money and forebearance.

September 22

BARCLAY. No stir. The Mexicans manage to assassinate three or four of our men daily, catching them intoxicated. The sick of the Regt. are in good quarters near the Plaza.

September 25

BARCLAY. Co. E on guard at the San Antonio Gate distant near two miles from Barracks. The American Army is now scattered throughout the City, each corps occupying certain portions. Strong guards are detailed and heavy pickets are posted at each gate, who examine all passersby. Every precaution is used to prevent surprises and to crush an outbreak. The Mexicans still carry on their system of assassination. Our men have generally been paid off, liquor is plenty and they will get drunk. In all Mexican towns the sale of liquors is carried on extensively. Almost every shop and store are furnished with a bar where they retail aguardiente and brandy. I do not know whether they are taxed for this privilege or not.

COULTER. This morning mounted guard. Sent out as a picket on the Garita de San Antonio Abad, about a mile and a half from our quarters. At the fortifications on this route. This is the point which General Twiggs attacked and it bears many marks of his cannonade. There is a battery in the road with a ditch in front, flanking batteries on each side completely ditched and a long line of breastworks running almost to the Garita de

Belen. These batteries are admirably secured from the bursting of shells. The whole surface of the ground, except the mere platforms where the guns stand, is covered with water. Our picket is officers and men thirty strong with two pieces of artillery. Here is, I think, a deficiency in our guard. While the quarter and city guards are extremely strong, the picket is left rather weak, and expected to use artillery, although there are neither gunners nor artillerymen allowed for the guns. Nothing of importance happened except that we stopped all the good market people and exacted a toll of fruit, etc., before allowing them to pass the guard. Our revenue from this kind of tariff during the day amounted to about three gallons of milk, and oranges, apples, pears, bananas, sweet potatoes, pulque, etc., etc., in abundance. During the night there was an alarm from some cause or other in the city.

September 26

BARCLAY. Young Linsenbigler died in hospital after a long sickness. This boy when we left home was a smart active little fellow. He was a pet with all the company. Until we left Jalapa his health was good. From that time he pined away doing duty occasionally. He refused to remain with the sick at Puebla. Was sent to the hospital the day we left San Agustin where he remained until his death. Rev. McCarty,[5] the army Chaplain, preached today for the first time in the Reception Room of the National Palace. I attended. The audience was respectable and the old gentleman delivered a very able discourse. He is of the Episcopal Church, a man over fifty and very favorably known throughout the army on account of his gallantry in the different actions in the valley. At Churubusco in particular he was in the hottest fire, administering comfort and consolation to the wounded and dying and at the same time pointing out to the advancing columns the most practicable route across the ditches, charging them "to keep their cartridge boxes well up." It was a singular scene to behold in the City of Mexico, in the very National Palace itself, a Protestant minister and a Protestant audience. Five years ago a prophecy that such things would take place would have been ridiculed. But there they were. The old hoary headed preacher calling upon his "dearly beloved brethren" to return thanks for the manifold blessings they had received and men clothed in the habiliments of war, their sabres by their sides, kneeling and responding to the prayers of their pastor. The room is large, hung with silk

5. John McCarty, born in New York in 1798, was an Episcopalian minister who had served as a navy chaplain in the 1820s. Returning to the military in April of 1847, he served as chaplain with a New York volunteer brigade. At the Battle of Contreras he stayed with the men on the front line, and so impressed the army with his cool courage under fire that Captain Edmund Kirby Smith, tongue in cheek, suggested he was entitled to a battlefield promotion to "Brevet Bishop." He remained in the chaplaincy at various army posts until his retirement in 1867.

and velvet, the floor covered with Brussels carpet, the ceiling carved in the most beautiful manner, mahogany sofas and chairs covered with velvet were our pews and behind the preacher who stood upon a slight platform, was the chair of State overhung with a silk and velvet canopy, the whole surmounted by a crown upon which stood the victorious eagle of Mexico crushing in its beak the serpent. I have been informed that the English residents in the City some time ago secretly obtained the services of a Chaplain on board a British man of war lying at Vera Cruz who came to the City and privately baptized several children. But the laws of Mexico forbid such a proceeding and McCarty I have no doubt has the honor of being the first Protestant divine who ever declared the truths of Christianity in Mexico. The National Palace is built upon the ground where in days of yore stood the famous Palace of the Montezumas. A portion of the present building is said to have been erected by Cortes. The palace is oblong covering three or four acres, courtyard in the centre. The style is plain and simple, without any displays of the beauties of architecture. The lower story is occupied and intended as guard rooms, barracks for troops and stables. Upon the second story is the different chambers for the legislative bodies and public officers. I was in three or four rooms. They were like the Reception Room furnished splendidly. The chamber where the Congress assemble is a semi-circular room with two tier of galleries. It is quite small and as the soldiers before leaving rifled it of everything that could be carried away it now presents a somewhat desolate appearance. This room is lighted by windows stained with colored glass. Capt. Naylor is the superintendent of the Palace.

COULTER. This morning another of Company E, Jacob Linsenbigler, died in the hospital in this city and was buried in the afternoon with the usual honors. Today there was Episcopal service in the Audience chamber of the Palace by Rev. McCarty, a chaplain of the army. This is, I believe, the first public English Protestant service ever performed in the City of Mexico.

September 27
BARCLAY. Service is performed daily in the Great Cathedral. This magnificent building it would require days to examine and pages to describe. Not the most remote idea of the splendour can be given by one unacquainted with architecture or painting. In approaching its tall white spires are just visible and its deep musical bells sound loud and clear amid all the ringing and noise of the Metropolis. When we saw the church at Vera Cruz its wealth and splendour struck us as far surpassing anything of the kind in our own country. As the Jalapa and Puebla Cathedrals far exceeded Vera Cruz so does the Great Cathedral of Mexico City hide the splendour of the churches in the two latter places. The great altar is in the centre of the building and surrounded by a massive railing said to be

worth its weight in silver. The altar itself is dazzling with gilding and ornaments. The space occupied by the organ is as great as an ordinary sized church at home. On each side of the grand altar and extending the entire length of the building are shrines to the different saints. Candles are always burning before the images and devotees kneeling before favorite saints. The church is lighted with windows in the lofty domes. Everyone is struck with the roughness of the floor which, composed of boards which are in places two or three inches apart, is in strange contrast with the magnificence of everything around. Here are paintings of the first European masters. Here is statuary which would charm a connoisseur; but alas we uninitiated in the ministeries of these sciences cannot appreciate the fine touches. Like the poor Indians who are kneeling around the altar we are lost in amazement at the splendours around us. The devotees are principally women, the beautiful proud Castilian dame richly attired on her knees beside dirty lousy Ladrones, all crossing themselves, beating their breasts and going thro many ceremonies unknown even to the Catholics in the States. Besides the main church or room there are several lesser places of worship in the Cathedral. In one of those immediately above the altar is rich gilding imitating the beams of the sun. It is lighted from behind through a glass and presents a grand sight. I have observed in all the churches in the upper country imitations of the sun either about the altar or in some prominent part of the building. Whether or not it is intended to take the eye of the Indians I cannot say. That luminary was formerly worshipped by the Indians. In connexion with this I may mention the celebrated "Montezuma Dial" or as some call it the Sacrificial Stone. This stone is covered with hieroglyphics and is about ten feet in diameter. It is circular and built in with the wall of the Church. It is said to be a kind of connecting link between the present and ancient religion of the Indians, a kind of a compromise act. When the Indian enters the temple and kneels before the God of the Christian, it is with the knowledge and belief that the image of his own Deity shines in the altar before him and that his sacred sacrificial stone is honored by being a part of the temple. He is thus reconciled. However little real change has been affected in the minds of the natives. The Holy Fathers certainly deserve a great deal of credit for their ingenuity. If Mexico was a great and prosperous nation, if she held that rank which her position and her great resources entitle her to occupy, if justice and wisdom guided her councils, if her statesmen were honest and enlightened and her people prosperous and happy, then indeed might she worship in temples whose wealth and splendour would rival the churches of the East. But in wandering through these temples, where so much gorgeous magnificence is displayed, the mind is saddened at the idea that while luxury here prevails all else is poor and desolate. Neither the arts or sciences flourish. The plough stands rusting in the furrough and while the leaders and great men of the land are contending for rule and power the lower orders are ignorant and downtrodden. Here the Church and the Church alone flourishes and the whole nation are taxed and oppressed to support and build up a system of religion which triumphs over all power and sympathizes not with the people in adversity. In Puebla there were sixty churches and other religious houses and friars without number. They bear the same proportion in this city. The different orders of friars are in possession of the finest houses in the City. They own a great deal of real estate. Their personal wealth is not known. A great display is made in the churches and a still greater amount is said to be concealed. The most popular, numerous and influential order is the Dominicans. They wear silk gowns and stove pipe hats. They are a fat greasy jolly looking set of fellows, who appear as tho they much prefer new silk and old sack to sackcloth and ashes. The South Carolina Regt. moved today to the Palace. We have now the warehouse entirely to our own Regt.

COULTER. I find in my original notes several occurrences for which there is no particular date, but which have happened since Tuesday the 21st inst. Since that [time] the South Carolina Regiment have left the building in which we were and are now quartered alone. Understand General Scott has issued orders (rather secretly) to officers to be vigilant as a conspiracy or rising of the inhabitants is feared. There has been several cases of wounding and robbing of sick soldiers of our regiment near quarters by the Mexicans. General Scott has issued orders that in connection with the usual guard, one-third of the remaining force of each regiment shall remain under arms in their quarters, to be called an inline picket, for the purpose of being ready in case of any disturbance in the city. Today our company are on this inline picket. At midnight, the long roll was beat at the Marine quarters, and thinking it an advance, we were turned out, but discovered that the cause of the beat was to call the men up for roll call. They say they do it every night.

September 28

COULTER. Today went to see the building of the National Theatre,[6] but it was closed, so we dropped in an adjoining eating house kept by a Mexican, where there were some officers. Sitting down, very independently called for dishes. After waiting some time there appeared to be no signs of being attended and called a second time when we were invited out into the kitchen by a Mexican who said that this room was intended for officers alone and no privates were allowed to eat there. This distinction made between us and the shoulder-strapped gentry raised our republican blood.

---

6. Until its prudent name change the National Theatre had been known as the Grand Teatro Santa Anna.

Some sparring anything but polite ensued, and we left the house with eternal curses upon all in it and all who patronized it. In the afternoon there was a breaking out in the company; some of them were pretty well toddled and we had noisy quarters.

September 29
BARCLAY. Some days ago Gen. Scott issued an order that he had reason to believe the Mexicans meditated an outbreak. All are cautioned to be on their guard and hold themselves in readiness to move at a moment's notice. There is some little excitement on the subject, but the men wander about unarmed and alone as usual. It is astonishing how careless and reckless soldiers become. The whole army is now divided into three reliefs—one third of each regiment go on guard each day. After supplying the gate pickets, the main and quarter guard, the remainder form an inlying picket, who are always under arms. Today our Company are on guard at quarters.

COULTER. This morning mounted guard. Stationed at our regimental quarters. In the afternoon there was something of a row in the neighborhood, two soldiers having been stoned by the Mexicans. The guard was called out and after searching some houses, we captured three Mexicans who were given to Captain Daniel's Quartermaster, and by him taken to the waggon guard where they received their dues in the shape of a horse whipping, without judge or jury, the proper manner to deal with such characters. During the day stood double duty so as to have leisure time to attend the National Theatre at night. The performance was the "Lady of Lyons,"[7] played in English by a company of army followers, and in consequence was poor. The building itself is very large and well fitted up. Before entering the theatre proper, you pass through a Spanish vestibule in which are a number of fine large pillars supporting the arched roof. It is lighted by a very large skylight of cut and colored glass. The theatre itself is large, a very commodious pit or ground seats, then what is called the dress circle and above this four tiers of gallery. It is lighted by a large and magnificent chandelier. The stage is wide and very deep and the scenery beautiful and well shifted. Returned to quarters about one o'clock and immediately went on post for two hours, which was quite a sleepy job.

September 30
BARCLAY. A meeting of the Company having been held, Mechling, Bonnin and Bills were appointed a committee to purchase a sword to be presented to Lt. Coulter. McLaughlin, Coulter, Uncapher, Kettering, Carney and myself were appointed a committee to present the sword accompanied

---

7. An 1838 melodrama by Edward George Bulwer-Lytton.

with a letter expressing the high opinion the Company had of Lt. Coulter. Today we made the presentation. This was done by a unanimous vote of our Company and was intended as a slight return for the many acts of kindness which we have received at his hands. The sword is a beautiful blade. With the inscription it cost near $40.00. The inscription is "Presented to Lieut. James Coulter by the Westmoreland Guards, Mexico City, September 30th, 1847." Bravery is a quality which all American soldiers possess. It is therefore nothing extraordinary, but the courtesy and kindness of officers towards men, the hundred little acts of accomodation whereby the burdens of the rank and file are lightened or forgotten, these are deserving of remembrance and reward. As I was on the Committee of presentation, it fell to me to write the letter.

COULTER. Today the company presented a sword to Lt. Coulter for his good conduct and gallantry during the campaign, and particularly during the late actions. In consequence there was a spree and several were laid out.

October 1
BARCLAY. Among the public stores taken after the entry of our army was a large quantity of segars and chewing tobacco. As government monopolises the tobacco trade this was lawful spoil. Today one pound of chewing tobacco was distributed to each man of the rank and file of the Regt., the same quantity being issued to each private in the army. The tobacco chewers are in great glee. The weed for a long time has been scarce and very high, being about $1.50 per pound. The Segars which have been taken will be sold at low prices to the officers. In addition to this extra issue to the rank and file, Gen. Scott has ordered that the sum of $150,000 be raised immediately and paid in four weekly installments ending the 11th of October. Of this sum $20,000 goes to hospital uses and $90,000 to the purchase of a blanket and two pair of shoes for each soldier. The balance is for the general use of the army. This is right. If ever an army merited an extra issue of this kind, certainly the American Army which entered the City of Mexico deserve it.

COULTER. Today a portion of the captured tobacco was issued, a pound of chewing tobacco to a man. Segars were also distributed to the officers. In this country the growth and sale of tobacco is monopolized by the government and is a source of some revenue. The growing of it is confined by license to two districts, Orizaba and Oaxaca and is retailed throughout the country by agents. A large quantity was captured at Puebla and I think some other places, and a very large quantity in different shapes in this city. When we first entered the city the government, being disturbed and no person to take care of these affairs, considerable quantities were stolen by the inhabitants and retailed at exorbitant prices to the men. Now the price is reasonable.

October 2

BARCLAY. While eating breakfast this morning, I felt a sudden shaking in as I supposed the bench I was sitting on. Beginning to feel very dizzy and thinking that my dizzyness might be only imaginary, I looked round and saw from the countenances of my comrades that they all experienced the same sensation. We all rose and made a rush to the open yard. The rocking continued and we were convinced that there was an earthquake. The shock continued about one minute and produced a feeling something like a slight sea sickness. Two Mexicans who were at work in the yard fell on their knees and all the streets were filled with men, women and children. Priests and laymen on their knees and supplicating the Almighty. It was an impressive sight. The shock was considered more violent than any that had been felt for some years. The water dashed about and overflowed in the tanks and gutters. No damage of any extent was done. The houses in Mexico are built with very thick walls, probably on account of the earthquakes. I have observed in many of them cracks in the wall which it is said were caused by earthquakes. The City itself is built upon a shell of earth in the midst of the lakes. I would not be surprised if some day or other it was submerged, which interesting event I hope will not take place until we get out of it.

COULTER. This morning for the first time I experienced the sensations of an earthquake shock. About eight or nine o'clock, while the company were, for the most part, at breakfast under the arch in front of our quarters, all felt a peculiar sensation, a sudden dizziness as though about to faint, the walls appeared to be falling. All jumped up and ran into the courtyard and soon perceived the earth rocking and the water running back and forth on the pavement. It lasted two minutes and four seconds. It is said that in the streets the water was washed out of its courses and the trees were observed to wave. As soon as it was felt, all the Mexicans in the street fell upon their knees and continued praying until it was over. The Grand Plaza was completely crowded with priests and populace all on their knees. All doors which were standing ajar were dashed shut and open with violence. The water has stopped running into the fountain in our quarters and this evening understood that it is caused by the water pipes being injured by the shock.

October 3

BARCLAY. I attended divine service at the Palace. The majority of the boys went to the Plaza de Toros to see a bull fight. The Mexican[s] retain this amusement of their Spanish Lords. Sunday is always the day chosen for the exhibition. The bulls however are not the fierce animals of Andalusia. They are generally docile and make but a poor fight. The Mexicans with the usual caution to prevent the possibility of danger, saw off the points of the horns and place large balls on them.

COULTER. Today there was Episcopal services again in the Audience chamber. Went to the place for the purpose of attending, but the room was full, principally with officers and the English residents of the city. Went into a chamber opposite where I saw, much to my surprise, at the head of the room, a full length portrait of General Washington. While examining the paintings on the walls were politely ordered out by an orderly of General Quitman. Left and attended a bull fight at the Plaza de Toros where Company E congregated almost enmass. The building is old and very roughly constructed, but is calculated to accomodate an immense audience. The Plaza de Toros is situate about two squares to the rear of our quarters. Was much better pleased with this performance than one of a similar character which I saw at Jalapa. Four bulls were successively fought and killed, the last two, and particularly the last, fighting very well. Several horses were badly gored and overturned, one having his entrails torn out. Some of the performers were thrown off their horses and considerably hurt. The circus which succeeded the fight was a poor performance, but greatly pleased and astonished the greasers. Attended the National Theatre in the evening. The play was Spanish. Could not understand the language, but was considerably interested in it as a pantomime.

October 4

BARCLAY. Last night Col. Wm. B. Roberts and R. C. McGinley died. Col. Roberts came out as Captain of the Fayette Company. He was elected Colonel of the Regt. at Pittsburgh, receiving six votes over Hambright. Our company opposed him and he never liked us much afterwards. He was a good business man at home and personally a brave man. He wanted energy and did not possess either the education or talents to enable him to mix on equal terms with officers of rank in the army. Taking advantage of this deficiency, Gen. Pillow made him and his Regt. the "scape goat" at Cerro Gordo and Roberts had not the ability and energy to defend himself. He had very little sympathy with his soldiers and always threw every obstacle in his power in the way when the sick applied for discharges. He objected even to discharging Miller of our company who received a wound which has disabled him for life, saying "that if he could not perform military duties, he could cook" never considering that Miller volunteered as a soldier and not as a cook. My own opinion is that had Col. Roberts done his duty as a Colonel should have done some of our company who are now lying in the cold embrace of death would have been _____ home ornaments to society.

In the death of R. C. McGinley society has lost a valuable man. He was a man of fine mind and good education. A course at Washington College had fitted him for the study of the law. At the time the Guard were called on he was near the end of his legal course. He was the very picture of good health and was never sick until a short time before we left Puebla. At the wood yard he was very low. While we were in San Agustin he lay in Col. Roberts quarters and upon our leaving that place he was sent to the hospital at Mixcoac. He was sent from there to the hospital in the City where he remained until the time of his death. His body will be embalmed and taken home.

COULTER. This morning our Colonel, William B. Roberts, died as also did Corporal Robert C. McGinley of our company. Neither have been buried, but are undergoing a preserving process preparatory to being sent to Pennsylvania. Understood that during the night there was another slight earthquake shock. For my part I did not feel it.

October 5
BARCLAY. Company on guard today.

COULTER. This morning mounted guard. Stationed at the hospital. On account of wearing a pair of red Mexican pantaloons, not being in uniform, was not allowed to go to the Plaza, which suited me exactly, as the guards mounted there have more difficult post. The remainder of the company are scattered over the city.

October 14
COULTER. Find no notes for this interval in my original notes, nothing I suppose of importance having occurred during that period but the following general mention. Some days have elapsed since visiting my journal nothing of consequence having happened during the interim, the sum of our duty being to mount guard every third day. We have no drills now, only an occasional dress parade on which we would turn out rather shabbily were it not for the addition of two new companies. Our company musters but twenty privates for duty and some of the others even less. There are few amusements in the city and it is becoming rather a bore. Occasionally attend the theatre which is either in Spanish that we cannot appreciate, or English, which from the quality of the actors, being mere camp followers, is very ordinary. Last night was the first entry of a new star, Mrs. Sheppard, a discarded, super-annuated actress from some of the United States theatres. Her performance was poor.

October 23
COULTER. Have no intermediate dates for this interval but a general mention of the whole period. We have seen nothing more than the usual routine of garrison duty with nothing to disturb the monotony, except the occasional murder of soldiers or Mexicans. The other day a number of our company took an excursion to Chapultepec and Molino del Rey. Going out we fell in with some Mexicans who had a drove of unpacked asses. We were soon mounted and trotting along at a respectable gait down the

causeway. I had mounted a fine jack and was at the head of the party when one of the chaps put his bayonet into his rump. This made the jack pick up and he landed me over his head on my back. My musket struck the ground and the muzzle was filled with dirt and the whole seat of my breeches was torn out. Did not go directly up to the castle but went around by the Tacubaya road, the route which General Twiggs' storming party took. Here the pulque stalks are completely riddled with shot. Entered the meadow and crossed the route our division had taken to the castle. The distance did not appear so great and a number of the ditches are now filled. Went around the wall to Molino del Rey. This is a series of buildings, their walls so connected as to form an impassable breastwork, and an empty aquaduct running almost the entire length of the building forms a fine position for infantry. This battle, the issue of which was the loss of so much blood and with no advantage to us, is condemned by the entire army and reflects anything but credit upon General Scott, although it proves the reckless valor of our troops. With no greater loss, the intervening woods might have been entered and the castle carried, leaving the enemy isolated in Molino del Rey, a position which was untenable when we had possession of the castle, and which our troops, when they did take it, could not hold. Left Molino del Rey and midway between it and the castle, saw a number of Mexicans watching their mules and dancing to the music of the harp. Some were playing cards and all appeared to be enjoying themselves after the lazy southern fashion. Going up the steps of the castle, although we had time to pick our steps, found it more tiresome than when we went up under fire. The castle presents a different appearance from what it did then. The effects of the bombardment are still visible, but there are no signs of blood or dead hombres. They are now clean, comfortable quarters and garrisoned by the 14th Regiment of Infantry. The Second Pennsylvania Regiment has again to furnish the picket for the Garita de San Antonio Abad. Our company is on duty there today. We have twenty-six men and two pieces of artillery. My post is an easy one and one which will not very likely ever be needed—at one of the guns.

9

A Garrison Life is Very Dull and Troublesome
Mexico City

October 26

BARCLAY. For the last few weeks nothing of interest has transpired. Guard duty is the only duty. The company is on guard every third day. The balance of the time they amuse themselves as they see proper. The regulars are confined to their quarters, only two of each company being permitted to pass out daily. With the volunteers there is not such strictness. They run about when and where they please. Our quarters are clean and comfortable. After breakfast we usually loaf to the Officers' Quarters, to the hospital or the Plaza. The "Alameda" is also a favorite place of resort. It is a public grove containing some 8 or 10 acres laid out in good taste. Its broad walks, cool shades and numerous fountains are in agreeable contrast [to] the dirt and confusion of the City. We frequently meet Capt. Montgomery & Lieut. Drum who both appear to enjoy themselves very much.

There is a spirit of sociability in the Company now much greater than ever was before. The little band have been well tried, they know each other and are proud of each other. There is a general disposition to oblige and befriend one another. My own duties as First Sergeant are extremely light. Every man knows and is cheerful in performing his duties. I never have occasion to make use of a harsh word and this is to me indescribably pleasant. While other Sergeants are quarreling and contending with their men, our boys with cheerfulness obey every command. After night we have singing, dancing and fiddling. The days pass rapidly and pleasantly and indeed it is only the companionship of such men that keeps away the "Blues." A garrison life is very dull and tiresome and is injurious to both body and mind.

I have been at the National Theatre Circus and Museum. A Spanish Company and an American perform at the Theatre. The American Company is below mediocrity. The Spanish Company has some superior actors. Canete is the most famous of the company. We neither understand their language or the story, but the voice gestures and scenery all strike us. The building itself is grand, said to be one of the finest theatres on the western continent. Besides the seats which are on a level with the stage, there are five tiers of boxes. It is said it will contain over 3000 persons. The audience are chiefly of the army. The fashionables of Mexico refusing to patronage a company which will play before the Americans. Persons who have attended the theatres in our eastern cities tell me that the Spanish company chiefly excel in the working of their scenery. There is a company of dancers attached to the establishment who gambel about on the light fantastic toe in a manner astonishing to us heavy footed Yankees.

The performances at the Circus are tolerable. It is also patronized by the Americans entirely.

The museum is two rooms in the University. It is open each day gratis from 3 to 5 P.M. The rooms are crowded with curiosities. A Mexican, one of the Managers, very politely explains as well as he can to visitors the different collections. The most interesting specimens to us were the gold and silver ore and the manner of working the mines. Indeed the American visitors generally appeared to take a deep interest in examining the process of working the mines, whether because it was something new or the idea occured that they might themselves before long be engaged in the same business. There are the usual quantity of birds, animals, insects and reptiles. A beautiful collection of shells. The walls covered with paintings. They have also an _____ of the various productions of Mexican skill and industry. Among the coins there is a shin plaster,[1] a five dollar bill issued by a company in New York. But to the antiquary the most interesting collection is the images and different articles of household use of the ancient people of this country. Their bows and arrows _____ vessels for cooking and sacrifices are here assorted in any quantity. A gentleman connected with the museum is said to be well versed in Aztec lore. All the officers who make a visit are requested to leave their names.

A luxury which we enjoy is the perusal of two newspapers, the "American Star" and the "North American" published in the City, the former a daily, the latter a weekly paper.[2] They are both ably conducted.

Another great place of resort is the "Pulque Shops." The pulque plant is to the lower class in this country what the camel is to the Arabian and the reindeer to the Laplanders. The plant itself is composed of from 10 to 20 stocks which shoot out to the height of about 10 or 12 feet. The stocks at the roots are about 2 feet in circumference. When the plant has attained the proper size and age the centre is topped and the juice extracted. It collects again and is again extracted and so on until the plant becomes ex-

1. "Shin plaster" was a contemptuous term applied to paper money, especially fractional currency.

2. As befitting a nation of newspaper readers, Americans brought newspapers with them wherever they went, even along with the army of occupation. *The American Star*, a daily, was the "official" paper, using the army's own press and printing its official reports, but it was by no means merely an echo of Scott's views. The *North American* (also a daily) was its chief rival, but at least a dozen other papers, some quite ephemeral, catered to the soldiers' craving for news.

hausted. This juice is of a whitish color and sweet disagreeable taste. It is placed away and in the course of twenty four hours, having in the mean time fermented, makes a very pleasant cooling drink. At first we did not like it, but we have all become very fond of it of late. It is very refreshing and quenches thirst sooner than any drink I have ever met with. On a march it is the greatest imaginable luxury and I have often thought that the folks at home could relish and appreciate it in a harvest field. A half pint is pleasant and refreshing. A pint slightly excites and a quart will make a man as drunk as he wishes to be. This is with new drinkers. With old soap sticks I suppose a greater quantity will be necessary. At Jalapa the pulque was scarce, a barrel of it being brought to market on Sundays and feast days. The plant does not grow near Vera Cruz. The plant flourishes about Perote and from there the whole way to the City of Mexico itself. The first time I drank pulque was at Tepeyahualco. The water there was bad and we were forced to use pulque as a substitute. In Puebla, poor Melville and myself daily attended a shop and amused ourselves with the old Mexican keeper. The business however was not carried on very extensively in Puebla. But in Mexico City the pulque trade is very extensive. There are one or two, sometimes several shops in each square. Every morning early the Indians bring in the juice fermented. Sometimes they drive as high as 15 mules or asses each with two keg[s] or sheep skins filled with pulque on their back. The shop keeper then prepares the drink mixing water with the pure juice. It is poured into barrels. Some of them are sweetened to suit the palates of soldiers. The drink is sold for about a picayuna a pint. The shops are all painted to catch the eye of the bye-passer. A shop near the Plaza, known as the "Elephant" is our favorite. The Mexicans meet in their pulque shops, drink, sing and make merry. The higher classes do not openly use the beverage, but with the middle and lower, both men and women, it is a favorite.

But the pulque stock besides affording a common beverage is used for other purposes. The stocks planted in rows make an admirable fence, so dense that a bird can scarcely fly through it. A great many fields are surrounded by a hedge of this kind. From the great stocks the Indians make covers for their houses or huts. All the rope and coarse thread used in the country is made from the threads which are drawn from the stocks. From this thread bagging and matting is woven. I do not know what medicinal qualities the roots possess. A stock in full vigour is valued at $18.

COULTER. A train will leave shortly for Vera Cruz and one is looked for from the same place. Am again on picket guard at the Garita de San Antonio Abad.

October 27
COULTER. Today one of Company E, Henry Fishel, was discharged on account of disability. Dr. McMillen would not discharge him and so he,

after getting Lt. Armstrong's and Colonel Geary's aid and General Quitman's discharges, went to General Scott, who signed it without the surgeon's certificate. There appears to be a great reluctance among all the surgeons to discharge disabled soldiers.

October 28

BARCLAY. Henry Fishel who has been unwell for a short time was today discharged. He was in the hospital and made application to the surgeon who laughed at him. As he is a very persevering Dutchman, he was determined not to be bluffed off in that kind of style. So being recommended by the Lieut. and Colonel, he received a discharge from Gen. Scott himself. He will return home the first train. We are daily looking for a mail. The route now to Vera Cruz is open. Santa Anna was foiled in his attack on Col. Childs at Puebla.[3] We have heard of Col. Child's successful defence and of the death of Jack Gilchrist of the Duquesne Greys. Poor Jack, he was a great favorite with all who knew him and died fighting most gallantly.

October 29

BARCLAY. Engaged in writing letters home. A mail will go out shortly.

COULTER. We are again on picket guard at the San Antonio gate. Nothing to disturb us and had some sport, two or three of the guard being a little tight.

October 30

BARCLAY. The Guard at the San Antonio Gate is taken off. The other guard duties are as usual. I have not been very well lately. Symptoms of the fever and ague.

COULTER. This morning instead of the usual relief, received orders to remove the artillery and call in the entire picket, abandoning the station.

October 31

BARCLAY. Being a festival day and fearing an outbreak, Scott has ordered the pulque and liquor shops to be closed at a certain hour. Inspected

3. Immediately after the fall of Mexico City, Santa Anna and what was left of his army threatened the American garrison at Puebla, hoping to cut Scott's supply line. Most of that garrison, commanded by Colonel Childs, consisted of eighteen hundred hospitalized troops, with only 450 healthy soldiers fit for action, over half of whom were of the 1st Pennsylvania Infantry. Unwilling to risk a direct attack, Santa Anna commenced a siege, beginning 14 September, but under the cheerful and energetic command of Childs the defenders managed to hold their own while waiting for help. That help came from a column from Vera Cruz led by General Joseph Lane. After a hard march with much suffering and heavy fighting, he entered Puebla and broke the siege on 12 October.

and mustered in as part of Worth's Division by Capt. Marshall.[4] Montgomery is ordered to Vera Cruz. Lt. Coulter goes to Vera Cruz to bring up papers, etc., belonging to the Regt. Sergt. McLaughlin has not been well and for the last month has been living with Montgomery. He also goes to Vera Cruz for his health being detailed by Montgomery as a forage master.

COULTER. This is holy eve. Nothing doing except active preparations for the leaving of the train. There have been some religious ceremonies in the churches today; no other celebrations of holy eve; no demolishing of cabbage as in our country.

November 1

BARCLAY. The train started to Vera Cruz under command of Col. Harney. It will return immediately. Among the officers who returned to the States were Genls. Quitman and Shields, the former on business in relation to his office, the latter for the purpose of recovering his health. These two officers are great favorites in the army. They neither of them have that stinking pride about them which disgraces so many of the officers of the army. They are both men of great personal bravery and military skill. Shields looks bad and I judge will not live long. The wound he received at Cerro Gordo was very severe. He is not a man of as great talents as Quitman, tho probably a better officer.

At Dress Parade this evening orders read that an election would be held for Colonel of the 2nd Pa. Regt. on tomorrow and that in case a vacancy should occur in a field officer an election will immediately be held to fill the same and so continue until the field officers are filled. The election for Colonel has been spoken of for some time and it is believed by a great many that it was postponed until the present time in order that Capt. Montgomery might be out of the way. Montgomery was the prominent candidate in opposition to the Lieut. Col. A meeting was held tonight in which all the companies were represented for the purpose of putting in nomination a candidate. Todd a private in Co. D was selected. Being unwell I was at the officers' quarters and was not present at the meeting. I am told that both Geary and Brindle attended and made speeches.

COULTER. This is the first day of the festival of All Saints, or as it sometimes is called, "All Dead." There are some apprehensions lest there be a rising of the leperos, the city being crowded during the festival. In anticipation, General Scott has issued orders that all pulque and liquor shops be closed at least during the after part of the day and tomorrow. The train left today, and with it our two generals, Quitman and Shields. Captain

4. The text says "Marshall" but undoubtedly means William Whann MacKall (1816–1891), a West Point graduate (1837) from Maryland who, as a Confederate brigadier general in the Civil War, served as chief of staff to both Braxton Bragg and Joseph E. Johnston.

Montgomery also went down and Lt. Coulter ordered to Vera Cruz to bring up regimental property. James McLaughlin, who has been in bad health for some time back went to Vera Cruz with Captain Montgomery as foragemaster, and Henry Fishel, lately discharged. Mounted guard this morning. We have now to go to the Alameda for that purpose and mount with the regulars which does not suit the tastes of volunteers. The cause of this is that our Generals leaving, our regiment and the New York are temporarily attached to General Worth's division, and the South Carolina Regiment and the Marines to General Twiggs. Were ordered to the palace as Marine guard. Was posted at the outer doors. Was several times out on patrol in the Plaza, but no outbreak occurred, although the streets were completely crowded.

November 2

COULTER. Today is the continuation of the feast of "All Saints." No disturbance occurred. This evening on dress parade was read an order from General Scott for an election in our regiment to fill the vacancy of colonelcy and should it occasion, a vacancy for either lieutenant colonel or major, elections for such officers should follow immediately. Somehow there is rascality in this performance. It is certain that Colonel Geary has had this order for election some time, but has kept it concealed until after the departure of the train, in order, no doubt, that he might rid himself of a powerful opponent and one who most likely would have been elected were he here, Captain Montgomery, who was ordered to Vera Cruz. He has also sent Lt. Coulter, a prominent friend of Montgomery's down also, having positively assured him that there was going to be no election. The election is ordered by him to be held tomorrow morning so that there may be no opposition organized against him. On hearing these orders an opposition was immediately entered into. A delegate was sent from each of the twelve companies to nominate a candidate. Captain Montgomery was nominated by our company and supported by them and Company L, after a number of ballotings, his vote could not be increased and he was stricken out by the meeting. The contest was now between Captain Thomas Loeser, of Company A, and William A. Todd, private of Company D, neither of whom could command a majority. On introducing a third man, the vote stood thus: William A. Todd, 6; Captain Thos. Loeser, 5; Lt. Colonel Geary, 1. After our candidate (Montgomery) was dropped, Companies E and L supported Todd. The introduction of Geary's name as a candidate was improper, as the meeting was expressly to nominate an *opposition*. Geary was guilty of one very little trick this evening. A meeting of the whole regiment was first called to form an opposition to him, and knowing the meeting to be such, he and Major Brindle came in and made a couple of speeches to the men, expatiating largely on the condition in which John Geary would be placed in case the regiment elected another man to the colonelcy over him; that he had come out with us and now by fate we had been deprived of our highest ranking officer, and that he being the next in rank, was entitled to fill the vacancy, and throwing himself upon the good judgment of the men as he called them "the rank and file, the proper judges of merit."

November 3

BARCLAY. Three candidates in the field, Geary, Todd and Loeser. Neither Loeser or Todd will withdraw and so the opposition to Geary is divided. It is said that the Geary faction have offered Todd $200 or a commission as Lieutenant if he will withdraw, but he refuses. Electioneering is going on in great style. It resembles a constable's election more than a Colonel's. Geary himself is unpopular. His conduct towards the men until lately was to use a moderate term extremely arbitrary. Many hard things have been said about his behaviour at Chapultepec and a month ago he would have been easily beaten, but he has laid his plans well and by appealing to the interest and selfishness of individuals he hopes to succeed. As the opposition is divided the chances are in his favor. He has held out to many in the Regt. hopes of advancement. He has flattered many with the idea of appointing them Lieutenants. This had good weight in procuring him supporters. But the great lever was the ambition of aspiring officers, Captains and Lieutenants who are anxious to become Majors. It is amusing the disinterestedness of these gentlemen. Their argument is—If we can get Geary out of the road, Brindle will be elected Lieut. Colonel and then a vacancy will occur in the office of Major. So personal wrongs were forgotten, injuries overlooked and men supported Col. Geary (thro interested motives) who would have cut his throat had opportunity offered. Our company opposed Geary to a man. They voted for Todd, not because they preferred him to Loeser but because they thought he was the most prominent opponent of Geary. Inducements had been held out to Uncapher and myself, promises of promotion, but we understood the object and acted accordingly. The votes having been counted it is ascertained that Geary is elected. He has a majority of 15 votes over both his opponents, so the would be Majors have carried the day, but we are resolved to give them some trouble yet, before they get the *leaves* on their shoulders. The Geary party are in great spirit tonight.

COULTER. Todd was considered the candidate, but the vote being very close, Captain Loeser also appeared this morning as a candidate, thereby splitting the anti Geary vote. This was an election similar to elections in Pennsylvania. Liquor, promises and soft solder were given freely and as faithlessly. It was an exciting affair, all thinking it would be somewhat close. At evening the vote stood thus: Lt. Colonel Geary [256]; Captain Loeser [152]; Todd [89]; giving Lt. Colonel Geary a majority of [15] over the united vote of the opposition candidates. Although this united vote would not have defeated him, it is thought by many that had one only run in opposition it would have given sufficient probability of success to the party to have gained a number who only voted as they did in anticipation of the liquor they expected would follow. However, we have this consolation: It is not the voice of the regiment, and Colonel Geary, on his own reputation and popularity, could not have commanded one hundred votes. It was the scheme of a number of petty officers of the regiment, who threw their influence (and what they could take of their companies) for Geary, intending next to promote Brindle so as to create a vacancy for Major, each wishing himself to fill that office. These men were as follows: Captain Taylor, Company L; Captain Williams, Company G; Lieutenant Hambright, Company H; Lieutenant [Hiram] Wolf, Company K; Lieutenant [Alexander] McKamey, Company M, and Private [David] Duff, company B, and their influence amounted to this: Captain Taylor did not amount to much; Captain Williams took with him his entire company (at least forty votes); Lieutenant Hare drew over a goodly portion of his company; Lieutenant Hambright almost his entire company (about 75 votes); Lieutenant Wolf an entire company of nearly fifty votes; Lieutenant McKamey an entire company of over sixty votes, and the greater portion of the company to which Duff belonged voted for Geary. Many and most contemptible were the other sources from which he derived support. Sergeant [Christian W.] Leib, of Company G, a professed blackleg, on promise of a lieutenancy (which he afterward received) used money and influence, which was considerable with some classes of the regiment, for Geary. Sergeant [John A.] Cummings, of Company H, also supported him in his company for like reward and was afterward cut by the gallant colonel. An officer of this regiment, (no doubt at Geary's instigation) offered William Todd a forfeit of two hundred dollars in case he did not shortly receive a commission, if he would withdraw his name as a candidate for colonelcy. He himself also made temporary friends by his little conduct on this day. To many he promised offices. Some have since been granted. He mixed in with the most contemptible class of the regiment (fearing to attack a man who had a mind of his own) a set of drunken soldiers, and sociability, soft solder promises and threats made some votes there. So it went, a piece of complete pipe laying, but thank fortune, Company E voted *unanimously* against him. The scene which followed the result of his election was anything but creditable to the colonel. Liquor was gotten for the occasion and there was a general and promiscuous drunk among his friends (among which there are few good soldiers). His quarters were used freely and the noise and sprees lasted until very late.

November 4

BARCLAY. A vacancy having occured an election takes place for Lt. Colonel. Our company for the purpose of keeping up the opposition for tomorrow's election have determined to support Lieut. Armstrong. It is a compliment to the Lieut. and shows the confidence we all have in his military abilities. There is not the slightest prospect of electing him, but it will keep up the spirit of opposition. The votes having been counted, it is ascertained that Brindle is elected by a large majority. So tomorrow comes the tug of war. Tonight we have a meeting of delegates from each company who are either partly or entirely opposed to Geary. Companies A, B, C, D, E, F, I, and L are represented. The object of the meeting is to put in nomination a candidate for Major. The meeting is held in our quarters and I am the delegate from Company E. Altho not very well I attend. Lt. McMichael in the third ballot receives the nomination. The prospects of electing him are pretty good.

COULTER. This was the day of election for Lt. Colonel vice Geary *promoted*. Major Brindle had been generally spoken of throughout the regiment and it was hardly expected to defeat him. However, Lt. Armstrong of our company was named as the opposition candidate. It was thought thereby to unite the party for tomorrow's fight, which was considered would be the tug of war. In the evening the vote stood thus: Brindle . . . . ; Armstrong . . . . ; giving Brindle a much larger majority than any expected. There was a meeting of the regiment in the evening to nominate a candidate for Major, the candidates fearing the little party who voted against Brindle. It was to one intent, to keep as many candidates in the field as possible. Immediately after the result of today's election was known, Brindle, (as Geary did yesterday) gave his friends a spree. This prevented many of them from attending the meeting, but we all were there and by our votes equalized all the candidates and prevented any of them from coming to any conclusion and at last they adjourned in a row. After this we had a private delegate meeting in our quarters of members from each of the following companies: "A," "B," "C," "D," "E," "F," "G," and "L." Three of these companies had no candidate at all (A. C. & E.) and were sworn to defeat the faction that had gained the last two days. Portions of the other companies wished to join in this. At this meeting Lt. Richard McMichael, of Company "A" was nominated as the candidate for Major. Our company was on quarters guard today with Lt. McMichael, and he being our candidate, we had of course quite an easy time of it.

November 5
BARCLAY. The candidates for _____ major are Capt. Williams, McKamey, [Lt. Charles] McDermitt, Duff of Co. B and McMichael. The three former of the Geary faction. Duff was before us but will not abide the nomination. Lt. Hare of Co. F who was also before our meeting seeing that he has no chance himself is throwing his influence for Capt. Williams. Appearances are against us but we are determined to make as stout a fight as possible.

The votes having been counted our man McMichael has a majority of 22 over Williams his highest opponent. The boys are in glorious spirits at their success and resolve to make a night of it. As I am still sick and somewhat worse this evening, I move my quarters to the officer's room. A great deal of liquor was drank and noise made at the victory and considering that we, Company E, have been instrumental in defeating the long planned schemes of certain ambitious gentlemen, I think our boys had good cause to rejoice and make merry.

COULTER. Who our candidate was had been kept perfectly secret and this morning several of the opposition appeared, although a number did not. After the polls were opened and Company "A" had voted (being McMichael's company, they unanimously voted for him and that quietly) our candidate was announced and we ran him in by surprise. In the evening the vote stood thus: Lieutenant McMichael . . . . ; Captain Williams . . . . ; Captain McDermitt . . . . ; Lieutenant McKamey . . . . ; and scattering . . . . . So this time we selected our candidate. After being twice defeated by unfair means, at last so disunited them as to defeat the entire faction. As a consequence there was quite a spree, although I think neither so long or noisy as the others.

November 6

BARCLAY. I am still at Lt. Armstrong's Quarters being very unwell from an attack of the fever and ague.

COULTER. Today was spent rather peaceably discussing the late elections and occasionally each party damning the opposition.

November 7

BARCLAY. At Dress Parade this evening I am told orders from Gen. Scott were read approving of the election of Colonel and Lieut. Colonel and disapproving of the election of Major, the Regt. being too small to admit of three field officers. The Regiment are very much dissatisfied and consider that it is owing to misrepresentation of Geary who dislikes McMichael. For my part I have no doubt that Geary was well aware that Gen. Scott would not approve of the election of any Major. The idea of electing a Major was a trick of his own to secure his own success, and had either Williams or McDermitt been successful they would have met the same fate McMichael did. However much the plan speaks for the cunning and ingenuity of Geary, it shows the way he is willing to treat his friends and is in perfect consistency with the opinion I have long formed of his character.[5]

5. Barclay's suspicions were well founded. In a hasty note to General Scott, Geary described Lieutenant McMichael as "so deficient in education as to render him incompetent" to perform the duties of a major. (Geary to Scott, n.d., Geary Papers, Beinecke Library, Yale University.)

COULTER. Mounted guard this morning. Our company are sent to the Alameda, but not being wanted by the adjutant mounting guard, thereby escaping a day's duty. A great deal of littleness and rascality had been used by Colonel Geary during the late elections, but today the whole scheme was consummated. On dress parade an order from General Scott was read of the following purport: Approving of the elections for colonel and Lieutenant colonel ordering them to act until the will of the Governor of Pennsylvania[6] could be known on the subject, at the same time disapproving of and annulling the election for Major on the grounds that the regiment is not large enough to require a third field officer. General Scott must have been misinformed in the first place as to the strength of the regiment or he would certainly not have ordered an election for that office in case of vacancy. If the regiment is so small as not to require a third field officer, why order an election for colonel, when we had already two, unless John Geary had misrepresented the case in order that he might be promoted to the colonelcy, and finding his favorite (Captain Williams) defeated for major, altered his statement as having been mistaken. It is, I believe, a fact that he first reported the regiment eight hundred strong and afterward reported it either four or six hundred and also spoke very disparagingly of the major-elect.

November 8

BARCLAY. Monday. A Mexican convicted of attempting to murder a soldier was sentenced to receive 100 lashes, 25 each Monday. He received the first installment today in the Plaza. The greasers who had collected in large numbers were very indignant at the treatment of their brother and commenced stoning the Guard. A few Dragoons who were present charged in among the crowd, dispersed them and took two or three of the ring leaders prisoners. The outbreak has caused some little excitement but the whipping will go on as usual.

COULTER. Was quite a scene in the main Plaza. A Mexican convicted of attempting the life of an officer had been sentenced to receive twenty-five lashes each day for four successive Mondays. The first installment of his punishment was inflicted today. There was a very small squad in attendance and the Plaza was crowded with Leperos, etc. When the whipping commenced a number of stones were thrown at the guard from among the crowd. A party of some six or eight dragoons soon dispersed them, charging entirely to the portals. They made some bloody heads and took a

6. Francis Raun Shunk (1788–1848) was a self-made man who rose from poverty to be elected governor of Pennsylvania in 1844. A Jacksonian Democrat, Shunk was a popular, reform-minded administrator. Soon after his reelection, he was compelled to resign (9 July 1848) on account of poor health, and he died shortly thereafter. Shunk was succeeded in the governor's chair by William F. Johnston, presiding officer of the state senate and an uncle of Thomas Barclay.

number of prisoners who were sent to the guard house to undergo the same punishment. General Twiggs was present superintending the performance. The old fellow seems to take perfect delight in such amusements, rising up in his saddle at every stroke as though he was inflicting the punishment himself. Several of the hombres who were taken came to him pleading for their release. It was amusing to see the old chap whenever any one would come up turn away his head and put his hands to his ears. This was the first case of public Mexican flogging in the city and evidently created a great excitement among the citizens. The streets were densely crowded until night and a soldier was compelled to be on his watch walking the streets.

November 9

BARCLAY. The "Monitor" a Mexican newspaper contains a apology for the mob yesterday. It is decidedly rich to us who are acquainted with Mexican character. The reason why the amiable greasers were excited was because the Mexican was tied to a cross and scourged like the blessed Saviour. A cross piece on the post gave them the idea of the cross but how they could see in a dirty lousy Mexican who had been convicted of the most infamous of crimes, a cowardly attempt to assassinate, any resemblance to the Son of God is more than I can imagine.

In the City of Mexico and in all the principal cities of the Republic there is a class of people more numerous than even the priests and whose privileges like those of the holy brotherhood must be very considerably curtailed before the good and peaceable citizens of this country can enjoy any happiness. I refer to the Leperos[7] and Ladrones, a race which may be called distinct and which resembles the Gypsy tribes who roam over Asia. The Gypsies are a roving, the Leperos a stationary people. It is said that they have certain rules of government and the great bond which binds them together is poverty and the love of plunder. They sleep in the old buildings in the outskirts of the City, shunning every kind of labour. During the day they crowd round the corners of the streets wrapped in their dirty blankets and ready for any enterprise however villanous. Like all Mexicans they are cowardly and fear to attempt any very daring dangerous acts. But their ingenuity and numbers fit them for any crime, either to pick a pocket or overturn a government. Being men of great leisure they are politicians and formidable in numbers their support is eagerly sought by aspiring candidates for office. Santa Anna paid particular attention to those Republicans and was a great favorite. Backed by them he was absolute master in the City of Mexico. They would do anything for him that was reasonable, but even he could not bring his Ladrones to the right point when the Yankees

7. Rabble, the outcasts of society; not (as some American soldiers carelessly assumed) those suffering from leprosy.

got among them. They have the same objection to standing a charge of the cold steel as the veterans from the North. The Leperos and Ladrones are good sons of the church. They are in regular attendance and their sanctimonious appearance when in that duty is very edifying.

November 15

BARCLAY. For the last week I have been unwell suffering from as I judge the effects of the exposure on the night of the 13th of September. The Mexican was again soundly whipped today. As threats had been made a heavy force was under arms who would have given the greasers "gas" had they made an outbreak. Altho a great crowd had assembled no resistance was made.

COULTER. Since last entry have had a couple days of a severe ear ache. Was most uncomfortable, unable to sleep but little. Today the second installment of punishment was administered to the Mexican mentioned on Monday last, together with several others taken in the act of stoning same day. There was a heavy guard and dragoon patrol in the Plaza who kept the greasers at a distance. Those intimidated either by the guard or their reception last day and punishment of their comrades did not attempt anything of a row. Tonight there arrived at this place from Vera Cruz, an express who came through in three days and four hours.

November 16

BARCLAY. Company E on Quarter Guard.

COULTER. Our company are on quarter guard today.

November 18

BARCLAY. A mail came in bringing letters and papers from the States. We had expected to hear from the men at Puebla but are disappointed. I received one or two letters but none from home.

On the 9th inst, orders were issued to resume Company and regt. Drill. I have been for sometime in command of the Company. Lt. Armstrong is under arrest for leaving his Guard. His offence is very trifling and a Court Martial will acquit him under the circumstances. We have Company Drills every third morning in the yard. A large quantity of blank cartridges have been distributed to each company. Our company drill and fire remarkably well. For want of something to do I have lately been engaged in copyng the General and Regimental Orders. It may sometime be interesting to look over those orders when we return home. It is unfortunate that they have been so carelessly kept.

COULTER. Mail came in today from Vera Cruz.

November 21

BARCLAY. Received two months' pay from Paymaster Burns. The Privates each received $21, no clothing account being charged. This squares us up to the 31st October.

November 26

BARCLAY. The officers of the army have got up a complimentary benefit for Canete, the Spanish actress. She is a very superior woman and as her acting has been the cause of driving away many a dull hour the compliment is deserved. The house was crowded from the floor to the gallery. The performance did not please me as much as a Tragedy which I had witnessed on a former occasion. Canete personated a spoilt boy and acted to admiration. The New York and South Carolina Volunteers having made similar movements, it has been attempted to get up a Petition in our Regt. to Congress to recall us. About three fourths of those present have signed. A majority of the officers oppose the petition. Their avowed objection is that perhaps the petition might have some effect and thereby they will lose their offices, most of them being now in a better business than they ever were before. I do not see the impropriety of the petition. The fighting part of the war is over and it is not likely that the enemy for a year at least will raise another army. There is neither honor or prospect in a garrison life. Our ranks are already much thinned by deaths and discharges and it is intended to fill them up by recruiting. The idea of being obliged to receive a number of recruits into the company is outrageous. We are all opposed to it, but there is no help. Being soldiers we must submit. After a year of very active service, our affairs at home require our attention. If there was any likelihood of an engagement I do not believe that a single man in our company would wish to return until the fight was over, but the question is asked, "Supposing this war should continue 5 or 8 years, are we to be kept doing garrison duty?" The places of the dead being filled by every vagabond that a recruiting officer can pick up.

COULTER. This was pay day. Received two months pay and clothing allowance. At night attended the National Theatre. It was the benefit of Senora Canete, a celebrated Spanish performer, gotten up by the officers of the American Army. The vestibule was most magnificently decorated and lighted. The theatre proper was finely illuminated and crowded from pit to gallery. The performance was Spanish called "Le Gamin de Paris."[8] Canete appeared in the character of the boy Joseph. She supported her part exceedingly well. The scenery was fine. From the number of the audience it was quite a purse for the performer. After the night's expenses were paid she received something over two thousand dollars.

8. Described by *The American Star* as "the beautiful comedy in two acts, written in French by Messrs. Bayard and Dandenburg and translated into Spanish by Lombia."

November 28

COULTER. Mounted guard this morning. Sent to the main guard house from which our company were detailed as the market guard. Had an easy time during the day and at night were sent to the National Theatre as a guard. The performance was Spanish, and could not therefore understand the argument, but as a pantomime it was excellent and the scenery the most magnificent I ever beheld. The performance was called "Don Juan Tenorio,"[9] a tragedy composed of three acts as follows: The Pantheon of the Tenorios; The Statue of Don Gonzalo; and the Grace of God and the Apotheosis of Love. Canete appeared in the character of "The Spirit of Dona Inez."

November 30

COULTER. The New York and South Carolina Regiments have prepared petitions to send to Congress praying to be disbanded. It had been attempted in our regiment, but many of the officers, the colonel at their head, oppose it as "derogatory to the character of the regiment." So they say, but the true reason is they are better situated as officers of the army than they would be at home.

December 1

COULTER. Samuel Milner, a member of our company, who has been lounging about the city for some time back drunk, disappeared today. Supposed to have been murdered. This is more probable from the fact that he has made several very narrow escapes and once we examined the canal, ditches and whole quarters of the city. At the time he was last seen he was very far gone with liquor, and even if not murdered, could not last very long. This is the class of men generally killed in the city. A sober soldier seldom gets into trouble.

December 6

BARCLAY. A mail came in from Vera Cruz. It brought me no letters from home. Gen. Patterson also came up. There are a great many troops on the route between here and Vera Cruz. The mail was under the charge of Col. Hays' Rangers.[10] These Texian Rangers are a singular looking set of

9. "Don Juan Tenorio," written in 1844 by José Zorilla, was a popular theatrical adaptation of the Don Juan theme in which the hero was redeemed in the last act by the love of a pure woman.

10. Born in Tennessee in 1817, John Coffee Hays came to Texas in 1837 and became a leader of the famed Texas Rangers in 1840. In the Mexican War, the diminutive, boyish-looking Hays was Colonel of the Texas Mounted Volunteers, which the Mexicans called "Los Diabolos Tejanos"—The Texas Devils. After the war he settled in California as sheriff of rip-roaring San Francisco during the gold-rush days and became rich, peaceable, and respectable in his later years. He died in 1883.

soldiers. Without uniform and armed to the teeth they are a rough party. The Mexicans are very much afraid of them. On the march they were out scouting continually. From their appearance I do not think they are the men of San Jacinto.[11] The old Texians I judge are generally snug on their lands. These troops are most of them young men, many mere boys, and altho they may be admirable as scouters, there are a great many corps in the army upon whom I would place much more dependence in a heavy fight.

COULTER. The advance of General Patterson's train came in today, the regiment of Texas Rangers bringing the mail. They are a rough looking set of fellows, without anything like uniform either in dress or arms, some carrying long hunting rifles, some state rifles and some carbines.[12]

December 7

BARCLAY. Last night Capt. Taylor of Co. L died in his quarters of the brain fever. Capt. Taylor was from Bedford County and until his last fatal attack enjoyed good health. He was very clever and very intimate with many in our company. His friends intend that his remains shall be taken home. Dr. [Samuel D.] Scott of the 11th Inf., a native of Bedford and a great friend of Dick Johnston's has been very low with the brain fever. He has partially recovered and intends returning home by the next train. It was his sword that Dick wore on the fatal day of the Molino del Rey and I have seen the belting covered and stained [with] the blood of the gallant dead. Since I have been in the City I have made every inquiry in regard to the last moments of poor Dick. All accounts agree that he died most nobly. After we arrived in the City, Lt. Drum informed me that he had seen Johnston's body on the field and had sent it in a wagon to the hospital at Mixcoac, that the Regt. had taken it from there and buried him alongside of Col. Graham at the Hacienda occupied by the 11th Regt. previous to the Battle[.] Under the impression that this account was correct, I had rested satisfied. But upon making inquires a few days ago I find it was untrue. An officer does lie buried beside Col. Graham, but it is not Lieut. Johnston. The 11th Regt. on the night of the 8th September lay at Tacubaya and they never received the body. I have been several times at the quarters of the 11th Regt. I have received Richard's effects and sent his

---

11. At the Battle of San Jacinto on 21 April 1836, a Texas army under General Sam Houston defeated the Mexicans commanded by Santa Anna, holding him captive until he signed a treaty establishing the independence of the Republic of Texas.

12. According to the chief authority on the Texas Rangers, "their uniforms were an outlandish assortment of long-tailed blue coats and bob-tailed black ones, slouched felt hats, dirty panamas and black leather caps. Most of them wore long bushy beards." (Walter Prescott Webb, *The Texas Rangers: A Century of Frontier Defense* [Boston: Houghton Mifflin, 1935], 118.)

money home by Lieut. Tippin. His trunk I will send home the first opportunity. From all that I can there learn, he was buried at the hospital at Mixcoac. A private of the Regt. who was there sick says he saw him buried. What credit he deserves it is hard to say.

Another body of troops came in today. McGarvey and McCutcheon who had been left behind sick at Vera Cruz rejoined us. They both look well.

COULTER. Today General Patterson came in with the remainder of his train and force, having some three thousand men. Two of our sick left by the company at Vera Cruz, David McCutcheon and Charles McGarvey, came up with this train. Today Company E was on market guard and at night were sent as a patrol to the Principal Theatre or circus. Madame Armond is the great female equestrienne, but she is only remarkable for the unusual heavy proportions of her features and limbs. There was a pantomime performed "The Coopers in a Row," good in some respects.

December 8

BARCLAY. Capt. Johnston came up today in company with another reinforcement. Shields, McClaran, Stickle, Underwood and Waters are with him. They all look remarkably hearty, a little sunburnt and tired from the tramp. From them we learn that Dougherty, Heasley, Kuhns, Landon and Rager have been discharged and that Hagerty, Thomas, Simms are dead. Old Hagerty was a first rate soldier. He done duty up to a short time before we left Puebla and was never sick a day. He was a very passionate man and a great brute when in liquor. This was however but seldom. When sober he was a very agreeable fellow. Simms never done much duty. He was received into the company in place of Byerly in Pittsburgh. He there one night fell out of the second story of the warehouse, from the effect of which fall he was always lame. He died of the brain fever. Poor Nat Thomas never recovered from the injury he received when the wagon run over him. He was also imprudent, eating too much when sick and taking medicine. He was a good boy and was a great favorite of mine. When I was unwell at Jalapa he was very attentive to me and we often took long walks together. Poor Nat, peace to thy memory.

COULTER. Today the First Pennsylvania Regiment, under Colonel Wyncoop and about four hundred recruits, came in. With them the following of our sick left at Puebla rejoined the company: Captain Johnston, Corporal William Shields, Privates Samuel McClaran, Henry Stickle, James Underwood and Samuel Waters. Of our sick left at Puebla, George Hagerty, Thomas Simms and Nathaniel Thomas, have died. Discharged, Arch. Dougherty, Michael Heasley, Phillip Kuhns, Edmund Landon and James Rager. Dougherty had been left at Perote and came up as far as Puebla with Colonel Wyncoop, where he was discharged.

December 9

BARCLAY. A train went to Vera Cruz. Dr. Scott has gone home. I sent Dick Johnston's sword and trunk with him. This train is large and is under the command of Major General Twiggs. Lieut. Black of Co. B is discharged on resignation and gone home. I have written several letters and several of the company have sent small articles to their friends at home in Dick's trunk.

COULTER. A train left today for Vera Cruz. The petition gotten up in our regiment to Congress for a discharge was signed by some three hundred and sent down by this train with Dr. Scott of Bedford. One of our company, Daniel Kuhns, died in the hospital in this city during the night of a wound received the morning after we entered the City of Mexico.

December 10

BARCLAY. Last night near midnight Daniel S. Kuhns died in hospital having been confined to his room since the 14th of Sept. For some time after he was wounded the surgeons entertained no hopes of his recovery. For the purpose of cheering him up, Dr. McMillen promised him a discharge but finding that he was getting well he refused to discharge him. This was discouraging and from the time that he gave up hopes of getting home he pined away. His case is another instance of what I have frequently remarked in this country, the fatal effect of despondency of spirits. Kuhns was a printer by trade and a man of very general information. This expedition had much improved him in every respect and had he been permitted to return home he would have been a valuable member of society. He was buried today with due honors, religious and military.

COULTER. Today Daniel Kuhns was buried with the usual honors. Special service was read by the Captain on the occasion. The company are on quarter guard and inline picket today.

December 11

BARCLAY. Lieut. Coulter arrived from Vera Cruz. He came up in company with the escort of the British Minister. He reports that Gen. Butler[13]

13. William Orlando Butler (1791–1880), Kentucky lawyer, politician, soldier, and poet, alternated his military and civilian careers. He served with Andrew Jackson during the War of 1812, playing a decisive role in the victory at New Orleans. Returning to Kentucky, he was elected to two terms in Congress and was an unsuccessful Democratic candidate for governor. Appointed major general of volunteers in 1846, he was wounded at Monterey. When President Polk removed Winfield Scott from command he chose Butler, a loyal Democrat, to head the army of occupation. At war's end Butler was rewarded with the Democratic vice-presidential nomination as Lewis Cass's running mate in 1848. Butler also fell short in his bid for the U.S. Senate in 1851 as well as in his presidential ambitions in 1856. He remained loyal to the Union during the Civil War, though too old for further military service.

will shortly be here, that McLaughlin has gone home on furlough and that Adjt. Dutton is coming up with a number of recruits for the 1st and 2nd Penna. Regts. The wagon with the officers' baggage Coulter left with Butler's train.

December 12

BARCLAY. A row occured between the Greasers and some of the 1st Penna. Regt. One or two of our men were killed or badly hurt and near a dozen of the Greasers were used up. The fight commenced at a drinking house.

COULTER. Lt. Coulter of our company returned today from Vera Cruz in company with the British Special Minister (Doyle).[14] He reports General Butler's train at Puebla expected here in five or six days. He also says that Adjutant Dutton comes up with this train bringing about one hundred recruits for the two Pennsylvania regiments. The private wishes of the regiment are that the brave adjutant who went home on such a fierce errand may make his exit from this world before reaching the City of Mexico. Was quite a row today with the greasers near the quarters of the First Pennsylvania Regiment. For some cause or other they stoned some of the Pennsylvanians, killing one and wounding another severely. A portion of the regiment and a neighboring patrol soon cleared the street, killing from five to ten greasers. Am not certain but that Lt. Coulter came up yesterday.

December 13

COULTER. This evening one of our company, H. Stickle, who came up lately, unable to find his road to quarters, wandered to the suburbs of the city where he was attacked by some Mexicans and robbed of his bayonet and twelve dollars in money. Some of the company, wishing to go after the thief, we requested the officer of the guard (Lt. Valumsheybank)[15] to let us go as patrol, but he in his Dutch ignorance would not permit it, saying that we only wanted to plunder. This caused considerable of a jangle and language improper was used both by and towards a commissioned officer, and had we been in the regular service would have subjected all to twenty-four hours bucking and gagging.[16] However, he was as green as we were impudent, and having gotten the colonel's permission, went out in spite

14. Percy William Doyle (1806–1888) was a British career diplomat who served with the British mission to Washington in the mid-1820s before being assigned to Mexico.

15. No officer with a name even approximating "Valumsheybank" can be found on the rolls of the U.S. Army in Mexico.

16. The victim was seated on the ground with wrists tied together and his arms wrapped around the knees, which were drawn against the chest. A stick or pole was then inserted between the knees and elbows, so that he could neither stand nor move. That was bucking. He was also gagged. An hour or two of this punishment was considered sufficient.

of him. On coming near the place found that Stickle had been so badly scared that he could not point out the particular door into which the men went after plundering him. Searched a long time but could find no clue to them and returned without any prisoners, but we had sufficient for our trouble in gaining a victory over the Dutch tencenter.

December 17

BARCLAY. But little has been doing the last few days. At quarters we have cleaned out another room, the new comers somewhat crowding us. A couple of nights ago Stickle being on guard at the hospital started for quarters and lost his way. Three or four Mexicans got hold of him in a drinking house and robbed him of his bayonet and $10 in gold which he had saved from Jalapa. The Dutchman arrived at quarters in a rage and considerably frightened. Some of the company returned with him to the store but could find no Mexicans. A Tennessee and Indiana Regt. came in today. They are part of Gen. Butler's command. The Regts. are full, men look pretty hard. More troops are expected in daily.

COULTER. General Butler's train, or at least a portion of it, came in today.

December 18

BARCLAY. Orders received this afternoon to march tomorrow to Tacubaya. A few days ago some of the old Regiments left the City for that village. The object I believe is to make room for the new troops. As the orders are sudden and unexpected, everything is in bustle and confusion preparing for a start. I made out descriptive rolls after night for the men in the hospital. Bates, Hansberry, McClelland, Sargent, Shaw and Hoffer remain behind in hospital, Brady and Cloud as their attendants.

COULTER. The regiment received orders this morning to march tomorrow morning to the village of Tacubaya, where Colonel Riley's brigade went a few days ago. We are now attached to General Cushing's[17] brigade which is composed of the following regiments: First and Second Pennsylvania, New York, South Carolina and Massachusetts Volunteers.

17. Hailed by Wendell Philips (who despised his politics) as "the most learned man now living," Caleb Cushing (1800–1879) of Massachusetts was variously a jurist, scholar, diplomat, and politician, though his attempt to add "soldier" to that list (as these journal entries reveal) met with somewhat less success. A Harvard graduate at age seventeen, master of half a dozen languages, and congressman (first as a Whig and then as a Democrat), he was the minister to China who negotiated the treaty opening the Middle Kingdom to American commerce. After the Mexican War, Franklin Pierce, whose presidential nomination Cushing had engineered, named him attorney general. Despite his brilliance, Cushing managed to be

December 19

BARCLAY. Up early. Went to hospital with the descriptive rolls. Our company detained near an hour waiting for the wagon with the officers' baggage. About 9 A.M. Regt. formed and a flag was presented to the Regt. by the Stockton Artillerists (Co. K). Geary made a speech which was poorly cheered. Regt. marched to the Plaza, stacked arms and about 10 A.M. marched from the City to San Angel, in company with the New York, South Carolina, 1st Penna. and Massachusetts Regts., all forming a Brigade under Brigadier General Cushing. The command marched past Maj. Gen. Scott who from a balcony reviewed the troops. Day very warm and road dusty. It is evident that Gen. Cushing does not understand how to march troops. I would not fancy making a long tramp under him. A party from our company who were left behind to pack the wagon judging that our destination was Tacubaya went to that village. They had somewhat of a tramp before they arrived at San Angel. The 2nd Pa. Regt. is quartered in a monastery. The quarters are good. Our company occupy four cells. There is room for 10 men in a room. The company officers have two rooms to themselves. Water is abundant. A large reservoir about 150 yds in length, 50 in breadth and 10 feet in depth lies some 20 yds from the porch in front of our rooms. A tank conveys water in abundance under the windows. The water can be reached with the hands. All things considered, these are the best quarters we have had in Mexico.

COULTER. This morning the regiment marched. Some of us not being at quarters when they started, took a short cut and soon arrived at Tacubaya. Found that the regiment was not there and after waiting some time learned that on arriving at the plaza the order had been countermanded and they had marched to the village of San Angel, about nine miles from Mexico. After another tramp of about five or six miles, arrived at that place where we found the whole brigade. The First Pennsylvania were quartered about half a mile from this in the old building where we were quartered before the storming of Chapultepec. Our regiment are now quartered in a very large monastery. Drew no rations and had quite a starving time of it.

---

wrong on virtually every major issue in the years before the Civil War and is best remembered as the butt of poet James Russell Lowell's cruel verse, as found in *The Biglow Papers:*

"Gineral C. is a dreffle smart man;
He's ben on all sides that give places or pelf,
But consistency still wuz a part of his plan,_____
He's ben true to *one* party and thet is himself."

10

Decidedly the Best Quarters
We Have Ever Had in Mexico
San Angel

December 20

BARCLAY. From our porches took a view. San Angel like most of Mexican villages covers a great deal of ground. Gardens and orchards intervening between the houses. The scenery around the village is very fine. All the battle fields of the valley are visible. The monastery is the principal building of the place. It is very large covering several acres. It belongs to the Carmelite Monks and is a kind of summer residence. The majority of the monks are now in the City, a detail of about 20 being left as a guard of the premises. There is attached to the monastery an orchard containing over 100 acres, the whole surrounded by a fine wall over 12 feet high. A wall like this in the States would be very expensive. Here it is more cheap, stones of all sizes being thrown together and cemented by the admirable plaster which they have in all parts of this country. They have no frost here and a wall will stand for years which would not remain a single season in the States. The orchard is laid out in plots, alleys of 8 feet running the entire length and breadth of it. The plots are overgrown with sprouts and bushes. The orchard is watered from the tank, each bed or plot being alternately overflowed. A small creek flows through the lower part which is spanned by three very fine bridges. The scenery along the creek is beautiful. A large summer house, a bath house and an oratory, built in different quarters, afford the monks places for rest, bathing and prayer. At present the weather is too cool for bathing. But in the warm season when a torrid sun hangs direct over the head this orchard must be a Paradise. Among these woods the monks can wander and meditate over the writings of the holy fathers. The quiet stillness of the grove invites to meditation. Amid "such a wilderness as this" love too might find "transport and security" but that is forbidden. No woman dare enter the precincts of the monastery and these sylvan shades have never witnessed any scenes of love. Were I disposed to say goodbye to the world, its cares and pleasures and devote the remainder of my days to meditation and prayer I know of no spot which would be more congenial to my taste than the old monastery of San Angel. But as it is not at present my intention to surrender the beggarly elements of the flesh, I must rest intent in admiring the fancy and taste of our neighbours, the Carmelite Monks.

It was through the village of San Angel that the retreating masses of Mexicans fled from Contreras pursued by a handful of Americans. It was necessary for them to go thro San Angel to reach either the City or Churubusco. From the housetops of this village there were many anxious spectators watching the field of Contreras on the evening of the 19th and morning of the 20th of August. An English resident points out where the balls from the pursuers struck the houses. This Englishman formerly lived in Pittsburgh, where he left behind him a wife. He has been in Mexico for many years, is married and has many children. He is wealthy and was near being hung up for concealing and conniving at the escape of Major Borland[1] and some American prisoners.

San Angel will be remembered in history as the place where the deserters, taken at Churubusco, or a part of them, were whipped and executed.

COULTER. To keep off hunger did not get up until ten o'clock and then breakfasted on hot coffee. San Angel is quite a neat, clean, little village, not large however. It is said to be the healthiest spot in the State of Mexico. The buildings do not present that dilapidated appearance as in many other small towns. It is principally church property. The buildings in which we are quartered are called "El Convento del Carmel." It is a large building containing several hundred cells for monks and a large chapel attached to it. It belongs to the order of "Carmelite Monks." There are about a dozen of them here now who have the building in charge. They wear a very coarse brown dress and sandals. There is a very large orchard attached to this building containing a hundred acres or more and surrounded by a high stone wall. It is watered by two streams and also from a large basin of water in one end. The building is also supplied by a fine aquaduct. The orchard has been allowed to run wild for some time and some parts are now grown up with underbrush. Our company are quartered alone in one wing of the building. We have four cells and the officers two. We have also a porch at the end of the hall from which there is a fine view of the country and the whole line of our operations up to the battle of Churubusco can also be seen. These are decidedly the best quarters we have ever had in Mexico. Drew a ration of bread which it was a punishment to eat and so lived until evening on apples found in the orchard.

1. Solon Borland (1808–1864) of Arkansas, along with Colonel John P. Gaines, allowed himself and his command to be captured at Encarnación early in 1847. After winning his freedom, he went straight from Mexico to the United States Senate and from there to a diplomatic post in Central America. In retaliation for a slight he suffered there, the American navy obliterated the offending city of Greytown (in present-day Nicarauga). He joined the Confederacy in 1861, rising to brigadier general shortly before his retirement due to poor health.

December 21

BARCLAY. Meat rations issued today for the first [time] since we have left the City. Our bread has been mouldy and we only eat it because we have nothing else to eat. This is always the case on a move. The Commissary Department manages to get out of order and we suffer. Another misfortune is that there is as yet no Mexican market here. However in a few days all will go well. The Commissary will get into order and the Mexican market women will flock to the quarters of the soldiers, their best customers.

General Cushing has issued a batch of orders, five daily roll calls, company drills 4 hours each day, Regt. drills daily, etc. A new broom sweeps clean. As a mattter of course his orders will not be obeyed. The last time I called the roll was immediately after Chapultepec was carried in order to ascertain who was behind. At Jalapa and Puebla we were verdant and had reveillie and tattoo calls, but of late we have been getting over our greenness bravely and Cushing's orders won't work. The policy of frequent roll calling and drilling is good when applied to regulars but the volunteers should be exempt from all duties except such as are absolutely necessary. They are composed of a different material from the regulars and should be differently managed.

Smith, who we left behind at Puebla, rejoined the company today. He is in fine health.

Adjt. Dutton arrived with his recruits. Forty are to be distributed in our Regt. They are a hard looking party, many of them Dutch.[2] The greatest anxiety prevails in our company lest we should get any of these gentlemen. It is a dirty business this recruiting of volunteers. No man when he left home had any idea that he would be forced to associate with a lot of recruits, generally the refuse of society. In no former war I believe did Government resort to such means of increasing and filling up the volunteer corps. But in the present war there appears to be a continuous effort to assimilate the volunteers to the regular forces. Whenever the men can resist they do so, but in a case like the present it is useless to make resistance and however outrageous to our feelings we as soldiers must bow in submission and the vacancies occasioned by sickness and death in our ranks are to be filled by strangers. A lot of lousy Dutch and still more worthless natives are to supply the places of Hartford, Melville, McGinley, Johnston and a band of noble souls, our former comrades who forever will be dear in our memories.

COULTER. Fared rather better today, having drawn a ration of meat. We are settled now and will draw rations more regularly. Our General, who is rather a green hand, has ordered severe drilling, but there is a poor chance

2. In nineteenth-century American usage, "Dutch" did not refer to those from Holland but to those from Germany (a corruption of "Deutsch").

of having his orders obeyed among old volunteers. Adjutant Dutton came here today with nearly a hundred recruits for ours and the First Pennsylvania Regiments. A very hard feeling exists in both regiments with regard to these recruits and all companies are reluctant about receiving them. Another member of our company, Joseph Smith, left sick at Puebla, came up with these recruits and joined us again today.

December 22

BARCLAY. Regt. early under arms. The Brigade will be reviewed today by Gen. Scott. Each Regt. drawn up on their own ground. As the General advanced the Band struck up "Hail to the Chief,"[3] the troops presented arms. The General looks care worn, much thinner than when we saw him at Vera Cruz. He still rides his old bob. He was accompanied by Generals Patterson, Butler and several officers with an escort. The party are on a visit to Contreras. Patterson is a heavy set man without anything remarkable in his appearance. I did not get a good view of Butler. Johnston, Coulter and several officers followed the party and had a pleasant trip to the battle ground. While Scott was pointing out and explaining to the others the various movements he gave it as his opinion that the Battle of Contreras was one of the most glorious on record.

COULTER. Today the brigade was reviewed by General Scott. After review mounted guard. Stationed at the Plaza over the Mexican stores to prevent the soldiers from plundering them. In the evening General Cushing issued orders to the officer of the main guard to take charge of all the liquors in the stores and have them placed under lock and key to prevent its being sold to the men. We had quite a time collecting the liquor. At one store the owner persisted that he had none and every demijohn which we touched declared to contain "vinegar," but all proved to contain different kinds of liquor. This order caused some swearing among the old topers who said the general was a twenty-eight gallon-law-man.[4]

December 23

BARCLAY. Gen. Cushing has placed all the liquor in the village under lock, sealed with his seal. This is an old trick. Officers can soak their skins full. They thus enjoy the privilege themselves and at the same time know that others are deprived of their wonted potations. But Cushing might as well attempt to make Methodists out of the Carmelite Monks as to keep

3. Not yet reserved solely for an appearance by the president of the United States, "Hail to the Chief" was just one of the numerous "national airs" that served at patriotic occasions in lieu of an official national anthem.
4. An exaggerated reference to the notorious "fifteen-gallon law" enacted in Massachusetts in 1838 and designed to discourage alcoholic consumption by prohibiting the purchase of liquor in quantities smaller than fifteen gallons at a time.

soldiers from liquor. The old topers, veterans in many a Bacchanalian war, are as great strategists as Gen. Worth himself. Their resources are inexhaustible. The pleasures, the comforts of life they can despise. Like philosophers they can surrender or do without even their rations of bread and beef. Clothing and blankets are mere vain appurtenances. But liquor is the sine qua non of existence, the great elexir which drives away all cares and gilds with delights the hardships, trials and wants of the soldier.

December 24

BARCLAY. Altho 24 hours have not elapsed since Gen. Cushing placed the great seal of state upon the liquor shops, the tactics of the soldiers are being developed. Sundry ill looking greasers folded in their blankets meet the soldier at every corner and with a very knowing look, lisp "Wysky." At the same time a pat on the breast informs him that a bottle of that interesting liquid is concealed under their blanket. The guard are ordered to arrest all such customers but they never see them selling, always turning their back to the fellow that is taking a swallow. When I was making my morning report this morning in passing thro the market place, one of the Guard swore he was there to protect the market people and there was nothing to sell but whiskey. Which bye the bye was true. This being Christmas Eve, for the purpose of keeping up an ancient and time honored custom our company has determined to have a little convivial meeting. The arrangements are on a scale with the bulk of our purses. The one thing needful having been procured in a sufficient quantity, the night was spent in making merry, in singing, fiddling and dancing. The lemon punch was pronounced "vino." If it had any fault it was that the quantity of alcohol was somewhat great in proportion to the water and sugar. But this was rather an amiable failing than a fault. We made the punch in coffee pots which answered the purpose very well. I doubt if the Carmelite Monastery ever witnessed such a night and if the spirits of any of the former monks were hovering about they would find the inmates of their cells making great reforms, introducing customs quite Lutherish and substituting sack (or rather most villianous aguardiente) for sack cloth and ashes. The only penance they done was about midnight when several young men might have been seen hanging over the portico and with very disconsolate looks and amid much moaning and sighing, trying (to use a polite expression) "to calve."

COULTER. This evening being Christmas Eve, had quite a jolly time in our company quarters. In spite of our general's precautions, liquor was unusually plentiful, and Company "E" were generally pretty tight. In the course of the spree a number of good jokes happened, which may be remembered by the following: "Don't tell Sarah,"—two tight lads measuring lengths on the floor, who mixed up a glass of "All Sorts" composed of draining of the punch cups, sugar, tobacco spit and an old chew of tobacco, and some other ingredients.

December 25

BARCLAY. Christmas Day. Coffee this morning a little lemo-wisk-ish. Day beautiful. The recollections of many a happy Christmas at home fills the mind with pleasant sensations and now thousands of miles away our hearts turn to the delights of home. The bright Christmas fires, the happy faces around the hearth, the many familiar household scenes rush to the mind. Imagination conveys us back and we hear, we see, we feel that we are again among those we love, but sad reality breaks the spell.

While our friends are luxuriating in a Christmas dinner in true Pennsylvania style, we content ourselves with pudding and government rations, the former being the only indulgence that market today would afford. I visited today both the catholic churches of this village. Ceremonies as usual are performed but they do not pay that attention to Christmas festival as I had supposed they would.

COULTER. CHRISTMAS DAY. Went to Mexico this morning that I might see their mode of celebrating this day. The ceremonies were altogether religious and all business appeared to be suspended, except in the fruit, confectionery and fancy line. The portals and Plaza were completely crowded with tables of these articles. In the evening attended the National Theatre. The performance was Spanish and represented a Turkish seraglio or harem. Canete, as usual, performed a prominent part. In the last scene the ladies of the harem had revolted, getting men's attire and arms they fight the slaves of the Turk. It was amusing to see them dressed in Mexican uniforms with heavy muskets on their shoulders. Canete was the drummer of the party. They drilled in both the manual and in marching, and considering who they were, it was remarkably well done. The firing was also good. In fact the female portion of this population would fight better than the hombres. Slept in the hospital. There being considerable fatality in these quarters some of the party got beds, the remainder of us slept on the floor.

December 26

BARCLAY. Read in the American Star the President's message[5] which the enterprising proprietors of that paper had expressed from Vera Cruz in seventy hours. The message takes in my opinion the proper ground,

5. In his Annual Message on the State of the Union, 7 December 1847, President Polk reiterated his policy of ending the war with substantial territorial concessions by Mexico. Until such a treaty was agreed to, he advocated making Mexico pay for the continued costs of the occupation.

that we should be indemnified for past and secured from future injuries should be the maxim of every American citizen. War is no child's play and when once entered upon the honor and dignity of our country require its rigorous prosecution. The future reputation and standing of the United States among foreign nations will depend in a great measure upon the manner in which the present war is terminated. Those statesmen who advocate the Quixotic policy of treating Mexico with a magnaminity injurious to our own interests should have as little influence among the people as the pusillanimous misers who cant philanthropy and weep over the blood and treasures expended. War to be sure is an evil, but a submission to insult and injury is a still greater evil. In a contest like the present a great nation like the United States should be willing to make pecuniary sacrifices and the gallant souls whose blood has flowed so freely in the cause of their country were willing victims, men who despised the sneaking, truckling policy of the opposition at home, martyrs whose glorious memories their fellow citizens should shield from the attacks of traitors who have dared to impute to them other than the highest and noblest of motives. On these things my mind has long since been made up.

COULTER. This morning President Polk's message appeared in this city in print, having been expressed from Vera Cruz in seventy hours. Returned to San Angel today.

December 27
COULTER. There is as yet no prospect of leaving our present quarters. No movement has yet been made towards the north and everything remains in uncertainty. It was supposed when we came out here that we would shortly move towards Queretaro, but now there is no signs of any such expedition.

December 29
BARCLAY. Today the dread recruits were distributed. Our company were so extremely fortunate as to escape. They were allotted to the smallest companies, viz., A, C, D, H, & I. This has given great joy to our boys. They are a hundred times more afraid of recruits than of Mexicans. Brigade orders read.

COULTER. Today the recruits were apportioned among the companies of the regiment. Luckily Company "E" got none, they being given to the smallest companies so as to equalize all as nearly as possible. They were given to companies A, B, C, D, H and G. This evening orders from General Cushing were read ordering a general inspection and mustering in of all the regiments of the brigade for Friday the 31st of this month.

December 30

BARCLAY. Engaged in preparing muster rolls. Somewhat troublesome on account of the clothing which it was necessary to charge.

COULTER. Since coming to these quarters, although we receive the usual rations, there is almost a famine in the company. No one mess are able to make more than a single meal out of a whole day's rations. Every morning we must purchase some rations or go hungry until issuing time comes. This causes a good deal of sport, every evening some mess's rations being stolen and quite a row ensues to discover the thief. This morning we drew two day's rations of bread, and though only one meal has been eaten since, our mess have but a mere morsel left. Cannot account for this otherwise than that the meat rations are very bad and therefore not much to eat in them, and the bread so sad that a very small bulk weighs 18 ounces.

December 31

BARCLAY. Mustered into the service by Adjt. Gen. Hooker.[6] Company E as usual looked well and passed muster without a word of objection. The company numbers for duty—1 Capt., 1 1st Lt., 1 2nd Lt., 3 Sergts., 4 Corps., 1 Musician, 25 Privates; sick present 3 privates. The night being the last of '47 was passed after the fashion of old times—performance similar to those on Christmas Eve.

The year being now ended for the purpose of showing the health and duties performed by different member of the Company I subjoin the substance of my guard rolls which were kept with exactness from the 8th April, 1847. Previous to that time no roll of the guard was kept.

[*Rolls and summary of monthly reports for 1847 were here given in the original diary.*]

COULTER. Today we were inspected and again mustered into the service, making precisely one year. This is our seventh muster, and yet we have not seen two musters at one place: first at Pittsburgh, second at

6. Joseph Hooker (1814–1879) of Massachusetts graduated from the Military Academy in 1837 somewhat below the middle of his class. After a slow rise to the rank of captain (with a brevet lieutenant colonelship for Chapultepec), he resigned from the army after the Mexican War, his career blocked for having sided with Gideon Pillow in the cabal against Winfield Scott. Early in the Civil War he showed such bravery, energy, and initiative that he replaced Ambrose Burnside as commander of the Army of the Potomac. His fatal indecision at the Battle of Chancellorsville demonstrated that he was not cut out for independent command, and he was replaced by George G. Meade on the eve of the Battle of Gettysburg. During the Civil War, Hooker acquired, through a newspaper's typographical error, the nickname "Fighting Joe," but judging by his unseemly fracas with enlisted men (see entry of 19 January 1848), the name could have been applied earlier.

Lobos Island, third at Camp Patterson, near Jalapa, fourth, Camp at Tepeyahualco, fifth at San Agustin, sixth at the City of Mexico and seventh at San Angel. At today's muster we numbered forty officers and men. The original company ninety-four. [Coulter's listing of the Company Roster is omitted.] Mounted guard today at regimental quarters.

1848

January 1

BARCLAY. Day warm and pleasant. In agreeable contrast with the many New Year's Days we have spent in Pennsylvania. The Mexicans do not celebrate the 1st and consequently the market is dull. Neither turkeys or ducks can be obtained and how can a New Year's Dinner be made without something in the turkey line. As a substitute we have a roaring dinner of eggs which approach *near* the desired object.

COULTER. Being on guard yesterday, was on post when the old monastery clock struck midnight and ushered in the new year, 1848. In honor of the occasion, and in hope of having a happy time of it, I welcomed the new year with _____ Pennsylvania _____. The boys were making good use of their muskets and many a cartridge was burned out of the cell windows to the declining year. Some others set up to welcome the grand entry of Forty-eight and by the time that happy moment arrived were gloriously corned. Several amusing incidents may be remembered by the following: The captain, under arrest, or "Hail to the Chief." A drunken corporal, wishing to extinguish a fire. The officer of the quarters guard (Captain Loeser) was most loyally drunk and many were the odd remarks which came out of him. He was very much concerned about the men firing so much about quarters and received great assistance from Lt. A. and Sergeant M. who were continually firing a couple of revolvers near the old fellow's head and cursing the men to stop the disturbance. He could not understand what had gotten over the D.D. soldiers that by G____d they would not obey him. The day has been dry and fine, dry in another respect also, no whisky. Tried to get up a dinner suitable to the occasion, but could not, the market being very poor. Company "K," First Pennsylvania, celebrated this evening. A number of us attended. As is usual among soldiers, considerable liquor was drunk.

January 2

BARCLAY. McClelland came out from the City. Sargent started with him but gave out and had to return. McClelland looks well and his wound is rapidly healing.

January 3

BARCLAY. Capt. & Mechling gone to the City. I am reading Col. Fremont's Journal.[7] These poor fellows suffered terribly and we can appreciate both their descriptions and the fatigues of their campaign.

COULTER. Mounted guard today. Sent to General Cushing's quarters. By the way, it is reported that he is made Governor of the City of Mexico. It is not true of course, but the men all wish to get rid of him. A few days ago Colonel Wyncoop, with a party of Texan Rangers, captured General Valencia and brought him to the City of Mexico.[8] He was taken at his residence and protested against taking a citizen prisoner.

January 4

BARCLAY. Called on the Adjt. Gen. with muster rolls which were examined. Saw for the first time Gen. Cushing. He is a man near forty, above the middle size, very slim and of rather unmilitary appearance. His face is very intellectual, forehead high and eyes piercingly black. He was speaking to a Mexican and carried on the conversation for half an hour very fluently in Spanish. Battalion Drill.

COULTER. Number 6 had a mess of wild duck today. It was quite a treat, but too much trouble preparing for our lazy mode of cooking.

January 5

BARCLAY. Among the many rumours going the round of camp, there is one today that our Regt. will shortly move for Orizaba and garrison that haunt of the guerillas. Battalion Drill. The health of our company is pretty good, McCabe and Gordon being the worst cases.

January 6

BARCLAY. Lovely morning. Regt. Drill. Practiced firing. The Regt. being deployed as skirmishers fired by file and wing, ten rounds to a man. The firing was creditable. In the afternoon a brisk skirmish took place between the Mexicans and a party of the 1st Penna. Regt. and Rangers. The

---

7. John Charles Frémont (1813–1890), famed "Pathfinder" of western trails, instigator of California's Bear Flag Revolt, first Republican nominee for the presidency and an unsuccessful Union general in the Civil War, prepared in 1844, with the help of his wife, Jesse Benton Frémont, an account of his western adventures. Printed by the Senate in an extraordinary edition of ten thousand copies as Frémont's *Report of the Exploring Expedition to the Rocky Mountains in the Year 1842 and to Oregon and North California in the Years 1843–44*, Senate Exec. Doc. 174, 28th Cong., 2d sess., U.S. serial no. 361 (1845), it was widely reprinted by commercial publishers and made its author famous both in America and abroad.

8. Valencia was actually captured on 2 January only one day before this entry, not the "few days ago" of Coulter's assertion. Here, as elsewhere, the diarists seem to be expanding on their notes by drawing on their not always reliable memories.

Mexicans had murdered two Americans when they were attacked. Some 14 were killed. I believe the two Americans killed were drunk and the affray commenced on account of their cutting some pulque stocks. Among the Mexicans killed I fear that there were some harmless and inoffensive.

COULTER. Some soldiers belonging to the First Pennsylvania Regiment coming from the city were attacked by a party of Mexicans and one killed and several wounded. One was larieted and dragged some distance when the rope slipped. The Mexicans, it is supposed, were lying in wait for the omnibus which runs daily between this and the city. Their regiment was alarmed and started in pursuit. It is said they were stoned by the hombres when in pursuit. They killed all greasers that were seen, some no doubt innocently. One Mexican, I understand, was killed while plowing. However, this is the only way to deal with such men. The party attacked were wholly unarmed and the man killed was shot with ball and buckshot, showing that it was evidently our own cartridges, many of which have been sold by the men to the Mexicans for want of money, an act which shows but little principle, in a soldier.

January 7

BARCLAY. Nothing going on. Lt. Coulter and Mechling have gone to the City. A Regimental Drill.

COULTER. This evening our gallant Lt. Colonel Brindle attempted in a speech to justify the Mexicans in the attack, but was drunk and his principles and character are too well known in the regiment.

January 8

BARCLAY. The anniversary of our departure from Pittsburgh. At Dress Parade Company E took their new position in the Regt. being now the left company, the second post of honor. Capt. Johnston is now the next in rank to Capt. Loeser. This second post of honor is not very profitable. In Regt. drills the left of the Regt. generally have the most marching. On days of inspection it is inconvenient and on the march being in the rear we are exposed to the dust and to the irregular movements of the advance.

COULTER. The regimental position of the companies were altered this evening. They now stand as follows: "A," "G," ____ ____ ____ ____ "L," "K," "M," "B" and "E," thereby placing Company "E" on the left wing on account of Captain Johnston, being now the second oldest captain in the regiment, Captain Loeser, being the oldest. This is considered the second post of honor, but is the most difficult position both on march and drill.

January 9

BARCLAY. Corp. and 13 men on guard. We have now barely two reliefs and the men are on guard at least once a week. The duty except in the main guard is not considered onerous. It is said that Col. Wyncoop of the 1st Penna. having already taken Valencia is now in pursuit of Santa Anna. Wyncoop is a very active enterprising officer. He would [be] splendid in command of Dragoons. The capture of Valencia has added much to his reputation. No dress parade. Last night a light was seen on the mountains distant between 30 and 40 miles. From its appearance it was difficult to account for it. Some of the wiseacres said it was a volcano and no mistake.

January 10

BARCLAY. As usual Camp rumours afloat. The Quartermasters have received orders to report immediately the number and condition of their transportation. This seems to indicate a move in some direction. No drill or parade. Several of the 1st Regt. boys up tonight—Mann, Kelly and Kelley of Co. K, the associates of poor Jack Gilchrist are always welcome visitors to our company.

January 11

BARCLAY. A small mail brought up as I understand by Col. Dominguez[9] of the Spy Company reached San Angel today. I received a letter from Uncle Ed addressed to Capt. and myself. It gave me very great satisfaction to hear that at home all was well. Heard of the death of an old friend, David Eichar. Dress Parade.

COULTER. Received a small mail today, only four letters for our company. Several days ago had some sport raising a false alarm. In consequence the principle portion of the company who had gone to bed early were roused in quite a hurry. A scrambling for breeches and shoes followed. As yet we have no definite prospect in view, but it would be impossible to conceive of all the conflicting reports we receive here hourly. At one moment about to be disbanded, then to be consolidated, about to march to Queretaro, next to Orizaba and a thousand and one others.

January 12

BARCLAY. Coulter and myself went to the City. Had a pleasant ride. As we entered saw the funeral of Capt. [James R.] Irwin, Chief of the Quartermaster Dept. The Captain was a regular officer, much esteemed. I never saw him to know him. The funeral pageant was solemn and imposing. The coffin wrapped with the flag was in an open hearse drawn by four black horses covered with crepe. Black ostrich plumes waved from the

9. Manuel Dominguez, a disgruntled former weaver turned robber, whose band of pro-American spies at times numbered two thousand men and did invaluable service for Scott's army. Aware that if he remained in Mexico after American troops were withdrawn he would be "killed like a dog," he was allowed to relocate in New Orleans at war's end. Despite promises of support, the American government never approved any further assistance and he was compelled to fend for himself in a strange land.

hearse. Immediately behind the hearse was led the Captain's horse, fully rigged. There followed some 60 officers and numerous citizens. Gen. Scott, Butler and Patterson were in attendance. The escort was a Battalion of the Rifle Regt.

Was at the "Sociedad" the fashionable resort of officers and black legs. Four or five rooms crowded with gamblers, Monte being the chief game. These gambling houses pay a tax of $1000 per month. Their victims are chiefly officers of the army, many of whom have sold their payrolls for two & three months in advance. Visited Coulter's former neighbors. Dined at a French house. After hunting in vain for Patterson's Quarters whom Coulter was anxious to see, we returned home in time for dress parade.

COULTER. Early this morning there was quite a noise in quarters caused by some of the boys rousing Geesyn out of his sleep and frightening him. Today's Star says Colonel Dominguez of the Native Spies captured a number of prisoners whom he delivered to Colonel Childs at Puebla, among them three Generals, Rinson, Minon and another whose name I do not know.[10] The first is commander in chief of the Mexican Army, appointed instead of Santa Anna. Today the surgeon recommended two of our company, Hansberry and McClelland, both crippled in the hospital in Mexico, for discharges. A train going down shortly.

January 13

BARCLAY. Rumor today that the train was attacked at Santa Fe and a Rifle Regt. considerably cut up. It is also stated and generally believed that a consolidation of the different companies of our Regt. is about to take place. The Colonel has assured several of the officers that it will be done. The 12 companies formed into 6 or 8, the surplus officers to be sent home on the recruiting service. The rank and file unanimously oppose the proposition and their reasons for doing so are highly satisfactory. A great anxiety prevails on the subject and this new scheme is still more objectionable than the recruits. I am told that several officers are favorable to the consolidation, thinking that they will thus get home, and thus for the gratification of their own selfishness they would turn a deaf ear to the wishes and sacrifice the pleasures and comforts of their men. The volunteer officers chosen from the ranks by their men should never forget the obligations they owe their companies and indeed in general they act right and their treatment of the men is very different from that of many of the Regular officers. Some of the Regular officers are contemptible, insolent

10. The report was confused. Manuel Rincón had already been rendered hors de combat. The general captured along with J. J. Miñón was Anastasio Torrejón.

scoundrels and the lower their grade the more insulting they generally are. Lt. Davis told me today that when last in the City he was at Laurent's (an eating house). While there three regulars came in, Sergeants, clean, well dressed, decent looking men. They sat down and asked Laurent for their dinner. While waiting for it a 2nd Lieut. of the Regulars came in and seeing them there informed them that officers attended that place and that they must leave. An old Colonel of the 6th Inf.[11] who had been there all the time and seen that the men had behaved themselves now interfered and said they must have their dinner, that he was not ashamed to eat before men who behaved well and paid their bills. The Sergeants thanked him but refused to remain, saying that they were not aware of the house being exclusively for officers when they came in, and left. I mention this incident to show the general feeling among the 2nd Lieuts. of the Regular Army, whelps fresh from West Point and also as a very creditable instance of a rather unusual interference upon the part of an officer of rank. There are many establishments in the City where a private can neither eat or drink. The principal gambling houses are highly aristocratic and it is necessary to have the bars on the shoulder to obtain admission to the many balls and houses of pleasure, where the gentlemanly officers flock by hundreds. One night at the Theatre an officer had the impudence to order Hartman from a seat he had taken, saying that the officers had the preference of the seats. As the theatre was pretty well crowded, Hartman properly refused to obey, saying that he had paid for his seat and if he must leave he wanted his money refunded and he would leave the theatre. The old Padres are making a fuss today about two of their wax candles being stole. It appears some of the boys fastened two ramrods together with a bullet screw on. Running them thro a hole in the wall, they reached the candles and drew them to the hole with the screw. A few days ago they managed to get some salted fish in the same way. The holy fathers have a lot for Lent underneath in the lower story. By raising a couple of bricks in the floor and running down a pole they succeeded in screwing on several piles. As a matter of course none of Company E were engaged in such performances. They are above everything of the kind.

11. The Colonel of the 6th Infantry, Newman S. Clarke, had been brevetted a brigadier general for his service at Vera Cruz and would undoubtedly have been referred to by Barclay at that rank. There was no lieutenant colonel of this regiment, but four officers held that rank by brevet. Of them, three were in their thirties, so only Benjamin L. E. Bonneville (1796–1878), slightly over fifty, qualifies as "old."

Born in France, of a philosophically radical family numbering Lafayette and Thomas Paine among its circle, Bonneville was sent to the United States as a child, attended West Point, and became a western explorer in the 1830s, the famous Bonneville Flats being named in his honor. Washington Irving was so impressed with his character and accomplishments that he wrote Bonneville's life story in 1837.

COULTER. Colonel Jack Hays with his rangers was out lately after the guerilla chief Padre Jarauta.[12] Overtook him with about two hundred Mexicans and in the ensuing fight some thirty of the enemy were killed. The priest it is believed was either killed or wounded, but was carried off by his men; his horse, cloak and pistols were taken. The two of our company recommended for discharges yesterday, got none. This shows the attention paid by officers to the necessities of the men. A private soldier must linger and die in a hospital unless he have some shoulder-strapped friend to intercede for him continually. Another of our company, (Shaw) whom they would not discharge last train is now so much reduced that he is unable to travel and cannot last long. Thus as long as a man is able to stand the trip to Vera Cruz he is denied a discharge. But when it is too late he is either discharged to die on the road, or left to waste away in a hospital, where the attention is anything but what a man on a sick bed requires. It is reported that the general is about to consolidate the old volunteer regiments. It might be avoided but the officers of our regiment in particular wish it to succeed, as they expect thereby to remain the longer in the service. But the men will most strenuously oppose it. It is unjust in the extreme, and some doubt the power to destroy the identity of any volunteer company. But the question here in any case is not the right or justness of the measure. Our generals have the power and must be obeyed. The old volunteer regiments have been treated badly. They have been recruited and in the case of our regiment officers have been appointed over companies otherwise than by election, contrary to the express laws of Pennsylvania. It has been submitted to thus far, but if this measure is urged it may cause a disturbance which will affect the character of this war considerably. The upper room (Number 3) had some fun with Geesyn this evening by blackening his face and _____, much to his own amusement also until they applied a second coat of grease which changed the tune.

January 14

BARCLAY. A train left the City this morning for Vera Cruz. Both Hansberry and McClelland had been promised discharges, but for some reason or other were neglected. These poor fellows will never be fit for duty and it is cruel barbarity to keep them here. Regt. Drill.

COULTER. Had a duel this evening with the well known Geesyn. It had been agreed privately that I should be shot and a patrol be sent after Henry

12. Father Cenobia Jarauta, born in Spain sometime before 1800, though a priest led irregular troops in the Spanish civil wars, earning a reputation for cruelty. After settling in Mexico in 1841, he continued to practice both callings (the priestly and the guerrilla) with great effectiveness until, in June of 1848, he overreached himself and called for a revolution to overthrow the Republic. The revolution was speedily and bloodily suppressed and Jarauta himself was summarily shot.

whom it was supposed would try to conceal himself. The affray came off in the orchard with muskets at fifty paces. Shots were exchanged and I fell. There were too many present who could not keep the proper gravity, but burst into a laugh when the muskets cracked. In the end I became the butt of the joke myself. The patrol, according to appointment coming, I attempted to conceal myself and lying down got my breeches rather daubed with _____. However, my antagonist was taken considerably frightened and by the officers who knew the joke, ordered to his quarters under guard for further investigation. There was a meeting of some officers this evening to take into consideration the propriety of increasing the rations, complaints having been made throughout the regiment, and in fact the entire brigade. Our mess are completely out. Mess Number 1 had an old beef bone this evening. There was no meat on it when they commenced and by the time it had passed through third hands was completely polished.

January 15

BARCLAY. Part of Company on guard. The officers of the Regt. are getting up a petition to have the rations of beef and bread increased. They will not succeed. For some reason or other there has been for some weeks an awful deficiency in our rations of these two articles. Whether it is on account of the inferior quality of the provisions or an increase of our appetites I cannot say. Fortunately we have a little money left which keeps off starvation. Capt. and Lieut. Coulter gone to the City. Additional rumors of the consolidation of the regiment. I made out a report of the state of the company for Col. Geary.

January 16

BARCLAY. Sunday. Yesterday orders for an inspection today. Orders countermanded. Sickness in our company increasing. Something like the measles have broken out. Bills and McCabe are the worst cases.

An agreeable rumor going the round today that the volunteers are about being discharged.

January 17

BARCLAY. Last night the South Carolinian died whom the New Yorkers a few nights since robbed and attempted to murder. The assassins were apprehended by the Rangers and were this morning sent to the main guard house in the City.

Received the Report of the Secretary of War, a document prepared with labor and a part of which we by no means approve of—his recommendations as to the volunteers.

COULTER. Heard the dead march a day or so ago for the first time since coming to these quarters. The only species of sickness prevailing here is the measles which are rather prevalent in the regiment, and even more so in the remainder of the brigade. It is much worse, however, in the city and the whole army are troubled with it. There are many cases of very sore throats also. There have been in our company three cases of measles since coming to San Angel, but none of them have been fatal. Had an agreeable rumor today, which like all such, is of course false, that ten regiments of regulars were being raised by order of Congress to relieve the old volunteers now in the service. Our valiant Colonel has fallen into bad company and bad habits of late. For some days back he had devoted the greater part of his time gambling. Like all beginners, he is winning a little, but will be strapped in the end. He has been very penurious since coming to Mexico, and by his living off the commissary and plundering of the men's rations, he has collected a considerable sum, but this will soon go to satisfy his gambling propensities. Hope he may have a happy time of it.

January 18

BARCLAY. Sargent came out from the City. The surgeon at the hospital refused to discharge him for duty so he ran off. He brings us news of the death of Joseph Shaw who died yesterday morning in the hospital of chronic diarrhea. Shaw was a very healthy man when we left home and continued in good health until a short time before we left Puebla. He was ordered by the surgeon to remain in Puebla but refused on leaving San Agustin. He, with McGinley and Linsenbigler, went to the hospital at Mixcoac. From that he was taken to the hospital in the City where he lingered until his death. He was a quiet, well disposed young man of a good easy disposition. When able he was always willing for his duty. Capt. and Lt. Coulter return today from the City. Some scoundrels have stolen some pictures belonging to the monastery. No clue can be hit upon to lead to the knowledge of the thieves. A kind of mob meeting was held this evening, when Col. Brindle made a speech and proposed the ridiculous expedient of each man clearing himself on oath. He was laughed at and the men turned the argument by making complaints about the rations. It is to be regretted that there are many men in the army who are so lost to all sense of honor and honesty as to commit depredations which at home would send them to the penitentiary. But such is the case. The 2nd Penna. Regt. have a character for being honorable, but there are exceptions. There are men in it who probably were convicts in the States and there are others who the fear of the law and not any principle of honor kept from being robbers and burglars at home. Good men suffer by being brought in contact with such fellows. Their society is disagreeable and there is danger of contamination. Besides guard duty is increased. It is necessary to guard every point where anything can be stolen.

COULTER. Today one of our wounded men, C. F. Sargent, returned from the hospital in Mexico. From him learned the death of one of our company, Joseph Shaw. He died in the City of Mexico yesterday, 17th January. Mounted guard today on the upper picket. The guard was composed of South Carolinians and Second Pennsylvanians under a Massachusetts Lieutenant. Were not long on duty before we found our officer to be "fresh from the sodd and rather green." About eleven o'clock at night one of the men on post, wishing some sport, reported to the lieutenant that there were a number of armed Mexicans in the neighborhood. He immediately roused the guard with "Up, men, up and load your peas, the inimy are on us." The men who had a contempt for both the Mexicans and the Irish officer were hard to wake. By the time one end of the room were up the others were asleep. "Men, men," says he, "did you not come here to stand guard?" "Yes" said one "but, by God, not to be roused for a damned fool." "Up and load your paces then" said he. "Pound me some brick bats" said another "and I'll load mine." After a good deal of trouble he got three muskets loaded. The men did not wish to dirty them for nothing. He wished to make the whole guard sit up all night, but those not on post were soon asleep. He then doubled the men on post, placing a second at some distance down the road to give timely alarm. About two hours before day was sent out myself as the fartherest picket. Finding a corn stack near crawled into it to keep warm. Shortly after saw the lieutenant coming down the road and crawled out of the stack. The noise of trampling the fodder frightend him and he would not advance another step until I answered him twice in plain English. He cautioned me about the responsible duties which were resting on me. "Be watchful; these are the hours of slumber and if they attack at all it will be shortly." It was amusing to see an officer one year in the service so frightened at nothing. He was very much disturbed about a light which he saw. Asking me where it was told him that it was Contreras, the very name of this battle ground. Scared him worse, and although two miles off he believed it was the Mexicans preparing to attack us. The poor fellow did not sleep a wink during the whole night. "Sure" said he "I can neiver close me eyes when I think danger is near."

January 19

BARCLAY. Morning cloudy and somewhat cool. A fight took place between a New Yorker and the Flag Sergeant of our Regiment. Adj. Gen. Hooker, being present and interfering in the row, got a blow or push which brought him to the ground. He rose in a terrible passion, drew his sword, but could not find the man that hit him. After pitching about for some time in a very amusing manner, he ran up to the market guard who was quietly walking his post and gave him a furious kick in the seat of honor. His steam being now up to the highest point he bolted. The Adj. is a very clever regular officer. The possibility that a private would dare to strike him never entered his cranium. In future he will be more careful how he enters into Pennsylvania rows. There is a report today that the down train was attacked near Rio Frio and many of the discharged killed. At Dress Parade orders read from the Secretary of War returning thanks, etc., to the army.

COULTER. This morning when the guard was relieved, our lieutenant cautioned the new officer to be very particular as there was great danger.

January 20

BARCLAY. Mechling and Sargent gone to the City today. Returned in the evening. I made out company pay rolls and sent them to the Paymaster by Capt. Williams. At dress parade the proceedings of a court martial were read. One of F company for striking an officer has been sentenced to hard labor with ball and chain at Chapultepec for six months, pay stopped, etc. The Colonel was very anxious that the regiment should hear and profit by the example. He double[d] the line and had the proceeding twice read over, but an indisposed old wagon which was passing at the time made a devil of a racket and the very complimentary design of the Colonel's was frustrated.

COULTER. On dress parade this evening the proceedings of a general court martial were read. Among other sentences, one of Company "F" of our regiment was sentenced to six months imprisonment at Chapultepec with iron yoke and ball and chain. In this case the sympathy was universally in favor of the prisoner. There were more rumors this evening about consolidation. Some even said the colonel had orders to that effect. Tonight four armed Mexicans were taken lying in wait for straggling soldiers.

January 21

BARCLAY. Dick Coulter and McWilliams detailed to guard prisoners to Chapultepec. The "consolidation scheme" being still the bugbear, a meeting of the Sergeants of the Regt. was held today to take some measures against the proposed movement. I drew up a petition to Gen. Scott which met with the approbation of the meeting and all pledged themselves that their companies would unanimously sign it. Mess No. 6 was today increased by the addition of two new members, Geesyn and Sargent. The former is to do all the cooking while the mess performs his guard duty. Heard that a train had arrived in the City—Big gambling tonight among the officers.

COULTER. This morning received an addition of two new members to our mess, Sargent and Geesyn. Today was detailed as one of a guard to convey to Chapultepec the prisoners sentenced yesterday. There were six in number from the New York Regiment, one from the Massachusetts and one of the Second Pennsylvania Regiment. Went by way of the village of

Mixcoac, making one day's journey going and returning, about fourteen miles. There were a large number of prisoners under similar sentences at Chapultepec. At this place for the first time saw the punishment of the iron yoke which is cruelly severe. It consists of a heavy iron band around the neck with three prongs which turn upward and extend some distance above the head. This prevents the prisoner from turning his head or bending his neck without moving the whole body. One of the prisoners told me that he was unable to sleep longer than a quarter of an hour at a time on account of this yoke. While at the castle learned that General [Thomas] Marshall's train came into Mexico today with about fifteen hundred men. Returned however, at a rapid gait, having gotten into a walking match with a couple of Massachusetts volunteers. Today the meat rations were so small and of such inferior quality as to cause an examination into the matter. It was found with true scales that out of fifty rations they were eleven and a half pounds lighter than the allowance, a discovery not much to the commissary's credit. It was found that the colonel had received no orders relative to consolidating the regiment, and to prevent it, if possible, there was a meeting of the O[rderly] Sergeants of the regiment who agreed to petition the general not to issue such orders, and by resolution, requested the officers to present a like petition. It is thought by some that if General Scott finds such a decided opposition to this measure among the volunteer regiments that he may not press it, having regard to his popularity. The old fellow still appears to have an eye upon the Presidency of the United States.

January 22

BARCLAY. The mail brought us many letters from home—latest dates 13th Dec. I received letters from Uncle Ed, Eichar and Corp. Carpenter.

COULTER. Today part of the mail which came in with yesterday's train was distributed. Our company received quite a number of letters, among others I received one from Uncle. Learned by this mail the death of one of our Company "E," Edward McCredin, who was discharged at Vera Cruz and died shortly after reaching home. Orders from General Scott were read on dress parade this evening relative to the burial of the dead, that all persons belonging to the army, without regard to rank, shall be buried with the proper honors, and if possible in coffins. This order was issued in consequence of a number of bodies at some of the general hospitals having been given to Mexicans to bury as they thought proper instead of the usual detail of soldiers for that purpose. From the news by this mail it appears that the Whig party generally are settling down into a decided opposition to the war. Clay's Lexington speech, Calhoun's resolutions and Corwin's ideas have given great encouragement to the Mexicans, has protracted the war and completely counteracted the effect of the late victories.[13]

January 23

BARCLAY. Day cool and cloudy. Newspaper mail came from the City. Heard of the death of Maj. Webster.[14] He died early this morning.

COULTER. This morning heard of the death of Major Webster of the Massachusetts Regiment. He died during the last night. He was a son of Honorable Daniel Webster of Massachusetts. Received a large number of papers today. A number of articles were read to the regiment on dress parade: An invitation to the officers to attend the funeral ceremonies of Major Webster tomorrow; also a letter from Governor Shunk of Pennsylvania to Major Patterson relative to The Pennsylvania Regiments, tendering them his thanks and best wishes for their health and speedy return. Also General Patterson's reply. Heard quite an interesting rumor today, that Governor Shunk had refused to allow recruiting or calling out new companies to fill up the old regiments, but offered to furnish two full regiments and as many more as might be wanted if the President would discharge the old ones. Of course it is all gammon, but afforded some gossip for the newscatchers. There were some peace reports also. Saw in one of the papers we received today (The Pennsylvania Argus) a letter purporting to be from a member of this regiment highly complimenting the gallantry of Colonel Geary. Understand that William Wise of Company "D" was the author of this letter. His name may be attached to it, but it is undoubtedly the production of John Geary himself.[15]

13. Opposition to the Mexican War by prominent American political spokesmen, mainly Whigs, did, in fact, mislead some Mexicans into believing that American war weariness might lead to an abandonment of the war effort.

Henry Clay's sensational Lexington, Kentucky, speech of 13 November 1847 castigated the Polk administration for "unnecessary and . . . offensive aggression. It is Mexico," Clay declared, "that is defending her firesides, her castles and her altars, not we."

John C. Calhoun of South Carolina, privately feared that Mexico was "forbidden fruit; the penalty of eating it [is] to subject our institutions to political death." On 14 December 1847 he introduced two resolutions into the Senate opposing the acquisition of Mexican territory.

On 11 February 1847 Thomas Corwin of Ohio declared, on the floor of Congress, that were he a Mexican, he would ask Americans: "Have you not room in your own country to bury your dead men? If you come into mine, we will greet you with bloody hands and welcome you to hospitable graves." The speech was much opposed at the time but served Corwin in good stead during the Civil War when he was United States minister to Mexico.

14. Edward Webster, the black-sheep son of Daniel Webster, the Massachusetts statesman, died of typhoid fever while serving in a war his father opposed. His older brother, Fletcher, died in the Civil War, which his father had tried to prevent. Webster's great rival, Henry Clay, also lost a son in the Mexican War.

15. See letter by "S." dated 25 October 1847 in the *Pennsylvania Argus* of 10 December 1847.

January 24

BARCLAY. Attended the funeral of Maj. Webster. His remains were temporarily deposited in a vault in the Catholic Church of this place. They will be sent home. Major Bowman of the 1st Pa. Regt. commanded the escort. The corpse was conveyed in a hearse. His own war horse was led behind, fully caparisoned. The sword hung by the saddle and boots reversed with spurs were placed in the stirrup. The horse was led by an attendant in mourning. There is nothing to my mind so touching in a funeral pageant as the led horse of the dead. Its presence forcibly recalls recollections of the departed. We see the steed but no rider is there. Between the soldier and his horse, the faithful companion of his hardships, there is a strange affinity which approaches nearer companionship than any relation between man and the brute creation. Maj. Webster's horse is a most magnificent animal, I think the finest I ever saw, since I have been in Mexico. I have seen many fine horses collected and selected from the choicest breeds in the States. But to return to the funeral, the Rev. McCarty, the army Chaplain, repeated the service of the church on the gate sill. The firing was only tolerable. Maj. Webster was a small man of light frame. He did not possess any of his father's greatness. He was said to be an agreeable and well informed man, of an amiable character. His vice was intemperance which was the cause of the disease that carried him off. A small mail which came in brought me a letter from W. A. Johnston, being the first received in reply to my own letters written from the valley.

COULTER. On quarter guard today. Have quite an easy post, not having to stand during the night. Today a couple of instruments were brought from the city, the stocks for the legs, intended to contain two persons. Also another called the wooden horse. It is a piece of timber about four inches wide raised by uprights about five feet from the ground. The criminal is placed astride this horse and his legs tied underneath. There have been several soldiers of this brigade sentenced to both these punishments by the late court martial. Received another batch of letters and papers from the city. By this learned the death of another of Company "E," Michael Heasley, discharged at Puebla died shortly after arrival home. Received answers to the letters sent from the city by the first mail that went down. It appears that they are making great exertions at home for our recall. By this mail received Colonel Geary's report of the operations of the 13th of September last. It is a beautiful document. I don't know how a man who was so short a time with his regiment can have the presumption to speak of an action of which he knows so little. He seems so fearful of giving offense to any officer that he commences at Company "A" and goes entirely through the regiment speaking of almost every officer who was in the action. This evening attended the funeral ceremonies of the late Maj. Webster. Major Bowman, of the First Pennsylvania had command and the funeral was attended by General Cushing and nearly all the officers of the brigade. The body was carried to a church yard in this place where the funeral ceremony was performed by Rev. McCarty. The body was not interred but it is intended to send it home.

January 25

BARCLAY. Went to the City to see about the payment of the company. Met Benjamin Martz who we left behind at Vera Cruz very sick. He is now the picture of good health. He has had his adventures as well as the rest of us. Dr. [John B.] Porter, the surgeon at Vera Cruz, sent Wise and Martz to the general hospital at New Orleans in order that they might there be discharged. He neglected to send their description rolls and they could not be discharged altho very low. Owing to this highly criminal conduct of Dr. Porter, those men were obliged to remain at New Orleans and passed thro the terrible yellow fever campaign in that city. Gradually recovering their health they preferred rejoining their company to remaining idle, again crossed the Gulf and started for Mexico City. Wise took sick and remained at Perote Castle. Martz came on. He joins the company today. Received from Maj. [Robert B.] Reynolds over $1200, being two months' pay for the company in general, the Vera Cruz and Puebla men receiving 10 and 12 months pay. My own amounted with clothing account to $35.00. The men of our company in hospital also received their pay. They are doing well with the exception of Hoffer. His case is somewhat doubtful. Dined with the Capt. at the Sociedad. Saw several pretty girls today.

COULTER. Saw a man undergoing the punishment of the stocks in the Plaza. His sentence is to remain eight hours a day in the stocks for three months, merely for refusing to turn out on dress parade until he received rations. This offense was tortured into mutiny and in consequence the sentence. He belongs to the Massachusetts Regiment and it does not reflect much credit upon his officers. One of our company, Benj. Martz, left sick at Vera Cruz, came up with the last train and joined the company today. In company with Samuel Wise, also of our company, he was sent to New Orleans and even further up the river. The surgeon at Vera Cruz had not sent their description rolls with them and in consequence they could not be discharged. Wise came up with the train as far as Perote where he was compelled to remain on account of sickness. Understand that Captain Montgomery has been ordered to Mexico City to undergo a court martial, Colonel Geary having preferred charges against him for writing a letter which was published in the States speaking in severe terms of the field officers of our regiment.[16] Woe to Colonel Geary if anything happens [to]

16. This letter, which Montgomery wrote to his family, found its way into the newspapers in Westmoreland County. In it, Montgomery was highly critical of the 2d Pennsylvania Infantry, claiming it had "the reputation of being the worst officered in the service." He further claimed that before the Battle of Contreras none of the regiment's officers could be

him. Orders were read upon dress parade this evening relative to guard mount, that the men should mount guard with knapsacks and one day's provisions. The South Carolinians were quite lively today, having a report that an order for their disbanding was in the city. As in all such cases, this proved to be a hoax. Lieutenant Coulter went to town today and drew the money to pay the company. Were paid this evening and the boys are quite merry.

January 26

BARCLAY. Rumors today that a treaty of peace! has been signed and expressed to the States. Bates rejoined company having run off. In making a very active leap today I sprained my ankle, badly. I am laid up.

COULTER. Having been paid yesterday, went to the city this morning. No news of any account. Rumors about the South Carolina Regiment being discharged and articles of a treaty having been signed and sent to Washington, but these reports are not credited. Another small lot of letters were received today. Made a purchase of this book in which this journal is written, and after strolling about for a couple of hours returned to San Angel sore in the limbs, having ridden a rough horse. Another of our wounded, A. G. Bates, returned to the company from the hospital at Mexico today. Money is doing its work and many of the regiment are rather corned.

---

found on duty, which dereliction led to the regiment's failure to participate in the battle (a feeling shared by Coulter—see diary entry of 19 August 1847). Although the letter was private and not intended for publication, it could be construed as a violation of the same regulation under which Scott had attempted to try Quitman, Worth, and Duncan. Bad blood had long existed between Montgomery and Geary (see Mrs. John Geary to her husband, 8 April 1847, Geary Papers, Beinecke Library, Yale University) and the colonel seized upon this opportunity to bring his rival low. Montgomery put up a skillful defense (which can be found in the *Pennsylvania Argus* of 7 July 1847) but, as was usually the case in courts-martial, to no avail. He was summarily convicted and dismissed from the service. The governor of Pennsylvania, however, reinstated Montgomery to his former rank and position.

11

History Will Do Justice to All
San Angel

January 27

BARCLAY. Amused with more reports. I note them because they are the chief topic of conversation. The bad rumors we discredit, the favorable ones we uphold and try to believe. It is said today that Gen. Lane has taken Santa Anna prisoner somewhere near Orizaba.[1] We are trying to believe the story, but it is hard to swallow. Wrote to Uncle Ed and Dr. Marchand.

COULTER. Mounted guard this morning at the main guard house. Luckily did not stand post, having been detailed to make out the guard report. Our guard duty here is now almost as heavy as it was in the city. There are seventy-two on main guard besides the general's guard and several pickets. There are also heavy guards at each of the regimental quarters. Company "Q" (as the guard house inmates are called) is rather strong today, over forty American prisoners and four Mexicans. There is yet a great deal of sickness in the brigade, but not generally fatal. In our company there have been two more cases of what is supposed to be measles besides a number therein indisposed. Am rather used up myself today, I think from cold, joints stiff and head stuffed up and in anything but like a pleasant condition. I think the colonel has met some reverses in his gambling. He gave the regiment a drill today (the first for some time). He was in quite a bad humor and ordered all reported on duty to be out tomorrow on pain of the guard house.

---

1. At the time of his Mexican War activity, which led to a major-general's brevet, the peripatetic Joseph Lane (1801–1881) was a popular Indiana political figure. After the war, President Polk appointed him governor of the Oregon Territory, and upon Oregon's admission as a state he became its first United States senator. A Southern partisan and an enthusiastic supporter of secession, he ran in 1860 for vice-president on the Democratic ticket headed by John Breckinridge.

The expedition to Tehuacan that Barclay refers to did not quite succeed in capturing Santa Anna who, forewarned, had fled in haste, leaving the table set, the candles still burning, and his (and his wife's) clothes neatly packed. General Lane chivalrously forewarded Donna Santa Anna's dresses to their owner.

January 28

BARCLAY. Day windy. A fire broke out in the large orchard attached to the monastery. It burnt very freely on account of the number of dry leaves. It was very funny to see the Padres jumping about in their long gowns and attempting to put out the fire.

COULTER. This morning caught a flea on my clothes, the first either of these or lice I have seen in these quarters. It is decidedly the cleanest building I have seen in Mexico. Have had a rumor afloat today which has been going the rounds for a short time back, but until today had not the support of newspaper credit (which is, however, very slim), that is, that articles of a treaty had been signed and forwarded to Washington City. By this treaty it is said that Mexico concedes the territory demanded on condition that the United States leave a sufficient force here to sustain the government against the revolts of the states. This afternoon the orchard attached to this monastery was by accident set on fire. There being a great quantity of dry brush and high withered grass the fire spread rapidly. The monastery bells rang the alarm and in five minutes there were more greasers collected on the spot than I thought the village contained—enough, had they been good men, to flog the regiment. Our regiment also turned out en-mass, not because they were interested, but to see the sport and if possible catch a hare, in which the orchard abounds. The alarm scared out several new Padres whom I had never before seen, they having kept close to their cells since the occupation of their building by the heretics. Some of these reverend fathers charged most gallantly into the fire, but the spirit did not sustain them, fire and smoke were superior and they retreated with tearful eyes. Their feet also being only protected by sandals were severely scorched, and I have no doubt the poor Padres thought seriously of purgatory. The hombres worked hard (they are better at this than fighting) water was let on in abundance from the reservoir, and after burning some twenty acres the fire was checked. Some of our boys tried to keep up the sport by throwing brands where brush was plenty. A drunken Mexican came into our quarters craving [?] some of the men for "des royals" which he said had been stolen from him, but he met with rather a cool reception. Was bucked and placed in the hall. After enjoying or rather enduring this for some time was allowed to vamoose. As was ordered yesterday, had a regular drill this afternoon. After performing one or two field maneuvers, stacked arms to rest. Colonel Black, coming up, Geary invited him and the regiment to drink pulque.[2] (Company "E" did not accept the treat.) But once in the pulque shop the boys were not so easily gotten out and

2. In civilian life Geary was a vocal foe of demon rum. "I have been temperate from my youth up," he boasted. "In all my life I think I have never used, medicine or otherwise, a quart in all of spiritous liquor" (Paul Beers, "John W. Geary," *Civil War Times Illustrated* 9 [June 1970], 11).

remained there until it was too late to drill, and we escaped with a dress parade. Many have been the surmises and speculations upon this act of the colonel's. Some say that he has been successful in his gaming (understand he broke a Monte bank today), others that peace is about to be declared and the colonel wishes to conciliate the men before reaching the United States.

January 29

BARCLAY. Stickle commenced cooking today for the officers. The rumors of a treaty having been signed are confirmed.[3]

COULTER. This evening had a regimental drill and from the colonel's disposition think the Monte bank must have increased some at his expense. The adjutant made some remarks about the dark blue jackets, and we were ordered to appear in the light blue or grey tomorrow. Am obliged to the colonel for noting my appearance to the captain, as I did not have my jacket buttoned and belts under. On returning from drill he vented some of his ill disposition on a drunken Irish Green. Taking him by the collar, attempted to force him into quarters, and pushing him backward, upset him into an old woman's milk crock. This caused the colonel to lose another "peso."

January 30

BARCLAY. Sunday. A few days ago a wooden horse and a pair of stocks were placed in front of our quarters for the punishment of the offenders in the different regiments of the Brigade. Two men have already been punished. Last night the improvements were carried away and destroyed. This morning an advertisement was stuck up offering a reward for the runaway horse. Gen. Cushing the introducer of these patent methods of treating volunteers is in a terrible passion and it is said offers a discharge to any soldier who will inform upon the men that destroyed his pets. Lieut. Armstrong who has been for several days suffering from a sore eye went to the City today to place himself under the care of Dr. McMillen. Sargent detailed to attend on him.

---

3. The long-rumored, long-awaited treaty ending the war between Mexico and the United States negotiated at the town of Guadalupe Hidalgo would not be formally signed until 2 February 1848. With minor reservations it would be ratified by the United States Senate the next month and accepted by the Mexican Congress the following May. By its essential provisions, Mexico recognized American annexation of Texas and ceded most of its northwestern territories, including the present-day states of California, Nevada, Utah, and most of Colorado, New Mexico, and Arizona to its northern neighbor. In return, the United States agreed to assume American claims against Mexico and pay Mexico an additional amount of fifteen million dollars. Contrary to the rumors heard by the diarists, the treaty did not require American troops to remain in Mexico after it was ratified.

COULTER. During the last night, much to the satisfaction of the entire brigade, the wooden horse and part of the stocks disappeared. A hand bill was found posted up this morning stating that the horse had gone express to Vera Cruz. The general is exceedingly wroth concerning it. Lt. Armstrong who has been suffering some time back from an infection of the eyes, went to the city this morning that he might have more convenient medical attendance.

January 31
BARCLAY. Made out monthly report. Played alley ball[4] and loafed. Gambling going on. The new band is boring everybody.

COULTER. It is said that the general has offered an honorable discharge to any man that will inform him who made way with the stocks and the blooded horse "Boston" (so the wooden horse has been christened in honor of the home of the general). I think he will have a happy time finding it.

February 1
BARCLAY. Day beautiful. Capt. [James] Barclay of the [2d] N.Y. Regt. buried. The Adjt. of that Regt. [Lt. James S. McCabe] read the funeral service. As the Adjt. has a most terrible voice—I am told he read the service in the same tone that he forms the Regt.—it must have been very impressive. I made out Wise's Descriptive Roll. It will be mailed to Perote.

COULTER. The funeral ceremonies of Captain Barclay, late of the New York Regiment, were performed today.

February 2
BARCLAY. On Dress Parade an Eulogy pronounced at Uniontown on Col. Roberts was read. It was brief and like all similar productions said nothing but good of its subject. Mention was made of Lieut. [John] Sturgeon of Fayette County. This very promising young man died at Puebla while we were there. His body embalmed was laid in the vaults of the church. It was intended to take the remains home but the villanous Mexicans stole away the coffin. The object of those people in thus violating the hallowed precincts of the tomb is in consistency with other features of their character. It is the low despicable feeling of gain which induces them hyena like to dig up the grave and break open the coffin of the dead. And the blanket and clothing of the corpse is their reward. Lieut. Sturgeon was very intimate with our company and always showed towards us the warmest friendship.

---

4. A makeshift version of the ancient game of bowls in which balls are rolled down a long, grassy lane with the goal of coming closest to a designated spot or else dislodging the opponents' balls.

COULTER. Mounted guard at the main guard house today. Had quite an easy time, being on patrol. On dress parade this evening was read a funeral sermon preached in honor of the late Colonel William Roberts.

February 3

BARCLAY. Alley ball the amusement of the day. The alley is in the summer house in the orchard. At Regimental Drill the Colonel complimented the regiment upon their discipline. In consideration thereof he says he will have a new guard house for his Regt. It was a rather singular way of winding up a huff. But to confine a white man in the present guard house is outrageous. The inmates are principally New Yorkers and the room is crowded. A newcomer is generally set upon and robbed and otherwise ill treated.

A ration of molasses and pickled onions! issued. Hartman who was on guard there tells me that the Indians are planting corn at the village.

COULTER. Drew a ration of molasses and pickled onions and had a regimental drill. On this drill performed a new maneuver, the marching square. The colonel, after cursing the regiment for an awkward set of sons of bitches during the whole drill, smoothed it all over in the end by complimenting the men on their "superb performance."

February 4

BARCLAY. In this morning's paper a notice that the treaty had been signed and expressed to Vera Cruz. If it meets with the approval of both governments many a poor fellow here will thank his stars. A South Carolina man this morning shot himself. For some trifling offense he has been confined in the guard house over night. He was so mortified at the disgrace that he committed suicide. This excessive delicacy is not usual in the army but the Palmetto Regt. is composed of a noble set of men. They were always favorites with me since the encampment on Lobos. Being chiefly young men they have a kind of State pride. They do not mix with the other regiments. It is very seldom that you see a Palmetto intoxicated and but few of their names appear on the guard house lists. In all those respects the New Yorkers are the exact opposite.

This morning the regiment ordered out to police the quarters. Our company whose part of the building requires no policing are sent to clean up the filth made by other companies in a distant room. They preferred hiring Mexicans to do the job. The English sailor, Clark, who on board the Cooper made himself acquainted with us called to see our boys today. He belongs to one of the new Tennessee Regiments and is a Sergeant. He looks well and is full of music. He said the other day while drilling he was in command of his company and as he does not understand cruising on land he several times capsized the whole Regt.

COULTER. The whole regiment were ordered out today for police duty. Our company were ordered to police a part of the building which was very dirty and in which none of them had ever before been.

February 5

BARCLAY. Coulter and Bowman gone to the City. Last night the prisoners in the guard house threw one of their number out of the window. The man was much hurt by the fall. A glorious shower last night. Everything this morning looks green and fresh like a May morning at home. The trees in the orchard have been for several days in blossom. The Mexicans are busy setting out and grafting young trees. The grafter receives fifty cents for every twelve grafts. The blossoms on the apple trees do not smell so sweet as in our orchards at home. We miss the swarms of bees. Nor are the birds so numerous as in springtime in Penna. Our old acquaintances the robins appear to be the most numerous of the feathered tribe.

COULTER. On guard today. Quarter guard and posted in the back part of the building to protect the padres.

February 6

BARCLAY. Leave having been obtained, the most of our Company paid a visit to Contreras distant near three miles from this village. The position of the enemy was good. On a commanding height near 4 acres of ground was open and clear. All the surrounding country is rough. It would have been madness to have attempted to carry the works by an attack in front. The spectator is surprised at the extreme roughness of the ground upon which our troops and batteries maneuvered, at the boldness of our light batteries which opened upon much heavier pieces from a most disadvantageous position and at the extreme and unaccountable negligence of the enemy's pickets and guards who suffered a heavy force to gain their rear and entirely to surround them without their knowledge. The deep ravines gave our men shelter but it is to me a mystery how they could approach within 400 yards of the main body of the enemy without their presence being known. Capt. Drum showed Mechling the point where they were first observed and it is certainly not over 400 yards from where the Mexican guns were planted. We passed on the road the bridge under which the Mexicans drowned in their flight and where they were shot down by scores. Near the bridge is a large mound of earth surmounted by a cross under which reposes the Mexican dead. This afternoon a gloomy drizzling rain fell. We have been here now near two months and this is the first rainy disagreeable day. All the rest of time has been sunshine. In this respect Mexico will bear a favorable comparison with any country in the world. The climate at this season of the year is delightful and I am told that the rainy season is equally pleasant. The heavy rains in the forenoon are followed by clear and beautiful afternoons.

COULTER. Today has been cloudy and considerable rain in the evening. The company visited the battle ground of Contreras. Not being about at the time, did not have the pleasure of going. Rooms Number 3 and 6 are on quite a spree today.

February 7

BARCLAY. Uncapher went to the City to relieve Sargent in his attendance on Lieut. Armstrong. The Lieut's eye still continues very sore and painful and it is doubtful whether he will ever recover the sight of it. He is shut up in a dark room at the Sociedad and his diet is tea and toast. At dress parade this evening the new brass band made their first appearance. They play tolerably well.

COULTER. Drew a ration of corn meal today. Colonel Geary's long talked of brass band made their first appearance this evening on dress parade. They have made considerable progress for the time they have been at it. But for my part I think such music is wholly unnecessary for a volunteer regiment, and we may reasonably hope to be out of the service before they are anything like perfect. Room Number 6 appears to have kept on their spree pretty well today. Jimmy Hays was a little corned this evening and gave us his Geary Song. It is a production which he only sings when he is tight. It is as follows:

The Gallant Colonel Geary

When war broke out in the sultry South,
The land of bugs, so dreary, Oh!
Among the first that volunteered
Was the Gallant Captain Geary, Oh!

CHORUS: Oh, Gallant Captain Geary, Oh!
    Oh, Gallant Captain Geary, Oh!
    Oh, Gilmebres, did you ever see
    The like of Captain Geary, Oh!

At Pittsburgh when the troops arrived,
So kind was Captain Geary, Oh!
That all the boys with one accord
Made of him Colonel Geary, Oh!

   Oh, Gallant Colonel, etc.

At Lobos Island first he fought;
The foe they were quite scarey, Oh!
Although they were but seven miles off,
Quite bold stood Colonel Geary, Oh!

   Oh, Gallant Colonel, etc.

And on this Island he was left
With some of our men quite weary, Oh!

He had his *final hope* destroyed
By a naughty volunteerio.

Alas, poor Colonel, etc.

At the black pass he next did charge,
And swore by the Virgin Mary, Oh!
His name he would immortalize,
That Gallant Colonel Geary, Oh!

Oh, Gallant Colonel, etc.

At Chapultepec where cannons roared,
The Colonel ne'er did vary, Oh!
A cannon ball, it struck his groin;
Alas, Poor Colonel Geary, Oh!

Alas, poor Colonel, etc.

And now he's gone and in his grave
That man so brave and hairy, Oh!
The foe still tremble when they hear
The name of Colonel Geary, Oh!

Alas, poor Colonel, etc.

And now all in another world,
If not in purgatorio,
A roulette table is kept there
By this Gallant Colonel Geary, Oh!

Alas, poor Colonel, etc.

The "final hope" mentioned in verse 4 refers to a joke told of Colonel Geary while at Lobos Island. While there some of the officers told a soldier to fire a brush pile. The heap was soon in a blaze which set the colonel in quite a rage and he was about to send the soldier to the guard house when the officers who had ordered it stepped up and told the colonel so. He then very sorrowfully remarked to them: "That was very wrong. Suppose we were attacked here, that (referring to the brush pile) was my *final hope*."

February 8
BARCLAY. Company E on guard. Capt. J[ohnston] returned from the City. Rumored that the Rothschilds have advanced $600,000 to the Mexican Government. Hopes of a speedy peace.

COULTER. Quite a number of peace rumors afloat today. This evening had a regimental drill and the pleasure of again hearing the Diarrhea Brass Band. The colonel again treated the regiment to pulque, excepting Company "E," none of whom accepted it. It was the most ludicrous drill I ever saw and some accuse the colonel of being drunk. The field was very muddy in places and when the regiment came to such spots the men always broke ranks with a yell and either walked around or picked their steps through the mud.

February 9

BARCLAY. Johnston and Coulter off on a ride to some ruins beyond the City. Obtained from Geary and Adjt. Gen. Hooker a pass for Carney and myself. Six Mexicans, ill looking rascals, brought in prisoners this evening. They were taken by *two* horsemen while concealing themselves under a bridge between this and the City. As they were fully armed there is no doubt but their intention was to fall upon and murder solitary and unarmed soldiers.

COULTER. This afternoon a number of armed Mexicans were taken concealed under a bridge near the quarters of the First Pennsylvania Regiment. It was supposed that they were lying in wait for soldiers, but on examination it proved that they had a pass from General Scott to escort a family to some place near, but seeing a party of our soldiers they became frightened and concealed themselves. Had a battalion drill this evening.

February 10

BARCLAY. At daylight Carney and myself started on foot for the City. Took a short cut across the fields. Saw the hospital boys who are all improving and Lt. Armstrong who is suffering very much. Eat and lodged at old "Guahalotes" an ex-colonel of the Mexican Army named Lorenzo Perez whose house is patronized by our company, the favorite dish being "Guahalote" (turkey and peppers). The old fellow and his family think a great deal of the Pennsylvanians. One of his sons was killed at Cerro Gordo. Another is aid de camp to Gen. Bravo and with the General was taken prisoner at Chapultepec being among the military students. The Col. was at Buena Vista, Monterey and Churubusco. Visited this afternoon the Cathedral and Museum. Bought Life of Kemble.[5]

COULTER. Had a dress parade this evening. A parcel of the boys are on a pulque bust again. Both our officers and Daddy Barclay are in the city and Mechling has command of the company.

February 11

BARCLAY. Up early. Breakfast over called on our sick and started for San Angel. This trip was very pleasant. Night most beautiful moonlight. Bowman and myself watched Madame Luna among the clouds for a long time.

---

5. Probably *Memoirs of the Life of John Philip Kemble, Esq., Including a History of the Stage From the Time of Garrick to the Present Period,* by James Boaden, published in two volumes at London in 1825. The gifted and extensive Kemble family, which included John's sister, Sarah Siddons, and his niece, the American actress and reformer, Fanny Kemble, dominated the British stage during the nineteenth century.

COULTER. On quarter guard today. Was no drill as the colonel has gone to the city to attend Captain Montgomery's Court martial. Captain Montgomery came up a few days ago and his trial will come off shortly.

February 12
BARCLAY. Coulter gone to the City to attend as a witness on the Montgomery court martial. The guard drilled by Capt. Brooks[6] of the South Carolina Regt. As this drilling was new there has been a great deal of grumbling among the men.

COULTER. This afternoon there occurred quite an amusing scene. The officer of the main guard (Captain Brooks, of the South Carolina Regiment) undertook to drill the guard and did give them a tedious drill of three hours in length, much to the amusement of our regiment who groaned him completely.

February 13
BARCLAY. This morning Capt. Brooks again drilled the guard. The Capt. went home from Jalapa and has only of late rejoined his company. He told the guard that altho he had not been with the army during the campaign he still wished to show them that he understood his duty. While he was drilling a mob raised and commenced hooting, etc., and finally throwing eggs. The Capt. was in a most terrible rage. Being relieved a part of the new guard was sent with him to his quarters. Amidst the hooting and egg pelting of the mob he cocked a musket but did not fire. There is great excitement and had he fired he would have been killed. At noon the Regt. being about to start for the field, the Capt. passed. The yelling was renewed. He snapped his pistol three times at the crowd. Marched near two miles to a large plain where Gen. Cushing reviewed the Brigade. Several movements were performed. Returned late in the evening to quarters. Col. Geary made a speech in regard to the transactions of today which he hoped would never again happen, etc. Brooks has Lieut. Wolf and [Bivan R.] Davis placed under arrest for conniving at, etc., the mob. The Capt. is a formidable character being a notorious duelist, having shot or winged his opponent on two or three occasions.

COULTER. This morning Captain Brooks, the hero of yesterday's performance recommenced his drilling of the guard. One fellow refused and

6. Preston Smith Brooks (1819–1857) won his greatest notoriety on 22 May 1856 when, as a congressman from South Carolina, in retaliation for harsh words directed at a kinsman, he surprised Massachusetts senator Charles Sumner at his desk, beat him repeatedly over the head with a gold-headed cane, and left the battered senator near death in a pool of blood on the Senate floor. To many shocked Northerners this brutal act was the epitome of the arrogant violence which slaveholding bred, and they nicknamed the congressman "Bully" Brooks, a title his actions in Mexico foreshadowed.

he had him bucked, but the chap was cut loose before the officer had fairly turned his back. Several eggs were also thrown at him. Some time after the guard was relieved and he started for home followed by the groans of the crowd and as soon as he had passed the gate was saluted with a shower of eggs upon his back. He returned, obtained a guard and again started followed by groans. He snatched a loaded musket from one of the guard and damned them to groan now. Some time after, the regiment were out preparatory to a brigade drill. Captain Brooks again passing, was saluted with groans. He snapped a horse pistol three times at the crowd. His pistol would not go off and the men again cheered him. It did not end here, but afterward when we were on the drill ground he walked past the regiment and ordered Lieutenants Wolf and Davis under arrest, although we had a colonel in command. He was again laughed at and complained to General Cushing. On our return home the colonel made some remarks about this morning's affair, that Captain Brooks had preferred charges against Lieutenant Wolf and Davis of conniving at mutinous conduct. He hoped the men would not carry it any farther, and that he intended to prefer charges against Captain Brooks. Received orders for an inspection and review, by the Inspector General, tomorrow at half past eight o'clock.

February 14

BARCLAY. St. Valentines Day. Instead of sending love notes we are early under arms to march in the field of yesterday. Major Buchanan[7] the inspecting officer, reviewed the Brigade. Marched back to San Angel and stacked arms. Each Regt. is to undergo a minute inspection as on muster day. The 1st Penna., New York and Mass. Regts. are inspected but our Regt. is not reached. About 4 P.M. our company mount guard. Coulter and Bates sent in with Lieut. Armstrong's trunk and cot.

COULTER. This morning was detailed to go to the city with Lieutenant Armstrong's baggage. Found him still confined to a dark room and his eye very bad. The court martial in Captain Montgomery's case is going on. Major General Patterson is president of the court. Today the brigade was reviewed at San Angel with knapsacks on and fully equipped. This bore I escaped by being in the city.

7. Robert Christie Buchanan (1811–1878) of Maryland was a career soldier from the time he entered the Military Academy at age fifteen to his retirement with the brevet rank of major general in 1870, after a stint as military commander of Louisiana during Reconstruction. In between, he fought in the Black Hawk War, the Seminole Wars, the Mexican War (with special distinction at Molino del Rey), and the Civil War (commanding a brigade at Antietam and Fredericksburg), displaying always a steady and dependable, if not dashing or brilliant, military performance.

February 15

BARCLAY. Maj. Buchanan inspected the 2nd Penna. Regt. He is very particular. That part of our company not on guard passed inspection well. Their arms and clothing were in good order and no remarks were made. Haines is very low. But little hopes are entertained of his recovery. Two men detailed to wait on him. Fight between some members of the 2nd Penna. and the S. Carolinians and Texians. The ill feeling originating with the Capt. Brooks difficulty is evidently increasing.

COULTER. This morning returned to San Angel where I arrived about noon, again very luckily escaping a regimental inspection made this morning by the Inspector General. This morning General Cushing left for Puebla, being on a court of inquiry to be held at that place in the cases of the arrests of Generals Worth and Pillow and Colonel Duncan by General Scott.[8] The whole brigade are pleased at this departure and many are the fervent prayers for his long stay.

February 16

BARCLAY. Another fight between the regiments. This disposition to quarrel is fortunately confined to the rowdies. "Santa Anna" of F Company has lost a piece of his nose, bitten off by a Texian in a fight. The Texian however cried peccavi.[9] One of the Mass. Regt. early this morning was drummed out of the service to the tune of the Rogues March. As the ceremony took place shortly after daylight but few witnessed it.

COULTER. Dress parade this evening and orders read stating that Colonel Wyncoop of the First Pennsylvania Regiment was now in command of the brigade and should be obeyed as such. For a couple of days back some of our regiment have had considerable quarreling with some of the South Carolinians and Texans.

---

8. Despite an army regulation to the contrary, officers in the Mexican War did not hesitate to write letters to newspapers back home, usually exaggerating their own prowess. The most egregious offenders on that score were Gideon Pillow and artillery captain James Duncan. Pillow's letter to the *New Orleans Delta*, signed "Leonidas," not only praised its secret author for displaying "masterly military genius and profound knowledge of the science of war, which has astonished so much the mere martinets of the profession," but also denigrated the part played by the chief of these "martinets," General Scott.

Duncan's missive was less eloquent but equally insubordinate, praising himself and Worth at Scott's expense. When the authorship of the letters was exposed, Scott arrested Duncan and Pillow. Worth, who felt under unjust suspicion, defended his innocence in such violent terms that he too was arrested.

When news reached President Polk that his favorite, Pillow, had been arrested, the president was so outraged that he overturned the charges and set into motion the events that would lead to Scott's trial and dismissal from command.

9. Latin for "I have sinned." It is likely that the Texan's actual words were somewhat less elegant.

February 17

BARCLAY. Understand that Gen. Lane was again out in search of Santa Anna. Long drills in the afternoon. After night, Kline[10] with his fiddle had a little private concert in our quarters. He is a musical genius, among the best performers on the fiddle I have ever met with. He sings and plays "Old Joe" to perfection.

COULTER. This morning mounted guard at the main guard house. Posted over the prison and had considerable trouble, some of the prisoners continually escaping. We had an Irish lieutenant of the Massachusetts Regiment on guard (the hero of one night's picket guard) he was fearful as usual of the prisoners escaping and the guard being attacked. During the night while I was on post for some cause or other the monastery clock stopped and the Sergeant, having no other means of ascertaining the time, we were allowed to stand a long time before the mistake was discovered.

February 18

BARCLAY. Day cool and very windy. When the wind blows strong in this region clouds of dust and sand fill the air and obstruct the view. The outline of the mountains is barely seen through the hazy atmosphere. I am reading Kemble's life. An express has arrived from Vera Cruz. News that the Ten Regiment Bill has not passed and that Gen. Butler is to take command of the army, Gen. Scott being suspended. This state of affairs has arisen from the unfortunate difficulties among our officers. It is to be regretted that Genl. Scott was so sensitive in regard to the letters written home. His fame was built upon a foundation too firm to be shaken by any such unofficial productions. But a Court of Inquiry will now assemble and the campaign be investigated. Gen. Scott probably managed as well as any other officer would have done. But he is only human and there is no doubt errors have been committed. The armistice and the battle of Molino del Rey will likely be the chief points made against the Commander in Chief. Had the *puffing* letters been passed over in silent contempt this Court of Inquiry would never have assembled and out of the army there would have been but one opinion as to Gen. Scott's abilities. The facts laid before and the finding of the Court of Inquiry may lessen the impression of the people as to the talents military and diplomatic of the General.

COULTER. This morning the clock had resumed the even tenor of its course and our fourth term was as short as the last was long. Had a regimental drill this afternoon and performed a new field maneuver, forming square from line.[11] An express came up this afternoon in fifty-two hours from Vera Cruz.

10. There were two Klines in the 2d Pennsylvania Infantry. More than likely the one with the musical gift that so impressed Coulter was Fred Kline, the bugler of Company K.
11. A maneuver designed to allow infantry to withstand cavalry charges.

February 19

BARCLAY. Day cool and windy. Johnston went to the City. Gen. Scott in an order published in this morning's Star takes leave of the army.[12] Night most lovely moonlight.

COULTER. From the dispatches brought by yesterday's express, General Scott is suspended from the command of the army until the result of the court [of] inquiry, now sitting at [Puebla] is known. Major General Butler, of Kentucky, is now in command of the army. Had a dress parade this evening and the proceedings of a court martial ordered to investigate the conduct of the New York Regiment for damaging the building in which they were quartered, were read.

February 20

BARCLAY. Sunday. Last night after midnight some fellows of our Regt. attempted to dig a hole through the wall under the porch by our quarters. Their object was plunder which they supposed was concealed in the room beneath us. Fortunately Byerly was up and moved the gentlemen. They returned a second time when he heard them and threatened to call the guard. They then left. This morning we see their work in a large hole commenced in the solid wall and a considerable quantity of rubbish and stones loosened. So much for the Sappers and Miners. Regimental Inspection. I got hold of an old Catholic prayer book to which I devoted the greater part of the day. At dress parade orders read that hereafter there would be a Regt. Drill each morning at 9 A.M. and a Dress Parade at 5 P.M.

COULTER. A regimental inspection this morning. After inspection mounted guard at regimental quarters and placed over the Padres. Colonel Geary received rather a bitter pill today. Being in our company quarters, he saw a private journal of one of the men lying on the table. With all the impudence of his disposition, he picked it up, and as luck would have it, it opened upon a page where it spoke of his election and used very disrespectful terms relative to himself. Having read the paragraph, he inquired whose it was and shut it up without any remarks on its contents. It was a just rebuke and richly deserved. It was an unpardonable piece of impudence for any man, without permission, to read the private journal

---

12. Considering Scott's penchant for bombast, his farewell was simple and dignified:

"By instructions from the President of the United States, just received, Major-General Scott turns over the command of this army to Major-General Butler, who will immediately enter upon duty accordingly.

"In taking official leave of the troops he had so long had the honor personally to command in an arduous campaign—a small part of whose glory has been, from position, reflected on the senior officer, Major-General Scott is happy to be relieved by a general of established merit and distinction in the service of his country." (General Order No. 50, in *North American*, 19 February 1848.)

of another. On dress parade this evening orders were read for daily battalion drills at eight o'clock A.M. and company drills in the afternoon. We can stand this as long as our officers can and it will not last long.

February 21

BARCLAY. Regt. Drill. Our company did not turn out, part being on guard and all having obtained permission to go to Churubusco today. Churubusco Church is near three miles distant from San Angel. The principal part of the road being built up with the straggling village of Coyoacan, Haciendas and Ranches. The church is a large stone building and was covered by breastworks and ditches. About ¼ of a mile from the church is the "tete du pont," the bridge which is fortified spanning a deep and narrow bed of a creek (at present there is no water) on the road which enters the city at the San Antonio Gate.

The position of the enemy was very strong and it looked as madness to attack them in front. But their works were stormed and carried by an inferior force by an attack in front. The reckless dashing bravery of the American soldier and not military science won Churubusco. Our loss at Churubusco was 800 men killed and wounded. Before the terrible fire of the enemy several of the most veteran regiments gave way and it was the consciousness that victory and victory alone would save them from utter destruction which brought the men to the charge. Amid the brilliant successes which attended the army of the valley of Mexico, the defects of commanders have been overlooked and the blaze of glory which surrounded the whole campaign has hid from the public eye the ill plans of different battles, but History will do justice to all and the services of the rank and file to their country will be justly appreciated, when the great superiority of the enemy, their selected and strongly fortified positions and the frequent ill arranged plans of the American officers are taken into consideration. Molino del Rey and Churubusco, the most bloody battles that American troops were ever engaged in were gained not by any scientific movements or combinations but by the intrepid valor of the common soldiers.

In passing over the field of operations the first question which occurs is, Why was the battle fought at all? Why was an attempt made to carry the works by front attack? To me it appeared that our troops entered into the engagement without knowing the obstacles they had to contend against. The columns of Worth and Smith and Pillow flushed with their successes at San Antonio and Contreras rushed forward in pursuit of the retreating enemy and without the necessary delay and reconnoitering immediately commenced the attack upon Churubusco. Two things are certain. The rear towards the City of the Mexicans position was not fortified, their artillery being all mounted towards the front, and 2nd, Shields Brigade gained the enemy's rear without suffering any loss from the enemy's artillery. The question then presents itself, Why was not the enemy's rear turned? and What was the necessity of sacrificing so many men uselessly. The San Patricio Legion did not retreat in time. Their retreat was cut off by Shields Brigade and they were obliged to surrender. From Churubusco to the City is over six miles. It was along this road that Harney's Dragoons charged. The impetuosity of some of the pursuers carried them over the works at the Garita. Lieut. Coulter pointed out to us the old ranches behind which Pillow's men had found a temporary shelter. The day after the Battle, he and Dick Johnston had visited the field. Poor Dick pointed out to him where his company had lain and where he had pulled a wounded soldier out of a ditch who lay exposed to the Mexican fire.

From Churubusco the party paid a visit to San Antonio which we had passed on our march from San Agustin on the 8th September. Altho this position was formidable it was carried by Gen. Worth with scarce any loss. The Mexicans falling back upon Churubusco after being made acquainted with the results of Contreras. While reconnoitering these works on the 18th of Aug. Cap. Thornton of the Dragoons was killed by a round shot.

At San Antonio is a very large Hacienda, the proprietor of which is said to be one of the wealthy men of the country. The fields appear well cultivated and there is a large quantity of grain about the out houses. I am told that the most profitable crop in the valley is the pulque or maguey plant, but from the very high prices all kinds of grain must yield heavy profit. The farmers of the valley are not blessed with regular showers, but in lieu thereof they water their fields from the mountain streams and lakes. Almost every foot of ground for miles in the neighborhood of Mexico City can be overflowed.

A portion of our party, principally of the 1st Penna. Regt. who have sneaked along, are disposed to plunder. Col. Geary remained behind until the whole party had left San Antonio and started for home. He then rode ahead. Lieut. Coulter and Mann remained back. Some half dozen ruffians from the 1st Regt. immediately raised a row with some Mexicans and commenced robbing. The guards interfered and they set on the guard. One of our company Hays, tried to save the guard and received a severe blow on the face. I was on ahead myself and did not see the row. The offenders will be arrested and court martialed and I sincerely hope well punished. A man that will rob and abuse these defenceless people would commit the same offences at home were he not restrained by dread of the laws.

COULTER. After guard mount our company turned out for a trip to the battle ground of Churubusco. Some others of the regiment went with us, and in passing the quarters of the First Pennsylvania Regiment, were unfortunately joined by many more. Colonel Geary also went along. After a march of about three miles came to the Convent of Churubusco. This was surrounded by a very strong breastwork and batteries. This is the place where the deserters, under Major Riley, made such a desperate stand. The convent is a large, fine building and contains many beautiful paintings. From the belfry of this convent we had a full view of the whole battle ground. About three quarters of a mile in front was a large white hacienda at which Generals Shields and Pierce took their positions. They had left the main road before reaching the convent and taken possession of this hacienda for the purpose of cutting off the retreat of the enemy. It was here that the New York and South Carolina Regiments suffered so severely. The convent itself was attacked by General Twiggs from the road on our left (standing in position to front the hacienda). About two miles to our rear are the batteries of San Antonio, which General Worth entered without a fight. The works of San Antonio lie in a direct road to Churubusco and this road is protected by a very strong battery at what is called the "Tete du pont," about three hundred yards from the convent. General Worth advanced against this work and was joined midway by General Cadwalader, who entered the road from the left. This advance was partially protected by the enemy's train which had been stopped on the road. After passing this train the fire was very heavy and the loss was unusually great. This point of attack has been censured by some. From these works went to San Antonio. This road runs from San Agustin through San Antonio direct to the City of Mexico, where it enters at the Garita de San Antonio Abad. These works are very strong, but General Worth, by his generalship, entered them without loss. It was by the first shot fired from this battery that Captain Thornton was killed while reconnoitering on the 18th of August last. At this place there is a very large hacienda with a fine grain plantation surrounding. Here our army got a great quantity of forage before entering the city. It appears to have been a forage depot for the Mexican Army. Our division, when it marched from San Agustin on the 8th of September last, followed this road to this place. Here some of our party commenced plundering. Did not return to Churubusco, but followed the road our division had taken to Coyoacan. On this road some of the First Pennsylvanians plundered again and we had considerable trouble bringing them up. They first broke open a pulque shop, drank and destroyed the pulque and carried off a number of articles. Next they robbed a Mexican boy of his blanket. A few of them became impudent on our hands and a row ensued in which one of our company (Hays) received a black eye. Reached home about four o'clock, making our journey about ten miles. It is said that there are Mexican emissaries in the city. An armistice will likely be concluded.

February 22
   BARCLAY. Regt. Drill at 9 A.M. Day lovely. Mexicans busily engaged in grafting in the orchard. Ball after night at the Lafayette House. The Ball was quite aristocratic and exclusive—none but officers admitted. A stage

load of ladies came out from the City and the whole of the performance were highly creditable to the memory of the Father of his Country.

COULTER. This day one year ago, we were rusticating on the island of Lobos. Today we spent the forenoon drilling and washing up clothes. Dined on our usual rations and in honor of the day had an addition of a fine bread pudding made by our famous cook, Geesyn. Three of the men engaged in yesterday's plundering during our excursion to Churubusco, were arrested to undergo a court martial.

February 23
BARCLAY. Drill at 9 A.M. Company of guard. Haines sent to the Hospital. He is very low. Capt. returned from the City. It is rumored that all the recruiting officers have been ordered to rejoin their companies. At Dress Parade orders read that a mail would start for Vera Cruz semi-monthly, leaving Vera Cruz on the 1st and 15th of each month and starting from Mexico City three [days] after the arrival of each up mail. This is a great accomodation to the army. Surgeon examined those that he intends to discharge. Kegarize from our company was examined.

COULTER. Mounted guard this morning. Stationed at the General's Quarters. In the afternoon underwent an examination before Captain Hooker, Adjutant General, as to what I knew relative to the plundering of the 21st inst. On dress parade this evening orders Number 3 of General Butler were read establishing a regular mail between the capitol and the coast. This mail to be independent of occasional trains and it is to leave Mexico City on the first and fifteenth of each month; to be escorted by a dragoon guard of at least twenty-five men, to be relieved at each post on the route. As the distance is long between the posts of Puebla and Perote, a new post is to be established midway between them. Ojo de Agua has since been selected for that post. This will give us a regular semi-monthly mail, and the guard being relieved at each post, will be able to move through in about seven days; also without inconvenience or requiring any extra force at the garrisons on the route. My guard post was relieved at dark and during the night was posted as a picket at the end of a long walled cave.

February 24
BARCLAY. Drill changed from 9 to 8 A.M. As the orders were only given this morning, the turn out was small. Did not march from the grounds. Orders to turn out tomorrow morning at 6 A.M. Ball at night at the La Fayette House. Highly creditable, etc.

COULTER. A regimental hospital has been established at this place and today all our sick were moved into it. This evening orders for drill were altered from eight to six o'clock A.M.

February 25

BARCLAY. Turned out at [six] A.M. and drilled. Bates and Smith gone to the City and back.

COULTER. Had a regimental drill at six A.M. The colonel looked very sleepy and cross at being waked so early and I think drill at that hour will not be repeated. Have had an addition to our company today of dos Senoritas.[13] Several orders were read on dress parade; one from Colonel Wyncoop, ordering a general inspection and mustering in of the brigade on Tuesday the 29th of the month; another from Colonel Geary disposing with battalion drill tomorrow, it being set aside as a regimental wash day. Had a couple of horse races this evening, one between a horse of Lieutenant Klotz and another of Dr. Rutledge of our regiment.[14] The persons mentioned rode themselves and Rutledge won the race. But running on, his bridle broke, and his horse running foul of an ass loaded with wood, he was thrown, though not much injured.

February 26

BARCLAY. A mail came in which brought a number of letters and papers. I received a number of letters from home and a Commission or notice of an Appointment of 2nd Lieut. in the 11th Regt. of U.S. Infantry, with rank from 30th Dec., 1847. Date of Notice 21st January, 1848. This appointment as it is the wish of friends at home I will accept. To their kindness I am indebted for the appointment. At the same time it is a hard matter to leave my old company. In the capacity in which I have so long acted as 1st Sergt. I have become so well acquainted with all the men and from the most intimate knowledge have formed so high an opinion of them that it requires a good bit of philosophy to part with them. To me they have all been as I could have wished and if I must now leave them in discharge of what I consider a still higher duty it is with the most lively remembrance and full appreciation of their many noble qualities and with the hope that we all will soon meet together again in our own land. As during a long intercourse their gentlemanly bearing towards me was always most pleasant, so now when about to part from them I am deeply affected with their manifestations of regard.

COULTER. On quarter guard today. Stationed in the back part of the building over the Padres. Appeared before the court martial as a witness in the case of one of the prisoners of the Churubusco spree. Received a mail this evening. By this mail Sergeant T. J. Barclay received a commission as Second Lieutenant in the 11th Infantry. Also Colonel Geary re-

13. What the activities of the "two girls" may have been is not further specified.
14. Dr. Hugh Rose Rutledge was not of the 2d Pennsylvania regiment but was an assistant surgeon in Calhoun's Battalion of the Georgia Infantry.

ceived an order from the Secretary of War to discharge Sergeant James McLaughlin, who had left for home on sick furlough, where he arrived but in very bad health. The boys are very sorry at Daddy's being about to leave and there is a gloom over the whole company.

February 27

BARCLAY. Newspaper mail from the States.

COULTER. This morning had a regimental inspection, after which a meeting of the company was held to take into consideration the propriety of purchasing a sword to be presented to Lieutenant Barclay, which was most enthusiastically agreed to. Went to the City of Mexico as one of the committee to purchase this sword. Found Lieutenant Armstrong much better, but still confined to his room. Was very sorry to learn that Captain Montgomery had been broken of his commission by the court martial. However, it will only be another crime for John Geary to answer for in the States. It being Sunday afternoon, and a time of general amusement, the stores were shut and we were unable to make the purchase. Could find no place of public amusement in the evening, the National and Principal Theatres were both closed and we were compelled to go to bed early for want of employment.

February 28

BARCLAY. I made out the muster roll and monthly report of E Co.

COULTER. The Court Martial sitting this morning again, it was necessary that I should be at San Angel soon. Left the city by daylight with Corporal Bowman, and by taking a short route across the fields, reached quarters in time, and was examined before the court in the cases of the other two engaged in the Churubusco affair. From the wording of the charges it was impossible for any of the witnesses to swear anything criminal against these prisoners, and I have but little doubt that in consequence these two, a pair of perfect scoundrels and deserters (they deserted at New Orleans and were retaken) will escape, while the first, who is comparatively innocent, will as certainly receive some punishment. After the court martial returned to the city on Lieutenant Coulter's horse, having there met with rather an unlucky accident or perhaps misfortune. Dismounted at Captain Montgomery's quarters, and giving my horse to a Mexican to hold, went up stairs. Looked out of the window a minute after and the Mexican had vamoosed with horse, saddle, bridle and a number of letters belonging to ours and Company "H" which I was bringing to town to put in the post office. Made some search but could hear nothing of the thief. Offered twenty dollars to a ladrone to bring him back. The only way to catch a thief here is by hiring another to expose. He appeared very certain of catching him and left in company with one of our native spies apparently as big a rascal as himself. They did not return and I suppose they found it more profitable to sell the horse and divide the spoils; for being only across the street at the time the horse was stolen, they undoubtedly knew who took him. After searching the city over, could not find a suitable sword and postponed the purchase until the arrival of the train from Vera Cruz. This night lodged at Lieutenant Armstrong's quarters.

February 29

BARCLAY. The 2nd Penna. Regt. was mustered in by Capt. Hooker. They looked remarkably well, particularly my old company. Corp. Bonnin has been promoted 1st Sergt., Bigelow, 2nd Sergt. and Gordon and Steck, 3rd and 4th Corpls. The appointments are all good and the promotion of the two former is but sheer justice to the two oldest non-commissioned officers of the company whose claims have heretofore been overlooked.

COULTER. Left for San Angel by six o'clock in the omnibus, where we arrived in time for inspection. The regiment was mustered in, our company numbering fifty one officers and men and present and absent including Milner, who has been missing for some time and Sergeant McLaughlin who will be discharged. This is the first time since being in the service that we have been mustered in twice at the same place. The regiment have drawn bed sacks filled with straw to sleep on. On dress parade this evening was read the finding of the court martial in Captain Montgomery's case. This night I slept on what might be called a bed for the first time since leaving the steamboat "North Carolina" off Camp Jackson, a period of about thirteen and a half months.

March 1

BARCLAY. Went with Col. Geary to the City. Called on Maj. Thomas,[15] Adjt. General, who ordered me to report to and join my Regt. the first opportunity. Afterwards called in company with Col. Geary on Gen. Butler. The General's Quarters are superb and he received me with great politeness. Gen. Butler is above the middle height, spare in person, with a keen, intellectual face. His hair is grey and he wears it a la mode, Gen. Jackson. He is most perfectly gentlemanly in his manner and conversation. While we were there Gen. Lane entered, having just dismounted from his late

15. Lorenzo Thomas (1805–1875) of Delaware, graduated from West Point in 1823. Except for some active duty in the Seminole Wars and at the Battle of Monterey, he was essentially an administrative officer, serving as Winfield Scott's chief of staff from the end of the Mexican War until the outbreak of the Civil War. As a brigadier general, he served as the adjutant general of the Union army during the first half of the Civil War and then supervised the organization of black troops, emerging from the war with the brevet rank of major general. In 1868 he served a brief stint as interim secretary of war when President Andrew Johnson attempted to remove Edwin Stanton from that post, playing a bit part in the drama which led to Johnson's impeachment.

expedition.[16] He was accompanied by a couple of his officers and three Mexican officers, prisoners of war. The whole party were covered with dust and Lane himself was the beau ideal of the field soldier. His clothing, and big boots covered with dust. His beard long and a segar which he smoked assisted in placing him in complete contrast to Gen. Butler who was dressed in taste.

Lane appeared to affect a vulgarism in his dress, movements and talk. His expedition has been fortunate and he was giving Butler an account of it. After all had taken a drink of whiskey, which Butler with very good taste had brought out, we left the two Generals.

I met by mere accident Lieut. Col. Savage[17] of the 11th Regt. and reported to him and had an understanding with him as to my future connexion with his Regt. From what little I see of him I am well pleased with him. He was formerly a Major of the 14th and was wounded I understand before the City. Having written my letter of acceptance, I went before Lieut. Col. [Francis S.] Belton, Lieut. Gov., and made the necessary affidavit, both of which I forwarded to Gen. Jones. Carney and Hoffer at the same time made affidavits before the Lieut. Gov. in regard to a private matter of business. Col. Belton is an old artillery officer, now of the 3rd. He is man of near 50 and in old times was known to the Greensburghers. He is dry and was not disposed to say a word more than was absolutely necessary. We had no conversation. I was amused with the precision of the old fellow in administering an oath.

Remained over night at "Old Guahalotes." The young ladies sang several songs. Carney and Hays each sang. M. Hays' song was exceedingly entertaining.

COULTER. Today General Lane returned from his last expedition. He had an engagement with Padre Jarauta. The enemy lost about one hundred killed and fifty taken prisoners. Father Martinez[18] was killed. Our loss was one killed and four wounded. A large quantity of arms were taken. This evening had considerable sport and quite a row with Lieutenant Coulter. Four of us undertook to buck him, and after much trouble accomplished it. In the row he had a shirt torn off his back, and getting loose, he tore one off each of us by way of retaliation. Leb Allshouse got pretty drunk afterward and kept up the sport until one o'clock. Several appointments of

16. On 25 February Lane, along with Colonel Hays' Texas Rangers, captured the town of Sequalteplan, killing and capturing a number of guerrillas. This was said to be the last military engagement of the Mexican War.

17. John H. Savage commanded the 16th Tennessee Volunteer Infantry for the Confederacy during the Civil War.

18. Like his commander, Padre Jarauta, Juan Antonio Martínez (or Martin) was a Spanish-born priest who learned the techniques of guerrilla warfare during the Spanish civil wars before applying them in Mexico.

non-commissioned officers in our company to rank from today have been
made by the captain as follows:

> 4th Corporal Bonnin, to be 1st Sergeant
> vice - Barclay, promoted.

> 3rd Corporal Bigelow, to be 2nd Sergeant
> vice - McLaughlin discharged.

> Private Gordon, to be 3rd Corporal
> vice - Bigelow, made Sergeant.

> Private Steck, to be 4th Corporal
> vice - Bonnin made Sergeant.

March 2

BARCLAY. Visited the Cathedral. Each time I enter this most magnificent edifice, I am more struck with the wealth and grandeur. Returned at 1
P.M. in the stage to San Angel.

Here Ends the Mexican War Journals of Thomas J. Barclay.

12

The Brigade Has Completely Broken Loose
San Angel

The following entries are from the diary of Richard Coulter.

March 2

Nothing of importance today. Has been unusually windy. Had some amusing conversation with one of the Padres. Tom Barclay struck up a talk with him in Latin which he understood tolerably, and had the chap's blood up about Luther, Calvinists, ana-baptists, etc., etc., etc.

March 3

Mounted guard this morning. Luckily posted at the upper picket. In the afternoon learned that Lieutenant Barclay intended leaving on Monday and getting relieved from guard, went to the city to make another attempt to purchase a sword. Found nothing fit for the purpose, and Captain Montgomery very kindly offered to attend to making the purchase in the United States. Lodged at ["Old Guahalotes."]

March 4

As I was passing through one of the portals near the Grand Plaza saw what I have often heard of but never before seen, that is, an old bitch giving birth to a litter of pups and a couple of Comanche women looking at the performance. Noticed on the streets for sale large baskets of colored eggs, at least they appeared to be such. Understood that they are used by the inhabitants to throw at each other during the feast of Carnaval [Mardi Gras]. (Don't know about the truth of it.) There are but few amusements in the city and it is quite a bore to be there now. About three o'clock left in the onmibus for San Angel. A meeting was called in the evening. Some resolutions were passed complimentary to Lieutenant Barclay and agreed to send to the States with Captain Montgomery for the sword. One hundred dollars were raised for that purpose.

March 5

Learned today that seven companies of the First Pennsylvania Regiment under Lieutenant Colonel Black, are ordered to Vera Cruz as train guard. Towards evening the weather became cloudy and rained a little.

Tonight had a bucking match of First and Second Sergeants and Third and Fourth Corporals, the new non-commissioned officers. After which attempted to buck old Mechling, but he got his Dutch up, smacked his fists and swore he would smash any one that said "buck" to him. So ended the sport.

March 6

This morning Colonel Black's command marched to join the train which leaves the city today. Mounted guard. Stationed at the regimental hospital. Three of our company lately discharged, go down with this train, Hansberry, Kegarize and McClelland. Hansberry has papers for one-third and McClelland for one-fourth pension. Thus it is that men disabled in battle are refused their just rights. The powers that be attempt in this particular to curtail the war expenses, while contractors in the States receive enormous prices for supplies and transportation. The real source of expense is left untouched. The colonel has not signed Sergeant McLaughlin's discharge. He owes Jim a grudge for a letter of his published in the Greensburg papers, and wishes by this means to give him some trouble. Saw the published articles of armistice lately concluded between Generals Worth and Smith with the Mexican commissioners. It provides that there shall be a cessation of hostilities throughout the Mexican Republic; that neither army shall advance beyond its present lines, nor pass through the territory occupied by the other; that places occupied by the American troops shall be evacuated temporarily in case of elections; this armistice to be terminated by either party on notice of different lengths of time in different places and some other articles.

March 7

This is the last day of the carnival. No ceremonies that I observed in San Angel, but understood that it was celebrated in the city. Had noisy and wet quarters during the afternoon. Some of the boys got up a row and drenched each other with water.

March 8

This is the first of Lent. This morning observed an odd religious custom in vogue here. All the Mexicans, men, women and children had stamped on their forehead a small black cross. Also some of the Catholic soldiers have this mark.[1] It was done in the church attached to our quarters. The brigade was reviewed by Generals Worth and Cadwalader and afterward drilled by Colonel Wyncoop. Some of the boys had another drinking match this afternoon.

---

1. 8 March 1848 was Ash Wednesday. Coulter's acquaintance with Catholics in Pennsylvania must have been extremely limited.

March 9

Mounted guard this morning at the main guard house from which four of us were detached as a guard to protect a neighboring hacienda. It appears to be quite a pulque establishment, and I saw here what I have never before seen in Mexico, the owner of the house selling pulque to the soldiers on credit. Were well treated here and supper was furnished for the guard. At night slept in the shop. The old man before going to bed left a considerable quantity of pulque in one of the vessels in our room which we attacked pretty freely. Pulque is calculated to make a fellow tipsy and we got rather tight and had a merry time of it. The guard were Decker, McCabe, Waters and myself.

March 10

The armistice lately concluded was read to the regiment on evening parade. Tonight Geesyn caused a good deal of laughter. He was tight and had a fight with one of the company.

March 11

The sick in the regiment in the general hospital at the City of Mexico were sent today to our regimental hospital at this place. Two of our company came out. Hoffer, the only sick man left there and attendant.

March 12

This morning one of Company "K" shot a large wolf in the orchard connected to our quarters. Mounted guard this morning. Part of the company are on quarter guard; for myself, was sent to the main guard and posted over the prisoners. These prison posts are the most disagreeable species of guard duty. The sentinel is in continual danger of being put in the guard house himself for the escape of prisoners which often cannot be prevented. Received a mail from the city today. English envoys came in last night and a small train with the mail this morning. Received one letter only. News of no account; all peace prospects in the States. Today several of the surgeons of our brigade disinterred the bodies of the deserters buried in the field opposite our quarters for the purpose of getting the skeletons. There was a number buried there before the battle of Chapultepec.

March 13

On dress parade this evening the proceedings of a court of inquiry held in Mexico City were read. A wolf again made his appearance in the orchard. Some of the men went out but did not catch him; in fact, they are exceedingly numerous here, coming into the town, and even approaching sentinels at night.

March 14

Instead of the usual regimental drill or dress parade, the companies were ordered out for company drill. The captain marched Company "E" by flank movements across the field to a pulque establishment; having drank, returned on a similar march to quarters. Such was our drill. Today learned of the death of Ex-President John Q. Adams.[2]

March 15

This morning our guard detail was unusually heavy, a corporal and fifteen men. We have only twenty-one men for duty. On quarter guard; am posted over the cells of the Padres. The main guard house has been removed from our quarters across the Plaza to a building lately used as the Massachusetts hospital. Our mess cook, Geesyn, is sick today and I have had quite a job working. Goes a little awkward after being rid of it for a month or so.

March 16

This has been an exceedingly dull day. Am mess cook today. Some of the company had been swimming in the reservoir at the head of the orchard.

March 17

This is St. Patrick's day in the "mornin." There was rather a laughable thing happened upon Steck or old "livers" as he is called. We had a mess of boiled eggs for breakfast and Fred, very unluckily got a rotten one which, before he discovered it, was broken on his plate and mixed with a good egg. His greediness would not allow him to throw away the whole plate, but he attempted to separate the good egg from the bad until we laughed at him, when he very reluctantly threw away the whole mess. It is only a specimen of his piggish propensities. It was for an affair somewhat similar that he received the appellation "Livers." It happened on the evening of the second day's march from Vera Cruz (April 10). We had been short of rations and were unable to shoot any beef. Fred. had shot a cow, but only brought home what he thought he could eat himself, namely a very large liver, the heart and kidneys. he refused to give the rest of his mess any, but having boiled them, ate the whole batch, after which he demolished a gallon of soup which he managed to get. This is his great fault, an enormous appetite and no disposition to restrain it within the bounds of decency. Today was a guard policing of our entire quarters. See

2. On 21 February 1848, former president John Quincy Adams, then a congressman representing his Massachusetts district, suffered a massive stroke on the floor of the House of Representatives, just after delivering a speech against the Mexican War. Carried to a sofa in the speaker's office, he lingered there in a coma until his death two days later at the age of eighty.

from today's paper that General Scott has withdrawn his charges preferred against General Worth and Colonel Duncan, and that General Worth has withdrawn his charges against General Scott. The only case now before the court of inquiry is that of General Pillow on the charge preferred against him by General Scott. Lieutenant Colonel Brindle ordered squad drills this evening without arms. The remainder of the companies were out, but we were not, having no commissioned officer present. It is a pretty drill anyhow for men fifteen months in the service. Even regulars never heard of such a thing. This being St. Patrick's day, in the evening the Irish Greens had a supper and subsequently a spree. Colonel Geary and some other officers were, I believe, present. A number of speeches it is said were made, one by Colonel Geary, who is courting popularity at every expense.

March 18

The regiment were formed this morning and the death of Ex-President John Q. Adams announced and orders that in token of respect the flags at the different garrisons should remain half staff high, a salute of thirteen guns to be fired at sunrise, half hour guns during the day and twenty-nine guns at sunset. After this the colonel made some remarks to the regiment. Said it was reported that he wished to march the regiment to Pittsburg (when they were disbanded) and have them discharged there. He pronounced the author "a liar," and added "that's plain English." Said that the regiment was now soon to be discharged and he wished no man to entertain any ill will against him, that it had always been his object to do justice to the men, and a great deal more gass to the same effect. For some days back he has been particularly friendly to the men. It is amusing to see the littleness of the man and he works to his end most admirably. He expects his reign will soon be at an end and he wishes to gloss over his faults and conciliate the men before returning to the States. He is a perfect politician and on his return home he will be a leading party man and support a character for honesty, etc., which he does not deserve. The men generally under his command are of such a character that a few well spoken words will gain their good will. Some plundering was committed in the neighborhood and the rolls of the different companies were called to see if any were absent. Company "E" all present or accounted for. Attended the funeral of Lieutenant [Gustavus F.] Gardner, of the Massachusetts Regiment. He was buried in a Mexican graveyard near a little old chapel about half a mile from this village where several others of his regiment, Catholics, were buried, and by paying for the ground, respect is insured for the grave. He, being a Catholic, the old priest of the chapel officiated at the funeral. The old priest was a native Mexican, almost pure Indian blood. A little ragged urchin preceded him in chanting. The chapel bells tolled during the entire ceremony. Considerable mummery was gone through, a quantity of holy water used upon the coffin and the assembly, when it was placed in the grave with military honors. It was an odd scene and decidedly ludicrous. His chanting was most horrible.

March 19

The Texas Rangers, whose time of service is near expired, leave for the lower part of the line shortly. This morning a portion of the company, under Captain Johnston, took a tramp to the battle ground of Contreras. The road continues along the line of Pedregal (rocky ground) which extends from Churubusco until beyond Contreras. It is a most rugged piece of country and a perfect den for wolves and even guerrillas. Saw on the side of this Pedregal the remains of a very ancient chapel or monastery built among the most tremendous rocks. It shows the singular fancy of the sect and the mode by which Catholics gain a permanent foothold in a country. Chapels, monasteries, nunneries, etc., etc., are scattered without regard to expense, over all part[s] of the land. They are generally built on territory which is useless to others and built in the most substantial manner. The battle ground is nearly three miles from San Angel. It is as follows: Standing in the principal heavy battery, with the face towards San Agustin. On the left is a flanking battery protecting the main work and at the same time covering the road to San Angel. On the right is a similar battery which also contains the main and rakes the continuance of the road beyond Contreras. The principal battery contained heavy artillery, the right and left light pieces, in all twenty-two guns. About three hundred yards in front and separated by a deep ravine, are the old buildings in which a portion of Magruder's battery was posted, the remainder with several mountain howitzers extending along the woods to the right. This wood was also occupied by our infantry. The howitzers were brought in there without knowing the nature of the enemy's works and were soon dismounted. About two miles further is a large hill bare upon the summit from which General Scott viewed the operations. On the night of the 19th, General Twiggs' Division and Shields' volunteer brigade crossed the ravine on the left of the works within one hundred yards of the enemy's sentinels and gained the road leading to San Angel. They moved beyond this, colonel Riley's brigade occupying the old chapel and Generals Smith and Shields extending from the road to the chapel. Before day of the 20th, Colonel Riley moved through another deep ravine, at the time running with water, and took his position about five hundred yards to the rear of the enemy's works. From this point he charged the right flanking battery, the guns of which were turned upon him and from which he received one fire. It was in this battery that Captain Drum retook the two Buena Vista guns. This battery taken, the retreat in that direction was cut off and the remainder untenable. The retreat was then commenced on the San Angel road and they were hotly received by Generals Shields and Smith at a large bridge a few hundred yards from the works and by them followed into San Angel. General Shields lost but one man (accidently wounded) in this pursuit. The principal loss was in Magruder's battery. His position was an exposed one, and from the nature of his pieces, being merely light ones, he effected but little damage upon the heavy earthen breastworks and heavy guns of the enemy. The great point of this battle was the movement on the night of the 19th to gain the San Angel road and a position to the enemy's rear. After leaving the battle ground went to a neighboring pulque shop. While here a Mexican came up complaining that he had been robbed by some Americans. This gave us a fruitless chase of near two hours. After having found no trace of them in any other direction, mounted the captain's horse and went into the Pedregal. Here heard of them, but did not see them. This was the way by which McGruder's pieces were transported from San Agustin. It is almost incredible and speaks well of the perseverence of American soldiers. It is with difficulty that a horse could travel it, over abrupt rocks over which the pieces must have been lifted by the men. Our search was fruitless and we returnd to San Angel. When near that place Carson shot a large dog which fell into the aquaduct. Not thinking it was the same acquaduct that supplied our quarters with water, went home and with Carson had the pleasure of returning to throw out the carcass.

March 20

Undertook to wash a blanket this morning. Quite a job. The Texans quartered here left this morning for the city previous to going down with the train. Received a mail from the United States this afternoon. By it learned the death of Honorable A. G. Marchand[3] and several others of Greensburg and neighborhood. Also a letter was received by Sergeant Cummings of Company "H," stating that the Governor had refused to commission the officers of Colonel Geary's appointment and that the Adjutant General had forwarded to him an order to fill all vacancies by election. It is believed that Geary now has that order, but he denies all knowledge of it, and even disputes the power of the Governor to issue such an order. It has caused some excitement in Company "H." This evening there was a brigade drill under Colonel Wyncoop. This I very luckily escaped, having stopped to get a drink, the regiment got so far ahead that I did not regain them.

3. Albert Gallatin Marchand, a Greensburg lawyer and Democratic political figure who was a United States congressman from 1841 to 1845, died on 5 February 1848 at the age of thirty-six.

March 21

Mounted guard at the main guard house. Posted in the upper plaza to protect a store. This afternoon there was a battalion drill and dress parade in which we received several orders; one from Colonel Wyncoop, requiring the guards to be drilled, a thing unprecedented in military annals, and for which Captain Brooks, of the South Carolina Regiment, was egged in our quarters. Another order from the same authority prohibiting all soldiers and army followers of all descriptions from passing pickets without a special permit signed by himself. Was not required to stand post during the night.

March 22

Were not relieved at the usual time, the old guard having to remain on duty until after the review. At eleven o'clock General Patterson reviewed the brigade. This done, I escaped, for it is decidedly a bore to march some distance to a field, there to be drilled for hours in the sun. We received a very fine coffee mill today, which by the kindness of Captain Montgomery, was left for the company. This was really an acceptable present, as the ones we brought from New Orleans are completely worn out. This evening a printed circular was distributed to the commanders of companies containing several general orders from the War Department at Washington City, one of which reduces the clothing allowance of volunteers one dollar per month and provides that the six months clothing money formerly paid in advance to volunteers on entering the service shall be discontinued, in lieu of which certain articles of clothing therein enumerated shall be issued. The clothing allowance of volunteers was formerly three and one half dollars; by this order it is reduced to two and a half. Here is another specimen of retrenchment and reform. All that will be saved during the war by this regulation will not provision the army a single day.

March 23

Today some of the company had a frolic throwing one another into the reservoir. Jim Coulter and several others were completely ducked. Company "H" intends proceeding with an election without an order, but I expect Colonel Geary will foil them in the end. He has now Sergeant Cummings under arrest for mutiny. A rumor afloat this evening, but of course a mere rumor without foundation, that our regiment will leave shortly to garrison Rio Frio and that the First Pennsylvania Regiment will remain at Jalapa.

March 24

Mounted guard. At main guard house. Posted in the market and in consequence was not required to stand at night. Was quite a row among the prisoners in the guard house. One had his head badly cut. Several had their necks well felt, and a number of shirts were torn in the melee. The Massachusetts men have been paid off and are generally drunk, making a great noise and carousing; several fights in the market. While on post two of our waggoners stopped with Mexican Maragretos.[4] Some of the boys drew a linch pin, the horses were frightened and started down the plaza at a gallop. The wheel coming off, the sentries had a merry ride on the axle trees. They afterward had some more sport with them. Our bread was unusually bad today. The meat was not drawn until late, and then was not full rations and of very inferior quality. General Valencia died today at the City of Mexico, caused principally by hard drink.

March 25

This morning General Cass[5] was hung in effigy and afterwards buried at the quarters of the First Pennsylvania Regiment on account of his being the reputed author of the regulations reducing the clothing allowance of volunteers. There was a piece of beef, or rather skinny ribs, stretched like a coon skin against the outer wall of our quarters with a label stating that it was the rations of six volunteers and in truth it was a very true sample of our day's rations. The meat was old, poor and principally skinny flank, the bread mouldy and short allowance, almost impossible to eat it. This afternoon a petition was gotten up to the colonel to examine into this matter.

March 26

Nothing stirring. A very pretty day and in the evening a slight shower which made it more pleasant. Some of the boys were enjoying a swim in the reservoir and in the evening had a shirt tail row with water and sticks. In the afternoon one of the company (Byerly) was suffering greatly with colic and it was laughable to see the consolation and condolence given him by his mess mates, Bills, McCabe and McGarvey.

March 27

Mounted guard this morning. On the upper or Contreras picket. Having a number of men and only two posts, we had quite an easy time of guard. The wind was high and the air filled with perfect clouds of dust. A man and woman (Comanches) had quite a fandango here on account of his having attempted some ungentlemanly familiarities with the lady.

4. Probably a misprint for *mercaderas*, "market women" or "vendors."

5. Lewis Cass (1787–1866) was a United States senator from Michigan, a state he had been identified with since his military service there as a general in the War of 1812 and his subsequent tenure (1813–1831) as territorial governor. An ardent expansionist and a prominent Democrat, he was secretary of war under President Jackson and later minister to France. In 1848 he received his party's nomination for president, losing to the Whig, Zachary Taylor. In the Buchanan cabinet he served as secretary of state.

They were both drunk. She attempted to make complaint to the officer of the guard, but it was all "no entiendi" ["I don't understand"].

March 28

Before guard relief this morning, a greaser was washing blankets in the aquaduct which supplies our quarters. Stopped him, which greatly disturbed his feelings and he threatened us with "poco tiempo mucho fandango" ["a big brawl pretty soon"]. We retaliated with a threat of "calaboso." So he thought it better to vamoose. A slight shower this afternoon. After going to bed Mike, Leb and "Livers" had quite a kicking match in which "Livers" was worsted. A report that our regiment moves down shortly to garrison some of the lower posts.

March 29

Daddy and myself looked over the pedregal this morning. It is an unusually rocky piece of country and evidently the effect of volcanic action. In places the rocks apparently have been liquid matter congealed in the form of waves; in other spots more settled. It is intersected by many long and deep ravines and chasms and numerous caverns, good hiding places for wolves in which the pedregal abounds. Some distance in this pedregal is a large and isolated plantation containing about two hundred acres, having in it a large deserted hacienda. We did not go near to the building for fear of fleas in which it abounds. This is an odd spot, a large fine farm completely surrounded by almost inaccessible rocks. There are other spots of tillable ground varying from a quarter to two acres, but none so large as this. Returned to quarters around the lower side of the orchard wall. There are some very pretty little spots there and a number of ranches completely hidden in large and blooming rose bushes. Here got from a Comanche woman the coldest and best drink of water I have had near San Angel. Had quite a row in our orchard. A famous fighting bully of the South Carolina Regiment, known by the name of "Grey Buck," for some cause had a grievance with another rowdy called "Sands" of the First Pennsylvania. They adjourned to the orchard to settle the difficulty, a large crowd attending. They stripped and after some preliminaries went to work. "Grey Buck" was thrown, but with his doggish propensities, laid hold of the other with his teeth. This caused some interference and quite a melee ensued in which a number were knocked down and a great deal of foul play shown. Order was restored and they went at it again and again a row followed which caused more bloody heads. It was amusing to see Sergeant Joe Fostiner, of Company "F" standing over the combatants trying to give fair play, dealing his blows right and left dropping a chap every stroke. Although he was several times attacked by as high as half a dozen, he kept all off with ease and he was a lucky chap who did not get a sore head. This was a fight which I could enjoy not being concerned which was whipped.

March 30

Mounted guard this morning. On the quarter guard. Posted in the back part of the building to protect the Padres. During the night a shrine near my post was broken open, the locks were picked, and a quantity of wine and some little articles stolen, luckily not while I was on post.

March 31

A small mail was received from Vera Cruz. Not over a dozen of packages for the company, and for the first time since being in Mexico did not receive a single letter and only one paper. Today we built a dam in the creek at the lower end of the orchard and had a fine bath.

April 1

Got an unlucky fall, or rather was thrown head foremost into one of the rooms. Upset Mess Number 5 coffee pot. Came near scalding the mess. Skinned my hand, sprained my back and in consequence have been completely used up all day. Had a very heavy rain this evening, the first I have noticed for some three months, which completely drenched the ground. This being the first of April, a great many hoaxes have been played off on different persons.

April 2

Mounted guard this morning. Stationed at main guard house on prison post. All the American forces except the necessary guard for hospitals, quarters, etc., are to evacuate the city today from eight o'clock until three P.M. holding the citadel and gates. This is in accordance with the provisions of the existing armistice, the inhabitants being about to hold an election today. Today's Star says the treaty has been ratified by our Senate with some few alterations, which with the vote will be given tomorrow. On dress parade the proceedings of a court martial were read in the cases of Lieutenants Wolf and Davis of our regiment, charged with being present at and not endeavoring to suppress a mutiny of some of the Second Pennsylvania Regiment in the case of egging Captain Brooks of the South Carolina while in command of main guard at Second Pennsylvania quarters. Were both found guilty and sentenced to be suspended for two months from all rank and command and forfeit all pay proper for same period.

April 3

Today Captain Johnston returned from a pleasure excursion to Real del Monte. He brought with him several specimens of ore from the mines. Today's Star contains a list of the Senators who voted for and against the treaty and the modifications made on it. It is of necessity all surmises as the Senate deliberated in secret session on this subject.

April 4

The Surgeon has received an order to report all sick unable to walk or be carried in waggons. Many are the surmises and speculations the boys have made about this order. After dress parade the Sergeant told "Livers" that he had reported him absent without leave. The captain entered into the hoax and after some deliberation and advice to Fred. consented to release him from the guard house (which he feared). This set so hard on Steck that he was even unable to eat (a remarkable feat, the first time since being in Mexico). He lay down in an old tent in the portico lamenting his misfortunes. His tormentors did not let him rest there, but dragged him, tent and all, into the quarters. Fred in disgust then went to bed and Dr. Marchand (Jake), fearing some bad consequences, administered to him in the shape of a tobacco injection. The joke was carried on until late. Our rations failed this evening and I was almost ravenous with hunger. We pledged a part of tomorrow's rations to Keslar for bread. Then stole Decker's breakfast and he ran me over the entire building for his bread. Were unable to get our jaws stuffed. Rained greater part of the night.

April 5

Mounted guard. On patrol at main guard house. There is in the guard house a man named Stanford of South Carolina Regiment confined in irons for the murder of a private of same regiment who was killed last night. General court martial is in session. Among other cases, Sergeant Cummings of Company "H," who was arrested some time ago is to be tried on charges relative to the attempted election. Lieutenant R. C. Drum, 9th Infantry, visited the company today. His regiment is stationed at Pachuca, near Real del Monte. Received a mail from the United States; no news of any consequence in it. Heavy rain all afternoon and continued greater part of the night. Noticed some snow on several of the mountains around the valley.

April 6

This morning noticed that the peaks of the surrounding mountains were perfectly white and the intervening ridge between the two snow mountains was covered completely with snow. This morning there came to light a most rascally transaction which greatly compromises the honor of the Second Pennsylvania Regiment together with some other regiments.[6] In the City of Mexico a few nights ago there was an attempt made

6. On the night of 5 April 1848, nine or ten American soldiers broke into what was variously described as a bank or a gambling establishment at 5 Calle de la Palma. In the course of the burglary they encountered Manuel Zorriza and killed him with a bullet to the head. The criminals were soon rounded up and included the two officers of the 2d Pennsylvania, Dutton and Hare, and Lieutenant B. P. Tilden of the 2d Infantry. On 17 May a military

to rob a large establishment situate on Calle de la Palma, containing some $300,000.00. The robbers were discovered, the clerk of the establishment firing upon them, wounding one, when he was shot dead himself. A number more shots were fired when the robbers made their escape. Several arrests were next day made and one of the party named Armstrong, turned State's evidence. By his testimony it appears that several officers of the American Army have been engaged in the affair, among them are Adjutant Dutton and Lt. Hare of our regiment. Hare was arrested in the city but Dutton made his escape to San Angel. Colonel Geary received an order from headquarters to arrest him, but Dutton had again made his escape. A number of parties were sent out to scour the country. Lt. Coulter with a portion of our company went down to Churubusco road for several miles where we entered the pedregal, and extending our lines for a great distance, swept the entire length back to San Angel. Saw no signs of him. On this tramp saw several very curious goat herds, or places to secure goats from wolves, constructed in the ravines, protected by projecting rocks, perfectly safe and easily watched by a boy and dog. Also saw one of those caves which had been fitted up and inhabited. When we returned to San Angel, learned that Dutton had been tracked towards the Indian village, but had not yet been taken. Some time after he was taken by Captain Brooks and another officer of the South Carolina Regiment and brought in, when he was taken by Colonel Brindle to the city. His conduct shows both his guilt and his cowardice. There is some sympathy for Hare, but the regiment are regardless as to his [Dutton's] fate. It has raised a terrible excitement among the men, and had he been taken by any of the parties which went in quest of him he would certainly have been shot, all wishing for the honor of our State that he might have been killed and not brought before a court of commission so that the matter might be made as little public as possible. Lt. Barclay returned from the city today. He has received a furlough until the 31st of May when his resignation is recommended to be accepted. Has been raining all afternoon with some little hail.

April 7

This morning in company with several others, went to the city to see Lt. Barclay off. No news of any account there. All the talk about the late burglary. Lt. Dutton and Hare are the only officers yet arrested, together with several regulars, a discharged teamster and a Frenchman. Numbers of the regulars are deserting from the city and Tacubaya. The train leaves

---

commission found them guilty and sentenced the officers and one of the enlisted men to be, as the traditional formula put it, "hanged by the neck until they are dead, dead, dead." Instead, they were spared and returned to the United States. According to Ethan Allen Hitchcock, at least one of the officers (whose name, out of delicacy, Hitchcock refrained from mentioning) became a highly successful civil engineer.

tomorrow and Lt. Barclay will have some difficulty getting off; he was disappointed in his arrangements. Remained in the city all night. Lodged at an Englishman's by the name of Wm. Young. Here slept with old Mechling in a bed on a bedstead between sheets, something for a soldier, only that the bedstead was so short that our legs from the knees hung over and the coverlet was so small that head and feet were both uncovered. We had quite a time of it and might have frozen had it not been for a hot punch just previously drank.

April 8

Mechling and myself were up this morning on our way to San Angel by four o'clock. We did this to obtain and send in a horse to Lt. Barclay in time for the train. It was rather dark, and having avoided the patrols, after a very muddy walk, reached San Angel by sunrise. Obtained for him a horse of Captain Smith,[7] with which Mechling returned to the city by eight o'clock in time for the train. Lt. Barclay went down. Yesterday, while we were in the city three deserters were taken near this village and the report is that there is a considerable number at San Agustin. A soldier belonging to the Louisiana Mounted men was taken near this yesterday for plundering, but just at dark he slipped the guard and made his escape, although several shots were fired at him. His regiment goes down today with the train and I suppose he is safe. Last night, Lt. [Joseph L.] Madson, of Company "M" of our regiment, was arrested and conveyed to the city on charge of being concerned in the late burglary. He was not in the city on the night of the affair, but is accused of being a prime mover in the plot and having been fully cognizant of it beforehand. It is really disgraceful that the only officers yet arrested should all belong to the Second Pennsylvania Regiment. On dress parade yesterday evening Lt. Klotz, of Company "K" was appointed Adjutant of the regiment. Mounted guard this morning. Sent to Contreras picket. Posted over the aquaduct. At night four of us, Brady, McCabe, McGarvey and myself were sent to a pulquerio about a mile further out from the picket to protect it. It has several times been plundered by the soldiers. The proprietor of the establishment treated us well and gave us supper.

April 9

Report of a mail having been captured near National Bridge. Very pleasant day and had a fine bath in the evening. This day one year ago our division marched from Vera Cruz.

---

7. During the Civil War, Lewis W. Smith was colonel of the 169th Pennsylvania Volunteer Infantry.

April 10

This is the anniversary of Fred Steck's great feat of eating a whole liver, etc. We have another hog's dose for him today. The surgeon has signed a certificate of disability for Hoffer of our company and has some hopes of his discharge. The surgeon now attached to our regiment is Dr. Rutledge. He is a young man, and what is not often the case among army surgeons, is very kind to his patients and shows a willingness to discharge those who are likely to be of no service. Had a regimental inspection this evening.

April 11

This was company guard day and not being on duty it was very dull. Mr. Clifford,[8] one of the United States Commissioners to this country, arrived at the city today. Captain Miller, of Company "K" our regiment, came with him, having been home on furlough. Hoffer's discharge papers have been signed. Meat rations were condemned today, and no others being provided, we had the pleasure of living on the bread rations, which of course, did not hold out.

April 12

Hoffer left this morning with the sick train, but by some mismanagement he did not get his papers and will have to remain some time in Jalapa. The train which left today took the sick of the whole army to Jalapa. As we got no meat yesterday, looked for double rations today. However, we got only one ration and that of a very inferior quality. Smith, who was one of the board that condemned yesterday's meat, says it is the same beef. In this way, the commissary makes quite a handsome speculation at the expense of the regiment. There was a skirmish of some character on the road between this and the city. It is said that some guerillas (I suppose greasers) were robbing a pulquina when some American officers, Colonel [Henry S.] Burton of the New York Regiment and Major Bowman of the First Pennsylvania among their number, came up and secured six prisoners. There was a Mexican brass band performing in the Plaza this evening. They played well but the music was not familiar. Our Captain was placed under arrest, by order of Colonel Wyncoop, for refusing yesterday to serve on a court martial, although on the sick list.

8. When the peace treaty with Mexico reached Washington, it was amended by the Senate on a number of minor points. Rather than refer the matter to Trist and Scott, who were out of presidential favor, Polk dispatched two special emissaries to Mexico to secure the consent of the Mexican government to the revisions. One of these emissaries was Nathan Clifford (1803–1881) of Maine, who was then attorney general of the United States and who would later sit on the United States Supreme Court from 1858 to 1881.

April 13

Put "Livers" on his rations. On dress parade was read the proceedings of a court martial held at Tacubaya by which a Lieutenant of the 4th Infantry was suspended for absence without leave, disobeying orders, and selling false pay rolls. A few more of the same stamp might also be very properly dismissed. There has been a great deal of lightning and some thunder this evening and night.

April 14

On guard today at main guard house. Posted in the upper plaza over a store. Did not have to stand at night and was allowed to sleep in quarters. The guard is becoming heavy there again. Our company was paid off two months pay ($14.00), not betting money, up to the last of February. The entire brigade are now paid off and spreeing and drinking have commenced. Gambling is going on extremely, roulette, Monti, Faro, Keno, Dice and various card games.

April 15

A train of near 500 waggons came in from Vera Cruz under Colonel Black and First Pennsylvania Regiment, 13½ days from that place, the shortest trip which has been made with such a train. Mr. Sevier,[9] the other commissioner, arrived today. During the night a robbery was committed at the parting near this place. Three Massachusetts men have been arrested for it.

April 16

The First Pennsylvania Regiment have returned to their old quarters near this. They only left one man behind on account of sickness. All the sick of our company were returned for duty this morning. We have twenty-seven privates for duty. All present except the Captain and Lieutenant Armstrong are on the duty list. A bottle of brandy won by Lieutenant Coulter of Captain Smith on a ludicrous bet of eleven.

April 17

On quarter guard today. Posted at the commissary rooms. Received a small mail from the United States. Got only one letter, that from Uncle. Recruits have been received for the First Pennsylvania, South Carolina and Massachusetts Regiments. Also nine were received for our regiment.

---

9. Ambrose Hundley Sevier (1810–1848), a hot-headed, ardently expansionist United States senator from Arkansas, was appointed commissioner to Mexico, along with Nathan Clifford, to iron out the remaining differences over the peace treaty. In poor health, he fell seriously ill while in Mexico and died shortly after his return to his plantation.

April 18

Anniversary of the battle of Cerro Gordo. Nothing new. Very disagreeable day. Number 3 have a spree and during the night a number more were quite boozy. A good deal of noise in quarters, and the materials kept at "The House that Jack Built" [malt] are in demand.

April 19

Received a mail from the United States, the regular mail. A brigade drill was ordered for this afternoon, but on the regiment's being turned out, the order was countermanded and terminated in a dress parade. A special order from General Butler was read transferring and changing several surgeons. One change which affected our regiment is Dr. [Thomas C.] Bunting, lately appointed surgeon of the First Pennsylvania Regiment has been transferred to our regiment. He is a good physician and the change has given satisfaction.

April 20

Had a brigade drill this morning at seven o'clock under Colonel Wyncoop, after we mounted guard. The New York and First Pennsylvania Regiments mount guard again with us in the upper plaza of San Angel. The Drum Major of the York Regiment has got a brass headed staff with which he flourishes largely at guard mount. Was sent to the second or Churubusco picket about a mile and a half from our quarters. This picket is stationed at the Canal Nacional, in the Plaza de Constitution of Coyoacan and about two and a half miles from Churubusco. In addition to our duty as picket we had charge of the prison, which contains about sixty Mexican prisoners confined for various offenses. On the opposite side of the Plaza from the prison is the Cathedral of Coyoacan. It is a very large building but rather antiquated. It was at this place that our division lay several hours with the Mexican prisoners on the 8th of September last. This is holy week and today holy Thursday. In consequence the church is decorated in great style and lighted by innumerable candles. This is a great season of festivity and amusement. There is a temporary ranch or huckster stand erected in front of the church where they have a variety of dulces, ice creams, etc. Two drinks that were new to me were one which had the appearance of milk made of smashed mushmelon seeds mixed with water and sweetened. The other a kind of seed called Cochea,[10] soaked in water and sweetened. The latter is said to be a Mexican cure for diarrhea. During the afternoon observed a ceremony which I have seen several times before—an image of the Savior in robes of scarlet with a crown of thorns upon a platform decorated with lamps borne upon the shoulders of four

10. Coulter is probably referring to chia, a drink made from the seeds of the plant of the same name, a member of the sage family.

men in grand procession accompanied by a Mexican band of music and followed by priests and populace with lighted candles. It was brought from a neighboring chapel and placed in the Cathedral. There is a considerable concourse of Mexicans here all dressed in their best celebrating this occasion. Had a good deal of sport with the hombres. Some of the guard gave several of them tobacco which they chewed and some even swallowed it. The consequence was several of them lost their last devoured rations. Slept in a little chapel inside of the prison dedicated to the virgin of Guadalupa. Made our beds under the shrine of the Virgin. The prisoners appear to be a merry set; they keep a great noise singing, etc.

April 21

Was awakened at daylight by the singing and shouting of the prisoners. This is Good Friday and a great holiday here. There are a large number of Mexicans here today and a fine market has been collected in the Plaza. Was relieved about one o'clock in the afternoon. There was a brigade drill again this morning which we escaped by being on guard. Yesterday all the churches were most handsomely decorated. Today they are stripped of all ornament and hung in black in commemoration of the crucifiction. In the City the display yesterday was said to have been magnificent. All their plate and valuables were in use. During this week, Holy Week, there is no music of any kind except for religious purposes. No ringing of bells on the churches, large rattles being used instead. Every child has a rattle made like our house rattles, making a continual noise. Mexican sentinels (these are local in the City) stand during this week with arms reversed. No riding in coaches, etc.

April 22

Today there is a great display of fire works. Numerous images of Judas of the most hideous shapes hanging everywhere filled with some combustible composition, which being fired, makes the image whirl for a time and then explode, tearing it to pieces. This is the great day of feasting among the greasers and they are generally in the habit of getting on a big drunk. Today we had a general cleaning up of belts, etc., for a review which had been ordered for tomorrow, but in the evening this order was countermanded and the review postponed. Today Lieutenant Keenan, lately from the United States, paid the company a visit. He brought with him a file of Greensburg papers (the Westmoreland Republican). Received by him a small handsomely bound pocket bible, a present from Aunt.

April 23

A portion of the company are on guard today at the upper or Contreras picket. On dress parade this evening were read the proceedings of a court martial held at San Angel before whom Captain Thos. Loeser was convicted of having been present at and not attempting to suppress a mutiny of the Second Pennsylvania Regiment in the case of egging Captain Brooks of the South Carolina Regiment, and like Lieutenants Wolf and Davis, was sentenced to be suspended from all rank and command for the period of two months and forfeit all pay proper during the same period. Also Sergeant Cummings, of Company "H" was convicted of conduct subversive of good discipline and attempting to supplant officers lawfully appointed by holding an election to fill vacancies of company officers which vacancies Colonel Geary had filled by appointment. He was sentenced to be reduced to the ranks. Thus Geary has completely triumphed over that company. After dress parade went to the city with Lieutenant Keenan. Here we got into company with Captain [John] Herron, O. H. Rippey and Hamilton, all of Company "K," First Pennsylvania Regiment, whom we found drinking hot punch at a Mexican restaurant. All adjourned to the National Theatre. It was the first performance of Signor Ropi, the magician. While he was performing some feats with the magic bottle, pouring out of it whatever kind of liquor was called for, one of our party (O. H. Rippey) who was rather tight, called a number of times very loud for Hot Wiskey Punch out of his bottle. No attention being paid to his demand by the performer, he called the louder damning him that he would expose him if he did not produce the punch. General Smith stopped this interesting performance by ordering a guard to take him. However, by the interference of Captain Herron he escaped. After the performance was over Rippey was very anxious to go to the palace to whip General Smith for interfering with him. We got some cheese and sardines at a French house and tonight lodged with Keenan at his quarters in an old church or convent.

April 24

This morning saw Charles T. Campbell.[11] He is now captain in the 11th Infantry. Lieutenant Keenan left this morning for Lerma. After the train with which he went had left I returned to San Angel. Bob Story went with the train to join his regiment. He is rather run down and a little sick already of campaigning. The Padres made a complaint today about the men going into the orchard and Colonel Brindle, in his wisdom, has increased the quarter guard, putting a sentinel at every passage to the orchard. This is the only place we have to wash, etc., and it is quite a hardship on the men as is also the heavy guard. Our quarter guard was before this increase, 33 privates, besides 34 furnished for brigade guard. No rations of beef were drawn for the last two days until this evening and then we only got a short ration for one day of very poor meat. Suppose the

---

11. Charles Thomas Campbell (1823–1895) was wounded seven times during the Civil War, from which he would emerge as a brigadier general of volunteers.

commissary will make a handsome speculation off the other ration. It is rumored that the Ten Regiment Bill has passed both houses. An exceeding heavy rain this afternoon.

April 25

The weather was fine in the forenoon, but rained and was very disagreeable during the after part of the day. Today Colonel Geary took off part of the guards stationed at the orchard. But all the horses belonging to the regiment have been turned out and part of the guard remains to prevent any more being put in. On dress parade, orders from Colonel Wyncoop were read for a brigade inspection and mustering in of the regiments at the end of this month. Also Geary made some remarks about the guard which had been placed over the orchard and gave himself considerable credit for removing it. Understand that James McDermott, a member of Company "E," who deserted at New Orleans, returned home, and not being well received, went back to Orleans, where he died and was buried in the strangers' ground. The end of a deserter.

April 26

Mounted guard this morning. The whole of our company detail under Lieutenant [William F.] Mann, of Company "K," First Pennsylvania Regiment, were sent to the lower or Churubusco picket. We had a very pleasant time of it, having a good officer. We had some sport with the prisoners, putting wet powder into their room and giving them cigars with powder in them. Some rain during the afternoon. Lodged at night in the little chapel inside of the prison. Some of the boys being rather *windy*, raised quite a fandango by continual discharges of sulphurated hydrogen much to the annoyance of Billy Shields who got sick and Brady, who wanted to sleep, as he was shortly to go on post.

April 27

This morning got a very good cup of chocolate at a small vendor near. Had some fun shooting rockets at the greasers. Were relieved and returned to quarters about noon. Captain Johnston has been very low for some days back. Geesyn was tight and rather noisy this afternoon.

April 28

A pleasant day, but unusually dull, not even a rumor to break the monotony. Dress parade in the evening.

April 29

Company guard today. Was not on duty. The mode of detailing guards has been changed to daily details from all the companies to take effect tomorrow. This is the better and more equal mode and by it, duty will be the same in large and small companies. Have been engaged cleaning up for tomorrow's mustering in. Captain [Edward A.] Paul, of the Massachusetts Regiment, on main guard today, had some difficulty with his prisoners. They broke the guard house doors he having ordered them to be kept closed, for which offense he bucked eighteen of them and two sentinels. Irish Jimmy, of the New York Regiment, was in the guard house and made a great deal of sport. To use his expressions, he pushed a stunner to the captain, commencing "Paul, Paul, why persecutest thou me," and so bored him that he released him from confinement.

April 30

During the last night, or rather very early this morning, a prisoner named Stanford, of the South Carolina Regiment, under trial for murder and confined in chains in a separate room, made his escape. The nails which held his handcuffs were very small and flimsy (likely the black-smith was bribed as the prisoner had several thousand dollars of money made by gambling) and were easily loosened. By means of a knife and small claw hammer, he drew the nails of a closed window and made his escape without the knowledge of the sentinels who were just around the corner from the window. His trial was not yet over, but there was little doubt of his conviction. The sentinels and a person (the owner of the claw hammer which was left) suspected of assisting him, are in confinement. This morning we had a mess of what we call sapota butter. This is the second dish of this kind we have had. It is made of sapota nigra,[12] skinned, stoned and beaten up with cinnamon, nutmeg and sugar. It has much the taste and appearance of our apple butter, but much richer. Today we were mustered by Lieutenant Colonel Abercrombie,[13] making sixteen musters in the service and the third muster at San Angel. After this we mounted guard. On quarter guard and posted in the rear of the building over the Padres' quarters. In this morning's Star there appeared a letter purporting to be from Queretaro, stating that there had been a revolution at that place, and that the combined forces of Bustamente, Almonti and Parades[14] had overthrown the government and driven out Congress. There was quite a spree in our quarters at night. A great quantity of liquor drank and a number laid over. Turkey was most gloriously soused; danced around in great glee, hardly knowing what was wrong with him.

12. A tropical fruit resembling a pear, with green skin and black pulp.
13. John Joseph Abercrombie (1798–1877) of Tennessee graduated near the bottom of his West Point class of 1822 but by steady application and considerable battlefield experience worked his way up the ranks, being named colonel on the eve of the Civil War. As a Union brigadier general of volunteers, he commanded a brigade in the Valley and Peninsular campaigns, retiring from the service at war's end.
14. Anastasio Bustamente (1780–1852), Juan Nepomuceno Almonte (1803–1869), and Mariano Parades y Arrillago (1797–1845)—three Mexican generalissimos.

May 1

Today this brigade was reviewed by Commissioners Sevier and Clifford, Generals Patterson and Worth and Colonel Riley. It is represented as having been a fine affair. Was not out myself, not having been returned from guard. After night McClain stripped himself and went down through a hole in the hall into a kind of a store room of the convent where he filled several haversacks with beans. The letter published in yesterday's Star concerning a revolution at Queretaro was a hoax.

May 2

Some fifteen or twenty of the company under Lieutenant Coulter, went to the city to search for the body of David Kuhns, who died and was buried there. The grave yard has since been used as a waggon yard and it was with some difficulty we ascertained the neighborhood of the grave. Dug over a very considerable space of ground, but only disinterred four bodies, none of which proved to be the one for which we were searching. Got a very good dinner at the Fonda Francisca. Jake Marchand and several others got rather tight, particularly Jake, who thought he had slept all night under a waggon in the waggon yard. While in the city, one of our waggoners (we had two teams along) got tight also and we had a rare time getting to San Angel. First he fell out of the waggon. Luckily for us he was not driving at the time. He afterwards took the lines himself, and a Mexican team attempting to pass, he tumbled the fellow, considerably jockeying him by running in turn across the road before him every time the Mexican attempted to pass. He ran in the leg of one of the Mexican's mules. When we got home had a mess of beans stolen out of the Padres' store room. Today's Star says that there is more than a quorum in the Mexican Congress at Queretaro. If so, we may look for some movement either for peace or war shortly.

May 3

This morning another party went to the city to continue the search for Kuhns' body. Not being ready at the time the waggon started, three of us, Brady, Kettering and myself went in on foot. Had a rapid walk and reached the place just about as soon as the waggon which had some ten minutes start. Raised seven bodies unsuccessfully besides some others uncovered. The eighth proved to be the right one. He had been buried in a strong tight coffin and was in better condition that any of the others. Was easily recognized both by color of coffin, pictures, hair, blanket in which he was wrapped, newspaper and envelope in his pocket, having his name on some trinkets in the head of his coffin. Also we found at the head of the grave about a foot under ground the stone placed there by Sergeant Barclay at the time of the burial. After making the discovery, reinterred the body and marked the spot until another suitable coffin could be obtained. Afterward, as we were going up to the Plaza saw two lepers fighting in the street with small swords. On the lieutenant's calling to them they ran, but after a short run they were captured and taken to the main guard house, where the lieutenant had gone to have two of our party released, McCabe and McGarvey, who came in with us yesterday, and remaining in all night and not having passes were taken by the patrol after tattoo. Lieutenant Coulter had them both released. After this we had another dinner at the Fonda Francisca. Returning home Jake Marchand and Brady were pretty well "how come you so." Jake was very much troubled with the rough road and jolting of the waggon. Tonight Fred. Steck went out to lodge with a Mexican friend of his (an old Comanche woman), but fleas and bad smell so annoyed him that he was back in quarters by three o'clock in the morning.

May 4

Today Captain Johnston who is still unwell, moved his quarters across to where Captain McKamey lodges to be more convenient. On dress parade this evening an order from Colonel Wyncoop was read in which General Patterson and the Commissioners through him tendered their thanks and regards to the brigade for their fine appearance and drill on the late review. More gammon to gull volunteer regulars. One of our company, Carson, is very unwell with rheumatism and has been moved to the hospital, the only sick man we have there now.

May 5

This morning received a mail from the United States. Received a number of letters, etc. By this mail learned of the death of Sergeant James McLaughlin, formerly a member of Company "E." It was received with an unusual feeling of sorrow. It still continues very sickly in Westmoreland. Got a letter from Lieutenant Barclay written at Vera Cruz. He says Wise is well, at Perote, and wishes to join the company. Aikens is lying sick at same place, having been ruptured by a fall from a horse. Elliott is hospital steward at Vera Cruz with eighteen dollars a month besides the stealings from dead men and winning at Monti. Another letter states that Hoffer is yet at Jalapa. Not having his papers, he is unable to get off, and came very near being taken up as a deserter. Mounted guard today. On quarter guard, posted in the rear of the building to protect the Padres. Lieutenant Keenan has returned from Lerma, bringing with him a soldier of the 11th Infantry who says he knows where Lieutenant Johnston is buried. We had another mess of Padres' beans. Geesyn has been suffering a couple of days with the tooth ache. So today, as a cure, he got pretty tight on aguardiente. Tonight he took a drunken notion and made a pot of chocolate which was very acceptable. After this his spirits rose and he afforded a great deal of amusement relating his adventures and quarrels with his daddy.

May 6

This morning some fifteen of this company under Lieutenant Coulter, together with Lieutenant Keenan, went to Mixcoac to search for Lieutenant Johnston's remains. The soldier who was along could only tell the enclosure in which he had been buried. Dug over a large space of ground and raised quite a number of bodies. They were buried in some places two or three deep without coffins. After considerable trouble found the body. He had been buried without a coffin. Was lying on a straw mat on which the soldier said he had been carried. It was nearly reduced to a skeleton. Was easily recognized, however, by marks on clothes, etc. Hair which was still there corresponded. Had on an officer's pantaloons, Mexican make with white stripes such as he had on. The traces of bullet holes in the pantaloons to correspond to the wounds which he received. Around the left wrist was tied a leather strap which one of the company (Byerly) said he had tied on himself. Placed the body in a coffin and filled it with charcoal. Some of the men covered the top with roses. Returned with the body to San Angel. While at Mixcoac, got a fine mess of mulberries.

May 7

Mounted guard. On the Contreras picket. Posted on the lower factory road. Was very much troubled today with diarrhea. During the night (when not on post) slept in a little house used for a guard house. Very close together and was much annoyed with the smell of aguardiente (one or two of the men being a little tight) and rotten feet, some fellow who was not very cleanly having taken off his shoes.

May 8

This morning there was an insect, pronounced to be a scorpion, caught in our room. It is about 1½ inches long with a sting in the tail, claws like a crab, having eight legs and of a brownish color. I have it in a bottle preserved in aquardiente. Have been starving myself today on account of the diarrhea and took two large doses of castor oil, about 5 oz.

May 9

During last night a man belonging to the Massachusetts Regiment, named [Patrick Duffee], who brought his wife along with him, killed her. This he had attempted to do several times before. He was drunk at the time. The cause is said to have been jealousy, she having allowed *familiarities* with a number of officers and men of the brigade. He was arrested today, together with a man named Kelly, charged with having been concerned in it. Fred. Steck has been used up with the ear ache. On dress parade this evening there was read an order for commanders of companies to make a return of all camp equipage necessary for their companies in case of a march. The order comes from Lieutenant Colonel Brindle and is therefore not of much consequence.

May 10

This evening some of the company got on a spree. Sam McClaran was in an unusually good humor. Leb. was tight again and cut some high extras, such as rolling into a corner, saying that the room turned so he could not lie still. Livers was decidedly drunk, and not being much used to such excitement, performed some green turns.

May 11

Sam has been continuing his spree today. One of our company, Jacob Wise, left at Vera Cruz, joined us today. "Old Telegraph" looks better than ever. He had been sent to New Orleans together with Martz. Afterwards returned together with Martz as far as Perote where sickness again detained him. After remaining there some time he got off with difficulty. He says that another of Company "E," John Aikens, is there. Also that he had been discharged and had married the daughter of the Alcalde of Perote. This latter part of his story was afterwards proved to be incorrect. Don't know how he got it into his head. Of course the boys were glad to see him and undertook to initiate him again into the company. The consequence was that in half an hour they had him royally tight and singing "Nothing." Within another hour they had taken him down to the creek to swim and he narrowly escaped drowning by being pulled out. He had a happy time and shortly after dark he was stretched out on the floor drunk as Bacchus, disposing of the extra load in his stomach.

May 12

Mounted guard. On main guard from which was detached with three others as one of the small pickets to guard an Indian village near this. It is a picturesque little place, a cluster of ranches almost entirely hid among trees and shrubbery. We had no post to stand, being only there to protect them from being plundered by the soldiers. Amused ourselves with a pack of Mexican cards. The officer of the day came around in the afternoon just at a time when the other three were away and requested that we would all be there the next time he called. Did not call again however. Slept in a small old ranch.

May 13

Going over to quarters for breakfast heard that the boys had quite a spree last night. Uncapher had his drawers torn off and together with

Brady lost his shirt. Poor "Telegraph" was bucked and gagged and so roughly handled that he cried and called out "murder." They put him through another stage of naturalization. In the row which ensued while the stripping of Uncapher was in progress Carney and Sam Byerly were both knocked down by a person at the time unknown. It afterwards proved to be Sam Moorhead who was taking advantage of the occasion to lay in the dark to take satisfaction out of a particular person and struck at him twice, but missed his man both times and struck the above mentioned two. From accounts they must have had a loud time. A party were getting ready this morning to go to San Agustin to raise the body of William Melville, buried there. Wishing to go along, got Geesyn to go to the village to stand the remainder of my guard tour and went along. We had a rough ride in a waggon. Had some difficulty in finding him. Opened eight graves, in six of them the bodies were without coffins. Found him, however in the eighth grave. It was in a bad state of preservation. The coffin being made of short pieces of boards, was broken. The lid cracked in and the body covered with earth. It had luckily been sewed in a blanket. Removed it to another coffin which was then filled with charcoal. Made our dinners on bread and cheese gotten at a Fonda. San Agustin looks considerably cleaner and better, but as dull as when we were there. A new flag has been drawn for the regiment.

May 14

Lieutenant Coulter, this morning drilled the squad who were tight the other evening. Considerable rain today, sufficient to prevent evening parade.

May 15

Great peace news today. On dress parade this evening, the new colors were brought out and received by the regiment with three cheers. They are dark blue silk with yellow fringe, having the eagle and stars and "Second Pennsylvania Infantry" on them. They were drawn by requisition for the regiment. Colors have also been received by the other regiments here. Before the parade was over there fell some drops of rain and was considerable appearance of a shower, and the color bearer left the ground, fearing to get his flag wet, which was construed by some of the boys into a bad omen, the colors retreating for the first time they were at the head of the regiment.

May 16

Dull day. Nothing except vague peace reports. In the evening a subscription paper was handed to the company intended to raise money for the purchase of a saddle to be presented to Lieutenant Colonel Brindle as a token of regard for his gallantry, gentlemanly conduct, etc., etc., etc., etc.

In the opinion of Company "E," he is a small unworthy object upon which to bestow such a token, and accordingly nothing was subscribed.

May 17

A party went to the city today to view the body of Daniel Kuhns. It had been concluded not to get a lead coffin, it being considered that a wooden one double and filled with charcoal will be sufficient. Soon raised and placed the body in a new coffin. We returned to San Angel by three o'clock. On dress parade this evening were read two orders from Colonel Wyncoop, one ordering all the ball cartridges in the possession of the men to be turned over to the Quartermaster. Cartridges for guard purposes to be furnished before going on duty and returned at the end of the tour. Another ordering a brigade drill tomorrow afternoon, with five rounds of blank cartridges, but with an express caution to commanders of companies to see that the men have no ball cartridges about their persons before going on the field. Some think he is afraid to trust himself with the men when there is lead about. To tell the truth, it would be dangerous for some of the little whippets of officers in the brigade.

May 18

On quarter guard today. Great many stories afloat about ratifying the treaty and going home. Some one heard General Patterson say we were going down next week; another heard Colonel Riley say something of the same kind, another Colonel Geary and another some doctor; in fact nearly every one has *some such positive information* on the subject. It is said, and I believe on good authority, that Hare, Dutton and the other burglars are to be hung. From some cause the brigade drill did not come off this afternoon. All the ball cartridges have been turned over today.

May 19

During last night and this morning had a very severe attack of ear ache which, although I cannot be called sick, renders me very uncomfortable. Received a mail from the United States today. Not much news of any kind in it. This afternoon there was a brigade drill with blank cartridges. The officers took great care that the men should take out no ball cartridges. However, there were a number of both balls and ramrods fired, I presume accidentally. Some one of our regiment fired some gravel at old Revelon, the horse thief. The drill was cut short by a heavy rain. There was a great spree in company quarters this evening, Captain Loeser, Lieutenants Armstrong, Coulter and Davis, old Bonnin and quite a number more were most completely sewed up and continued the row until nearly daylight. Several shirts were torn off and two or three cuffed. Armstrong had both wrists and McCabe his shoulder badly sprained. Old "Telegraph" was almost pulled asunder.

May 20

A number of last night's party have been continuing the spree all day. On dress parade this evening was read the finding and sentence of the court of commission in the burglary case. All, Adjutant Dutton, Lieutenant Hare, Lieutenant B.[ryant] P. Tilden, Second Infantry, the gambler Lafferty, a sergeant and two privates of the Second and Seventh Infantry were found guilty of murder and burglary and sentenced to be hanged by the neck until they are dead, dead, dead. General Butler approved of the sentence of the court and ordered the first four to be executed on Thursday the 25th inst., and at the instance of the court, commuted the sentences of the other three to close confinement during the war and a dishonorable discharge. He also ordered that Armstrong and another who gave state's evidence, should be confined during the war. Some more of the boys are getting on a bust this evening. A very heavy rain.

May 21

This morning the Padres made a complaint that one of the shrines had been broken open and entered and a silver cup, some wine and other valuables stolen. The regiment was ordered out for inspection, it being Sunday and while under arms a commissioned officer from each company was sent to search the quarters for the stolen property. *Of course it was not found, although it is not so certain it was not stolen.* An extra from El Monte appeared this morning stating that they had learned by extraordinary express the ratification of the treaty in the House of Deputies by a vote of 51 to 35. It is expected to pass the Senate shortly, as there is little opposition in that body.

May 22

This morning our Commissioners Sevier and Clifford left for Queretaro. It is said they have official notice of the ratification of the treaty by both houses, at least prospects are very favorable. Two more small scorpions were caught this morning in our quarters. Am considerably troubled and somewhat reduced by diarrhea. My head is still stuffed up and a disposition to ear ache. Had hot tobacco smoke blown into my ear from a pipe. This evening our pay rolls were received to be signed. We will most likely be paid tomorrow, near the whole brigade are already paid.

May 23

We were paid off today. I received $18.60, two month's pay and four month's clothing allowance, deducting charges against me for clothing. The whole regiment were paid today and gambling is going on in all corners, roulette, monti, faro, dice and many other card games. Before three days, half the men will be completely strapped. Caught another scorpion in our room this afternoon. It is much larger than any I have before seen. I have it with three others preserved in aguardiente. The doctor gave me a prescription for diarrhea today sufficient for a horse.

May 24

On dress parade this evening was read an order from General Butler for the regiments to hold themselves in readiness to march at a moment's warning and that commanders of companies have rolls and discharges made out that there may be as little delay as possible at the coast. Many of the men have gone to town to see tomorrow's execution. After dress parade this evening had a conversation with Colonel Geary, which revealed to me, as I think, one of his schemes for gaining popularity (concerning certain appointments to be made).

May 25

Instead of the expected execution this morning, the condemned men all pardoned, or reprieved until the will of the President can be known. The Mexicans were greatly disappointed at this as well as many who went to witness the execution. For my part, excepting Hare, I would rather they had been hanged. Geesyn had $18.00 stolen out of his roundabout pocket which was hanging in one of the rooms. Suspicion fixed on a certain one of the company, but no discovery was made. Some of the company were tight this evening, among the rest Coulter and Old Joe.

May 26

On hospital guard today. On dress parade this evening was read an order from General Butler relative to turning over all surplus arms and ammunition. This evening a mail was received from the United States, but, very unusual, I did not get a single letter or paper. No news of any account in it.

May 27

The treaty has been ratified in the Mexican Senate by a vote of 33 to 4. Had a short regimental drill this afternoon in light infantry movements. An order has been received from General Patterson to fill all vacancies in regimental and company officers. Our company comes under this order, having but one second lieutenant. Geary has filled all these vacancies by appointment except in our company where he has ordered an election which he will confirm by appointment. I do not know why our company was favored in this general sweep, unless he feared a decided opposition to his usurped power and curbed his compromised dignity by adding an appointment to the person elected. This evening we had an election which resulted in the unanimous choice of Sergeant Mechling as second lieutenant. Of course there was a great spree after it and we got but little sleep. There has been a general spree throughout the brigade this evening. A large number with the brass band and Colonel Geary at the head, went up to Wyncoop's quarters, making a great noise, shooting, yelling, etc. They say Colonel Wyncoop was somewhat frightened at first, but seeing it was a drunken crowd, he ordered them to quarters. They kept up the noise until 3 o'clock. A beautiful party for a colonel to be in, but such is his mode of maintaining his standing around the regiment, not by making them obey him.

May 28

Today our dead bodies were sent to the city, there being not sufficient waggons to take them down with us, they will be brought by the last troops. This evening there was a great deal of shooting of muskets and firing of rockets. It is said that several balls were fired from the convent in the direction of Colonel Geary. Such is the esteem in which he is held by his men. The brigade has completely broken loose and the officers do not attempt to control them. Some even encourage it. Their reign will soon be over and they know it—so do the men.

May 29

This morning one of our company (Gordon), who quarters in our room, caught a scorpion in his drawers which had been hanging on the wall during the night. Another was also caught in one of the other rooms. We have been busy all day preparing for march. On dress parade this evening orders were read for march tomorrow morning at daybreak. Our brigade marches by way of Mexicaltzingo to Ayotla. The remainder of the division, who are in the city, meet us at that place by way of Penon on the National Road. All are in great glee at our approaching departure. The fiddle is going, liquor abundant and quarters are in a glorious state of confusion.

13

Goodbye, Uncle Sam
San Angel to Pittsburgh

May 30

Reveille at one o'clock. Had considerable difficulty in getting our baggage into the waggons. Perhaps our officers have more than allowable, at least more than convenient for the men, and some of it useless, especially Lieutenant Armstrong's pillows, which he says are as useful as any part of our baggage and that the men ought to carry their knapsacks. We have, moreover, a very poor train. In company with Bates, went ahead of the train. Passed through Coyoacan, Churubusco and Mexicaltzingo. The latter is a very poor place composed principally of huts. After a march of about nine miles entered the National Road beyond Penon so that I was disappointed in seeing the works at that point. At this place we were joined by that portion of the division who came direct from the city, viz: Lieutenant French's[1] Light Battery and the Georgia Cavalry. Saw Lieutenants Hare and Dutton in a waggon, under charge of a detachment of the Georgia Cavalry. Dutton appeared to be in light spirits for a man in his situation. From here to Ayotla it was very bad marching, the road being deep with sand. Company "M" of our regiment, was in the advance and Bates and myself went with them. They camped about two miles beyond Ayotla, and after having had a good wash in the lake was treating myself to a nap in the shade when I was awakened with the news that our brigade had encamped at Ayotla, so we had the pleasure of retramping the last two miles. The distance from San Angel to Ayotla is about twenty-one miles. Since camping, the captain, who sent to the city, joined us, having with him the remains of his brother, Lieutenant Johnston. He says he was unable to bring the others. Our cartridges, which had been turned over to the Quartermaster a few days ago, were not returned, which makes quite a difference on march, forty rounds of buckshot and ball being rather heavy.

---

1. William Henry French (1815–1881) of Maryland, an 1837 West Point graduate, was a major by brevet and General Pierce's aide-de-camp. Loyal to the Union, he refused to surrender his Texas command at the outbreak of the Civil War and became a major general of volunteers, commanding a division at Antietam, Fredericksburg, and Chancellorsville. Falling into disfavor with Meade, the stout, ruddy-faced French sat out the last year of the Civil War in garrison duty.

We are encamped on the borders of Lake Chalco. The water is rather warm but of very good taste and is much improved by remaining over night in a canteen.

May 31

Reveille beat at 12 o'clock. One of the drummers, Revelon, who was publicly whipped at Jalapa, for some cause or other, roused the band at midnight and beat the reveille. The consequence was that our regiment was ready for march about the time the other troops were being roused by their reveille. So we had to wait some time. Our regiment being rear guard today did not remain for it but started in advance. When near Cordova, passed a Mexican merchant train bound for the City of Mexico. Reached Cordova by sunrise. There was a cold bracing wind blowing which makes marching much more easy. The march over Rio Frio Mountains was long and exceedingly fatiguing. Reached Rio Frio where the advance guard were and remained several hours for the regiment. Some companies of the Second Ohio Volunteers are stationed at Rio Frio. They have built themselves log cabins, as it is very cold here at times and has been known to snow here. They march with us tomorrow. The market at Rio Frio was unusually poor. It was with difficulty that we obtained even a few bananas. We did not encamp here but went about a mile further and encamped on the banks of the same stream. Had a very refreshing bath in the Rio. It is, I believe, the best water on the route. Encamped about 3 o'clock. Our march today is estimated at 24 miles; we thought it some further when we traveled it before. Colonel Wyncoop, wishing to make brass marching, is pushing the men too hard. Some plundering was done today at Cordova and this evening orders were read for no man to leave his regiment or company on march on penalty of being dishonorably discharged. There will be some difficulty in enforcing it. This morning from the top of Rio Frio Mountains took what I suppose is for me the last view of the Valley of Mexico. Was greatly inconvenienced with piles today. Since arriving at camp the Massachusetts Regiment buried a poor fellow who died on march. It was exceedingly unpleasant to hear the dead march on our way home. Had he died when our heads were turned the other direction it would not have been so much noticed. Twenty-four rounds of cartridges would have been burned over him and then forgotten as one out of misery.

June 1

Reveille at 3 o'clock. It was very cool at this early hour. Moved shortly before daybreak. Our regiment in advance and companies "B" and "E" under command of Captain Humphreys forming the advance guard. We had an advantage of this of the cool of the morning for a considerable portion of the march. We reached Rio Nigra about six o'clock. This river is about 8 miles from our last camp. It runs through a very deep gorge and is surrounded by very high bluffs. It is crossed by a very large and substantial bridge called the Bridge of Texmelucan. Thus far our march was rather down hill. We were compelled to remain here about two hours for the train. We halted again about a mile further on to stop all who attempted to get ahead of the advance. Between this and the town of San Martin, met a merchant train bound for the City of Mexico consisting of an immense number of pack mules and few waggons. About noon reached San Martin where I made a purchase of some very salty cheese at 50 cents per lb. This place is about 19 miles from last camp. Here we were stationed as a guard at the streets and fondas to prevent the men from scattering off or plundering. There were few provisions to be found here. This town is much larger and more handsome than I thought when we passed through on the up march. Remained here until all the division, except the rear guard, had passed through. Encamped about four miles beyond at the hacienda of San Baltazar, making the days march 23 miles. Our camp is a grassy plain on the banks of a small stream. Had some trouble getting beef rations. There was considerable sport with Carney this evening. He got rather tight at San Martin which had quite a bad effect on him, paralyzed some of his organs and prevented their operation. Dr. Bunting was sent for and an amusing scene occurred. A mixture of _____, nonsense about an _____ headed _____ etc. The detachment of the Second Ohio Volunteers stationed at Rio Frio evacuated their garrison and marched with us today. They started keen as rabbits with the intention of marching down the other regiments, but before reaching camp were stretched the entire length of the train with scores of blistered feet. Had considerable rain during the night.

June 2
On route by daylight. The Massachusetts Regiment in advance and ours next. They started off with a promise that we should stir our stumps but we pressed them rather hard. After a march of seven miles, very unexpectedly encamped at 8 o'clock A.M. at Rio Prieto on an extensive grassy plain. A fine place to pitch tents, but otherwise very poor place for a camp. Wood very scarce and water very bad, dirty and stinking. This is a specimen of Colonel Wyncoop's discretion. After three successive heavy marches we have almost lost a day. I understand his object was to prevent the men from being over night in or near Puebla. To make up for this we will have a heavy march tomorrow. He told the beef contractors that we would encamp some six miles further, so that he went in advance and had the cattle butchered ready to issue when we arrived, and in consequence we had considerable trouble getting meat, it having to be hauled back to camp. This is called a Rio, but it is little better than a mere succession of muddy ditches and swamps. The Quartermaster and Commissary waggons have

gone in to Puebla to load up stores and be ready to move without delay on our arrival. Since camping another poor fellow has been buried belonging to the First Pennsylvania Regiment; he died on march. It was from the effect of a severe burn at San Angel, caused by the explosion of a quantity of cartridges. Undertook to wash some clothes in the muddy water here, but they were blacker when done than when I commenced. A heavy rain during the night.

June 3

On march by daylight; third regiment from advance. The First Pennsylvania Volunteers leading at a rapid walk, our regiment pushed them hard, stretching out the train almost three miles. About two miles from Puebla met a merchant [train] consisting of waggons bound for the City of Mexico. Since the occupation of the country an immense quantity of foreign merchandise has been imported. Nor will the owners trust any more to Mexican escorts. Americans are engaged at high wages to conduct their trains. When near the city of Puebla the regiments were formed and marched in order. Halted and stacked arms for an hour or so at the main plaza which we reached about 9:30 o'clock. The market was exceedingly fine, far exceeds the City of Mexico both in quantity, variety, quality and price. In fact Puebla is in every respect the best city on the route and has a far more modern appearance. Ate several large slices of most delicious water mellons equal to any we have at home. Dates were in abundance. Our boys laid in a goodly store of bread and other provisions as far as the funds would allow. For my part, I purchased a haversack of Mexican cheese. It is 12 miles from our last camp to this place. Continued our march to the village of Amozoc, a distance of 11 miles, making the day's journey twenty-three miles. This latter part of the march was severe. Water was scarce and having worn a hole in my canteen I was unable to carry a supply. In fact it was a most rascally march. It was expected we should have encamped at the bridge beyond Puebla the night previous and marched through the city this day. Encamped in the plaza at Amozoc, the same place as on the up march. Every store was shut and water very scarce, being drawn with great labor from deep wells. It was almost impossible to draw it fast enough to supply the men. Shortly after camping there was a slight shower. Had a fair prospect for a heavy rain during the evening, but unfortunately it all passed around. A number of our men are missing, several supposed to have been murdered by the Mexicans. A day or so ago in Puebla, an officer was lassoed, drawn into a bye street and had his throat cut.

June 4

On march at daylight. The morning was cool, but the road very deep with sand. However, we had a pleasant march, having shade mostly the whole way. After a march of about eight miles came to the village of

Acajete. Got some very good water here. Continued our march through a deep cut and also the Pass of El Pinal and encamped about noon at El Pinal, about seven miles from Acajete, making the day's march about fifteen miles. The camp is near an old hacienda and near the same place as on the up march. We got water from a neighboring pond, supplied by the rains, which is very full of leeches, etc. Drew a ration of American bacon here which many think is not very good. Dr. Miller, who was formerly attached to our regiment at Jalapa and who obtained leave of absence there, has returned and has again been attached to our regiment or rather has always been. His conduct before was far from satisfactory *to all*, and today a remonstrance was gotten up among the officers against his superseding Dr. Bunting, who is quite a favorite within the regiment. Had a fine prospect for a rain in the evening, but were again disappointed.

June 5

On march by daylight. After seven miles reached the village of Nopalucan. The Fourth Indiana Volunteers are garrisoned here. The market was exceedingly poor. Passed another small village and a hacienda three miles from Ojo de Agua, where we camped on the up march. Encamped about 12 o'clock at Ojo de Agua, distant nine miles from Nopalucan, making the day's march sixteen miles. This was the place of our Fourth of July camp on the up march. It is a fine place to pitch a camp. The water is good but warm. The only difficulty is a want of wood. We were compelled to haul wood from our last camp. Lieutenant Armstrong was placed under arrest this morning by Colonel Wyncoop for attempting to pass the advance. The large spring here ends in a lagoon, where I had a fine bath, and of which I stood in great need. Had some rain in the evening. Also a horse race, but neither running out the course, the bets were drawn.

June 6

Reveille at two o'clock. Our regiment was rear guard today and did not get off until daylight. Did not wait for the regiment, but started with the advance about four o'clock. The day's march was over a sterile, barren plain and tedious on account of its being so level. Today the force was divided into two brigades, the Second Ohio, South Carolina and New York Regiments forming the first under Colonel Wyncoop, the First and Second Pennsylvania and Massachusetts Regiment constituting the second under Colonel [Isaac H.] Wright of the Massachusetts, Colonel Wyncoop commanding the whole. By taking a direct course across the plain cut off about two miles at a single bend. The road makes this circuit to avoid that portion of the plain which is at times inundated, but at present is in good order. Some of the men burned a straw thatched ranch on today's march, much to Major Bowman's concern. About two miles from camp halted at a kind of well and tank to wait for the regiment. The water is better here than we heard it to be at the camp, and so we had a period to rest our poor limbs, some crackers and a smoke before the regiment arrived. Halted at Tepeyahualco, twenty one miles from Ojo de Agua. Before we could pitch our tents there came up a heavy storm of rain and high wind which not only completely drenched us, but made a perfect mud of the ground on which we were to sleep. However, a stiff horn of American whiskey and after the rain a good fire brought us back to a comparatively comfortable condition. Had no supper, but a little coffee, which was very bad on account of the quality of the water, and some crackers. On today's march, Steckle picked up a Mexican boy whom Lieutenant Coulter intends taking to the United States with him. The water here is the worst on the whole route, being greatly impregnated with copper. This is the second ducking I have gotten at this place and is sufficient to remember it. The town lies near the foot of Mount Pizarra, a mountain which is very well known and as well cursed by every soldier who came this far up. It stands isolated on the plain apparently where one part reaches the table land but a few miles off, but after a day's march the soldier finds himself apparently not much nearer than in the morning. Was fortunate enough to collect about half a canteen of rain water from the markee. On this entire day's march the country was exceedingly barren, not even a covering of grass. The only signs of cultivation was a small patch of beans and a little stunted grass.

June 7

Up early and breakfasted on crackers and coffee. Except the small quantity of coffee I drank, I have not tasted the water of this camp. Having been rear guard yesterday, expected to be advance today, but found that the whole of the other brigade and one-half of the train were to move ahead of us, and that we were only to be advance of our brigade. Did not get off until day-light and then had about a mile march in deep, tough mud. After a length of time got Mount Pizarra to our backs and reached the hacienda of San Gertrudis without a halt. This hacienda is half ways from our last camp to Perote. Here we halted about ten minutes to get water; it is the only water on the march. The water is better than when we went up. The day was fine for marching, the sun shone out but little and the dust was completely laid by the late rain. The latter end of the march the country showed more signs of cultivation. Extensive corn fields on both sides of the road. Reached Perote before noon and camped in front of the castle. Our day's march was nineteen miles. This was the most rapid and steady march we have had. Except a halt of about ten minutes at San Gertrudis and another of about the same length about four miles from Perote, we were kept at a steady, rapid walk. We are camped on the old camping ground. Shortly after pitching our tents had a slight rain. The plain to the left, as formerly, is planted in corn. There is only a single company of artillery in the castle now. Perote has been a perfect grave yard for the American Army. In one year over 2,000 men were buried around it. The first thing we heard on reaching it was a squad firing over some poor fellow's grave. The town of Perote is the same ill looking place. After some hard crowding and the risk of broken ribs, succeeded in reaching the door of the bakery in the castle and purchased two loaves of fresh but half baked bread which together with some chocolate and boiled potatoes (small ones) made us quite a supper. Drew a ration of light bread in the evening. One wheel of our waggon came near breaking in today's march, so in the evening had its place supplied by another, which did very well, except that it was 6½ inches higher than the opposite one and so tight that it would hardly turn on the axle.

June 8

On march before daylight. Colonel Wyncoop's force of two brigades has fallen through and the whole has again been thrown together. So we expected to be the second regiment from advance, but were placed next the train. After a rapid march of a few miles passed the small village of Cruz Blanca, and a mile further passed Molino Blanca, 9½ miles distant from Perote, and the place where we camped on the up march and after a march of 4½ miles further, reached Las Vigas. Encamped at La Hoya, 6 miles from Las Vigas, making the day's march 20 miles. The portion of this day's march as far as Las Vigas, showed considerable signs of cultivation. Extensive fields of corn and wheat on both sides of the road and several rough hills under cultivation. From Molino Blanca until beyond the town of Las Vigas still showed signs of the burning we did on the up march. Las Vigas was deserted, that is, what remained of it, some of the houses were unburned and the church was used as dragoon quarters for the horses. From this place the march was around the rugged mountains of Cofre de Perote. On entering the village of La Hoya, it commenced a steady soaking rain which continued until after reaching camp. The road through the pass was exceedingly bad. Several waggons were upset and broken down. The train was considerably scattered and our baggage waggon did not get into camp for two hours after we arrived. The town of La Hoya is still for the greater part deserted. The seven pieces of cannon spiked by General Worth in his advance are yet lying by the roadside.

June 9

Reveille at 3 o'clock. This day our regiment was again rear guard. This is the third day we have been rear guard while some other regiments have only once at that post. Did not wait for the regiment, but was off ahead of the advance guard by 4 o'clock. Had a blundering tramp in the dark and several times pitched head foremost into the road, and ruts in the road. It was very dark and foggy and some rain. Reached the small town of San Miquel de Soldado, 4½ miles from La Hoya by early dawn. After a tramp of 3½ miles further, reached the very small town of La Banderilla. On yesterday's and this portion of today's march, noticed the character of the ranches dissimilar to those on other parts of the road. They are built of clapboards with very high peaked roofs with large rough shingles fastened on with wooden pins. Two miles from La Banderilla reached Camp Patterson, or as it is more generally known, "Camp Misery." There were some troops here just about breaking up their camp. Also found a guard on the bridge to prevent soldiers of our brigade from going into Jalapa in advance of the train. Being perfectly acquainted with these parts, had no trouble in avoiding this guard and reached Jalapa about three miles further at almost 8:30 o'clock. The market here was very poor this day. Bought some cheese from a sutler, purporting to be good American cheese which proved to be perfectly rotten. Saw Hoffer here, one of our sick, who had been sent down to be discharged, but had been disappointed. He has recovered and is in pretty good health. Aikens is also here who had originally been left sick at Puebla. It was a hoax about his having been married. The brigade arrived about ten o'clock and remained here about an hour. Curtis Keely, an acquaintance of mine of Company "K," First Pennsylvania Volunteers, died here last night. Saw our old Blackberry woman here. She took quite a cry when our regiment left. Our regiment started as rear guard, but by this time they were all in advance. There were a great many rumors afloat in Jalapa about the scarcity of transportation and the probability of our lying some three months in this neighborhood, also of sickness at Vera Cruz, etc., etc., etc., etc., etc. By some mistake the train was started from Jalapa without any advance guard. The stragglers (which is by far the largest portion today) followed the train and the train followed the stragglers for four miles, when Colonel Wyncoop, in a great rage, overtook the head of the party and turned them with many oaths. Encamped at the hacienda of [Las Trances?] about three miles from Jalapa, making the day's march 16 miles. Rained very heavily nearly all night.

June 10

Did not move this morning until near 8 o'clock. Our regiment in the advance. After a march of six miles encamped near the hacienda of Encero on the stream called at this point Los dos Rios. Found the remainder of our division encamped here. There was some pains and time taken in laying out this camp, as it is expected we may lie here some time. It is at present very uncertain when we leave this. Our baggage waggon did not come up for some time after the others, in consequence of having broken down before leaving last camp and required to be unloaded and repacked. It is expected the whole army will move down and encamp here until transportation can be obtained, which is said to be very scarce. On guard this evening, the colonel's quarter guard. The colonel, out of complacency, let us off with standing post during the night only for the purpose of protecting the horses, etc. from prowling Mexicans. Had some trouble with a couple of Mexicans who came to the camp after midnight claiming some mules, etc., running about which they said belonged to a train of theirs on the road to the city. Old Dr. Miller, alias "Dutch," was wakened by the noise and ordered me to take them under guard instead of sending them away as I had intended. So the poor devils were compelled to lie down on the ground without coats or blankets for the rest of the night under guard.

June 11
Drew a ration of soap and have been engaged washing clothes for the coming march. It is quite a romantic place on the stream below the bridge. The river rushes over great ledges of rock between high and abrupt banks. A dress parade in the evening and orders from Colonel Wyncoop read relative to protecting camp, roll calls and daily drills, company and battalion. They brought General Marshall's division around today and encamped in the neighborhood. At tattoo some orderly sergeant attempted to call a roll and it rained a perfect babble over the whole camp, everyone crying out "here," hissing, groaning and shouting for Colonel Wyncoop. After the band which had struck up was done, some of them got out a pot and kettle band and performed around camp until dispersed by the colonel.

June 12
Some of the companies had a nominal drill this morning. Company "E" did not turn out. Had no battalion drill in the afternoon. Only a dress parade in the evening. The colonel finds the most popular course is to let his men off as easily as possible. Drew soft bread today. Camp is now decidedly a bore. We have no longer a campaign ahead of us to think of, speculate on, etc.

June 13
This morning had a company drill (they called it drill) of five minutes. The First Pennsylvania and New York Regiments have orders to hold themselves in readiness to move. Changed the position of our camp about a hundred yards to the front and have our tents pitched in one line, two companies forming one camp, leaving in consequence a very wide and commodious street. By the change, our company are placed rather near the sinks [latrines] for pleasant smells. However, these are being filled up. Last night there was some plundering done at a hacienda some two miles distant from camp and a guard was sent there today to remain while the troops were here. Three of our company, Brady, Martz and James McWilliams are on this guard.

June 14

Short company drill this morning and brigade drill under Colonel Wyncoop, in the afternoon. From some cause, very agreeable to us, our regiment did not turn out on this brigade drill. The day has been very dull and as warm. We are lying here with nothing to stir up camp and it is a bore. More troops have arrived and are encamped at Camp Patterson beyond Jalapa.

June 15

This afternoon had a refreshing bath in the creek. I am now so considerably reduced with diarrhea that it is with difficulty I can walk far. Went some distance down where the water forces itself through narrow ledges of rock. This evening the First Pennsylvania, New York and South Carolina Regiments received orders to march and moved under Colonel Wyncoop about an hour before dark. The Massachusetts and our regiments have orders to march tomorrow morning. Three day's hard bread and bacon have been issued. Camp is quite lively again.

June 16

Reveille at 2 o'clock. Our baggage waggon was not so full this time, the officers having another in which to put their luggage. Did not wait but started in advance of the regiment about 4 o'clock. The moon was up and it was exceedingly pleasant marching. Reached the hill of Cerro Gordo, 8 miles distant from camp, before it was very warm. Left the road at the road battery and at this place had a fine view of the immense ravine through which Plan del Rio passes, some four hundred yards wide and of immense depths. Followed a path until I struck the enemy's artillery road and followed this over the hill. Saw in the distance the batteries which General Pillow's brigade attacked, but could not reach them, a ravine intervening. By taking this road I think I must have saved some two miles. Reached Plan del Rio about ten o'clock, 14 miles from last camp. The entire face of the hill and the old camp ground is changed, grown up with chaparral. The first bridge was blown up some time ago by Padre Jarauta to stop a train and is now lying in ruins. The stream is crossed by a road cut around it. The Jersey battalion is camped here mending this road for the coming trains. Our whole train was taken across this place, the road being not very good, and in order that we might get an early start tomorrow, we are now camped at the second bridge. Our tents are pitched without order wherever the best shade or best ground offers. The day has been extremely hot; in fact it would be impossible to march in the middle of the day. We are now thoroughly into the regions of ticks and sand flies which are very troublesome. Had a wash in the deep hole down at our old camp. Some of the boys gathered a quantity of lemons and had quite a time drinking lemonade. The water is by no means as good as on the up march, or at least as we thought it. Perhaps we have just come from a region where the water is better, or the season may make the difference.

June 17

Reveille last night about 11 o'clock. The advance off by 12. Companies "B" and "E" of our regiment being rear guard did not get off until one o'clock. The moon was up, and being nearly full, made it very easy marching. It was almost as light as day and very warm, although at night. After a march of eight miles, reached the place where we got so much beef while lying at Plan del Rio. Shortly after leaving this a waggon broke down which detained the rear guard some three hours. Some of us went on to attend to camp. Reached National Bridge about an hour after sunrise. The advance arrived about sun up and the rear guard did not get in for a considerable time after it. A part of one of the Tennessee Regiments is stationed here. Had a wash in Rio Antigua; it was called Rio Nevinta [?] on the up march. The water is much cooler than Plan del Rio. The heat today was excessive. Impossible to sleep. The marches are to be made at night. This morning's march, according to Shrover's measurement, is 10½ miles. But a better estimate of it is at least fifteen. There was something of a breeze under the arches of the bridge and they were crowded with panting soldiers. On march again at 5 o'clock in the evening. Not having eaten anything but bread and water since we first reached Encero, the march and heat completely prostrated me, and after a walk of perhaps a mile was compelled to get into a waggon. The road was very rough and made it more painful riding than walking, but I was too weak to walk. There was a caged parrot hanging upon the waggon which the jolting of the waggon every few minutes brought into contact with my head when the bird would reach out and pull my hair, quite an annoyance to one too sick to enjoy it. There was also a troublesome little Comanche boy in the waggon. Encamped about midnight at San Juan. From National Bridge to San Juan is a distance to which we took two day's on the up march and thought them very heavy marches. Shrover's table makes the distance 15½ miles, the men say 20. Many of them did not get in until after daybreak.

June 18

Had just gotten our tents pitched, and the heat being almost suffocating, and this being the last night we expected to be in the country, we cut out the back end of the tent to get, if possible, a current of air, when it commenced raining very heavy and we had the satisfaction of a complete drenching. It had not even the benefit of cooling the air which seemed as sultry as ever. San Juan was the camp after the first day's march from Vera Cruz on the up march. It has been made a post and there are some Tennessee men stationed here. There are also, as at National Bridge, some American stores, but the principal article of trade is American Whiskey, at least so called. Had a wash in the stream, and after some considerable trouble succeeded in washing a shirt, that is, in a kind of way, although it was considerably more the color of the black sediment in the bottom of the stream. There are also the greatest abundance of limes here and also cocoanuts, which are not ripe however. Spent a considerable portion of the day under a bridge where there was some breeze. Heat is very great. One of Company "D" was court martialed here for insolence and insubordination to Colonel Geary. He had called him a damned rascal, coward, son of a bitch, etc., etc., and attempted to strike him. Was convicted and sentenced to forfeit all pay and allowance due him and be dishonorably discharged at New Orleans. On march again at 6 o'clock in the evening. Did not attempt to walk this time, but got into the waggon and had a time of it with the parrot. The road was very deep with sand and the train moved slowly. Had considerable rain on this march. Encamped about midnight at Camp Vergara. Shrover makes this march as follows: San Juan to Santa Fe, 7 miles; Rio Madre, 3 and Vergara, 2½; in all 12½ miles, but I think it is considerably longer.

June 19

We had hardly gotten our tents pitched when we had another heavy rain. Camp Vergara is in sight of and 3 miles distant north of Vera Cruz on the beach. It was General Twiggs' headquarters during the siege and here the road to Mexico leaves the beach. The water is not good. There are several American sutler stores here, but as usual, the principal commodity is whisky. Had a fine bath in the gulf this morning. The other detachment of our division, who came down, embarked yesterday. There are no transports ready and we may have to lay here a day or so. A steamer and several sail vessels came in today. This afternoon had another bath in the Gulf, and in fact we have been in the water nearly all day and I feel already its good effects. All our men are taking advantage of salt water and are in the gulf continually riding on the waves and being washed into shore. Had a very heavy rain during the night. Did not come a great deal into our tent, but many were completely flooded.

June 20

Had another bathing in the breakers. This morning the colonel received orders to divide the regiment into two detachments, one of 200 men and 30 officers under command of a field officer to embark on board a sail vessel; the other of 400 men and 15 officers with all the sick under command of a field officer to embark on a steamer. The first detachment was ordered off immediately under command of Lieutenant Colonel Brindle, consisting of companies "A," "C," "G," and "M." Our detachment under Colonel Geary consisting of companies "B," "D," "E," "F," "H," "I," "K" and "L," moved about 11 o'clock A.M. A portion of the officers of each company except Company "E" of our detachment were ordered to the sail vessel to make the complement of 30 officers. There are not as many men in the regiment as this order called for, but they were proportioned. We marched to Vera Cruz to embark from the Mole. Vera Cruz is much altered and for the better. It is now decidedly a handsome business place, almost completely Americanized. Excepting a baggage guard, we went on board a lighter at 12 o'clock. Were carried down to Sacrificios Island about three miles below the city and embarked on the steam tow boat "Mary Kingsland." She was lying here taking in coal. There is a large quantity of coal collected on the wharf for the use of the American vessels. This island is near the old landing place of the army on the 9th of March and from the vessel we could see the old magazine and some remains of the seige works. There is no middle deck to the vessel and we are much crowded, being compelled to sleep on the hurricane deck and wherever we can find room to lay a blanket. On coming aboard, we got some Mississippi water which was in a tank and it was most refreshing. In fact I did not know that the water of Mexico was so bad until I again tasted the Mississippi. Some of the men gathered many specimens of coral on the Island before leaving. While here we got our boxes of clothing, etc. which were left at Vera Cruz when we marched into the upper country, but when opened were all mouldy. Among them were a number of pairs of the old blue uniform pantaloons which the owners to preserve had left and the sailors were soon rigged up in them, making an odd appearance. Had some sport with an Irish deck hand in regard to the box containing Lieutenant R. H. L. Johnston's remains. Barclay, McLaughlin and myself had packed up all our extra clothing in a small box and placed it in one of the boxes. They were about the best preserved of any. I preserved our three gum coats and a few more articles of McLaughlin's for his friends and threw the rest over board. Finished loading and on our course by dark. Lay to a short time opposite the city for the colonel and some other officers. Immediately put to sea and we poor devils on deck laid ourselves out for sleep as well as the nature of circumstances would admit.

June 21

This morning found ourselves well out to sea and once more quit of Mexico. Sail in sight in the morning apparently bound for Vera Cruz. Drew a ration of pickled onions. Every place is completely crowded. Moved my quarters to the hurricane deck. A number of the men are sick. For my part I feel no inconvenience from it; on the contrary am greatly refreshed and braced by the sea breeze. One great inconvenience here is want of shade. Nearly all are compelled to lie in the sun the greater part of the time. About noon our canvass was spread and we are now making fine headway.

June 22

Slept very comfortably on the upper deck, except we were considerably wet from the steam pipe. About two o'clock this morning and until ten o'clock they were engaged drawing the salt out of the boilers. In the meantime we only made about two knots under sail. At ten o'clock the engine was in full blast again. This afternoon drew some raw sauer kraut (it was somewhat tainted) and had a mess of pork and beans. This is the first I remember of, since leaving the vessel on landing at Vera Cruz and was well relished. At noon 300 miles from Vera Cruz. Had a slight shower of rain in the evening. During the night the sea was rather high and the waves washed over the lower deck, wetting those who slept there. Did not reach us above.

June 23

A steamer in sight this morning. Drew a ration of dried apples. In the afternoon the steamer was again stopped and boilers cleaned, which took some six hours. Towards evening a school of porpoise appeared and sported about the vessel about a half hour. An old chap, a recruit of Company "I," who was pretty tight, gave the colonel some impudence, upon which the colonel gave him a choking together with a caning. This morning another recruit of Company "I" was detected in the act of stealing, upon which the men took him in hand and gave him fifteen on the back well laid on, and having bucked him, placed him under the shoot of the wheel. Salt water did him good.

June 24

A man named George Weaver of Company "F" died early this morning, I believe of mania potu [delirium tremens]. He was sewed up in his blanket and very unceremoniously thrown into the Gulf; in fact so gently that although I was sitting within a few feet of him when it was done did not know it until I heard the splash. Raw sauer kraut was again issued today, as usual a little rank. A dead calm, all our sails have been taken in. About noon steam was stopped and we lay to six hours more to clean boilers. While lying to a quantity of truck was heaved over, which together with the dead body before heaved over, brought up a very large shark. It first cantered about the vessel some times coming close under the stern and at the surface of the water. A number of musket and rifle shots were fired into him but he did not appear to mind them. He was twice caught with hook and line, but both times broke loose. Once we had his head to the lower deck. He managed, however, to consume near a barrel of pork (soldier's rations) which was thrown to him. He had with him a small pilot fish about a foot or so in length. It appeared very officious in attending to him. The shark was at least fifteen feet in length and sailors say more. A great many were anxiously looking for the Balize Light House, but were disappointed.

June 25

This morning came into green water and gradually into the muddy water from the Mississippi. Great many vessels lying off and near the mouth. Entered the river about noon. Anchored a short distance up again to clean boilers. We at last found ourselves in Yankee land in fresh water. Several boats came up alongside with potatoes and other vegetables. Steam up at sunset and on our way up the river. While lying at anchor the steamer "Fanny" passed having on board General Butler and staff. Had a bad night between the heavy dews and steam pipe; our blankets were completely soaked.

June 26

About 11 o'clock A.M. anchored at Algiers on the opposite side and 1½ miles below Orleans. Many boats alongside in a short time and provisions were brought in plenty. The colonel went to the city for orders and returned with the very important news that we were ordered to Pittsburg, there to be discharged, and that all the troops are to be taken to their respective states to be mustered out of the service. Both officers and men will sustain a loss from it, losing our milage, which would be far more than necessary to carry us cabin passage home. It has raised quite an excitement among all the regiments here. The greater portion of ours have worked despite of order with a determination of not returning [?]. Went ashore this evening and took a walk through Algiers. Sold my gum coat to one of the mates for $3.00 thereby raising some funds.

June 27

This morning went up to Orleans. Saw the boat on which our regiment is to embark, the "Taglioni." Berths are being fitted in the steerage for the men, but will be very much crowded and uncomfortably hot, many of the berths being almost in contact with the engines. Yesterday our company officers came up to the city to see about getting our company off, and by order of General Butler we were detached from the regiment with permission to report at Pittsburg within a reasonable time. The object was that we might take another boat. After some difficulty passage was obtained for forty-five officers and men on board the steamboat "Charles Hammond" for $675.00, being a rate of $15.00 per man, to Cincinnati, being the distance this boat goes up the river. In the evening went down on this boat to the "Mary Kingsland" where the company was transferred, except Jacob Wise, who was absent and who was left behind. We then started on our upward and homeward trip. Run in to the landing at Camp Carlton, seven miles above New Orleans to take on board a detachment of the First Pennsylvania Volunteers under command of Colonel Wyncoop for whom the steerage of the boat had been chartered. This gallant officer was in a glorious state of intoxication and refused to ship his soldiers in the steerage of a boat while other men were engaging a cabin passage. He was forgetting that his men were taking government fare which cost them nothing and that we were paying out of our own money for all we got. There was considerable altercation about the matter and a number of the men wished to go ashore and leave his excellency the entire boat. When it was found that he would not come on board as long as we remained in the cabins, for the sake of the boat captain, who had treated us well, it was agreed to go on the upper deck. Wyncoop's men were not agreeing that we could go below. This was the worst treatment we ever received at the hands of any officer and the result of a contemptible pride. We slept during the night on the upper deck. I have slept in worse quarters, but this was doubly hard on account of the disappointment. There was considerable trouble preventing some of the men from going ashore. However, after we had become settled on the deck and the burn cooled off, as it always does in the case with persons in hard circumstances, it was laughed at and each cracked his joke on his neighbor (with an occasional curse on Wyncoop, etc.) and many inquiries were made as to where we were to get our morning's breakfast.

June 28

This morning found a hungry crowd on the hurricane deck and no prospect of any breakfast. We had no rations, and not expecting to cook anymore, had thrown our plates, etc. away on leaving the "Mary Kingsland." The captain of the boat seeing our condition, tried to make an arrangement with Colonel Wyncoop so that a table might be set for us in the cabin by ourselves, or that the boat cook should be allowed to cook for us. All was of no use; his lordship could not retreat. Eight days rations were then issued to us out of the government stores on board, such as they were, crackers were full of weevils and pork received having been carried to Mexico and back again to be issued to men when fresh and wholesome rations were staring them in the face, all the time without the means or power of getting them. However, hunger was forcing upon us and at last Kuhn and McCutcheon were engaged to cook for the company during the trip. After a long delay we succeeded in getting for our breakfast (it was dinner time, however) a kettle of bean soup. There being about half a dozen plates and tins collected, we went at it by reliefs. Each fellow got a little bit, by no means enough for a set of chaps who were eating their breakfast at noon. However, the jest passed during the meal and each consoled himself that he had seen the time when he could not get even this small allowance of beans. Two or three of the company (Moorhead, McClaran and some others) got on a spree this afternoon and gave a great deal of trouble by their noise, calling the attention of the whole boat. In the fuss Wyncoop did not pass unrebuked. During the afternoon we passed Baton Rouge where General Taylor now lives. He was on the river bank as we passed and saluted the boat, which was returned by loud cheers. Towards evening passed the Taglioni. Rained the greater part of the afternoon and night. The captain of the boat spread a tarpaulin on the front part of the deck which accomodated a part of the company. The rest of us had to take it as best we could under the edges of the cabin skylights.

June 29

Ran into Natchez at daylight this morning. Only remained long enough to change mail. Managed to buy some bread. This morning a man named Robinson, Company "G," First Pennsylvania, fell overboard and was drowned although the boat was immediately backed down stream to his assistance. About noon, made another short stop at a little town where we got some dried venison. Our cooks have had considerable trouble with the men of the First Pennsylvania Regiment below, who will not allow them to cook, saying that we have no right on the boat. The kettle had been set off repeatedly, so that they have been compelled to quit and we are now compelled to trust to what we can buy at the stopping places. Managed to spread our tarpaulin a little better and have now got tolerable quarters for the greater portion of the company. It is decidedly disagreeable to be placed as we are, among men who are ill disposed towards us. Shortly after dark we reached Vicksburg, where we stopped about an hour to get pork put on board and which was issued to us, having been condemned. Here were plenty of provisions to be purchased, but we were short of funds. Some of the First Pennsylvania Regiment made a charge on a grocery store and carried off a large quantity of provisions. A Mississippi battalion is about being discharged here, and among them I accidently found an old college chum, John A. Anderson, who is adjutant of the battalion. Here a member of this battalion came on board and took a cabin passage, but his excellency did not object, having had as much trouble about the matter as he wished. As we were passing the "Taglioni" came up to the landing. She kept within hail of us all night. The river is very low and they were compelled frequently to sound the channel. Had a difficulty with some of the First Pennsylvania Regiment who had taken possession of our quarters and swore they had a better right to them than us, as we did not belong to the boat. After some difficulty their officers persuaded them off. In fact their officers are completely under; they have not the least control over the men now.

June 30

This day completes 18 months in the service. Making reasonable headway. Nothing of any consequence. Passed and were passed by the "Taglioni." During the night it was comfortably cold.

July 1

Have made tolerable running all day. Passed the "Taglioni" lying to, some say burying a man. During the night it rained and ran foul of a quay, which detained us about an hour.

July 2

Reached Memphis about 10 o'clock. Were detained there about one hour loading freight. Rained all forenoon. Saw nothing of the "Taglioni" today. Were passed in the evening by the "Hancock" carrying soldiers. Was decidedly cold during the night.

July 3

Dull warm day and making but poor speed. About 7 o'clock in the evening entered the mouth of the Ohio and stopped at the town of Cairo. Here the First Pennsylvania did some plundering out of a wharf boat of divers hams, sausages, beef, mackeral and a keg of whisky. Took in tow the barge "Yorktown" for the purpose of lightening cargo in case of running in a sand bar, which is probable.

July 4

FOURTH OF JULY. This morning passed Rock Cave, or as it is sometimes called, "Morrell's Cave."[2] The "John Hancock" was lying to near it and a Fourth of July celebration of the citizens was being had on the shore. A number of the First Pennsylvania got drunk on this *Glorious Independence Day* and made blackguards of themselves. They talked as they thought proper to Colonel Wyncoop who had not the resolution to resent or order them out of the cabin. An old swivel was got out of the boat and cartridges having been made, quite a firing was kept up in passing boats and towns. Wyncoop wished to treat our company to a quantity of brandy, which was very properly and promptly refused.

July 5

The "Taglioni" passed us early this morning. A dull day. Rained nearly all afternoon and night which made it uncomfortable on deck.

July 6

Reached the lock below Louisville about 10 o'clock A.M. The "Taglioni" had just gone through. Did not wait for our boat, but walked up to town. At Louisville I met a cousin of mine, Mr. Eli C. King, who was very kind to us and assisted us in getting another boat. Here we also found

2. Now Cave-in-Rock State Park on the Illinois side of the Ohio River. "Morrell" should be "Mason," after Samuel Mason who, in 1797, transformed this highly visible river landmark into a robbers' den disguised as a hospitable inn to lure gullible travelers.

Jacob Wise, one of our company who had been left at New Orleans. He had come part of the way up the river on the "John Hancock" and then shipped to the "Taglioni" which brought him here. He was good and tight. With the assistance of King, we succeeded in getting a cabin passage for the whole company at $6.00 a passenger on the Packet Germantown, to be paid at Pittsburg, which was the best part as we were strapped. The steamboat "Charles Hammond" had great trouble getting through the lock. Here some guards had to be cut away and a negro was killed at the crank while closing the gates. After getting through the lock she smashed a wheel in the canal. We got our baggage transferred to the Germantown in the afternoon. The Charles Hammond left this at dark and we are at last rid of Colonel Wyncoop. A number of our regiment and the First Pennsylvania were left behind by their respective boats, many of them having scattered through town at the time of starting. We lodged on board the Germantown which did not leave the wharf this afternoon. A mattress did not prove as comfortable for sleeping on [as] the deck; tossed and tumbled all night. Our boat is not much crowded and most of us got state rooms. Hagan Carney and I are in one together.

July 7
Left Louisville this morning at 10 o'clock. Made good running. In the evening were edified by a lecture from a minister who was on board at the same time. There was considerable card playing going on at the other end of the boat. Bills and McGarvey were much touched with the lecture and applauded him.

July 8
Wakened at Cincinnati wharf where we had arrived during the night. The "Taglioni" had left here about three o'clock yesterday afternoon. The Western World and Charles Hammond carrying Colonel Black and Colonel Wyncoop's detachments of the First Pennsylvania are here. They remain for the rest of the regiment before proceeding to Pittsburg. Left Cincinnati 10 o'clock A.M. Cleaned up our muskets and belting this afternoon.

July 9
Had a company inspection on the upper deck. The company made quite a respectable appearance. Our friend, the preacher, was horrifed at what he called a parade on Sunday. Some rain in the afternoon.

July 10
Reached Wheeling this evening. There had been a large number of citizens down from Pittsburg to receive the troops and went up with the "Taglioni." There was a good deal of sport when the mattresses were placed in the cabin for the night. Lieutenant Mechling was court martialed for bad

conduct, etc., proceedings of which are recorded below. Lay up at Steubenville about 12 o'clock P.M. for some hours. All went ashore and had quite a spree. Bills stood guard at the court martial, barefooted and in red Mexican uniform.

Steamboat Germantown, 10th July, 1848.

Before a Court Martial organized by order of Captain John W. Johnston, Company "E," Second Pennsylvania Volunteers.

President: Private Charles McGarvey.

Members: Corporal Gordon, Corporal Uncapher, Fifer Kettering and Privates Geesyn, Marchand and Moorhead.

Judge Advocate: Private Coulter.

Orderly: Private McCabe.

Charge 1st: Desertion.

Specifications to this: That when the steamboat Germantown was leaving the wharf at Cincinnati the prisoner, the said Lieutenant David Mechling, was found about to leave.

Charge 2nd: Unhumanlike conduct.

Specifications to this: That the prisoner, the said Lieutenant David Mechling, did on the evening of the 10th of July, 1848, enter a stateroom in an unhumanlike manner, namely, on all fours.

Prisoner objected to the Court not being in uniform.

Opinion of the Court on the objection delivered by the President.

That the Court having convened at an unusually late hour, some of the members having been in bed, all such forms should be dispensed with. Moreover, that Justice could be as well meted out by a court sitting in their shirt tails as by one in uniform. Therefore objection overruled.

Prisoner pleads not guilty to the charges and specifications.

Testimony on the part of the prosecution. Private C. Forward Sargent (sworn).

Went ashore with prisoner at Cincinnati?

Answer: He knew the hour to be 10 o'clock.

By the Court: Was he at the wharf when the boat left?

Answer: He was not.

Captain John W. Johnston, (sworn).

By the Court: Did the prisoner have your permission to go ashore at Cincinnati?

Answer: He had not.

Bar Keeper (sworn).

By the Court: When did the boat leave Cincinnati?

Answer: About 10 o'clock.

By the Court: Was the boat afterwards stopped to retake the prisoner?

Answer: It was, with a considerable loss of time.

Here the prisoner proposed a verbal question.

Opinion of the Court: Taking the late Court of Inquiry as their guide, the

Court order and direct that *A.A. Mode*, General Caleb Cushing the question be put in writing and asked through the intervention of the Judge Advocate.

By the prisoner: Did not the boat leave after ten o'clock.

Answer: Perhaps ten minutes after.

By the prisoner: Does not this boat generally remain later than the hour of leaving?

Answer: It does not.

Sergeant George W. Bonnin, (sworn).

By the Court: When did this boat leave Cincinnati?

Answer: Precisely at ten o'clock.

By the prisoner: What hour was set for departure at Louisville?

Answer: Cannot state except from hearsay.

By the prisoner: Do not steamboats start later generally than the hour set?

Answer: I believe they do, but this boat is decidedly an exception.

Jacob Wise, (sworn).

By the Court: How did the prisoner cross the floor and enter the state room this evening?

Answer: Why he went over the floor in a sort of double summersett and pitched into a state room head foremost.

By the Court: In what position was he when he entered the state room?

Answer: Why he was not in the position of a soldier anyhow.

By the Court: The Court cannot understand from your description the position of the prisoner and would prefer that you give them an ocular demonstration.

The witness attempted several times to throw himself into the attitude, but not succeeding, the orderly was commanded to put him through the motions, who tripping up his heels and taking him by the cuff of the neck and seat of the breeches, sent him sprawling into a state room. Much to the edification of the Court.

No testimony on the part of the prisoner who cast himself on the mercy of the Court.

The Court being cleared of all bystanders, after mature deliveration find as follows: That the prisoner, Lieutenant David Mechling, is guilty of the first charge and guilty of the specifications of the first charge. Guilty of the second charge and guilty of the specifications of the second charge. And sentence him, the said Lieutenant David Mechling, to have his straps cut off at the head of the company or in lieu thereof, to purchase the liquor for all present.

The above finding and sentence is approved.

John W. Johnston,
Captain, Commanding Company "E."

The sentence was complied with, the prisoner having elected to treat.

About the time the above court was ended and sentence executed the boat had arrived at Steubenville, where it ended in quite a spree.

July 11

Reached Pittsburg in the forenoon. There were a number of our Westmoreland friends there waiting for us and quite a lively time ensued.

July 12

Turned over our arms, accoutrements and camp equipage.

July 14

Were mustered out of the service by [Major George Wright].[3]

So, Good Bye, Uncle Sam.

3. George Wright (1803–1865) of Vermont graduated from the U.S. Military Academy in 1822 and was brevetted colonel for gallantry at the Battle of Molino del Rey, receiving the regular rank in 1855. During the Civil War, he commanded the Department of the Pacific and the District of California until his death in 1865 by drowning in a shipwreck off the Pacific coast.

Appendix

Roster of the Westmoreland Guards as mustered into the service of the United States, at Pittsburgh, Penna., January 1847

Name	Age	Height	Birthplace	Occupation	Service Record
Captain					
1. John W. Johnston	26	6'½"	Westmoreland Co.	Businessman	
1st Lieutenant					
2. *James Armstrong	26			Lawyer	
2d Lieutenant					
3. Washington Murry	29			Lawyer	Discharged for disability at Jalapa. Died on way home in May 1847.
4. *James Coulter	26			Lawyer	
1st Sergeant					
5. Henry C. Marchand	26	5'8½"	Westmoreland Co.	Lawyer	Discharged for disability at Vera Cruz, 21 April 1847.
2d Sergeant					
6. *Thomas J. Barclay	22	6'3"	Westmoreland Co.	Lawyer	Promoted 1st Sgt; appointed 2d Lt. 11th Inf. Date of commission, 30 Dec. 1847; of acceptance, 26 Feb. 1848.
3d Sergeant					
7. Henry B. Kuhns	19	5'7¾"	Westmoreland Co.	Law student	Discharged for disability at Vera Cruz, 31 March 1847.
4th Sergeant					
8. *James M. McLaughlin	20	5'8"	Westmoreland Co.	Law student	Returned to U.S. on sick furlough, 15 Nov. 1847. Discharged 29 Feb. 1848. Died at home, 30 March 1848.
1st Corporal					
9. James M. Carpenter	25	6'6"	Westmoreland Co.	Lawyer	Discharged for disability at Jalapa, 25 May 1847.

Note: * indicates those who reached Mexico City with the main body of the army.

Name	Age	Height	Birthplace	Occupation	Service Record
2d Corporal					
10. Andrew Ross	29	5'11"	Westmoreland Co.	Lawyer	Appointed 2d Lt. U.S. Inf. and returned to U.S. on account of disability. Died en route.
3d Corporal					
11. *William G. Bigelow	23	5'8¼"	Westmoreland Co.	Storekeeper	Promoted 2d Sgt., 1 March 1848.
4th Corporal					
12. *George W. Bonnin	27	5'10"	Philadelphia Co.	Lawyer	Promoted 1st Sgt., 1 March 1848.
Fifer					
13. Michael J. Kettering	19	5'8"	Westmoreland Co.	Tanner	
Drummer					
14. Andrew Jackson Forney	19	5'7½"	Fayette Co.	Cooper	Discharged for disability at Vera Cruz, 18 May 1847. Died on way home.
Privates					
15. John Aikens	21	5'11"	Somerset Co.	Tobacconist	
16. *Lebbeus Allshouse	21	5'9½"	Westmoreland Co.	Blacksmith	
17. *Andrew J. Bates	21	5'10"	Westmoreland Co.	Coachmaker	
18. *McClure Bills	20	5'9½"	Indiana Co.	Boatman	
19. *Hugh J. Brady	21	5'8½"	Westmoreland Co.	Storekeeper	
20. *Samuel A. Byerly	26	5'7½"	Cumberland Co.	Wagonmaker	
21. William A. Campbell	21	5'8½"	Westmoreland Co.	Lawyer	Discharged for disability at Jalapa, 8 June 1847. Died shortly after arrival home.
22. *Hagan Carney	21	5'8"	New York City	Carpenter	
23. *Humphrey Carson	19	5'10"	Westmoreland Co.	Tailor	
24. *Milton Cloud	29	5'7¼"	Loudon Co.	Shoemaker	
25. *Richard Coulter	19	5'9"	Westmoreland Co.	Law student	
26. *George Decker	26	5'7¼"	New York City	Saddler	
27. Archibald Dougherty	30	5'8¼"	Antrim Co., Ireland	Laborer	Discharged for disability at Puebla.
28. James L. Elliott	26	5'9"	Franklin Co.	Tailor	
29. *Henry Fishel	25	5'5½"	York Co.	Joiner	Discharged for disability at Mexico City, 27 Oct. 1847.
30. *Henry Geesyn	24	5'7¾"	Allegheny Co.	Laborer	
31. *Andrew D. Gordon	27	5'10"	Connecticut	Scalebuilder	Promoted 3d Cpl., 1 March 1848.

Name	Age	Height	Birthplace	Occupation	Service Record
32. Samuel Gorgas	21	5'10"	Cumberland Co.	Laborer	Died in hospital, Puebla, 30 July 1847.
33. John R. Grow	21	6'	Huntington Co.	Furnace keeper	Discharged for disability at Vera Cruz.
34. George Hagerty	32	6'1"	Washington Co.	Bricklayer	Died in hospital, Puebla, 10 Sept. 1847.
35. *Fred. Haines	18	5'5½"	Westmoreland Co.	Farmer	
36. *Edward Hansberry	26	5'9¼"	Philadelphia Co.	Weaver	Discharged at Mexico City, 5 March 1848, on account of accidental wound received 12 Sept. 1847.
37. James Hartford	20	5'10"	Westmoreland Co.	Teacher	Died in hospital, Vera Cruz, 16 April 1847.
38. *George W. Hartman	19	5'6½"	Franklin Co.	Tailor	
39. *James Hays	24	5'4"	County Down, Ire.	Tailor	
40. Michael Heasley	24	5'10"	Westmoreland Co.	Millright	Discharged for disability at Puebla. Died shortly after arrival home.
41. *Jacob Hoffer	21	5'8"	Cumberland Co.	Tailor	
42. Andrew R. Huston	34	6'4½"	Washington Co.	Painter	Died in hospital, Vera Cruz, 18 June 1847.
43. James Johnston	27	5'11"	Westmoreland Co.	Law student	Appointed Q.M. Sgt. 2d Pa. Regt., 7 Jan. 1847; discharged for disability at Jalapa.
44. Richard H. L. Johnston	21	6'3½"	Westmoreland Co.	Laborer	Transferred as 2d Lt. to 11th Inf. at Jalapa; killed in action at Molino del Rey, 8 Sept. 1847.
45. *Jacob Kegarize	22	5'4½"	Indiana Co.	Laborer	Discharged for disability at San Angel, 3 March 1848.
46. William Kelly	27	5'8¾"	Westmoreland Co.	Blacksmith	Discharged for disability at Vera Cruz, 19 May 1847.
47. John Kerr	26	5'9½"	Westmoreland Co.	Lawyer	Died on ship "J. N. Cooper" off San Antonio Lizardo, 11 March 1847.
48. *Henry Keslar	34	5'7½"	Germany	Turner	
49. *Jacob Kuhn	23	5'6½"	Westmoreland Co.	Blacksmith	
50. *Daniel S. Kuhns	27	5'8"	Westmoreland Co.	Printer	Died in hospital, Mexico City, 9 Dec. 1847, of wound received in same city, 15 Sept. 1847.

Name	Age	Height	Birthplace	Occupation	Service Record
51. Philip Kuhns	23	5'8"	Westmoreland Co.	Wire weaver	Discharged for disability at Puebla.
52. Edward B. Landon	37	5'10"	Addison Co., Vt.	Teamster	Discharged at Puebla.
53. *Jacob Linsenbigler	19	5'5"	Westmoreland Co.	Farmer	Died in hospital, Mexico City, 26 Sept. 1847.
54. *Peter McCabe	21	5'5½"	Lebanon Co.	Shoemaker	
55. *Amos McClain	23	5'11"	Westmoreland Co.	Carpenter	
56. Samuel McClaran	27	5'10"	Westmoreland Co.	Farmer	
57. *Richard McClelland	19	6'1"	Center Co.	Laborer	Discharged at Mexico City, 5 March 1848, on account of wounds received 15 Sept. 1847.
58. John McCollum	22	6'	Westmoreland Co.	Teamster	Died in hospital, Perote, 10 Aug. 1847.
59. Edward McCredin	38	5'11"	Baltimore, Md.	Plasterer	Discharged for disability at Vera Cruz, 19 May 1847; died on arrival home.
60. David R. McCutcheon	19	5'7¾"	Allegheny Co.	Saddler	
61. James McDermott	21	5'10"	Westmoreland Co.	Blacksmith	Deserted at New Orleans, 27 Jan. 1847; afterward died at same place.
62. Charles McGarvey	24	5'8¾"	York Co.	Furnace keeper	
63. *Robert McGinley	24	6'3¾"	Westmoreland Co.	Law student	Died in hospital, Mexico City, 3 Oct. 1847.
64. William McIntire	28	5'9¾"	Westmoreland Co.	Saddler	Discharged for disability at Vera Cruz, 31 March 1847.
65. *James McWilliams	22	6'	Washington Co.	Farmer	
66. *William McWilliams	30	5'8"	Westmoreland Co.	Carpenter	
67. *Jacob Marchand	18	5'7½"	Westmoreland Co.	Tanner	
68. Benjamin Martz	24	5'8¾"	Westmoreland Co.	Chairmaker	
69. George May	27	5'9¾"	Somerset Co.	Farmer	Discharged for disability at Vera Cruz, 18 May 1847; died there.
70. *David Mechling	27	5'11"	Westmoreland Co.	Farmer	Promoted Sgt.; elected 2d Lt. 27 May 1848.
71. William H. Melville	26	5'7¾"	Westmoreland Co.	Chairmaker	Died in hospital, San Agustin, 5 Sept. 1847.
72. Jacob Miller	27	5'7¾"	Westmoreland Co.	Farmer	Discharged at Jalapa, 7 June 1847, on account of wound received in battle of Cerro Gordo, 18 April 1847.

Name	Age	Height	Birthplace	Occupation	Service Record
73. *Samuel Milner	28	5'6"	Bucks Co.	Blacksmith	Missing at Mexico City about 1 Dec. 1847; supposed to have been murdered.
74. Samuel H. Montgomery	36		Westmoreland Co.	Clerk	Appointed Asst. Q.M. with rank of Captain at Pittsburgh, 8 Jan. 1847.
75. *Samuel Moorhead	26	5'8"	Indiana Co.	Farmer	
76. Lewis Myers	21	5'8¼"	Franklin Co.	Bricklayer	Died in hospital, Vera Cruz, 10 April 1847.
77. Jonathan Pease		5'7¾"		Coachmaker	Discharged at New Orleans.
78. James Rager	23	6'¾"	Cambria Co.	Boatman	Discharged for disability at Puebla.
79. Fred. Rexroad	19	6'¾"	New York City	Boatman	Discharged for disability at Jalapa, 19 May 1847.
80. *Chauncey F. Sargent	18	5'½"	Somerset Co.	Printer	
81. *Joseph Shaw	19	5'9"	Westmoreland Co.	Laborer	Died in hospital, Mexico City, 17 Jan. 1848.
82. William Shields	29	5'10"	Westmoreland Co.	Teacher	
83. Thomas Simms	23	5'10"	Centre Co.	Wagoner	Died in hospital, Puebla, 9 Sept. 1847.
84. Joseph Smith	21	5'9"	Westmoreland Co.	Blacksmith	
85. Thomas Spears	19	5'7½"	Pittsburgh	Carpenter	Died on board ship "J. N. Cooper" off San Antonio Lizardo, 16 March 1847.
86. *Fred. B. Steck	19	5'10"	Westmoreland Co.	Butcher	Promoted 4th Cpl., 1 March 1848.
87. Henry Stickle	22	5'7½"	Germany	Laborer	
88. John Taylor	27	5'9"	Westmoreland Co.	Tailor	Discharged at New Orleans.
89. Nathaniel Thomas	19	5'10"	Westmoreland Co.	Farmer	Died in hospital, Puebla, 7 Sept. 1847.
90. *Israel Uncapher	23	5'7½"	Westmoreland Co.	Lawyer	
91. James Underwood	22	5'7¾"	Cumberland Co.	Plasterer	
92. Samuel Waters	20	5'11"	Westmoreland Co.	Butcher	
93. William Wentz	25	5'11"	Westmoreland Co.	Farmer	Died in quarters, Jalapa, 15 May 1847.
94. Jacob T. Wise	18	6'1"	Cumberland Co.	Laborer	

Suggestions for Further Reading

The most recent survey of the Mexican War is the awkwardly titled but splendidly written narrative, *So Far From God: The U.S. War With Mexico* (New York: Random House, 1989) by John S. D. Eisenhower. The most thorough study remains the massively (but confusingly) documented account of *The War With Mexico* by Justin H. Smith, 2 vols. (New York: Macmillan, 1919) whose automatic assumption of Mexican inferiority might, however, prove disturbing to modern sensibilities. A partial corrective to this bias can be found in a contemporary compilation from the Mexican viewpoint called *The Other Side*, trans. and ed. Albert C. Ramsey (New York, 1850). The impact of the war on American life and thought is carefully traced by Robert W. Johannsen in *To the Halls of the Montezumas: The Mexican War in the American Imagination* (New York: Oxford University Press, 1983).

Some specialized studies of interest include: *Surfboats and Horse Marines: U.S. Naval Operations in the Mexican War, 1846–1848* by K. Jack Bauer (Annapolis: U.S. Naval Institute, 1969), especially strong on the siege of Vera Cruz; David M. Pletcher, *The Diplomacy of Annexation: Texas, Oregon, and the Mexican War* (Columbia: University of Missouri Press, 1973); Lester R. Dillon, *American Artillery in the Mexican War, 1846–1847* (Austin, Tex.: Presido Press, 1975); Robert Ryal Miller, *Shamrock and Sword: The Saint Patrick's Battalion in the U.S.-Mexican War* (Norman: University of Oklahoma Press, 1989); and Walter Prescott Webb, *The Texas Rangers: A Century of Frontier Defense* (Boston: Houghton Mifflin, 1935). *The Diaries of James K. Polk*, ed. Milo M. Quaife, 4 vols. (Chicago: A. C. McClurg, 1910), should be dipped into for a glimpse of the inner life of this bitter, driven man.

Two general studies of the U.S. military are essential for background: Marcus Cunliffe's delightful *Soldiers and Civilians: The Martial Spirit in America, 1775–1865* (Boston: Little, Brown, 1968); and Edward M. Coffman, *The Old Army. A Portrait of the American Army in Peacetime* (New York: Oxford University Press, 1986).

For some reason, except for *John A. Quitman: Old South Crusader* by Robert E. May (Baton Rouge: Louisiana State University Press, 1985), none of Scott's generals, not even Franklin Pierce, has been given a satisfactory modern biography. The best biography of Scott himself, *Winfield Scott: The Soldier and the Man* by Charles W. Elliott (New York: Macmillan, 1937), is aging, though it wears its years gracefully.

Junior officers have fared better, due to their later prominence in the Civil War. Many also wrote of their Mexican experience, most notably: Robert Anderson, *An Artillery Officer in the Mexican War* (New York: G. P. Putnam, 1911); P. G. T. Beauregard, *With Beauregard in Mexico*, ed. T. Harry Williams (Baton Rouge: Louisiana State University Press, 1956); George McClellan, *The Mexican War Diary of General George B. McClellan*, ed. William Starr Myers (Princeton: Princeton University Press, 1917); and E. Kirby Smith, *To Mexico With Scott* (Cambridge: Harvard University Press, 1917). Of their seniors, the best memoirs are by Winfield Scott, *Memoirs of Lieut.-General Scott, LL.D*, 2 vols. (New York, 1864), and Scott's aide, Ethan Allen Hitchcock, *Fifty Years in Camp and Field*, ed. W. A. Croffut (New York: G. P. Putnam, 1909). For an anti-Scott perspective, see Raphael Semmes, *Service Afloat and Ashore During the Mexican War* (Cincinnati, 1851).

Of indispensable assistance in tracking down the names and careers of American officers were: Francis B. Heitman, *Historical Register and Dictionary of the United States Army*, 2 vols. (Washington, D.C.: Government Printing Office, 1903); and the detailed roster appended to Cadmus Marcellus Wilcox, *History of the Mexican War* (Washington, D.C., 1892).

Memoirs of common soldiers are too extensive to enumerate. The outstanding example of the genre is *My Confession* by Samuel E. Chamberlain (New York: Harpers, 1956), whose exploits undoubtedly gained much in the retelling. Other soldier narratives of interest are: George Ballentine, *The Mexican War, By an English Soldier* (New York, 1860); and *Notes of the Mexican War* (Philadelphia, 1885) by J. Jacob Oswandel, a volunteer in the 1st Pennsylvania Infantry.

The Westmoreland guards were particularly prolific in recording their impressions. In addition to those by Barclay and Coulter, diaries were kept (and published) by George W. Hartman, *A Private's Own Journal* (Greencastle, Pa., 1849) and by William Joseph McWilliams, "A Westmoreland Guard in Mexico," *The Western Pennsylvania Historical Magazine* 52, nos. 3 and 4 (July and October 1969): 213–40, 387–413, ed. John Williams Larner, Jr. Some letters from the 2d Pennsylvania's first colonel, William B. Roberts, can be found in *The Western Pennsylvania Historical Magazine* 39, no. 4 (October 1956): 243–63. His flamboyant successor, John Geary, has been the subject of an unsatisfactory biography by Harry Marlin Tinkcom, *John White Geary, Soldier-Statesman, 1819–1873* (Philadelphia: University of Pennsylvania Press, 1940) and a sketchy article by Paul Beers in *Civil War Times Illustrated* 9 (June 1970): 9–16, but his career deserves better.

Finally, a charming sketch of Mexico on the eve of the war with the United States can be found in the copiously illustrated edition of Madame Fanny Calderón de la Barca's *Life in Mexico*, eds. Howard T. and Marion Hall Fisher (New York: Doubleday, 1966).

Further readings on these and other aspects of the Mexican War can be found in the copious entries (more than 4500!) in Norman E. Tutorow's massive compilation, *The Mexican-American War: An Annotated Bibliography* (Westport, Conn.: Greenwood Press, 1981).

Index

Abercrombie, Lt. Col. J. J., 291
Acajete, 122–23, 305
Adams, John Q., 274–75
Adventures of Telemachus, The, 57 n
Aikens, John, 76, 104, 132–33, 295, 310; injured, 293
Alburtis, Capt. William, 46–47
Alcoholic beverages: aguardiente, 103–4, 152; brandy, 20, 103; eggnog, 103; praised, 189, 227–28; pulque, 117, 204–5, 273
Alexander, John B., 3
Allshouse, Lebbeus, 162, 269–95; first of company to enter Chapultepec, 169–72
Almonte, Juan Nepomuceno, 291
American Highlanders (Co. B), 14, 93, 169–71, 157, 302
American Star, 204
Amozoc, 122–23, 304
Amusements of soldiers: alley ball, 251; bullfights, 95–96, 199; cards, 319; formal balls, 264–65; gambling, 236, 242, 251, 286; horse racing, 266; mock court martial, 319–21; music, 106, 203, 260; practical jokes, 153–54, 236, 238–39; pranks, 31, 103; roughhousing, 272, 280, 295–96; swimming, 274, 279; theater, 200–201, 289; water fights, 272–78. *See also* Drunkenness
Anaya, Pedro María, 149
Anderson, John A., 317
Anglo-Saxonism, 181
Antón Lizardo, 37
Armada, Spanish, 36
Armistice: terms of, 150–51; violated by Mexicans, 152
Armstrong, Lt. James, 52–53, 76, 142, 206; arrested, 215, 305; assigned to Co. H., 130; candidate for lt. col., 211; at Chapultepec, 168–69, 172; drunk, 232;

elected lt., Co. E, 12; ill, 153, 250, 254; returns to Co. E, 134–35
Army, U.S., 1, 2; numbers and losses in Mexican War, 180
Articles of War, 37
Aulick, John H., 39 n

Barclay, Capt. James (N.Y. vols.), 251
Barclay, John (son), 7
Barclay, Isabella Johnston (mother), 3
Barclay, Rebecca Kuhns (wife), 7
Barclay, Thomas, 3, 6–7, *8,* 256; resigns commission, 283–84; voted complimentary sword, 267, 271
Barnett, Col. Ward B., 147
Bates, Andrew J., 52, 60, 104; ill, 222; rejoins company, 247; wounded, 169, 172, 178
Bates, Henry, 12
Beauregard, Lt. P. G. T., 144, 160
Belton, Lt. Col. Francis S., 269
Bennet, Paymaster Albert G., 153, 154
Bigelow, William A., 19, 52, 268, 270
Bills, McClure, 197, 242
Black, Lt. Col. Samuel W. (1st Pa. Inf.), 44–45, 133, 220, 249
Bonneville, Col. Benjamin L. E., 237n. 11
Bonnin, George W., 32, 69, 178, 197, 268, 270
Borland, Maj. Solon, 141 n, 225
Bowman, Francis L., 15, 245, 285, 305
Brady, Hugh J., 19, 67, 107, 172, 222, 293
Bravo, Nicholás, 170–71, 256
Brindle, William, 165, 169, 176, 207, 289; at Chapultepec, 171; contempt for, 295, 296; drunk, 234; elected major, 14; as lt. col., 209–10; mocked by men, 240
Brooks, Capt. Preston (S.C. vols.), 281; bullies enlisted men, 257–58; captures

VOLUNTEERS

was composed in 10/12 Baskerville
on a Varityper system
by Professional Book Compositors, Inc.;
printed by sheet-fed offset on 50-pound, acid free,
Glatfelter B-16 paper stock
Smyth sewn and bound over .088″ binders' boards
in Holliston Roxite B-grade cloth,
wrapped with dust jackets printed in three colors
on 100-pound enamel stock and film laminated
by Thomson-Shore, Inc.;
designed by Will Underwood;
and published by
THE KENT STATE UNIVERSITY PRESS
KENT, OHIO 44242

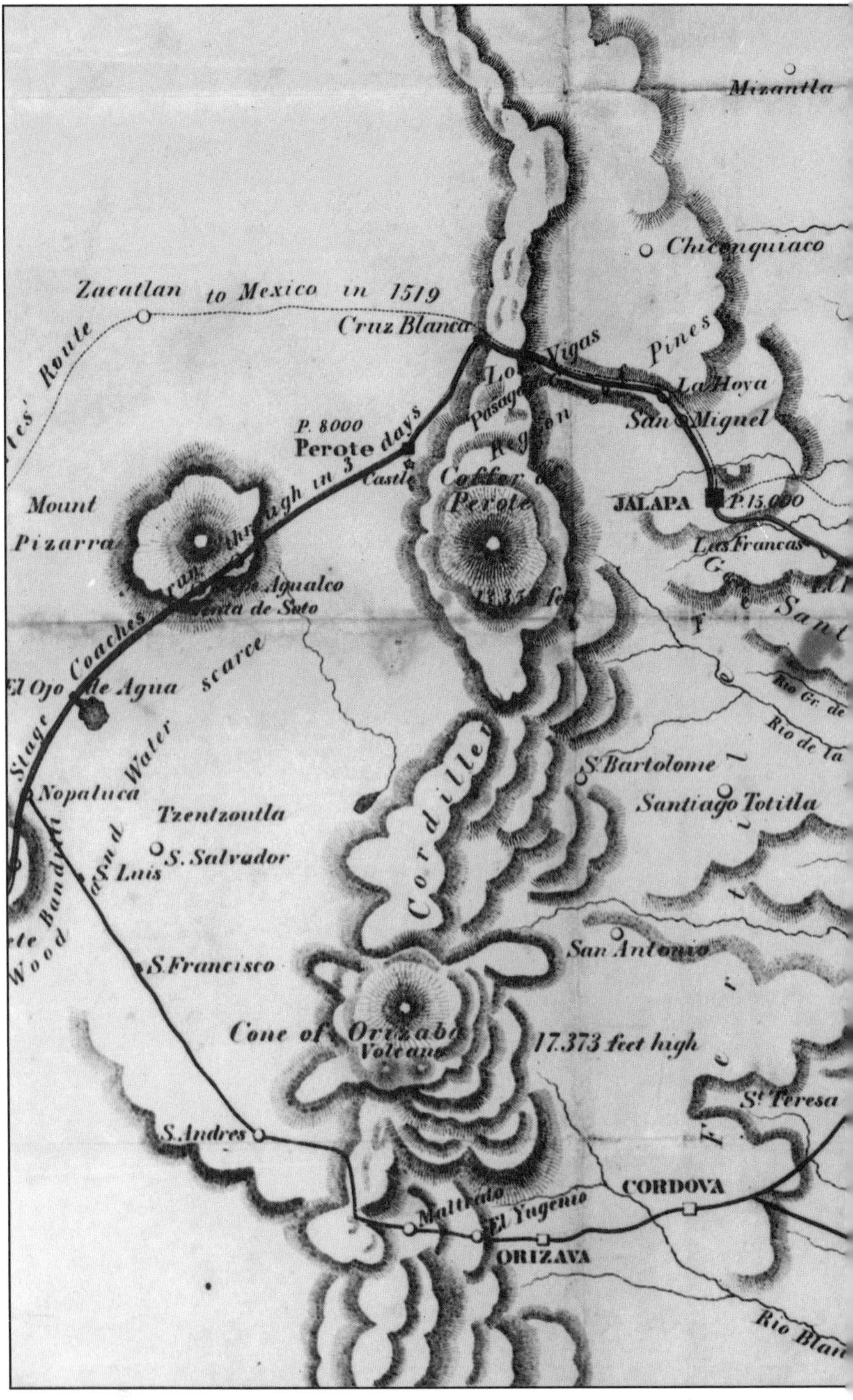
Mizantla
Chiconquiaco
Zacatlan
to Mexico in 1519
tes' Route
Cruz Blanca
Vigas
Pines
La Hoya
San Miguel
P. 8000
Perote
days
through in 3
Stage Coaches
Castle
Perote
JALAPA
P.15,000
Las Francas
Mount
Pizarra
Aqualco
El Ojo de Agua
scarce
Water
Nopaluca
Tzentzoutla
S. Salvador
Luis
Wood
S. Bartolome
Santiago Totitla
San Antonio
S. Francisco
Cone of Orizaba
Volcano
17.373 feet high
St. Teresa
S. Andres
CORDOVA
Maltrato
El Yngenio
ORIZAVA
Rio de la
Rio Gr. de